Anthropological Approaches
to Psychological Medicine

Anthropological Approaches to Psychological Medicine

Crossing Bridges

Edited by Vieda Skultans and John Cox

Jessica Kingsley Publishers
London and Philadelphia

Chapter 2 was originally published in the *International Journal of Social Psychiatry* (1996), volume 42, pp.245–265, and is reproduced with the kind permission of The Avenue Publishing Co.

First published in the United Kingdom in 2000 by
Jessica Kingsley Publishers Ltd,
116 Pentonville Road, London
N1 9JB, England
and
325 Chestnut Street,
Philadelphia PA 19106, USA.

www.jkp.com

Library of Congress Cataloging in Publication Data
A CIP catalog record for this book is available from the Library of Congress

British Library Cataloguing in Publication Data
Anthropological approaches to psychological medicine
  1. Cultural psychiatry 2. Psychiatry – Social aspects
  3. Medical anthropology
  I. Skultans, Vieda II. Cox, John, 1939–
616.8'9

ISBN 1 85302 708 1 pb
ISBN 1 85302 707 3 hb

Printed and Bound in Great Britain by
Athenaeum Press, Gateshead, Tyne and Wear

Contents

Introduction

Vieda Skultans and John Cox

The energy to cross the bridge between anthropology and psychiatry was part of our autobiographical narratives. One of us (VS) had worked as a medical anthropologist in a Department of Psychiatry at Bristol University and was therefore immersed in the ways of thought of doctors, and psychiatrists in particular. The other (JC) was trained in general adult psychiatry and had worked in East Africa for two years as part of his higher training. This experience of being translated from a Department of Psychiatry in London to a lecturer post at Makerere University, Kampala was a formative culture 'shock' which encouraged a cautious move from the safe training in British psychiatry to an environment where it was fundamentally essential to grasp the relevance of social and anthropological dimensions necessary to understand the causes and management strategies of mental disorder. For us 'crossing the bridge' was a part of daily work routines. We hope these readings will encourage others to cross this bridge from either direction and so enlarge their professional practice and research routines.

OUTLINING THE FIELD

Yet before bridges can be crossed we need to know what lies either side of the bridge and how strong the bridge: we need a map. Yet the conceptual terrain on either side of our bridge resists easy classification. The *Oxford Shorter Dictionary* offers us an older, etymological and all-embracing view of anthropology as the study of man which the anthropologist Leach would no doubt reject as 'a monstrous universal form of enquiry' (1982, p.13). These days we should at least add the supplement attributed to Malinowski that it is the study of man embracing woman while learning the language with the help of a sleeping dictionary.[1] Psychiatry was defined as the medical treatment of diseases of the mind. Inadequate as these definitions are, posing more questions than giving answers, we will rest with them for the time being. These definitions clearly suggest that anthropology – with the

7

sweeping scope of its interests – might have something to contribute towards the understanding of the mind and its vicissitudes. Thus as the boundaries and nature of anthropology have become more firmly delineated, so the specific contribution of anthropology to general medicine and psychiatry can be more rigorously specified.

Histories of anthropology remind us of its colonial roots.[2] As the colonial impetus of anthropology has diminished, the emphasis on other cultures has disappeared.[3] Instead local cultural difference has emerged as the focus of anthropological interest. Perhaps less tangible and easy to grasp than 'other cultures', it is however an enormously fruitful concept which puts both the observer and the observed under the microscope.[4] Difference is, of course, a relative concept. One cannot be different in the way that one can perhaps be beautiful; difference is always 'difference from', thus a simultaneously holding in attention as two contrasting concepts.[5] In this way an awareness of different cultural practices can lead in turn to a questioning awareness of one's own practices: hence the specific relevance of anthropology to the development of mental health services in a multicultural society.

Participant observation is central to the identity of anthropology and is characterized as akin to the experience of immersion in a bath.[6] Anthropological knowledge is, above all, knowledge grounded in the highly personal encounter between the anthropologist and the strange culture.[7] Through learning cultural norms and practices through trial and error – much as a child would – anthropologists acquire the insider's view of another culture. But to become accessible to others it cannot remain an insider's view only, it must be communicated. The participant therefore must also be an observer who is able to translate indigenous concepts and practices into another language using anthropological concepts. The etymology of the term ethnography gives us a clue to this important element in the anthropological enterprise: the writing or description of cultural otherness or difference.[8]

ANTHROPOLOGY AND SOCIOLOGY

In its insistence, some would say over-insistence, on the role played by culture and society in enabling human beings to establish their true identity, anthropology clearly shares much common ground with sociology.[9] Both disciplines see the individual as shaped and shaping their environment through an ongoing process of mutual influence. So what common ground do these disciplines share and wherein lies their distinctiveness? The sociologist Mills puts this well when he writes: 'The sociological imagination enables us to grasp history and biography and the relations between the two in society. That is its task and its promise' (1973, p.6). The anthropologist Leach eschews a definition but the concern of his kind of anthropology is clearly with the ways in which different societies chop up reality or perceive the world in terms of simplified binary categories, i.e. through difference. Although he sees anthropology as an empiricist discipline, he is also committed to the idealist potential within anthropology. For example, the structuralist perspective offers considerable leverage for making sense of belief systems.

THE HISTORICAL LEGACY

Both disciplines emerged at roughly the same point in history and share many intellectual ancestors. It is often said that anthropology and sociology are children of the Enlightenment. We could rephrase this more precisely by saying that the intellectual framework provided by the Enlightenment made possible the growth of specifically anthropological and sociological bodies of knowledge. What do we mean by this? Enlightenment thinkers such as Locke and Hume in England and Rousseau in France drew a distinction between nature and society, recognizing the power of enculturation but still emphasizing the underlying psychological sameness of mankind, its psychic unity if you like. Difference was thus a property of cultures and sameness of individuals and their bodies insofar as they are embedded in nature. A common rationality and a separation from nature enabled men to stand back and observe their own and other cultures: it facilitated the growth both of sociology and of anthropology. 'Society could not be studied in anything resembling a scientific manner until the idea of society as in some sense an object to be studied had been established' (Pocock 1961, p.5). Conversely, the study of other societies and cultures became central to the construction of a universal human nature: 'One needs to look near at hand if one wants to study men: but to study man one must learn to look from afar: one must first observe differences in order to discover attributes' (Rousseau, quoted by Lewis 1976, p.16). We shall come back to this text of Rousseau's when discussing the development of transcultural psychiatry. We might add, however, that belief in the essential sameness of mankind did not preclude the idea of men having a greater, or lesser, share in a common rationality. For example, the nineteenth-century anthropologist Tylor saw cultures in terms of an evolutionary hierarchy: cultures were ranked in terms of how developed they were (1958). Thus the essential tasks of anthropology and sociology were made possible by the Enlightenment. Namely, a belief in a shared human rationality made comparison and explanation possible and the objectification of society provided the emerging social sciences with an object of study. Together sociology and anthropology sought to undermine our taken for granted assumptions about own and other cultures. Sociology has been characterized as the discipline which renders the familiar or taken for granted unfamiliar. For anthropology the converse was the case, namely to render the strange familiar.

A more general distinction recognizable by psychiatrists, who are more likely by training to be familiar with sociological than anthropological approaches, is that the former discipline relies on identifying more discrete components of the social universe (e.g. marital status, social class, measures of economic deprivation, gender, parity, etc.) separated out from society as a whole, and then subject to the discipline of quantitative research methodologies and statistical sampling. Anthropology on the other hand looks at the whole culture and assumes that mental illness is itself a product of that society and that its expression and healing are intimately linked to the individual's particular life history and a society's pattern of social relationships and beliefs. As Littlewood has argued, a psychiatric approach which is based on anthropology will be meaning centred. But this distinction between the other and one's own culture is no longer clear cut. Many anthropologists now carry out their fieldwork 'at home'.[10] Should these researchers be called sociologists or not? The answer seems to be 'not necessarily' and depends not so much upon the site of fieldwork as with the paths taken to gain knowledge. Participant observation reflects the importance which anthropology attaches to local meanings, but it should be emphasized that, as many anthropologists have noted, it is not easy to achieve the right balance between participation and observation at home (Leach 1982, pp.124–126). This is not to say that sociology does not also have an interpretative tradition. It does, of course, have a long tradition that stretches from Max Weber to the ethnomethodologists. But the fact that there are overlaps and indistinct areas at the margins of anthropology and sociology does not mean that their distinctiveness collapses altogether. That there are certain hues of blue and green which cannot easily be categorized does not mean that blue and green are indistinguishable. It remains true to say therefore that anthropology is a subject defined mostly by its method.

MEDICAL ANTHROPOLOGY AND ITS CONCERNS

The branch of anthropology which is concerned with health and illness beliefs and practices has come to be called medical anthropology. Like social psychiatry it forms a bridge between our two disciplines and is concerned with shared understandings of health and illness, norms governing illness behaviour and ideas and practices to do with treatment. In its concern with suffering, and conditions which threaten the integrity and continued existence of individuals and groups, medical anthropology links with issues which lie at the very heart of the anthropological enterprise.

Medical anthropology is also the fastest growing subdiscipline within anthropology, yet despite its popularity still receives little mention in introductions to social anthropology. Why this should be so tells us a great deal about both the nature of social anthropology and of medical anthropology. The caution with which early British anthropology approached medical matters derives from the Enlightenment tradition: the idea that medicine deals with a uniform natural substratum which is of little interest to anthropology. On the other hand, there is the idea that everything which is of importance, interest and, most importantly, which can be accessed by others, takes place in a shared cultural domain took its justification from the philosopher Locke: 'There is nothing in the mind which has not first been in experience.' In other words our ideas have a social origin. The combination of these ideas led to a bipolarization of the cultural and the natural which enabled Durkheim to objectify the social world. Humans, of course, straddle both spheres, but while their activities in the cultural sphere were of interest to anthropologists, their residence in the domain of nature was felt to be beyond the competencies of anthropology and was referred to biomedicine and the natural sciences.

One consequence of this approach has been the by now well-rehearsed distinction between disease and illness. For medical and psychiatric anthropology there was a focus on cultures and on ethnopsychiatry which overlooked individual and bodily experience. The body, in Mary Douglas's inimitable words, was 'good to think with'. So in a curious way we could say that the body was absent from medical anthropology and sociology. Illness both physical and psychiatric was important, for example, because of what it could tell us about the cultural system of which it was a part. Biomedicine, and psychiatry as a medical speciality, were either the unproblematic lens which examined only exotic culture-bound syndromes or were exempt from scrutiny because they dealt with disease rather than a culturally permeated illness.

A while ago Lewis noted that the consequences of this dualistic Enlightenment inheritance have been a neglect of the psychological dimension and we are now painfully aware of that neglect: 'For us the individual is a microcosm of the social macrocosm. His private emotions and idiosyncracies, and difficulties he experiences in internalizing the norms of his community are his business. They are not on our agenda, at least not until they become such a common feature, shared by so many others, that they qualify as "social phenomena"' (Lewis 1976, p.22). The editorial decision to eschew psychiatric and psychological issues in the early Association of Social Anthropologists monograph forms part of that tradition (Loudon 1970). Traces of this bipolar approach to the individual and their culture survive in the writings of contemporary anthropologists. For example, Hendry in her otherwise excellent introduction to anthropology, in the context of discussing life course rituals, writes: 'A Church of England wedding tells us nothing of the bride or her beliefs, only about the social relations being established. In other words, we must separate personal beliefs from the social aspects of ritual behaviour' (1999, p.67). Such views transposed to the areas of health and illness, particularly psychological health and illness, would exclude many of the recurring concerns of medical anthropology from the legitimate remit of anthropological interest.

THE EMIC/ETIC DEBATE

Medical anthropology, however, continues to grow and flourish; the theoretical issues which confront it have nevertheless been shaped by the historical legacy of its parent discipline. For example, the debate about etic versus emic meanings which underpins much work in medical anthropology has its roots in this legacy. The terms etic and emic have a linguistic provenance in that they are derivatives of the terms phonetic and phonemic.[11] The term phonetic refers to patterns of sound sequences and is concerned with relationships of contiguity – where things are placed in relation to each other. The term phonemic, on the other hand, refers to relations of semantic or meaning similarity. This polarity has been summarized by Jadhav (Chapter 1) and the distinction can be readily recalled by the emic approach being more 'me' centred. This emic approach has facilitated the development of the search of the individual's explanatory model (EM) which is formalized within the emic interview (Weiss *et al.*). Kleinman (1988) gives examples of the advantage of this approach, especially when the health worker is working across cultures and is in the field of liaison psychiatry. Many psychiatrists as individuals and psychiatry as a discipline can, however, span this emic/etic dichotomy which is certainly contained within the recrudescence of the multi-professional team. In Barrett's (1996) ethnographic study of schizophrenia in a mental hospital in Australia, he concluded that the team as a whole came close to a complete grasp of this disorder – and yet a necessary approach contained within that team was the diagnostic understanding of the psychiatrist – although this approach on its own would have been insufficient. As Barrett has discussed, neither psychiatry tied to medicine and a diagnostic approach to an individual's difficulties, nor an anthropology which can be equally limited can include all necessary facets of a mental disorder. Van Dongen (Chapter 5) argues just this point.

The distinction between the two terms can also be elaborated in terms of form and content and in terms of imposed external meanings and subjective internal meanings. If we want to understand the essential differences between an interpretative and a positivist approach both in anthropology and sociology then we can observe it crystallize around the emic/etic debate. The *etic approach* has a loyalty to *facts* and their identification and argues that scientific categories can be transposed across cultures in order to apprehend these facts through processes of measurement and comparison. This approach is illustrated by the use of the present state examination in different cultures to determine the frequency of schizophrenia and to search for causal associations. The combination of facts and scientific categories are thought to be powerful enough to overcome the distorting effects of different cultures and subjectivities. This position has less power within anthropology than it does in the other social sciences. It has, however, been plausibly argued that the comparison which the etic approach advocates is not between facts but between discourses since we can never have linguistically unrestricted and direct access to the facts. Thus Holy, an anthropologist, writes: 'While generalization was seen as problematic, description was not' (1987, p.4). This is not to say, however, that anthropology has no commitment to comparison and generalization; although few anthropologists would endorse Radcliffe-Brown's (1952) claim that anthropology is above all a generalizing science – none would dismiss generalization entirely. All explanation involves some degree of comparison and, therefore, generalization. However, although the emic/etic debate continues to divide anthropologists as well as psychiatrists into two opposed theoretical camps, commitment to one or other theoretical approach does not necessarily determine their ability to perceive and convey subjective meanings. The ability to reconstruct the world from the native's perspective for example seems to depend much more upon the literary talent of the anthropologist. Malinowski (1944) was committed to the idea of social laws and comparison, and yet has left us a uniquely compelling portrait of the Trobriand islanders. Geertz and some of his followers argue that the authority of the anthropologist derives not so much from the experience of extensive and gruelling field work as from his or her command of literary strategies of persuasion (1988). Subtle implications or a choice literary phrase exert more power over us than protestations of a laboured methodology.[12] Scheper-Hughes's utterly riveting account of infant mortality, mourning and depression among the poor women of Brazil is a good illustration of just this point, even if her theoretical and political stance is controversial (1990).

Emic/etic distinctions have, of course, also shaped the development of psychiatry, indeed, of medicine itself. Medical understanding is at one and the same time a science and an art and certainly its implementation, which hinges so much upon an understanding of the intentionality and subjectivity of patients, is more art than science. But psychiatry, perhaps more than the other medical specialisms, straddles the emic/etic divide. Freud was both a natural scientist – his early research interests focused on the nervous system of the crayfish – and a humanist with a passionate commitment to understanding symptoms as a kind of language and to recognizing their intentionality. This dual commitment, evident in the writing of the early founding fathers, continues to shape the nature and direction of psychiatry as a discipline. Part of this dual commitment derives from polarities which are constructed not around the concepts of science and the humanities, thus acknowledging different kinds of knowledge, but around science and non-science where science is taken as a paradigm of all knowledge. To be unscientific is thus to fall short of a shared and agreed upon rationality. In order to be acknowledged as 'scientific', psychiatrists pursue epidemiological and 'evidence-based' research. Nevertheless, the voice of the patient draws psychiatrists back to a more humanistic and clinical approach. Indeed, it is the sterility and false polarization between so-called scientific and humanistic medicine which has drawn psychiatrists to anthropology; an anthropology which puts in question automatic assumptions of a special relationship with the truth by recognizing the social embeddedness of our beliefs about mental illness and the very partial nature of our connections with scientific truth. It offers a way of looking at the world which even if it does not relativize truth certainly emphasizes the social constraints upon our attempts to reach the truth, in other words it relativizes beliefs.

THE RATIONALITY AND RELATIVISM DEBATE

Our discussion so far suggests that the implications of an anthropological perspective on psychiatry are enormous. Indeed, the early history of anthropology and psychiatry shows an implicit awareness of this: many early twentieth-century anthropologists had a medical background and many more thought it important that their ideas should be validated in a cross-cultural setting.[13] For example, many of Freud's most important ideas about the development of personality and the relationship between the individual and society drew upon anthropological assumptions, albeit they are now generally acknowledged to be false.[14] So what are the questions that an anthropological perspective raises for medicine generally and psychiatry in particular? I suspect that most medical anthropologists, no matter what their theoretical persuasion, would agree that these questions cluster around the issues addressed in a famous collection of essays with the title *Rationality and Relativism* (Hollis and Lukes 1982) and which confront the anthropological enterprise more forcefully than they do any other discipline.

Following the title of this stimulating book we can group anthropologists into two theoretical camps: the rationalists and the relativists whose positions I will summarize as follows. Cognitive and moral relativists draw their inspiration from Wittgenstein's notion of *forms of life* and hold that beliefs and values can only be understood and assessed relative to particular cultures and societies. There is no room for absolute criteria of truth and rationality in this position. Discussions which refer to social constructionism and the incommensurability of different worlds very likely belong to this category. In the opposing camp are a smaller but highly articulate group of anthropologists. The essence of their position is summarized by Gellner: if relativism were indeed true then we might expect failure of anthropological ventures far more often than is, in fact, the case:

> It is an interesting fact about the world we actually live in that no anthropologist, to my knowledge, has come back from a field trip with the following report: *their* concepts are *so* alien that it is impossible to describe their land tenure, their kinship system, their ritual... As far as I know there is no record of such a total admission of failure... It is *success* in explaining culture A in the language of culture B which is, in the light of such a philosophy, really puzzling. Yet shelves groan with the weight of such books. (Gellner 1982, pp.185–186)

The French anthropologist Sperber makes a very similar point when he claims that 'the best evidence against relativism is, ultimately, the very activity of anthropologist, while the best evidence for relativism seems to be in the writings of anthropologists. How can this be?' (1985, pp.62–63). The answer he gives is, in effect, that relativism is a rhetorical device which by emphasizing the cognitive distance and remoteness of the other culture serves to enhance the intellectual prowess of the anthropologist.

Sperber's arguments, in fact, suggest that not all relativists are what they claim to be. However, the true value of this debate lies not in deciding whether culture or nature has more depth but rather in sensitizing medical anthropologists and cross-cultural psychiatrists to the ubiquity of culture. As Geertz argues, it is not anthropological theory but the wealth of anthropological data which has lent support to relativism (1984, p.264).

Perhaps one of the most daring enterprises is to turn the anthropological lens on the idea of culture itself. Readers will find in Roland Littlewood's chapter (2) a finely nuanced discussion of the changing meanings of culture. The culture nature debate can be seen to have developed as a special instantiation of the Aristotelian polarization between form and matter. But whereas the significant partner in Aristotle's duality is form, their relative weighting has come to be reversed in later debates about culture and nature as Geertz's famous quote suggests: 'the tendency to see diversity as surface and universality as depth' (1984, p.272). Early anthropologists like Kroeber were quite explicit about this: 'The organic sciences underlie the social ones. They are more directly "natural". Anthropology has found valuable general principles in biology' (1923, p.4). But whatever the relative weighting we attribute to culture and nature, whether we see ourselves as rationalists or relativists, we cannot ignore the work of culture.

Anthropology has moved on and penetrated the us/them divide. There may have been a period in the development of transcultural psychiatry and medical anthropology when culture was, indeed, a replacement of the old biogenetic racial categories.[15] But we no longer claim that anthropologists and psychiatrists are operating in a culture free zone: that we, the observers, are unaffected by cultural assumptions but that our informants are trapped in a web of cultural expectations. Indeed Jadhav (Chapter 1), on the origins of the western concept of depression, ably traces the cultural roots of this exceedingly common diagnostic category. We no longer occupy a central and privileged high ground from which we can impartially observe the cultural peripheries. Yet it is in the area of medicine and psychiatry that concerns about the pan cultural verities linger. Indeed, for Kroeber these were what Geertz describes as 'messy moral matters' and 'messy creatural matters like delirium and menstruation' (1984, p.265). The incest taboo is another category that has been put forward by anthropologists as a universal of human experience transcending cultures. For Kroeber the cultural universalities derive both from the demands necessitated by social living: 'No culture tolerates indiscriminate lying, stealing, or violence within the in-group' and from 'the biological sameness of the human animal' (Kroeber and Kluckhohn 1952, p.349). These converge to produce mental disorders which transcend particular cultures: 'The fact of the matter is that all cultures define as abnormal individuals who are permanently inaccessible to communication or who fail to maintain some degree of control over their impulse life' (p.350). Messy these matters may be, but that does not exclude them from the remit of anthropology. Indeed, Malinowski built his whole meta-theory of functionalism around the ostensible relationship between certain basic biological needs and the cultural response to them (1944). Although his theory may lack explanatory power due to the diversity of possible cultural responses it was at least an attempt to link two very fundamental dimensions of human experience.

THE HISTORY OF TRANSCULTURAL PSYCHIATRY

This debate and our changing understandings of culture have shaped the history of transcultural psychiatry. Intrinsic to the notion of a culturally impartial observer is the idea of science as a privileged route to knowledge which is able to transcend any one culture. But this commitment to translation and understanding across cultures did not necessarily dictate a refusal to acknowledge the importance of local contexts and understandings. Carothers in his monograph on the mental health of Africans insisted that culture could and did affect both the content and form of mental illness (1953, p.142). An early, rich collection of essays on *Culture and Mental Health* (Opler 1959) makes explicit acknowledgement of this:

> It is obvious that the individual is not a product of historically derived diagnostic terms or individually biased ratings and outlooks. Processes or

events, along with qualities or relations, are more basic categories for understanding the world. Descriptive labels like schizophrenic are still congenial concepts like matter and substance, but it cannot be assumed that essential qualities and relationships in the human world are really explored by such terms. Description requires further analysis, just as the case described or provisionally rated cannot be understood until it is seen in its meaningful setting and relationships. (Opler1959, pp.11–12)

However, Savage, Leighton and Leighton adopted a far more dismissive approach to culture:

If one selects particular cultures instead of trying to deal with cultures in general, he will probably be able to establish operational criteria that will permit the desired comparison at a useful and meaningful level of approximation. We also think that operational steps are facilitated if the detection of symptom patterns and the detection of impairment are used as a primary focus in cross-cultural estimates. (Savage *et al.* 1965, p.60)

However, much of the early work of the transcultural psychiatrists lies midpoint between these two traditions. For example, Ari Kiev while documenting the extent and diversity of cultural influences on psychiatric illness, insists on an underlying universal structure for such illnesses. He concedes: 'a variety of ways in which culture influences, the development, the form and the natural history of psychiatric illness, there is no certainty about the extent to which culture influences the fundamental structure or nuclear features of such illness' (1972, p.62). The most detailed exposition of the relative weighting given to culture and biology is given by Yap who resurrects Birnbaum's ideas on the structure and manifestation of psychotic illness (1974, p.32). The two terms used are pathogenicity and pathoplasticity (Birnbaum 1974, pp.208–209):

'Pathogenicity' dealt with the cause of the disease and determined the basic features of the psychosis; a subsidiary concept was 'predisposition'. 'Pathoplasticity' referred to the specific configurations and external features of the psychosis; subordinate to this was the concept of 'preformation'. A further auxiliary notion allied to the pathogenic was that of 'provocation' which concerns the triggering or activating factors of the illness. (Yap1974, p.33)

This position endorses the view that there are absolute standards for judging normality and abnormality which are independent of the way a culture interprets particular behaviours and states of mind. Culture here is very much 'the icing on the cake'.

The polarization between real disease grounded in biology and the cultural trappings of its symptomatic expression throws up a major problem for comparison. As Kraepelin recognized long ago, comparison depends upon being able 'to draw clear distinctions between identifiable illnesses' (1974, p.3). If culture disguises disease, how can the units of comparison be compared? Yap puts this as follows: 'Comparison raises the awkward but unavoidable question of what we intend to compare, and also the logical justification for doing this. The answer is that we compare what is functionally equivalent: that is, the behaviour exhibited in different groups when their members try to meet needs that are fundamentally biological and basically human' (1974, p.106). But any reference to functional equivalence necessarily makes assumptions that extend beyond the evidence of what is culturally visible to non-visible, quasi-metaphysical entities. Yap is quite clear about which he judges more important. He outlines two approaches to abnormality:

> The first and more profound is the causal-functional, which takes into account biological aspects of the total organism and allows us to view its behaviour historically in judging whether or not it is successfully coping. The second, more superficial, approach is the descriptive-statistical, which can be appropriately adopted where the phenomena to be studied are chiefly sociopsychological and belong therefore to a system much more open than the biological. For this reason abnormality defined in descriptive statistical terms can have only a relative significance. (Yap 1974, p.106)

Although Geertz's powerful attack on the anti-relativists does not have the transcultural psychiatrists in mind, they do in fact provide an appropriate target.

Nevertheless Yap (1965), in a pioneer CIBA symposium on transcultural psychiatry, when referring to manic depressive psychosis made clear his grasp of the relevance of the sociocultural variables such as mourning rituals, attitudes towards suicide, belief in an after life, shame and blame societies and the expression of anger for a full understanding of the aetiology of this disorder, its expression and optimum treatment strategies. Thus distinctions between 'icing' and 'cake', pathoplasticity and pathogenicity, though useful polarities to assist discourse are nevertheless a gross simplification of how most general psychiatrists think when working in clinical settings.

It is probable that the criticisms of the World Health Organization (WHO) international studies of schizophrenia may have been exacerbated by the descriptive symptomatic approach to this condition, as well as by the search for uniformity and a culture blindness towards an interview 'harmonized' for use across six language groups. Yet the better prognosis for this disorder found in developing countries and realization that expressed emotion can only truly be understood within an ethnographic framework are constant reminders that any biological/genetic causal influence is intimately related not just to the 'dominance' of the biomedical paradigm but to the interaction of cause and effect, biology and social influence, nature and nurture.

CULTURE-BOUND SYNDROMES

The history of the so-called culture-bound syndromes is of particular interest because of the theoretical allegiances which it exposes and which are further examples of the earlier discussion. We can discern three broad categories of thought vis-à-vis culture-bound syndromes. There is a line of thought closely linked to the stereotyping of primitive otherness in which the culture bound syndrome is seen as a kind of emblem of primitiveness or difference. It functions as a kind of symbolic marker of difference. Koro[16] provides good material for this kind of thinking.

Then there is the view that culture-bound syndromes are, to borrow Yap's term, 'conceptually equivalent' to western psychiatric categories and that they have simply acquired a variety of different cultural overlays. We are back to the assumptions about nature being deep and culture being superficial.

Third, we have the anthropological approach which suggests that culture-bound syndromes are to be found in all societies and that they point us towards the weak points within the social fabric: the areas where social demands on the individual are conflicting and paradoxical. Young's study of the concept of post-traumatic stress disorder (PTSD) reveals its very specific historical and moral roots in the American involvement in the Vietnam War (1996). It has been argued by several writers (see Littlewood and Lipsedge 1997) that anorexia nervosa is culture-bound in the sense that it represents and results from the pressures within western society about establishing autonomy in adolescence and the considerable preoccupation with sexual expression and performance. Other forms of local mental disorder such as Amakiro (a postnatal mental condition), Buganda (Cox and Amariko 1979; Orley 1970) and Ankole (Neema 1994) are believed to be caused by promiscuity during pregnancy which reinforces the social concern in these societies to ensure the legitimacy of the infant – without which it cannot be named or placed in a family. Culture-bound syndromes often lead us therefore to the core values of a society and so support the Durkheimian view that definitions of deviancy are essential to the identity of a community, be they crimes, sins or illnesses. In this way shared understanding of mental disorder including a 'new' category of Dangerous Severe Personality Disorder may help to maintain social stability.

NARRATIVE

The rise of narrative as both a method and object of study has brought changes to medical anthropology. Harvard psychiatrist and anthropologist Arthur Kleinman (1988) has played an important part in introducing narrative to medical anthropology. His early work called for what he termed a 'new cross-cultural psychiatry' which recognized the fundamental role of culture in shaping the essence of the illness experience and its conceptual formulation, not merely its outward cultural expression (1977). His work focused on narrative long before it was fashionable to do so. For Kleinman the importance of illness narratives is connected to the individual construction of meaningful life histories. Narrative reconstruction is about making sense of biographies disrupted by illness and other calamities. However, Kleinman's illness narratives are composite stories which combine the clinician's perspective with readers in the particularities of the personal narratives; the formal properties of the narrative and how these draw upon and recreate the cultures of which they are a part receive less emphasis. 'The "plot lines", "core metaphors" and "rhetorical devices" are never subject to systematic analysis in their own right' (Atkinson 1995, p.95). Thus, the transparent humanism of his earlier work may have neglected the social dimension. His more recent writing on social suffering sets out to redress that balance.

So we have come full circle in our journey from a common shared rationality, to the particularity of embedded and embodied experience, to a recognition of the importance of words as at one and the same time imbued with individual and shared meanings.

Much recent work in medical anthropology has as its focus the study of narrative and life histories. However, this interest bears little relationship to earlier sociological and anthropological studies of lives. Unlike the earlier interest in biographical approaches which saw it as a way of gaining insight into deviant and marginal sectors of society such as criminal and drug subcultures and prostitution, life histories are now recognized as occupying a central place for understanding the relationship between any individual and their social and historical circumstances and how individuals make sense of those experiences.

So let me (VS) say a little more about this reconstructed life history approach. In contrast to the window on a deviant reality where the interest was on what lay beyond the window and the window itself was perceived as translucent and unproblematic, the interest now is as much on the window as what it looks out on. Anthropologists, like oral historians, are as much interested in so-called mistaken perceptions as they are in true perceptions. Indeed, oral historians such as Portelli argue that discrepancies between fact and memory ultimately enhance the value of oral sources as historical documents (1991, p.26). Discrepancies may tell us more about the meaning of events than precise factual reconstructions. For example, narrative sequencing may not give a precise reflection of the chronological sequence of events, but it will convey their relative psychological and social importance.

So too the anthropologist is interested in the meaning of narratives and what they tell us about the narrator's relationship to history and society. For many psychiatrists such an approach may be old hat, the life history being the core of clinical assessment and therapy. For anthropologists it is an exciting discovery. Life stories then are of interest because they both provide a bridge which spans the earlier Enlightenment dualism of the individual and society and a means of accessing experience which would otherwise remain embedded in the body and beyond reach.

Skultans' fieldwork in Latvia demonstrates the way in which political oppression and violence are incorporated into narrative as illness and used as a form of moral evaluation of the past (1998, 1999). Medical histories are highly personal autobiographical accounts which derive their inner logic from the macro historical events by which they are framed. For example Mara, a countrywoman from Vidzeme, singles out historically important events in the Soviet occupation and features of Soviet society to explain each of her illness episodes. This is how she concludes: 'So I can't say that my health has been good. And with regard to my nerves, well...it's clear that my nerves suffered along with these events. They suffer from all that' (Skultans 1999, p.321). They are also a fundamental bridge between social anthropology and psychiatry. Historically and at the present time both disciplines are committed to the life history. 'Taking the history' is a routine feature of medical assessment. Of course it is selective in the information obtained and the framework within which this information is contained (see Sinclair, Chapter 11), but the same can be said of anthropology. It is indeed at the heart of clinical practice and of the relationship with the patient as a person; although the anthropologist, unlike the psychiatrist, is usually exempt from the additional requirement of being a 'healer' and having not only to understand the other but to provide assistance. It is perhaps in these settings that psychiatrists trained as anthropologists have particular possibilities of exploration – though they will experience the inherent difficulties of being not just a participant observer but also a participant healer.

CELEBRATING THE PARTICULAR

Malinowski's idea that authority derives from having been there is a celebration of the particular and the concrete and has its roots in Herder's urgings that we should embrace the concrete by an immersion in the specificities of time and place. His ideas have shaped the practice of ethnographic fieldwork and yet the participant observer has stopped short of the sick bed. Indeed, in many societies sickness seems to deprive the sick person of a voice. Janzen's classic study of illness and therapy in Zaire introduced the concept of the therapy management group who spoke and acted on behalf of the sick person (1978). Sansom's work among Australian aborigines describes how the sick do not speak and how others shape the sickness story for the sick person (1982). How do we embrace this silence? If narrative is one of the principle ways in which we learn about the experience of the other, then silence obstructs us in our endeavours. It bars the way to immersion in the concrete and particular. One solution has been a retreat to autobiography. If experience is truly embodied then this limits understanding to our own autobiographical experience. Indeed, recent writing in medical anthropology reflects the consequences of this particular conception of experience as embodied. Many of the most important recent texts in medical anthropology are autobiographical. The writings of Arthur Frank (1991, 1995), Irving Zola (1982) and Robert Murphy (1987) provide good examples. Church explores the meaning of her fieldwork among psychiatric survivors from the perspective of her own breakdown (1995). There are interesting parallels here with the role of training analysis in the development of psychoanalytic knowledge.

So does immersion in the concrete and bodily necessarily mean that we can only speak with authority about our own experience?[17] Although this is how it sometimes looks, the answer is no. To reinforce this answer we must draw upon the writing of Vico. Vico's characterization of historical knowledge is equally applicable to anthropological knowledge: 'Historical knowledge is not mere knowledge of past events, but only of events so far as they enter into human activity, and are an element in the biography of an individual or group. They are intelligible only to creatures who know what it is like to be a man. Whatever has been made by men…can be grasped by the rule guided imaginations of other men' (Berlin 1976, p.29). On this view autobiographical or self-knowledge paves the way for the understanding of others and undermines traditional categories of knowledge. To know not merely how or that, but why someone did or spoke as they did is to share or 'enter into' their experience (p.28). However, such knowledge does not come easily. Berlin describes Vico's 'appalling effort of trying to adjust one's vision to the archaic world – the need to see it through deeply unfamiliar spectacles' (p.96) Given the particularity and incommensurability of different cultures, to enter them is a slow and painful process. If 'the world of primitives is literally a different world from that of the sophisticated, as the world of the rich differs from that of the poor' (p.142), then how different will be the world of those who suffer from serious psychiatric illness from your world or mine?

Cheryl Mattingly, in setting the fieldwork context of her study of occupational therapy practice in a Boston hospital, writes: 'And who were these mysterious people, the very ill? Ostensibly they were from my own culture but they struck me as far more foreign than the Bengali officials I had once interviewed in the airless offices of Calcutta or the Kenyan film crew I had trooped around with, trying to capture life in urban squatter settlements outside Mombasa and Nairobi' (1998, p.50). According to this approach the human sciences yield a far more certain knowledge than the hard physical sciences. The realm of human sciences 'is intelligible to men [and women], who are its authors, in a way in which nothing else can be' (p.26). So what autobiographical experiences must we draw upon and what strategies must narrators deploy to enable you and me to enter these terrible worlds? How can we achieve the imaginative resurrection of these particular pasts, these troubled autobiographies? My answer points us towards narrative because 'above all words still speak' to us (Berlin 1979, p.113).

ARE CULTURES SICK OR CAN THEY MAKE YOU SICK?

One of the indirect, or perhaps not altogether indirect, consequences of the study of psychiatric illness in other cultures has been the evaluation of cultures as themselves pathological and pathogenic. The medical and psychiatric diagnosis of an entire culture has roots in two intellectual traditions. The earlier and larger tradition is that of nineteenth-century anthropology in which cultures formed an evolutionary hierarchy positioned in order of ascending complexity.[18] Needless to say, western Europeans were at the apex of this hierarchy. It is but a small step from evaluating the aesthetic, moral and intellectual qualities of a culture to judging its health and illness-inducing powers. The other tradition, which draws upon the ideas of this earlier one, is psychoanalytic and has its origins in the writings of Freud. Freud made constant comparisons between the history of mankind and the history of the individual; between conjectural anthropology and auto/biography. By and large the direction of his explanations was from the individual to the social in that he used his theories of the stages of infant development to shed light on religious and magical thought and practice. Through such comparisons Freud hoped to develop 'a pathology of cultural communities' (1963, p.81).

These views were adopted by some anthropologists who agreed that entire cultures were maladaptive or abnormal from a psychiatric point of view. Such diagnostic evaluations were thought to apply particularly to ritual and magical beliefs and practices which 'removed from their socio-cultural setting are plainly psycho-pathological' (Freeman 1965, p.66). The important question is, however, whether any human action is intelligible when removed from its social context. Magical thought is seen as an expression of obsessive compulsive disorder and witchcraft and sorcery beliefs of paranoia. The popular anthropologist Ruth Benedict used both diagnoses liberally. The jealousy and suspicion of the Dobuans she describes as running 'to paranoid lengths' (1961, p.109) and the institution of the potlatch among the Kwakiutl she sees as the expression of a megalomaniac trend (p.160). Such judgements draw upon an earlier widely prevalent view that magical beliefs and ritual exist only among people who are excessively fearful and suggestible (Seligman 1929, p.191).

Transcultural psychiatrists thus had a rich anthropological field to draw upon. Anthropological writing supplied them with any number of negative racial stereotypes. Carothers, for example, quotes Westerman:

> With the Negro emotional, momentary and explosive thinking predominates...dependence on excitement, on external influences and stimuli, is a characteristic sign of primitive mentality. Primitive man's energy is unstable and spasmodic. He is easily fired with enthusiasm for an undertaking and begins his work with great zest; but his interest dies down quickly and the work is abandoned... Where the stimulus of emotion is lacking the Negro shows little spontaneity and is passive. He waits for what is coming to him and avoids inconvenient, or adapts himself to it, instead of bravely confronting the obstacles of life and mastering them... The Negro has but few gifts for work which aims at a distant goal and requires tenacity, independence, and foresight. (Carothers 1953, p.85)

Strathern has recently argued that the insights of autobiographical experience have been of central importance for the literary construction of experience (1987). What this extract from Westerman's treatise on *The African Today and Tomorrow* shows is the way in which norms of selfhood are brought to bear on the construction of cultural and racial difference. Lurking behind this description we can detect the influence of a self imbued with a Calvinist work ethic.

THE SOCIAL SHAPING OF MEDICAL THOUGHT

The huge volume of work on the history of science and of medicine in particular makes this position untenable in its extreme form.[19] As Kuhn has demonstrated, science is not impervious to its social and cultural context (1970). This is even more true of psychiatry which deals with such culturally sensitive concepts as the sense of self, personal identity, values and emotions. Indeed, studies show that western notions of selfhood which place such a high premium on privacy and agency form part of a larger constellation of cultural ideas and values. Conversely, the quintessence of psychiatric illness – schizophrenia – involves the loss of these culturally valued attributes (see Barrett 1996). A compelling illustration of the way in which structures of medical thought mirror social and political structures is to be found in Unschuld's study of Chinese medicine (1985). He shows how the distribution of political power in different historical epochs is echoed by changing conceptions of the way power and energy are distributed throughout the body. For example, the devolution of political power is associated with a view of the body as possessing dispersed energy centres. Centralized political power is associated with a view of the body governed from a single bodily centre. Psychiatry, perhaps more than the rest of medicine, is influenced by what is going on in society. The roots of the large state psychiatric institutions are to be found in the processes of industrialization, the huge shifts of population from the country to the cities, the attendant demographic changes as families moved in search of work as well as the growth of a medical speciality eager to carve out its own area of expertise (Scull 1979).

It is a strange paradox that at the present time when psychiatrists are stereotyped somewhat negatively as being restricted to the medical model, only able to construe an individual's mental problems within a narrow diagnostic classification or preoccupied with reductionist quantitative research methods, that the evidence for new ways of thinking to take into account the qualitative meaning of experience and the need for a user-orientated service has become so much more prominent. Thus, for example, the interface between religion and psychiatry has become a popular area of discourse (see Dein, Chapter 7) and the Royal College of Psychiatrists, far from being a bastion of biomedical supremacy, has established a special interest group in spirituality. Furthermore, although central research funding is directed more towards the neurosciences than the social sciences, there is increased possibility for health services research funded by the NHS, as well as increased awareness of the relevance of qualitative as well as quantitative research methods. However, as Kleinman has emphasized and as Lipsedge rightly points out (Chapter 12), formal training in the social sciences (including social anthropology) is still as limited in postgraduate training programmes as it is in the teaching of medical students. In this regard the key influence of role models provided by individuals who have a double training is so important. Jackson has described the consumer-orientated health service where users and carers are active participants in the development of health care, and the increased prominence of public health doctors determined needs for a multicultural, multiracial society have brought such issues as stigmatization, equity for minorities, access to care and cultural competence of health workers (see Fitzgerald, Chapter 8) much more to the fore.

Medical thought is however still influenced by the search for closer links between mental disorder and social factors and the relevance of faulty personal relationships. Society is also searching for a more personalized therapy provided by health services which still is dominated by an impersonal technology and the use of medicine without explanations.

Western medical practitioners have therefore to compete with complementary therapists and consumers who may choose to bypass medical opinion in the search for a more meaning centered personal therapy.

MIGRATION AND CULTURE SHOCK

One important aspect of the social anthropological approach is concern with similarities and differences between cultures, as exemplified by the fieldwork of early anthropologists who were medically qualified (for example, Rivers 1916; Seligman 1929). The relationship between migration between cultures and mental health is a further example of a commonality of interest between anthropology and psychiatry.

The popular term 'culture shock' implies that the adjustment of an individual who is uprooted from a home society and transplanted, whether voluntarily or as a forced exile, can be distressing and lead to mental disorder. This experience of alienation is also a common experience reported by anthropologists when reporting their field work and, as Littlewood (Chapter 2) has described, they therefore have the need to talk about this experience – a process which has some similarity with the induction into psychoanalysis through training analyses undertaken by the psychoanalyst and their need to consider this experience.

The assumption of this book, scattered throughout its several chapters, is that this process of culture change and contrast between a minority and majority community, especially when the minority is subject to racial prejudice, is not only unpleasant but can lead to depression (see Fernando 1988), disadvantage and social exclusion. Assumption of differences and stereotyping of communities with beliefs and domestic practices different from a more powerful majority have led to the worst abuses of psychiatry in the history of European psychiatry and so heighten sensitivity to the dangers of labelling and of an impersonal mental health service. This may also influence the forces within society which are concerned to limit the role of doctors or at least to limit their therapeutic influence by an emphasis on multi-professional teamworking.

Both medical anthropologists and psychiatrists can only work constructively in these fields if they are not only similarly culturally competent but also aware of the extent of racial discrimination by individuals as well as institutions, including those to which they belong.

The idea that social change is bad for mental health has deep and by no means unfounded anthropological roots. Drawing upon Durkheim's idea of *anomie*, rapid social change was perceived as destabilizing for both societies and individuals.

RACE AND RACISM

To urge readers to cross the bridge between anthropology and psychiatry without being aware of the realities of discrimination and racism, both individual and institutional, which characterized the history of both our disciplines and still affects present practice, would we believe compound felony with personal offence. We were first sensitized to these issues by our own professional and personal biographies: JC's experience witnessing the expulsion of the Asian community in Uganda by Idi Amin and contact with expatriate colonial attitudes; VS's knowledge of expropriation and repression by the totalitarian regime in Latvia.

As several contributors to this book have pointed out, the history of anthropology and psychiatry is steeped in the attitudes of Victorian paternalism. Although anthropology has been repatriated (see Jackson, Chapter 6; Sinclair, Chapter 12) and the Rousseauesque image of the noble savage counteracted by increased recognition of the global extent of mental disorder and disability, nevertheless these histories can still subtly influence the practice of our disciplines.

The need for clarity, for example, with regard to the definitions of culture, ethnicity and race is crucial: Singh (1997) has presented useful definitions and issued a warning that transcultural psychiatry as a discipline has not only to recognize its historical legacy but also constantly to counterbalance the tendency to ethnocentrism and the institutionalization of disadvantage.

The 1999 World Psychiatric Association meeting in Germany agreed a common ethical code and included a session by German psychiatrists who were searching for the explanation as to how doctors had collaborated with the systematic killing of up to 10,000 patients with mental illness and learning disability on the ground of eugenics and 'legalized' euthanasia.

Transcultural psychiatry, as Murphy (1973) underlined, 'begins at home' and it is at home that the extent of discrimination, prejudice and stigma has to be recognized – both within an individual and institutional context. The Royal College of Psychiatrists whose history extends back to the middle of the nineteenth century when the first meeting of asylum directors took place in Gloucester adopted a report making 25 recommendations in the field of education and training for service delivery to a multicultural society. These recommendations were intended to counteract any tendency for mental health professionals to perpetuate racist attitudes and institutional procedures that are discriminatory on grounds of race, gender or religion. The persisting tendency to exclude teaching on transcultural psychiatry and race however within 'approved' training still persists and Lipsedge (Chapter 12) is right to have drawn attention to this neglect. Furthermore, the tendency to emphasize the importance of a biomedical explanatory paradigm, sometimes caricatured as being specifically western (see

Littlewood, Chapter 2; Hutchinson and Bhugra, Chapter 10) and the contemporary emphasis on the search for the genetic basis of mental disorder would suggest that, even if Littlewood's analysis of the overdose as an 'appeal' to the dominant biomedical paradigm is not totally explanatory, the supremacy of biomedicine underlined by commercial pharmaceutical interests is still apparent.

However, there are also signs of change and grounds for hope which include a greater awareness about issues of race and racism within medicine and psychiatry and an awareness that discriminatory and racist attitudes are not confined to the white population only but can affect any ethnic group. One of the first accounts of the problems experienced by a recently arrived immigrant was of a Swedish immigrant to the USA who was teased as being a 'green horn' and felt alien in a hostile environment.

Almost all the contributors to our book are clinicians and research workers. We are therefore aware that the need for a scientific method which is transparent, replicable and refutable and which leads to findings that influence mental health services remains fundamentally important. What is also important, however, is that such research, especially with minorities, is ethical and that those participating in such research are aware of its implications and have given fully informed consent. Ethical guidelines for research workers produced by the Transcultural Psychiatry Society and MIND by Patel (1999) are profoundly important; they are explicit and balanced and should therefore be considered by an ethics research committee.

The search for a common language explored by the WHO in its classificatory system and assessment methods, while important for communication between clinicians and researchers, may not necessarily always facilitate communication with the patient which is based on an individual personal narrative and dialogue: the narrative of the patient and the doctor and the informant and the anthropologist. Sinclair (Chapter 11) illustrates the importance of a participant observation methodology in understanding the medical student culture.

Other contributors, for example, Eisenbruch (Chapter 9), illustrate the value of an ethnographic approach to the understanding of postnatal mood disorder. The Cambodians, like the Ugandans (see Cox and Amariko 1979; Neema 1994), but unlike western diagnostic systems have explicit categories for postnatal disorders and even also identify specialist healers. They are concerned about causes and prevention of this condition – an approach characteristically absent from western classifications such as DSM IV and ICD 10.

Bridges, we believe, have to be constructed and then crossed in both directions. Yet they should not be fixed firmly at each end because our subjects – medical anthropology and psychiatry – are changing rapidly and the intrepid explorer may find that there is no familiar base to return to, once on the bridge itself.

The future of society is changing in response to new gender roles, more equal opportunities and an increased awareness of discrimination, exclusion and stigma. These changes, and in particular the changes in family structure and greater discontinuity between generations, will influence the rates of mental health problems and the types of service that need to be made available.

We hope our book will continue the process of widening the perspective of psychiatrists and that the bio-psychosocial model of mental disorder will give greater emphasis to its sociocultural component and medical anthropologists will become more familiar with the disorders of mental life, the madness and the badness, the influence of nature and nurture on medical conditions, as well as the changes in contemporary medical health services.

Both our disciplines are changing and perhaps the corridors of medical schools are just beginning to heed Kleinman's (1977, 1988, 1991) earlier call for a revolution in teaching priorities and to educate its faculty and students in both the art and the science of medicine, the qualitative and the quantitative, and so produce doctors more responsive to the society to which they are accountable.

The narratives of our patients and their informants and their search for mental health and for healers who will listen and understand their world are we believe the main supports for the bridges we are trying to build. The rewards for crossing to the other side, as these readings show, is not only an intellectual excitement as boundaries are explored, but also good news for clients, informants and patients who may seek our help and for those planners who establish a health-care structure by considering the assumptions of the helpers and the helped, the healers and the healed and the observers and the observed.

THE RELEVANCE OF ANTHROPOLOGY

This book will, we believe, inform the reader of the importance of social anthropology, both for the establishment of more sensitive psychiatric mental health services in developing countries where alternative healing systems are everyday realities, and for psychiatric practice in the west. Concepts and theoretical models of anthropology are relevant to many medical specialties. For example, and understanding of kinship systems, rites of passage, and the place of rituals and role of symbols are relevant to medical practice in the perinatal field (see Cox and Amariko 1979). Medical anthropologists have pointed out the limitations of psychiatric and reductionist perspectives – and so challenged medicine and psychiatrists in particular to increase their awareness of the limitations of diagnosis and the limited scope of medicines, without 'magic' and science (biomedical) without art. They have also opened up as routinely relevant an understanding of religion as a container of culture and important to the understanding treatment and cure of mental disorder.

If our book encourages more psychiatrists to undertake formal training as anthropologists and vice versa, then we will be satisfied. However, that is not our main goal. Instead we wish to encourage the reader to move across the bridge, to leave behind pre-formed stereotypes and to meet halfway the other discipline. In this way, and out of this discourse, we believe a more clinically relevant anthropology will emerge and certainly a psychiatrist's perspective more in tune with its own assumptions and so better able to contribute to a more holistic service based on the understanding not only of the patient as a person, or the psychiatrist as one spoke in the wheel, but also a service that is sensitive to the symbols and metaphors, the values and beliefs which reflect the society in which that person exists.

So which areas of anthropology are likely to be useful to the medical practitioner and psychiatrist? One not altogether helpful answer is – all of them. But perhaps attention can be drawn to some of anthropology's traditional areas of interest. Anthropological studies of symbolism and ritual have much to contribute to medicine and psychiatry. As Turner's (1967) profound understanding of the Ndembu showed, symbols (the smallest element of ritual) belong both to language and to the body; they are at one and the same time public and private. They mediate between polarities of corporeal and moral and social meanings. In the process of so doing physical experience is harnessed and gives power to community sentiments. Conversely, shared community values and beliefs give shape and intelligibility to bodily experience. Jung wrote that a sign is always less than the object for which it stands, whereas a symbol is always more than the object it represents. The healing power of symbols resides in this surplus of meaning that opens up as we move from the corporeal to the spiritual pole of symbolic meanings. Obeyesekere (1990, pp.3–68), in a combined psychoanalytic and anthropological approach, explores the way in which both the individual autobiography and the cultural ideology determine the ascetic ritual participation of a Muslim ecstatic in Sri Lanka. Pandolfi's study of south Italian peasant women draws upon her skills both as psychotherapist and ethnographer and shows how different kinds of social experience and recollection are inscribed in different ways upon the body (1991). What she describes as severed time, for example, memories of foreign domination or earthquakes, are remembered as the malfunctioning of the separate parts of the body. Social change is registered in the internal spaces of the body and emotions are registered as blocked movement (pp.61–62).

The early work of Van Gennep points to ritual promoting movement throughout the life course and effecting status change through processes of symbolic transformation (1977). Such transformations are also used in healing rituals which give linguistic shape to individual experience. The classic example is Lévi-Strauss's account of the Cuna shaman's healing assistance given to the woman in childbirth whose narrative transforms a painful physical experience into a mythical journey (1968, p.196). Contemporary ethnographers of healing rituals find the same transform-ations of the personal to the culturally mythic and language plays a key role in these transformations. Glass-Coffin's study of urban north-west Peru charts the power of words to inflict magical harm and to restore self-respecting identity and well-being (1992).

Anthropological studies of hospitals and medical practice have perhaps had the greatest impact on medicine. Goffman's studies of asylums (1968) and stigma (1963) have reached a readership beyond the disciplinary boundaries of anthropology and sociology; the workings of total institutions, among them psychiatric hospitals, were looked at not in terms of their stated overt aims but in terms of the hidden social control agenda of these institutions. A more recent study of psychiatric ideas and their relationship to the social organization of the hospital is by the anthropologist and psychiatrist Barrett (1996).

CONCLUSIONS

Kaufert and Kaufert attribute the refusal to address psychiatric issues to the 'narrower institutional affiliation of the British medical anthropologist' (1978, p.256). However, we want to argue that the caution with which early British anthropology approached medical matters derives from an Enlightenment tradition: the idea that medicine deals with a uniform natural substratum and that it is, therefore, of little interest to anthropology. This same Enlightenment tradition also underpins the work of the early transcultural psychiatrists and many later ones too. Psychiatry depends upon a commitment to the belief in a common rationality and presupposes that we may have shared criteria for judging irrationality.

Because so many of anthropology's perennial problems to do with understanding the particular and yet making it generally intelligible and accessible appear in an intensified form in the relationship between anthropology and psychiatry, medical and psychiatric anthropology have been marginalized. However, the paradox is that these central theoretical concerns which surface most acutely in medical anthropology have served to push it to the margins. Nevertheless, human experience and its observer and interpreter medical anthropology have sought to find a habitation in this obstacle-ridden terrain. The 'monstrous universal form of enquiry' that we alluded to at the beginning is one which questions definitions and self-assigned identities. Thus the dictionary definition of psychiatry as the medical treatment of diseases of the mind no longer looks straightforward. We have seen that medicine and psychiatry are not impervious to cultural values and that these shape conceptions of normality and abnormality, disease categories and, of course, ideas as to what constitutes appropriate treatment. The assumption too that in attributing diseases to the mind we have a clear shared understanding of the location of such diseases is no longer possible. In Taylor's words we do not have selves, or indeed minds, in the way that we have livers or stomachs, but rather selves and minds are constituted through each encounter with cultural goals and values: 'We are only selves insofar as we move in a certain space of questions, as we seek to find an orientation to the good' (1989, p.34).

So rather than a set of definitions we are left with questions. How can the understanding of individual experience in its own terms be combined with comparison and generalization? Can we move from individual and bodily experience to theory? We trust that this collection of essays will go some way to supplying positive answers to these questions for the reader.

NOTES

1. Attributed to Malinowski in Leach (1982, p.122).
2. See, for example, Wolf (1982).
3. Indeed, an ASA monograph edited by Anthony Jackson has just this title, *Anthropology at Home* (1987).
4. Including the self in the anthropological scrutiny can mean different things to different anthropologists. It may refer to the token gesture towards reflexivity such as Littlewood gives in *Pathology and Identity* in disclosing some fairly neutral features of his autobiography (1993); or it may provide a structure for the entire fieldwork study as in Favret-Saada's account of witchcraft beliefs in rural western France (1980).
5. The importance of difference has come to anthropology via linguistics. Ferdinand Saussure in his *Course in General Linguistics* outlined a theory of language and meaning as built upon processes of mutual definition and differentiation (1974, p.1916).
6. Participant observation which was until recently held to be synonymous with ethnography as a whole is now being recognized by anthropologists as one among a number of possible techniques. The claims of participant observers are increasingly being subjected to critical scrutiny.
7. For two very different accounts of the personal encounter with field work, see Nigel Barley (1983) and Renato Rosaldo (1993). Barley's *The Innocent Anthropologist* is one of the rare books by an anthropologist which has the reader in stitches of laughter. Rosaldo's chapter 'Grief and a Headhunter's Rage' is an intensely moving account of the anthropologist's journey from incomprehension and laboured theorizing to the illumination which comes from his own visceral grief reaction to the death of his wife (1993).
8. The role of writing in anthropology. Indeed, Marilyn Strathern argues that our recent recognition of the importance of the literary transformation of the fieldwork

experience may contribute to the intellectual reinstatement of such 'armchair' anthropologists as James Frazer (1987).

9. A number of prestigious writers, foremost among them Goffman, have been claimed as their own by both sociology and anthropology. Both are justified since Goffman was a sociology graduate but carried out his early fieldwork while based in the Department of Anthropology in Edinburgh.

10. However, like so many other concepts taken over by anthropologists, what or where home is is no longer clear cut. Judith Okely in *Own or Other Culture* provides a good example of 'confronting the unknown in [one's] midst' (1996, p.5).

11. The distinction was originally introduced by Kenneth Pike (1966).

12. This has come to be known as the writing culture debate after the collection of essays with that title focuses on anthropology not only as doing but as writing (Clifford and Marcus 1986). Rosaldo's chapter merits particular attention for the way in which it identifies the literary devices employed by Evans-Pritchard to convince the reader of his authority and his right to speak on behalf of the natives. His writing gives us a vivid portrayal not only of the Nuer but also of 'the fieldworker as a man endowed with calm presence of mind under the most arduous conditions' (Rosaldo 1986, p.89).

13. For the medical background of the early anthropologists, see Skultans (Chapter 3).

14. Freud made extensive use of the highly speculative anthropology of his day. He drew especially upon the work of James Frazer and William Robertson Smith. In *Totem and Taboo* he quotes from Frazer's *The Magic Art and the Evolution of Kings* to support his view that human beings are inherently anarchic. He draws upon Robertson Smith's wholly unfounded belief that sacrifice is the central component of all primitive religions. For a fuller discussion of these intellectual borrowings see Rieff's *Freud The Mind of the Moralist* (1961).

15. For a discussion of the way in which cultural explanations function as stereotypes of ethnic groups and have come to replace racial stereotypes, see Fernando (1988) and Nazroo (1997).

16. In Chinese culture *Koro* relates to a set of beliefs and behaviours focusing on a fear that the penis will retract into a man's body and result in death.

17. For a classical exposition of culture as hierarchy, see Edward Burnett Tylor (1959).

18. This emphasis on immersion in the concrete reminds us of anthropology's dual inheritance. Although anthropology clearly belonged to the Enlightenment project it also has roots in the counter-Enlightenment thinkers: Vico in Italy and Herder and Hahnemann in Germany. The easiest way of familiarizing oneself with these writers is through the writings of Isaiah Berlin (1976, 1979).

19. The recognition of the social shaping of science and medicine is, of course, in contradiction with Popper's idea that scientific truth depends upon falsifiability. Kuhn's argument is that scientific paradigms can ignore many instances of falsification and that it is not until a paradigm revolution occurs that such instances are taken into account. For a scholarly study of the development of scientific ideas in their social setting, see Webster (1975).

REFERENCES

Atkinson, P. (1995) *Medical Talk and Medical Work*. London: Sage.

Barley, N. (1983) *The Innocent Anthropologist Notes from a Mud Hut*. Harmondsworth: Penguin.

Barrett, R. (1996) *The Psychiatric Team and the Social Definition of Schizophrenia. An Anthropological Study of Person and Illness.* Cambridge: Cambridge University Press.

Benedict, R. (1961/1935) *Patterns of Culture.* London: Routledge.

Berlin, I. (1976) *Vico and Herder. Two Studies in the History of Ideas.* London: Hogarth Press.

Berlin, I. (1979) *Against the Current. Essays in the History of Ideas.* London: Pimlico.

Carothers, J.C. (1953) *The African Mind in Health and Disease. A Study in Ethnopsychiatry.* Geneva: WHO.

Church, K. (1995) *Forbidden Narratives: Critical Autobiography as Social Science.* Amsterdam: Gordon and Breach.

Clifford, J. and Marcus, G.E. (eds) (1986) *Writing Culture: The Poetics and Politics of Ethnography.* Berkeley: University of California Press.

Cox, J. and Amakiro, A. (1979) 'Ugandan puerperal psychosis?' *Social Psychiatry 14,* 49–62.

Favret-Saada, J. (1980) *Deadly Words: Witchcraft in the Bocage.* Cambridge: Cambridge University Press.

Fernando, S. (1988) *Race Culture and Psychiatry.* London: Croom Helm.

Frank, A. (1991) *At the Will of the Body: Reflections on Illness.* Boston: Houghton Mifflin.

Frank. A. (1995) *The Wounded Storyteller Body, Illness and Ethics.* Chicago: University of Chicago Press.

Freeman, D. (1965) 'Anthropology, psychiatry and the doctrine of cultural relativism.' *Man 65,* 65–67.

Freud, S. (1963) *Civilization and its Discontents.* London: Hogarth Press.

Geertz, C. (1984) 'Anti anti-relativism.' *American Anthropologist 86,* 263–278.

Geertz, C. (1988) *Works and Lives. The Anthropologist as Author.* Cambridge: Polity Press.

Glass-Coffin, B. (1992) 'Discourse, Dano and healing in north coastal Peru.' In M. Richter (ed) *Anthropological Approaches to the Study of Ethnomedicine.* Switzerland: Gordon and Breach, pp.33–55.

Goffman, E. (1968) *Asylums. Essays on the Social Situation of Mental Patients and Other Inmates.* Harmondsworth: Penguin.

Goffman, E. (1963) *Stigma.* Harmondsworth: Penguin.

Hendry, J. (1999) *An Introduction to Social Anthropology. Other People's Worlds.* Basingstoke and London: Macmillan.

Hollis, M. and Lukes, S. (1982) *Rationality and Relativism.* Oxford: Blackwell.

Holy, L. (ed) (1987) *Comparative Anthropology.* Oxford: Blackwell.

Jackson, A. (ed) (1987) *Anthropology at Home.* London: Tavistock.

Janzen, J. (1978) *The Quest for Therapy in Lower Zaire.* Berkeley: University of California Press.

Kaufert, L.P. and Kaufert, J.M. (1978) 'Alternate courses of development: medical anthropology in Britain and North America.' *Social Science and Medicine 12B,* 255–261.

Kiev, A. (1972) *Transcultural Psychiatry*. New York: Free Press.

Kleinman, A. (1977) 'Depression, somatization and the "new cross-cultural psychiatry".' *Social Science and Medicine 11*, 3–10.

Kleinman, A. (1988) *The Illness Narratives. Suffering, Healing and the Human Condition*. New York: Basic Books.

Kleinman, A. and Kleinman, J. (1991) 'Suffering and its professional transformation towards an ethnography of interpersonal experience.' *Culture Medicine and Psychiatry 15*, 3, 275–301.

Kraepelin, E. (1974/1903) 'Comparative psychiatry.' In S. Hirsch and M. Shepherd *Themes and Variations in European Psychiatry. An Anthology*. Brisol: John Wright.

Kroeber, A.L. (1923) *Anthropology*. London: George Harrap.

Kroeber, A.L. and Kluckhohn, C. (1952) *Culture. A Critical Review of Concepts and Definitions*. New York: Vintage Books.

Kuhn, T. (1970/1962) *The Structure of Scientific Revolutions*. London: University of Chicago Press.

Leach E. (1982) *Social Anthropology*. London: Fontana.

Lévi-Strauss, C. (1968) 'The effectiveness of symbols.' In C. Lévi-Strauss *Structural Anthropology*. Harmondsworth: Penguin.

Lewis, I. (1976) *An Introduction to Social Anthropology*. Harmondsworth: Penguin.

Littlewood, R. (1993) *Pathology and Identity. The Work of Mother Earth in Trinidad*. Cambridge: Cambridge University Press.

Littlewood, R. and Lipsedge, M. (1997) *Aliens and Alienists*, 3rd edn. London: Routledge.

Loudon, J. (1970) *Social Anthropology and Medicine*. London: Academic Press.

Malinowski, B. (1944) *A Scientific Theory of Culture and Other Essays*. Chapel Hill: University of North Carolina Press.

Mattingly, C. (1998) *Healing Dramas and Clinical Plots. The Narrative Structure of Experience*. Cambridge: Cambridge University Press.

Mills, C.W. (1973) *The Sociological Imagination*. Oxford: Oxford University Press.

Murphy, H.B. (1973) 'Current trends in transcultural psychiatry.' *Proceedings of the Royal Society of Medicine 66*, 711–716.

Nazroo, J. (1997) *The Health of Britain's Ethnic Minorities: Findings from a National Survey*. London: Policy Institute.

Neema, S.B. (1994) 'Mothers and midwives: maternity care options in Ankole South Western Uganda.' Unpublished PhD thesis, University of Copenhagen.

Obeyesekere, G. (1990) 'Unfreezing the text. Releasing the narrative.' In G. Obeyesekere *The Work of Culture*. London: University of Chicago Press.

Okely, J. (1996) *Own or Other Culture*. London: Routledge.

Opler, M.K. (ed) (1959) *Culture and Mental Health. Cross-Cultural Studies*. New York: Macmillan.

Orley, J. (1970) *Culture and Mental Illness: A Study from Uganda*. Nairobi: East African Publishing House.

Pandolfi, M. (1991) 'A memory within the body: women's narrative and identity in a southern Italian village.' In B. Pfleiderer and G. Bibeau (eds) *Anthropologies of Medicine*. Braunschweig: Vieweg.

Patel, N. (1999) *Ethical Guidelines for Research in Black and Ethnic Minorities*. London: Mind Publications.

Pike, L.K. (1966) *Language in Relation to a Unified Theory of the Structure of Human Behaviour*. The Hague: Mouton.

Pocock, D. (1961) *Social Anthropology*. London: Sheed and Ward.

Portelli, A. (1991) *The Death of Luigi Trastulli and Other Stories. Form and Meaning in Oral History*. Albany: State University of New York Press.

Radcliffe-Brown, A.R. (1952) *Structure and Function in Primitive Society: Essays and Addresses*. London: Cohen and West.

Rieff, P. (1961) *Freud: The Mind of the Moralist*. New York: Doubleday.

Rivers, W.H. (1916) 'Sociology and psychology.' *Sociological Review 9*, 1–16.

Rosaldo, R. (1986) 'From the door of his tent.' In C. James and G.E. Marcus (eds) *Writing Culture. The Poetics and Politics of Ethnography*. Berkeley: University of California Press.

Rosaldo, R. (1993) 'Grief and the headhunter's rage.' In R. Rosaldo *Culture and Truth. The Remaking of Social Analysis*. London: Routledge.

Sansom, B. (1982) 'The sick who do not speak.' In D. Parkin (ed) *Semantic Anthropology*. London: Academic Press.

Saussure, F. de (1916/revised edn 1974) *Course in General Linguistics* trans. W. Baskin. Glasgow: Fontana/Collins.

Savage, C., Leighton, A.H. and Leighton, D.C. (1965) 'The problem of cross-cultural identification of psychiatric disorders.' In J.M. Murphy and A.H. Leighton (eds) *Approaches to Cross-Cultural Psychiatry*. Ithaca: Cornell University Press, pp.21–63.

Scheper-Hughes, N. (1990) *Death Without Weeping. The Violence of Everyday Life in Brazil*. Berkeley: University of California Press.

Scull, A. (1979) *Museums of Madness. The Social Organization of Insanity in Nineteenth Century England*. London: Allen Lane.

Seligman, C.G. (1929) 'Temperament, conflict and psychosis in a stone-age population.' *British Journal of Medical Psychology 9*, 187–202.

Simons, R.C. and Hughes, C.C. (eds) (1985) *Culture Bound Syndromes. Folk Illnesses of Psychiatric and Anthropological Interest*. Dordrecht: Reidel.

Singh, S.P. (1997) 'Ethnicity in psychiatric epidemiology: need for precision.' *British Journal of Psychiatry 171*, 305–308.

Skultans, V. (1998) *The Testimony of Lives. Narrative and Memory in Post-Soviet Latvia*. London: Routledge.

Skultans, V. (1999) 'Narratives of the body and history: illness in judgement on the Soviet past.' *Sociology of Health and Illness 21*, 3, 310–328.

Sperber, D. (1985) *On Anthropological Knowledge*. Cambridge: Cambridge University Press.

Strathern, M. (1987) 'Out of context: the persuasive fictions of anthropology.'
    Current Anthropology 28, 3, 251–281.

Taylor, C. (1989) *Sources of the Self: The Making of Modern Identity*. Cambridge:
    Cambridge University Press.

Turner, V. (1967) *The Forest of Symbols: Aspects of Ndembu Ritual*. Ithaca: Cornell
    University Press.

Tylor, E.B. (1958) *The Origins of Culture*. New York: Harper Row.

Unschuld, P. (1985) *Medicine in China. A History of Ideas*. Berkeley: University of
    California Press.

Van Gennep, A. (1977/1905) *Rites of Passage*. London: Routledge.

Webster, C. (1975) *The Great Instauration Science, Medicine and Reform 1626–1660*.
    London: Duckworth.

Weiss, M., Doongaji, D., Siddhartha, S., Wypij, D., Pathare, S., Bhatawdeker, M.,
    Bhare, A., Sheth, A. and Fernandes, R. (1992) 'The explanatory model
    interview catalogue [EMIC]: Contribution to cross-cultural research methods
    from a study of leprosy and mental health.' *British Journal of Psychiatry 160*,
    819–830.

Wolf, E. (1982) *Europe and the People Without History*. Berkeley: University of
    California Press.

Yap, P.M. (1965) 'Religion and affective disorder.' In A.V.S. De Reuck and R.C.
    Porter (eds) *Symposium on Transcultural Psychiatry*. Boston: Little, Brown.

Yap, P.M. (1974) *Comparative Psychiatry: A Theoretical Framework*. Toronto:
    University of Toronto Press.

Young, A. (1996) *The Harmony of Illusions. Inventing Post Traumatic Stress Disorder*.
    Princeton: Princeton University Press.

Zola, I. (1982) *Missing Pieces. A Chronicle of Living with Disability*. Philadelphia:
    Temple University Press.

PART 1

Theoretical Approaches

The Cultural Construction
of Western Depression

Sushrut Jadhav

INTRODUCTION

Over the past two decades, a significant body of research has outlined major problems that relate to the deployment of psychiatric diagnostic classificatory systems and standardized research instruments in cross-cultural settings (Jadhav 1995, Kleinman 1987, Kleinman and Good 1985, Littlewood 1990, Murphy 1982). Among the diagnostic groups, depression[1] has been singled out as the one that raises significant issues of cultural validity and which poses special problems as a universally valid disorder (Jadhav and Littlewood 1994; Kleinman and Good 1985). Fundamental problems include:

- cross-cultural variations in definitions of selfhood (Heelas and Lock 1981; Marsella and White 1982)
- differing local categories of emotions (Lutz and Abu-Lughod 1990)
- cultural variations in language with attendant problems of translating emotion-related vocabulary (Littlewood 1990)
- the absence of a universal biological specification (Kleinman and Good 1985).

AN INDIAN PROBLEM

Despite these demonstrated concerns, medical professionals, psychiatrists included, consider depression as universal in form, with cross-cultural differences in symptomatology as a mere artefact (Kaplan and Saddock 1995; Sartorius *et al.* 1983). If there are such major differences in symptomatology[2], it begs the questions: Why do they receive the same diagnosis? How does this contradiction arise? To illustrate how this might have occurred and continues to take place; I will share some observations from clinical experience at several Indian rural and urban psychiatric clinics.[3]

The majority of psychiatric assessments in India take place in national and regional languages, either in Hindi or the language spoken in a particular state. However, the recording of case notes and discussions with clinical colleagues almost always take place in English with terminology that closely mirrors the vocabulary of western psychiatry. Most urban psychiatric clinics have standardized forms and entry sheets with printed headers and guidelines derived from established psychiatric history taking and mental state schedules used in Britain.[4] A final formulation and diagnosis of 'the case', together with planned interventions, take place in a manner so as to match the canons of psychiatric theory delineated in western psychiatric textbooks (Kaplan and Saddock 1995). Qualifying examinations for mental health professionals require trainees to have a thorough knowledge of such texts, with merit accorded to one's ability in espousing recent theories on mental disorders published in international journals with a high citation index.[5] An additional requirement, the completion of a research thesis vetted by a supervisory panel ensures conformation with internationally accepted methods and instruments.[6]

The pressures of learning the idioms of western psychiatric vocabulary with its associated 'touch of English', publishing in prestigious journals for acceptance by the international academic community (coupled with local association of the term 'western' with progress, refinement and technological advancement) seldom allow scope for developing alternative theoretical formulations on mental distress. Further, the teaching of western psychiatric history as a factual set of dates, events and names is directly linked to any local psychiatric discourse and thus appropriated as a common academic intellectual heritage. An audience with pharmaceutical representatives armed with semiotics that reinforce western folk psychiatric images (Kleinman and Cohen 1991; Neill 1989) are regular features at outpatient clinics. Such encounters often lead to the introduction of newer pharmacological products into clinical practice, sometimes with questionable monitoring of adverse drug side-effects.[7]

In this situation, local worlds, their core moral and cultural values, and a rich emotional vocabulary associated with bodily problems and expressed through a range of non-English languages (Lynch 1990), are often glossed over or pruned to fit into conventional psychiatric nosological systems (DSM and ICD). This process of systematically acquiring a culture-blind ability is considered credible and meritorious, both locally and internationally.[8] The exclusion of culture then systematically abolishes the ability (and sensibility) to consider the role of major social and cultural variables such as poverty, migration, urbanization, gender, caste, stigma and other socially oppressive situations that may well relate to depression or its local equivalent. Ironically, these are precisely the very issues cited by the international community as relevant for the health and economic development of the poorer nations (Desjerlais *et al.* 1995).

Issues of cultural validity then acquire a significance that has serious implications for and beyond the clinic setting. One might argue that such a selective 'cultural cleansing' of patient narratives takes away the opportunity for the major research questions that cultural psychiatry seeks to investigate. For example, how may local idioms of distress (currently fitted under the broad rubric of depressive or somatization disorders), such as *naara mein dard* (pain in the nerves), *meetha dard* (sweet pain), *sar mein garmi* (heat in the head), *tidik* (twitch), *badan mein dard* (pain in the body), or *dil mein udasi* (sorrow in the heart), etc., provide a phenomenological template to generate appropriate nosologies of distress[9] (Jadhav 1986). If such nosologies were to develop, they might perhaps lead to a fundamental reconceptualization of depressive disorders (Krause 1989; Nichter 1981).

How does one proceed further? A recent line of enquiry within the 'new cross-cultural psychiatry' framework suggests that 'western psychiatric theory' has often naturalized its own cultural distinctions, objectified them through empirical data and then received them back as if they were universal objective 'natural science' categories (American Psychiatric Association DSM IV 1995; Littlewood 1990). It postulates that each culture generates a local psychiatry (termed 'ethnopsychiatry') that constitutes and articulates the moral values and health concerns of that particular culture (Gaines 1992). In this schema, current psychiatric theory is just another instance of an ethnopsychiatry, embedded however in western society and developed in response to prevailing concerns at differing periods in history. Such an approach seeks to problematize existing psychiatric concepts that are otherwise considered culture free and universally applicable; by de-constructing theory (ies) to reveal their culturally constituted foundation (Good 1994). To use a postmodern cliché, such a project is about 'rewriting' psychiatric history: the others' perspective.

The remainder of this chapter will address this issue with a focus on the historical development of concepts and terminologies associated with depression in western Europe and, in particular, in Britain. Although limited to a lexical and semantic consideration of certain terminology, and therefore by no means an exhaustive cultural analysis, it is an attempt to provide a general overview of the ways in which some of the key concepts of depression have been culturally shaped, yet are now assumed to be universal natural entities that await further scientific research and investigation.

A BRIEF ETHNOPSYCHOLOGY OF WESTERN DEPRESSION
The mind–body distinction, concepts of self and the location of emotions

The literature of cultural psychiatry has often referred to separation of the mind from the body as a fundamental dualism that underpins western psychiatric diagnostic and classificatory systems (Gaines 1992; Kleinman and Good 1985). Although the history of mind–body dichotomies dates back before the seventeenth-century writing of René Descartes, the study of how the western self is culturally constituted has generated surprisingly fewer ideas. Some consider it as a bounded, unique, homogeneous and autonomous entity (Marsella and White 1982), with clear boundaries and personal space; others have postulated terms such as 'ego-centric' (Shweder 1991) and 'indexical' (Gaines 1992), as opposed to the 'socio-centric' and 'referential' self of third world societies. Analysis of contemporary western professional and folk psychological idioms suggests an image of an entity that generates thoughts and emotions from inside a metaphorical three-dimensional space enclosed within firm boundaries and containing a 'substance' (Goldman and Montagne 1986; Lakoff and Johnson 1980; Mant and Danoch 1975; Neill 1989). In this container, past experiences are stored in a vertical and linear fashion[10] that can be 'emptied' out in cathartic sessions. The 'pressure' brought about by 'life events' and 'traumas' could exhaust such a culturally constituted psychological space and lead to a bursting of protective dams (such as psychodynamic defence mechanisms) causing disintegration and disorder (Lakoff and Johnson 1980). This sort of 'rational' self therefore helps keep in check its emotions (mainly anger and depression) which if let out or let in (as in anger turned inwards) could prove damaging. The worth and social estimate of this self is then measured by achievements refracted through a self-monitoring structure (the affective apparatus). Thus, low self-esteem occurs when the affective apparatus is depressed and an inflated self-esteem when elated. Interpersonal and social problems are restructured as a series of person-centric 'constructs' (Kelly 1955) that are focused on the individual viewed as an unitary active agent acting upon the natural world.

Emotions are then both a property of, and simultaneously constitutive, of the self, but they can also acquire an impersonal form to be transacted and exchanged as commodities.[11] Emotional pathologies are represented through four 'primary' emotions: depression, elation, anxiety and fear. These are enshrined in the form of affective disorders within the official diagnostic systems (DSM and ICD) as pure forms, and as mood 'incongruent' disorders (schizo-affective disorders) if they occur in mixed forms (i.e. in association with thought disturbances). Psychodynamic forms of therapy invoke concepts such as 'engagement' and 'disengagement' with the affected self that then require the 'transfer' of key emotions onto a 'significant' other, the therapist. Although this metaphorical description is a brief and simplistic account of the self, it is derived from the discourse within western psychiatric theory. Here, depression is primarily a 'disorder of mood' that rests upon a pathology of key emotions considered arising from within the 'mind'. Predominant expressions of bodily distress are therefore situated within a separate diagnostic category: 'somatization disorders' and are viewed to have a distinct natural history, course, diagnosis and intervention from that of 'mood [affective] disorders' (American Psychiatric Association DSM IV 1995). Against this background, a range of depressive vocabularies and their cultural histories need to be examined in more detail.

A LEXICAL ANALYSIS OF DEPRESSION

Any attempt to examine the origin of depression and related feeling states, in an historical context, is beset with two major problems:

- relying upon ancient written texts, their interpretations within various disciplines and the general problem of historical interpretation
- the semantic and conceptual problem of retroactively employing a term or concept.

There are problems of assuming 'depression' to be a constant feeling state that is merely changing in its vocabulary over time; an idiom similar to the form–content debate across cultures (Murphy 1982). If the vocabulary of emotion is itself a cultural construct, that is shaped and in turn shapes affect, then there is a clear problem of assuming constants of affective states over time. Not surprisingly, several medical historians have chosen to take acedia, sadness, melancholia and depression as a single temporally linked and successive feeling state that has simply been subject to changing labels over time (Clarke 1975; Hunter and Macalpine 1963).

The earliest use of the term 'depression' in English language dates back to the seventeenth century. Its subsequent and ubiquitous use in describing a state of mind, the weather or economy suggests a general state of 'lowering of affairs' (Fontana Dictionary of Modern Thought 1988). The first standard English gloss of this term was introduced by Samuel Johnson in his dictionary (1755). The Oxford English Dictionary cites its etymology from Latin roots: de primere (to press down, Appendix). An idiom initially developed as a spatial metaphor, represented in astronomy and architecture, later acquired gravitational properties to represent a model of mood states along a vertical axis, well exemplified in the 1750s prints of William Hogarth (Littlewood 1994). How did such a metaphor arise? What were its historical antecedents? If the current western European vocabulary of dysphoric mood states is as recent as the seventeenth century, can one claim that emotional states were less differentiated or configured in a different manner before this period?

Although earlier research argued Old English as a poor medium for emotional expression, Nicholson (1995) proposes the presence of a prolific vocabulary of emotions during the Anglo-Saxon period. His analysis of Anglo-Saxon literature provides evidence of a rich abstract vocabulary denoting various mood states. An examination of Old English elegies revealed over 37 different emotions that serve as equivalents for Modern English terms such as sorrow, misery, grief, fear, caring at dawn, anger, sorrowful love, perpetual grief, etc. Based on this evidence, Nicholson challenges the premise that earlier societies neglected and undervalued emotional states due to a lack of emphasis on personal choice or to an undifferentiated psychological vocabulary (Leff 1973). While acknowledging that Anglo-Saxon vocabularies do not directly relate to Modern English words, Nicholson confirms the existence of a range of psychological states during the Anglo-Saxon period. Of particular interest is the term *unmod* in Old English which translates as depression, but also refers to a disease state arising from the stomach. This bears a close linguistic affinity with the Sanskrit term *unmada*, a generic term in ayurvedic medicine for severe mental disorders (Bhishagratna 1991), and suggests cultural transmission of concepts may have taken place during the Anglo-Saxon period (Clarke 1975).

Historical evidence argues that the major source of current concepts relating to psychological disturbances in Europe derived from the Church, followed later by classical Greek and Latin texts that came via Arabic sources. The most popular of these were *acedia* and *black bile* and both seemed to have had a complex relationship with a new term in English, *melancholia* (Jackson 1986).

ACEDIA, BLACK BILE AND MELANCHOLIA

Jackson's scholarly and exhaustive research on melancholia in general and acedia in particular (Jackson 1986) reveals the complexity in an historical analysis of psychiatric vocabulary and the difficulties of drawing valid conclusions. The absence of popular folk literature from such remote historical periods further complicates this issue. Historians have generally had access to surviving written documents only of the literate elite, which poses further limitations into research on the historiography of folk concepts.

The term 'acedia' originated from the Latin *accidia,* which may be glossed as 'heedlessness and torpor', and later became a 'favourite ecclesiastical word to describe the mental prostations of recluses, induced by fasting' (OED 1994). Black bile is the modern English translation of the Greek term, *melaine chole* (Latin *atrabilis*), with melancholia in English deriving directly from Latin, which in turn was derived from the Greek (Jackson 1986).

Western thought on melancholy derives from the Hippocratic corpus in the fifth century BC, systematized by Galen during the second century AD, thereafter preserved and elaborated by Arab and other Eastern physicians between the end of the Classical period and its Arabic reintroduction into the west (Rippere 1981). When these ideas re-emerged in the late Middle Ages, they were available through Latin translations that were then adopted into academic teaching in the universities (Clarke 1975). Such a process could therefore have led to a range of meaning systems, nomenclatures and theories. Despite such cultural transitions and reinterpretations, the term melancholia seemed to prove a relatively durable concept and an overarching category that was later to subsume a range of dysphoric terms including acedia and guilt (Bright 1586).

Although religious literature of the late fourth century AD referred to acedia as one of the major temptations with which the solitary monk had to struggle (Clarke 1975), Jackson's translations of the writings of John Cassian, an influential monk of the period, suggest bodily metaphors such as a 'weariness or distress of the heart', 'akin to dejection' and 'especially trying to solitaries'. He describes:

> The condition was characterised by exhaustion, listlessness, sadness or dejection, restlessness, aversion to the cell and the ascetic life, and yearning for family and former life. The afflicted monk became restless, complained that his situation was no longer spiritually fruitful and that he was useless in it, and he thought that he would never be well unless he left the place. In his continuing restlessness, time seemed to pass very slowly, he yearned for company and considered seeking solace in sleep. In short, he tended to either remain idle in his cell or to wander from it in restless pursuit of diversionary activities, in either case to no spiritual end. (Jackson 1986, pp.66–67).

The term continued to be used by theologians over the next decade, and by the twelfth century AD it survived internal ecclesiastical debate[12] to be officially accepted as one of the seven deadly temptations, the sin of sloth (Jackson 1986). How then did acedia acquire folk popularity if it was confined to monks, given their reclusive lives in monasteries? In contrast to the early Middle Ages, when medicine was taught exclusively in monasteries, an outward diffusion of medical ideas did not occur (Clarke 1975). However, the rise of clerical power during the twelfth and thirteenth centuries, led to confession being made obligatory by the Fourth Lateran Council (Legge 1963). This resulted in an extensive production of penitential literature, manuals for preachers and cathetical handbooks, with a steady diffusion of religious and medical ideas and concepts into the popular culture. During the subsequent scholastic phase, a systematic analysis of theological literature resulted in the integration of acedia with Greek theories of the passions that had started arriving into Britain. Acedia 'emerged as a disorder in man's emotional life. At times, it came to be thought of in medical terms' (Jackson 1986, p.70). Its status as a sin however, continued within the Church until further developments led to its association with black bile and religious guilt.

THE CULTURAL HISTORY OF GUILT

The word guilt derives from the early medieval German gelt (gold or *guld*: to pay for an offence), a monetary penalty for commission of crime but commonly used to indicate a failure of duty (OED 1994). The literature suggests this was primarily a religious and social category that became interiorized and transformed into a secular psychology. To follow the OED citations: Initially conceived as a sin (ninth century AD), later as the fact of having committed some specified moral offence ('Christ shed his blood so he might wash us from the sickness of guilt: *quarto sanguinuem suum fudit, ut nos a morbo culpe lavaret'*, fourteenth century AD), (Siegfried 1989, p.207); then as feelings of conscience (fifteenth to sixteenth century AD), and as a quasi-medical term, guilt-sick conscience (1625 AD), it later acquired physical characteristics such as being pent-up inside the body (1605 AD), and evolved into a more elaborate psychological category, guilt complex (1927 AD), with a further development into a plural form: guilts (1932 AD). (OED 1994)

If guilt originated as a moral and social category, how did it become incorporated within a medical psychological framework and acquire a pathological connotation (as it does in the psychiatric descriptions of contemporary depressive disorders)? To understand this, one needs to examine the changing relationship between the Church and medical profession. Jackson and others have postulated that this came about as a result of key texts and teachings of eminent theologians who were to later practise medicine, or vice versa (Clarke 1975; Jackson 1986). The role of this 'medical clergy' in merging moral guilt with an illness concept of melancholy and its postulated cause, i.e., black bile, is succinctly illustrated in the following passage by Saint Hildegard of Bingen, who wrote an influential medical treatise during the eleventh century, titled *Causae et Curae:*

> At the very instant when Adam disobeyed divine order, melancholy coagulated in his blood, just as clarity vanishes when the light goes out, though the still hot oakum produces malodorous smoke. And so it was with Adam, for while his own light was being put out, melancholy curdled in his blood, which filled him with sadness and despair. Indeed, when Adam fell, the devil breathed melancholy into him, that

melancholy which makes man fainthearted and unbelieving. (Delumeau 1990, p.246)

An influential earlier (fifth century) scholar, Saint Augustine, commented on the Christian notion of inheritance of sin:

> We inherit this ignorance and concupiscence, yet we are also guilty of them. For at the time of his sin, Adam formed one single man with all his posterity; all of us were contained in him. The unity of the human race within Adam explains how the first offence was also our offence. (Delumeau 1990, p.247)

Almost five hundred years after Hildegard's teachings, Burton extended this logic in his influential *Anatomy of Melancholy,* beginning with a discussion on the original sin that transformed man: 'the miracle of nature, into a miserable being subject to illness, fear, unhappiness: *Heu tristis et lachrymosa commutatio!'* (Delumeau 1990, p. 246)

THE INHERITANCE OF GUILT

From sin to gene

All this suggests how guilt simultaneously translated into a material substance (black bile) and an illness, to acquire a hereditary property. More significantly, through its association with black bile, it established a direct link with melancholia. Thus, there developed a situation wherein the triad of guilt, sin and black bile was firmly linked and crystallized into a robust category. This category was to become the basis for further elaboration of theories on melancholia and at the same time considered to constitute the 'clinical' features of melancholia, the disease. Black bile theories of melancholia remained popular until the seventeenth century and were variously viewed as heavy impurities that either produced noxious fumes or precipitated and blocked blood vessels, to produce melancholia. The spleen was considered to be the site that produced black bile, its spongy texture serving to absorb and store this thick viscous humour.

During the Renaissance, developments in medicine such as Paracelsus's challenge to Galenic medicine and his rejection of the humoral theory, Vesalius's work on anatomy, together with Harvey's theories of circulation, challenged the legitimacy of the black bile theory for melancholia. It was replaced by competing theories either in succession or in a mixed form. Some of the prevailing popular medical explanations include: spiritus vitae blocking the brain,[13] affectations of the mind[14] and melancholic vapours rising from the spleen to obscure the mind[15] together with a range of neo-Platonic theories invoking supernatural forces, demons and spirits as causal agents.[16] In this pluralistic atmosphere, the introduction of chemical theories,[17] nerve juices[18] and mechanical explanations were part of a paradigm shift that emphasized a primary pathology in the nerves (Jackson 1986; Porter 1991).

The cultural association of guilt with melancholia survived as a 'complex' to become symptoms of 'depression'. Medical historians consider this period one in which the body underwent a process of secularization (Delumeau 1990; Elias 1939; Porter 1991). Demons and malignant spirits of the pre-Renaissance period were objectivized through medical theories which introduced the concept of natural spirits located within the nervous system (as compared to earlier neo-Platonic demonic spirits from the supernatural world). With the discovery of such natural laws as those of Newton and Boyle, depression acquired metaphors derived from physics (such as stress, fatigue and energy). The four original humours, including black bile, were replaced by neurohumours (the forerunner of neuroendocrine theories), with the metaphors of balance and excess–deficit between humours being retained to explain various mental disturbances and normal brain functioning. Idioms such as sluggishness and heaviness translated into psychomotor retardation and drooping body postures, while darkness (derived from the shadow of black bile) retains popularity in contemporary folk vocabulary exemplified by pharmaceutical advertisements for anti-depressants. The current metaphor 'feeling blue' owes its popularity to the eighteenth-century notion 'to burn blue'; a burning candle emitting a flash without red glare, an omen of death or indicating the presence of devils with the plural form, blue devils, referring to an apparition seen in delirium tremens (OED 1994).

Later, the psychoanalytic theories of Freud reinterpreted religious guilt (as guilt sickness) into a schema that explained individual guilt as having originated from 'a great traumatic event: the murder of the father of the horde' (Delumeau 1990, p.251). In a similar manner, earlier quasi-hereditary ideas of inheriting depression (through its association with guilt) were gradually turned into a theory of heredity by Esquirol (Jackson 1986), later to be developed into the late nineteenth-century theory of degeneration (Hunter and Macalpine 1963), and then further shaped into twentieth-century genetic models for depressive disorders.

THE POPULARITY OF MELANCHOLIA

The cultural shaping and transformation of melancholia into a fashionable folk category lasted for well over a century and involved the whole of Europe. Popular interest in melancholia peaked in the seventeenth and eighteenth centuries during which it was dichotomized: as a disease with elaborate physiological explanations and as a sentiment cultivated by the elite (Babb 1951). Dubbed for over a century as the English Malady or the Spleen, its status as a disease of the genteel class was based on the idea that it was an attribute of superior minds, of genius (Doughty 1926). A number of medical historians suggest that this was an era in which Europe developed an immense interest in melancholia (Babb 1951; Clarke 1975; Delumeau 1990). Its diffusion into popular literature (Legouis and Cazamian 1964), together with further developments in European society such as the developing class structure (Macfarlane 1978), the private ownership of property (Marx 1887), the advent of enclosures and the notion of a private cultural space (Johnson 1993), and an interest in psychological idioms by the elite (Elias 1939), led to a personalization of melancholic feelings with a proliferation of terminology (Carritt 1948). Thus melancholy was described:

- *as divine* ('*Hail, divinest Melancholy.*' John Milton, *II Penseroso*, 1645).

- *as personality* ('*The Melancholy and pleasant humour were in him so con-tempered, that each gave advantage to the other, and made his company one of the delights of Mankind*'. Isaac Walton, *Life of John Donne*, 1640).

- *as landscape* ('*The Parke [at Bruxelles] so naturally is it furnish'd with whatever may render it agreeable, melancholy, and countrylike. Here is a stately herony, divers springs of water, artificial cascades, rocks, grotts.*' John Evelyn, 8 September 1640).

- *as folly* ('*All other joy to this are folly, None so sweet as melancholy*'. Robert Burton, *Anatomy of Melancholy*, 1622).

- *as a 'fit'* ('*Wrap in a pleasing fit of melancholy, To mediate my rural minstrelsy.*' John Milton, *Comus*, 1635).

- *as mood* ('*More, I prithee, more, I can suck melancholy out of a song, as a weasel sucks eggs...I do love it better than laughing.*' William Shakespeare, *As You Like It*, 1600).

- *as a desirable sentiment* ('*A sweet melancholy my senses keeps.*' Drummond of Hawthronden, *When'as She Smiles*, 1614).

- *as a national character* ('*The English are naturally Fanciful, and very often disposed by that Gloominess and Melancholy of temper, which is so frequent in our Nation.*' John Addison, *Spectator, Pleasures of the Imagination*, 1712).

- *as uniquely English* ('*The English Malady.*' Babb 1951).

A close examination of the historical literature suggests that this was perhaps an unique period in the history of western Europe when 'melancholy' in its mild form denoted a positive desirable and fashionable state and in its severe form, a disease state which caused suffering and stigma[19]. Against the background of two major recognized epidemics in Europe – Black Death and suicide – melancholia was viewed on the one hand as a social and health problem, particularly among the poor and unemployed, while the artistic community and women of the 'genteel class' on the other, were expected to be of melancholic disposition (Delumeau 1990).[20]

FROM MELANCHOLIA TO DEPRESSION

Against the background of Cartesian dualism, further developments in medical and psychological theories associated with the post-Renaissance period, led to a recategorization of melancholia into somatic and psychological types (Jackson 1986). Later, the term melancholia was displaced by depression that subsequently developed into a major ethnomedical category (Gaines 1992; Jadhav and Littlewood 1994). Although guilt continued to remain a feature of depression, it was to soon be valorized: in its excessive, pathological or inappropriate form, as a central feature of depressive disorders; and with its absence or lack as one of the core features of anti-social personality disorder (American Psychiatric Association DSM IV 1995). This tenuous link continues into twentieth-century concepts of heredity, reflected through a contemporary clinical classification that associates women suffering from early onset depression to have a high incidence of anti-social personality disorder among their first degree male relatives (Winokur 1973).

With the increasing popularity of physiological and chemical theories of mental disorders in an era dominated by advances in the natural sciences, depression seemed congruent with emerging natural physical science concepts that implied pressure, force, energy, motion and gravitation. By the beginning of this century, the term was deeply embedded in meteorology (high pressure and low pressure areas), stock market (the Great Depression), speech (lowering of pitch and musical notes) and lowering of vital bodily functions (depressed T-wave in electrocardiograms and depressed immune system) to became a robust western ethnopsychological construct. As an illness concept, it acquired battle metaphors. Popular public health campaigns in Britain now refer to 'defeating' depression, 'battling' with stress, 'strengthening' defences and 'buffering' vulnerabilities (Jadhav and Littlewood 1994). With this gradual interiorization of a range of dysphoric emotions that were relocated and postulated to originate from within an intrapsychic space (Lakoff and Johnson 1980), fears of losing 'control' over such emotions shaped the further development of contemporary psychological theories and insight questionnaires that view patients' attribution to 'external loci of control' as indicative of poor *'in-sight'* (my neologism) and an unfavourable prognosis for depression (Kaplan and Saddock 1995).

THE BIRTH OF FATIGUE AND THE CATEGORY OF SOMATIZATION

Originating from the French term *fatigué* and Spanish *fatiga*, in English fatigue denotes 'lassitude or weariness resulting either from bodily or mental exertion' (OED 1994). Its use in the current psychiatric vocabulary originated from several diverse sources, but unlike guilt and acedia, fatigue has had a more recent medical history, commencing around the end of the eighteenth century and closely related to the industrial revolution and the discovery of labour power (Rabinbach 1990).

The prevailing Protestant concerns about the importance of work meant that idleness was a danger to be guarded against. The emergence of commercial economies underpinned by capitalism, the industrial revolution, and the birth of chronological clock time led to the development of an ethic – 'not to waste time'– as the 'new measure of life'. Thus a new secular remedy for the medieval sin of sloth evolved: the discipline of work. Soon idleness was virtually regarded as the primary crime against industry, and this was supported by influential members of the scientific and political community in Europe. During this era, a significant intellectual framework, the doctrine of materialism, developed the idea that the body was a source of energy capable of transforming universal natural energy into mechanical work. This ability to generate energy and perform labour could then be harnessed by the state for the production of wealth and articulated in the form of a metaphor: the body as machine. Offray de La Mettrie's famous eighteenth-century treatise *L'homme machine*, provides an example of how this powerful metaphor from France and Germany swept through Europe: one that posited the human body as analogous to 'a watch-spring with unique self winding properties' (Rabinbach 1990, p.51). By the turn of the century, the body was modelled on the thermodynamic engine and linked with physical forces in the cosmos through a unifying category: energy, the antithesis of fatigue. As a generalizable category, it was picked up by Freud who 'juxtapose[d] two universes of discourse, that of force (or energy) and that of meaning, so that meaning relations [were] entangled with force relations' (Rabinbach 1990, p.63) and developed this theme to form the basis of his thesis in 'Beyond the Pleasure Principle' and a theory of 'libidinal energy' (Brill 1938). This concept of energy also gained popularity among late nineteenth-century physiologists keen to understand bodily functions through principles of physics and chemistry leading to the development of terminology such as calories and muscle proteins to explain energy production within the body.[21]

Concerns about human fatigue within industries and power plants peaked in the nineteenth century. The traditional western proscription of idleness, which spiritualized and consecrated labour, was displaced onto the working body (or class) and recast in scientific and medical language as a natural category. A major part of these developments originated in France: Philippe Tissie, the most prolific advocate of a national policy of hygienic resistance to fatigue in fin-de-siècle France, warned that a 'nation, like a fatigued individual is always prepared to obey any master which imposes itself on it brutally and with force' (Rabinbach 1990, p.146). This threat of 'fatigue' led to several debates within a medical profession alarmed at the 'mental' fatigue of youth in France and Germany, who expressed concerns over their exhausted state brought about by overwork and overstudy. The popular press dubbed this period as 'L'education homicide'. Several texts and monographs on fatigue were published and a state similar to the Elizabethan melancholic era had developed.

With the invention of the ergograph, aesthesiometer and algesiometer, attempts to measure the physical consequences of mental fatigue were balanced by others which tried to establish and develop a pure psychological category of fatigue. Among the most notable attempts was that of Emil Kraepelin who argued for devising sophisticated psychological techniques to measure fatigue. Kraepelin differentiated between fatigue (*ermüdung*) and tiredness (*müdigkeit*) as severe and milder forms of the same experience. He measured and plotted graphs on fatigability in mental terms through monitoring psychological performances of factory workers in his laboratory. Kraepelin argued for a system in which the 'unsuitable' would be left behind while the energies of the more capable could develop and be enriched 'so that the path would be open to a new species more capable of performance' (Rabinbach 1990, p.152).

Around this time, George Miller Beard, a neuro-psychiatrist, introduced the term 'neurasthenia' to cover 'all the forms and types of nervous exhaustion coming from the brain and from the spinal cord' (Rabinbach 1990, p.153). This term was then shared and reinforced by prominent physicians and social scientists, including Charcot, Simmel and Durkheim. Charcot's student, Charles Féré, became a leading proponent of a hereditary link between the 'neuropathic family' and its propensity to neurasthenia. Yet another set of physicians ascribed this hereditary notion to 'Jews and the slave race' and to a 'kind of inverted work ethic, an ethic of resistance to work or activity in all its forms'.[22] This incapacity that derived from impaired energy led Pierre Janet to develop the theory of 'psychological tension' that postulated a hierarchy of energies required for different types of activities. Janet argued that emotions were a 'variety' of fatigue and viewed the psyche as a permanent struggle between the economies of energy and fatigue.

By the end of the nineteenth century, the medical establishment's interest in fatigue as a biomedical disorder was highlighted by the US Surgeon General's Index listing more than one hundred studies of muscle fatigue, asthenia and spinal exhaustion, along with numerous studies of 'nervous exhaustion' and 'brain exhaustion'. The search for a physiological marker spurred medical research into the chemistry of fatigue with unsuccessful attempts at discovering a 'vaccine' against this state.[23] A biological origin of pathological fatigue eluded the medical establishment and the term continues as a psychiatric disorder, although controversy surrounds variants of fatigue. Nuances like chronic fatigue and myalgic encephalomyelitis (ME) reflect how their causes are contested by biological and psychological theories, while reified by an industry of sickness benefits and litigation. Although a cardinal feature of depressive disorder (as low energy), it retains a separate identity as chronic fatigue disorder in contemporary western ethnopsychiatry (American Psychiatric Association DSM IV 1995).

Somatization followed as a logical continuation of this discourse on fatigue. Defined as 'the occurrence of bodily symptoms in consequence of or as an expression of mental disorder' (OED 1994), the term was introduced into the psychiatric literature of the 1920s to validate emotional origins of bodily symptoms. It is now enshrined within the DSM IV as a disorder in itself, considered resistant to treatment and continues to preoccupy researchers who either seek a biological substrate (Goodwin and Potter 1978) or consider it prevalent among those who have a less differentiated psychological vocabulary (Leff 1973). Its psychological equivalent, alexithymia, was originally defined as 'an affective disorder characterized by inability to recognize or express emotions' and put forward by psycho-therapists of the early 1970s (Sifnoes 1972). However, standard textbooks of psychiatry now describe it as a means of communicating affective distress through somatic language. Curiously enough, a range of psychopathologies associated with powerful somatic idiom of distress such as body image disorders are not considered as 'somatization' and, further, are deemed appropriate for psychotherapeutic interventions (Kaplan and Saddock 1995). It is not surprising that the concept of somatization originated in an era when eugenic theories dominated academic scientific thinking. The association of high rates in non-western societies and frustration with efforts to accommodate it as an affective disorder together with a poor response to anti-depressive therapies (Kleinman and Good 1985) or psychotherapeutic interventions, have led to a not so concealed stigmatizing attitude towards 'somatizers'.

THE DISCOVERY OF STRESS

Originating from the Latin *stricta* (and thence French *estrée*) meaning narrowness, straitness, oppression, and Middle English *distresse*, the term connotes hardship and adversity (OED 1994). Its popular usage in current English began as a common overarching metaphor (of a natural force) principally in physics (fourteenth to seventeenth century), that denoted a sense of weight, pressure, strain or a deformation upon a material object. Its introduction into psychiatric literature occurred at the end of the nineteenth century when it was first associated with neurasthenia (Rabinbach 1990) and considered a general cause of mental disorders. It reached peak popularity in the 1980s following the introduction of an independent psychiatric disorder, post-traumatic stress disorder (PTSD), argued by medical anthropologists as a North American ethnopsychological construct invented in order to accommodate the collective trauma of the Vietnam War (Young 1995). This diagnostic term is therefore a good example of an aetiologically (and culturally) based disorder (trauma) within a diagnostic system that claims to be atheoretical and culture free (American Psychiatric Association DSM IV).

The concept of stress assumes the existence of a 'stressor' and the 'stressed': which are built into a higher order set of theories that include notions such as (social and psychological) 'supports' which buffer against 'stress': the absence of which are viewed to be 'vulnerabilities'. Stress then is an invisible impersonal 'thing' that is transmitted from the 'stressor' to the 'stressed' and which can only be empirically documented by its effect on the recipient and best judged through an objective clinical assessment by mental health professionals (American Psychiatric Association DSM IV). As a generic equivalent of bacterial or viral infection of the disease model, its credibility relates to non-stigmatizing qualities such as an impersonal nature, location outside the body and a semantic distancing from other emotion related vocabulary.

CONCLUSIONS

Focusing on the British cultural vocabulary of guilt, fatigue, energy, stress and depression, this chapter argues that such vocabularies have their own unique histories and meanings; deeply embedded, in this instance, within white British and western European institutions (including their health-care enterprises). If the cultural validity of depression can be taken as local experiences (of the population) that are clarified and validated on their own terms, then depression can be construed as a culturally valid concept for western settings. If this is the case, it is a fallacy to assume that depression is some real objective disease entity which can be found elsewhere or, for that matter, packaged and transported to a contrasting setting for ready use. The debate is not about the universality of suffering or its version of a local pathology across cultures, but whether it is the same as 'western depression'. As observed earlier, depression for the culture-free psychiatrist in India is no more than a consensus (of psychiatric nosology) among health professionals sharing a common (western medical) epistemology. This is not the same as being culturally 'valid' among the general population.

Although I do not wish to suggest that depression does not 'exist' elsewhere outside western European and North American cultures, one does need to problematize the question: Is the indigenous Indian version of depression essentially the same as western depression? The answer is that we do not as yet know, since current knowledge is derived mainly through a western epistemological framework. To proceed further entails the following:

1. A study of lived experiences of everyday suffering and recourse to help through local narratives and language that would identify key constructs and examine the cultural logic of constructing illness experience in both western and non-western settings. The semantic illness network is one such approach that revealed local distress models for the Punjabi community in Britain (Krause 1989) and Shiite Muslims from Iran (Good 1977).

2. Such local models would generate popular and locally meaningful patterns of distress to validate local experience on its own terms. These could then be operationalized and validated against western phenomenology and psychopathology for congruence or goodness of fit in form, content and quality. It is likely that some patterns of distress may not fit with western descriptions of psychopathology and disorders and may therefore need separate and distinct class category representation. Examples of these are the Japanese concept of *taijin kyofusho* in the official Japanese diagnostic system for mental disorders; the *qi-gong* (excess of vital energy) psychotic reaction and *shenjing shuairuo* (neurasthenia) as represented within the Chinese Classification of Mental Disorders, 2nd edn (American Psychiatric Association DSM IV 1995). Alternatively, some patterns may well reveal common universals that would enrich the debate on cultural validity.

3. Development of instruments, both quantitative and qualitative, that would measure such distress patterns and contribute towards the development of higher order categories or syndromes. Only then can such categories be comparable with western psychiatric concepts for cross-cultural equivalence and validity. For example, a study of 'life events' contributing to mental health problems would require at first a full picture of what a life event means to the population under study. What are its relative perceived threats to marriage, kinship ties and integrity of the community on the one hand versus economic risks or unemployment on the other? Would a western life events questionnaire be recalibrated by local members of the population who might choose to rearrange the hierarchy of events?

Cultural validity apart, there is an additional reason that merits such an enquiry: mental health professionals, particularly from developing nations, have often expressed surprise at the manner in which scholarly discourses on medical anthropology remain confined to western academic institutions with little impact on changes in everyday clinical practice in their own settings. It is ironical that some of the reasons are similar to both groups. These include their subordinate status within health institutions across cultures, the lack of teaching and systematic research in this area leading to a poor impact on mainstream medical disciplines including psychiatry. It is in this context that anthropologically informed methods of enquiry have potential to help establish clearer links between personal suffering and local politico- econ-omic ideologies. Such methods can generate alternative canons of culturally valid psychiatric theory and practice and contextualize them in both time and space. Although ambitious in its aims, research that will critique western psychiatric theory and practice and reveal its ethnopsychiatric premise also broadens the debate on cultural validity of psychiatric disorders in general. Moreover, this process might generate local interest into indigenous taxonomies and provide a meaningful framework within which both professionals and patients from non-western cultures could reclaim their local cultural and political histories.

ACKNOWLEDGEMENT

An earlier version of this paper ('Cultural origins of Western Depression') was published in the *International Journal of Social Psychiatry* (1996), 42 (4), 269–286.

NOTES

1. The term 'depression' unless specified, deliberately subsumes both mood (normal and pathological) and disorder, as the author considers it to be a culturally constituted complex.
2. A comprehensive review of the literature (Kleinman and Good 1985) suggests significant differences in guilt, self-esteem and somatic symptom between western developed and non-western developing societies.
3. Various hospital psychiatric clinics of rural and urban Bombay (1978–83) and Bangalore (1983–88). A significant number of self-referred patients are guided by their own idea of what constitutes 'psychiatric disorder', or by hospital porters and receptionists whose 'gate-keeping' decisions are based on local concepts.
4. Notes on Eliciting and Recording Clinical Information (1973): Institute of Psychiatry. London. This is a common reference point in clinics.
5. The more expensive texts are available in reference sections of the institutions' libraries, often mass photocopied at some expense for personal use. Journals highly sought after include *Archives of General Psychiatry*, *American Journal of Psychiatry* and the *British Journal of Psychiatry*.
6. Such as the Research Diagnostic Criteria, latest editions of DSM, Life Events and Locus of Control Questionnaires and Somatization Schedules.
7. It is common knowledge that prescribed 'newer' anti-depressants are often bought in the black market or sent by relatives and friends from abroad, particularly from the Gulf nations, at considerable expense to the family. Many psychotropic medications do not undergo local efficacy studies in view of their approved status in Britain and

North America. Most recently, the anti-psychotic drug clozapine was introduced without the mandatory blood count monitoring (personal communication, Professor R. Raguram, Bangalore).

8. The author would like to clarify that this description of everyday clinical routine does not imply that such culture-free care and practice is deliberate, nor does he question professional competence. On the contrary, great care is taken to provide consultations in a humane and competent manner that match with practices at internationally renowned clinics. But the issue here is about the criteria used.

9. During the course of this previous research, the author observed several clinicians who were perplexed and frustrated when patients presented with idioms of distress that did not match with phenomenology in psychiatric (western) textbooks or journals; leading to remarks such as 'wish they [patients] read before coming to the clinic' or 'if only they were educated' (Jadhav 1986).

10. Thus the academic and folk metaphor for mood disturbances as feeling down or high, and the linear link with past memories illustrated by the association of childhood loss and current depression (Littlewood 1994).

11. For a more detailed discussion, see Elias (1939) and Macfarlane (1978) on how capitalist economic structures shaped the development of private vocabulary. See also Johnson (1993) on how British housing architecture and domestic spaces articulated the distinction between private and public. A good example of commoditized emotion is the popular western psychiatric term 'free floating anxiety'.

12. The Church went through centuries of competition between Gregory the Great's and John Cassian's list of major temptations. While Cassian suggested eight sins, Gregory reduced the number to seven. Acedia was initially dropped from this but was finally rehabilitated as another related sin in Gregory's list. Tristitia was thought to be synonymous with acedia (Jackson 1986).

13. Paracelsus (1493–1541). His given name was Theophrastus Bombastus von Hohenheim. His work titled 'The Diseases that Deprive Man of his Reason' challenged earlier Galenic theories on melancholia. He suggested that melancholic complexions drive the *spiritus vitae* up towards the brain, leading to an excess and thus cause melancholia. Thus melancholics are disturbed by their own nature (Jackson 1986).

14. Thomas Elyot (1490–1546), physician turned clergyman, wrote a popular domestic guide 'The Castle of Health'. In it he devoted an entire chapter to the '*affectes of the mynde*' and another to '*hevynesse of minde*'. He used the terms passions and affectations as synonyms for sorrow, which was a result of black bile affecting the mind. His prescription included dietary restrictions, company of women, avoidance of darkness and keeping a busy mind.

15. Timothy Bright (1550–1615), another physician turned clergyman, postulated that black bile vapours rose from the spleen to obscure the clear mind and cause melancholia. His other significant contribution relates to a distinction between 'melancholia' and 'guilty conscience' ('*affliction of the soul through conscience of sinne*'). This bears some resemblance to the current dichotomy of neurotic and endogenous depression. Delumeau (1990) provides an example of 'a German [who] stayed at home during Holy Week to perform devotion, because he feared the excessive quantity of melancholic vapour exhaled by other worshippers'.

16. These were a combination of a range of astrological theories (relating to the influence of Saturn), demonic attributions and moral transgression against the Church. MacDonald suggests that traditional medieval and renaissance models of the universe

postulated both supernatural and natural forces at work in a hierarchical order of powers and beings (MacDonald 1981).

17. Thomas Willis (1621–1675) was one of the first to introduce chemical theories. He suggested that the spleen failed to ferment blood juices and favoured the role of 'Chymical Liquors' and their pathological alteration in melancholia (Hunter and Macalpine 1963).

18. There were several eighteenth-century theories that revolved around the brain and nerves. Influential concepts of well-known European physicians are summarized below:

    Friedrich Hoffman (1660–1742) postulated particles in body fluids that blocked the brain pores. Herman Boerhave (1668–1738) introduced a mechanical hydraulic circulatory physiology in which factors that slowed the blood circulation led to stasis around the hypochondriacal region causing melancholia. Richard Mead (1673–1754) who was influenced by Newton's notion of ether, suggested that animal spirits or nerve juice in the nerve fibres were instrumental for muscular activity. In melancholia, primary mental images caused by prolonged thinking or brooding on a fixed idea led to secondary alteration in the blood. William Cullen (1710–1790) postulated that the brain was controlled by a system of Newtonian forces, which caused excitement and collapse in various disease conditions. The brains of melancholic patients were firmer and drier in texture, which were therefore vulnerable to higher degrees of excitement. The reader will find a detailed account in Jackson (1986).

19. There were instances of pejorative terms used to describe variants of melancholia, such as Mopishness (Richard Napier), to reflect the sullen inactivity of husbandmen and artisans, while the term melancholy was reserved for the dumpish mood of idle gentlefolk. The foolish, weak and stupid people, heavy or dull souls were considered rarely troubled with low spirits (Porter 1990).

20. The term melancholy was recorded disproportionately among those of higher social rank with many merely adding the label to enhance themselves and give a dignified status to their conduct. Babb (1951) suggests that Elizabethan Englishmen believed that exerting one's brain led to depletion of heat and moisture from the body, and consequently at least a little melancholy was expected as a result. Consider the French parallel with the terms *spasmophilie*, one that is biomedically legitimized as a disease and *fatigué* or *la fatigue*, which is a culturally sanctioned folk illness (Gaines 1992). Compare also with the popular northern Indian Hindi term *Udaas Kabir*, commonly reserved for the dishevelled appearance of young men, after being jilted by their lovers (but one that is neither pathologized by the local culture nor related to social rank); although the commonly accepted term for depression among clinic populations is *Udasi*.

21. Notable scientists included German physiologists Adolf Fick, Carl von Voit, Ludwig Max Rubner, and Armand Gautier, director of the first chemical biology laboratory in France (Rabinbach 1990).

22. Théodule Ribot, a nineteenth-century French psychologist and editor of the influential *Revue Philosophique* that attempted to establish material foundations for mental mechanisms (Rabinbach 1990). Incidentally, he also introduced the term 'anhedonia' (in 1897) as a psychopathology to counter-designate the term 'analgesia', although now considered a cardinal feature of depressive disorder. This concept highlights a key western cultural preoccupation with the attainment of pleasurable states and unlimited happiness. Obeyesekere points out how this may well differ in non-western, particularly Buddhist, societies where states of general hopelessness are

an expression of an ideology that 'life is suffering and sorrow, and that the cause of sorrow is attachment or desire and craving.' (Obeyesekere 1985, in Kleinman and Good 1985). Such affects and their accompanying epiphenomena, he argues, are rooted in Buddhist existential discourse and do not constitute an illness; although features of depressive disorder may well be elicited.

23. Wilhelm Weichardt, a German physiologist whose attempts to synthesize 'kenotoxins' and 'anti-kenotoxins' for a fatigue vaccine were found ineffective in trials conducted by the Austro-Hungarian army during World War II (Rabinbach1990).

APPENDIX (OED, 1990)

Depression: brief history of the idiom

The term depression originates from: De primere (Latin) to press down. The action of depressing, or condition of being depressed; that which is depressed: in various senses. (Opp. to elevation). The digits in parenthesis (italicised), denote the year when the term was first used.

a)   The angulatory distance of a star below the horizon, the apparent sinking of the celestial pole towards the horizon as the observer travels towards the equator (*1391*: Chaucer Astrol., II. 25, And than is the depression of the pole antartik, that is to seyn, than is the pol antartik by-nethe the Orisonte the same quantity of space).

b)   Fig. The act of putting down or bringing low, or the fact or condition of being brought low (in stature, fortunes, etc) (*1533*: Frith Wks, 5, Aduersitie, tribuation, worldly depression).

c)   Disparagement, Depreciation (*1628*: Feltham Resolves 11. lxxiii. Thus depressing others, it (pride) seeketh to raise it selfe, and by this depression angers them).

d)   Suppression (*1656*: Hobbes. Six Lessons Wks. 1845, VII., 278, You...profess mathematics, and theology, and practise the depression of truth in both).

e)   The action of pressing or weighing down, of sinking (*1656*: Blount Glossogr., Depression, a pressing or weighing down, *1697*: Potter, Antiq. Greece III. ix. Flags, the Elevation whereof was a signal to joyn Battle, the Depression to desist).

f)   The condition of being depressed in spirits; dejection (*1660*: Baker's chronicle).

g)   A depressed or sunken formation on a surface; a hollow, a low place or part (*1665*: Phil. Trans., I. 42 Of the Nature of the Ground...and of the several risings and depressions thereof).

h)   Reduction to a lower degree of power (*1727*: Chamber's cyclopaedia, depression of equations)

i)   A lowering in quality, vigour or amount, esp of trade (*1793*: Vansittart Refl. Peace 57, The depression of public funds...began before the war).

j)   Lowering of vital functions or powers; a state of reduced activity (*1803*: Medical Journal X. 116. Great depression...has without doubt lately shewn itself in a very remarkable manner in the influenza).

k)   Lowering in pitch, flattening of voice or a musical note (*1845*: Stoddart in Encyl. Metrop. I. 176/1, A slight degree of elevation or depression, of length or shortness, of weakness or force).

l)   A term for one of the operations for cataract (*1851-60*, Mayne Expos. Lex., Depression...a term for one of the operations for cataract).

m)   The lowering of a muzzle of a gun below the horizontal line (*1853*, Stocqueler Milit. Encycl., Depression, the pointing of any piece of ordinance, so that its shot may be projected under the point-blank line).

n)   A lowering of the column of mercury in the barometer (*1881*: R. H. Scott in Gd. Words July 454 Barometrical depressions or cyclones).

REFERENCES

American Psychiatric Association (1995) *Diagnostic and Statistical Manual IV.* Washington DC: APA.

Babb, L. (1951) *The Elizabethan Malady: A Study of Melancholia in English Literature from 1580 to 1642.* East Lansing: Michigan University Press.

Bhishagratna, K. (trans.) (1991) *The Sushruta Samhita.* 3 vols. Chowkhamba Sanskrit Studies Volume 30. Varanasi: Chowkhanba.

Bright, T. (1586) *A Treatise of Melancholie.* London. Thomas Vautrollier.

Brill, A. (ed. and trans.)(1938) *The Basic Writings of Sigmund Freud.* New York: Random House.

Carritt, E. (1948) *A Calendar of British Taste: From 1600 to 1800.* London: Routledge and Kegan Paul.

Clarke, B. (1975) *Mental Disorder in Earlier Britain.* Cardiff: University of Wales Press.

Delumeau, J. (1990) *Sin and Fear: The Emergence Of Western Guilt Culture 13th –18th Centuries.* Trans E. Nicholson. New York: St. Martin's Press.

Desjarlais, R., Eisenberg, L., Good, B., Kleinman, A. (eds)(1995) *World Mental Health: Problems and Priorities in Low-Income Countries.* New York: Oxford University Press.

Doughty, O. (1926) 'The English malady of the eighteenth century.' *Review of English Studies 2*, 257–269.

Elias, N. (1939) *The History of Manners.* Trans. E, Jephcott. New York: Pantheon Books.

Fontana Dictionary of Modern Thought. (1988). London: Fontana.

Gaines, A. (ed) (1992) *Ethnopsychiatry. The Cultural Construction of Professional and Folk Psychiatries.* New York: State University of New York Press.

Goldman, R. and Montagne, M. (1986) 'Marketing "mind mechanics": Decoding anti-depressant drug advertisements.' *Social Science and Medicine 22,* 1047–1058.

Good, B. (1977) 'The Heart of What's the Matter: The Semantics of Illness in Iran.' *Culture, Medicine and Psychiatry 1,* 25–58.

Good, B. (1994) *Medicine, Rationality and Experience: An Anthropological Perspective.* Cambridge: Cambridge University Press.

Goodwin, F. and Potter, W. (1978) 'The biology of affective illness.' In J. Cole *et al.* (eds) *Depression: Biology, Psychodynamics and Treatment.* New York: Plenum Press.

Heelas, P. and Lock, A. (eds) (1981) *Indigenous Psychologies: The Anthropology of The Self.* London: Academic Press.

Hunter, R. and Macalpine, I. (1963) *Three Hundred Years of Psychiatry: 1535–1860.* Oxford: Oxford University Press.

Jackson, S. (1986) *Melancholia and Depression: From Hippocratic to Modern Times.* New Haven: Yale University Press.

Jadhav, S. (1986) *Help-Seeking Behaviour, Choice of Healers and Explanatory Models.* Unpublished MD Thesis. National Institute of Mental Health and Neurosciences, Bangalore, India.

Jadhav, S. (1995) 'The ghostbusters of psychiatry. Editorial commentary.' *The Lancet 345,* 808–810.

Jadhav, S. and Littlewood, R. (1994) 'Defeat depression campaign: Some medical anthropological queries.' *Psychiatric Bulletin 18,* 572–573.

Johnson, M. (1993) *Housing Culture: Traditional Architecture in an English Landscape.* London: University College London Press.

Johnson, S. (1755) *A Dictionary of the English Language.* 2 Vols. London: Longman.

Kaplan, H. and Saddock, B. (eds) (1995) *Comprehensive Textbook of Psychiatry.* 6th edn. Baltimore, Maryland: Williams and Wilkins.

Kelly, G. (1955) *The Psychology of Personal Constructs.* New York: Norton.

Kleinman, A. (1987) 'Anthropology and psychiatry: The role of culture in cross-cultural research on illness.' *British Journal of Psychiatry 151,* 447–454.

Kleinman, A. and Good, B. (eds) (1985) *Culture and Depression: Studies in the Anthropology and Cross-Cultural Psychiatry of Affect and Disorder.* Berkeley: University of California Press.

Kleinman, D. and Cohen, L. (1991) 'The decontextualization of mental illness: The portrayal of work in psychiatric drug advertisements.' *Social Science and Medicine 32,* 867–874.

Krause, I.B. (1989) 'Sinking heart: A Punjabi communication of distress.' *Social Science and Medicine 29,* 563–575.

Lakoff, G. and Johnson, M. (1980) *Metaphors We Live By.* Chicago: University of Chicago Press.

Leff, J. (1973) 'Culture and the differentiation of emotional states.' *British Journal of Psychiatry 123*, 299–306.

Legge, M. (1963) *Anglo-Norman Literature.* Oxford: Oxford University Press.

Legouis, E. and Cazamian, L. (1964) *A History of English Literature: 1650–1963.* Revised edition. London: Aldine Press.

Littlewood, R. (1990) 'From categories to contexts: A decade of the "new cross-cultural psychiatry".' *British Journal of Psychiatry 156*, 308–327.

Littlewood, R. (1994) 'Verticality as an idiom of mood and disorder.' *British Medical Anthropology Review 2*, 1, 44–48.

Lutz, C. and Abu-Lughod, L. (eds) (1990) *Language and the Politics of Emotion. Studies in Emotion and Social Interaction.* Cambridge: Cambridge University Press.

Lynch, O. (ed) (1990) *Divine Passions. The Social Construction of Emotion in India.* Berkeley: University of California Press.

MacDonald, M. (1981) *Mystical Bedlam. Madness, Anxiety and Healing in Seventeenth Century England.* Cambridge: Cambridge University Press.

Macfarlane, A. (1978) *The Origins of English Individualism.* Oxford: Blackwell.

Marsella, A. and White, S. (eds) (1982) *Cultural Conceptions of Mental Health and Therapy.* Dordrecht: Reidel.

Marx, K. (1887) *Capital,* 3 Vols. 1954 (ed) London: Lawrence and Wishart (1954).

Murphy, H.B.M. (1982) *Comparative Psychiatry: The International and Intercultural Distribution of Mental Illness.* Berlin: Springer-Verlag.

Neill, J. (1989) 'A social history of psychotropic drug advertisements.' *Social Science and Medicine 28*, 333–338.

Nicholson, S. (1995) 'The expression of emotional distress in old English prose and verse.' *Culture, Medicine and Psychiatry 19*, 327–338.

Nichter, M. (1981) 'Idioms of distress: alternatives in the expression of psychosocial distress.' *Culture, Medicine and Psychiatry 5*, 379–408.

Obeyesekere, G (1985) *Depression, Buddhism, and the work of culture in Sri Lanka.* In Kleinman and Good (1985).

Oxford English Dictionary (1994) CD-ROM 2. Oxford: Oxford University Press.

Porter, R. (1990) *Mind-Forg'd Manacles: A History of Madness in England from the Restoration to the Regency.* Harmondsworth: Penguin.

Porter, R. (ed) (1991) *The Faber Book of Madness.* London: Faber and Faber.

Rabinbach, A. (1990) *The Human Motor: Energy, Fatigue and the Origins of Modernity.* New York: Basic Books.

Rippere, V. (1981) 'Depression, common sense and psychological evolution.' *British Journal of Medical Psychology 54*, 379–387.

Sartorius, N. *et al.* (1983) *Depressive Disorders in Different Cultures: Report on the WHO Collaborative Study on Standardised Assessment of Depressive Disorders.* Geneva: World Health Organisation.

Shweder, R. (1991) *Thinking Through Cultures: Expeditions in Cultural Psychology.* Boston: Harvard University Press.

Siegfried, W. (ed and trans.) (1989) *Fasciculus Morum: A Fourteenth-Century Preacher's Handbook.* Philadelphia: The Pennsylvania State University Press.

Sifnoes, P. (1972) *Short Term Psychotherapy and Emotional Crisis.* Boston: Harvard University Press.

Winokur, G. (1973) The types of affective disorders. *Journal of Nervous and Mental Diseases 156,* 82–96.

World Health Organisation (1980) *The Ninth Revision of the International Classification of Diseases and Related Health Problems* (ICD-9). Geneva: WHO.

Young, A. (1995) *The Harmony of Illusions: Inventing Post-Traumatic Stress Disorder.* New Jersey: Princeton University Press.

Psychiatry's Culture[1]

Roland Littlewood

CORE AND PERIPHERY

In contemporary industrialized societies, the origins of distress and suffering frequently seem to be hidden from our immediate awareness. Yet apparently they can be located and identified by physicians. Personal misfortune is increasingly experienced through a medical lens which encourages us to understand and shape our troubles in a clinical way: as something like a disease which suddenly constrains us from outside our intentions, with its particular cause and characteristic pattern, and for which doctors possess potential treatments. Is bereavement perhaps to be considered a psychological disorder? The impact of unemployment, incest or witnessing disaster? Is sexual dissatisfaction an illness? Our inclination to theft, violence or greed? Or even something like social change or the 'stress' of urban life?

In its attempt to become recognized as a purely naturalistic science, independent of the particular moral values in which it has developed, western medicine has played down the social relationship between patient and doctor and between the experience of suffering and the local understandings through which suffering occurs. Medicine seeks the laws and regularities of a physical world immune to changes in historical frames of reference or in human cognitions. It objectifies experience as if our experience was constructed out of natural entities and, ascribing to them the conditions of our clinical observation, it reifies our personal contingencies as biological necessity. As the French anthropologist Pierre Bourdieu (1997, p.296) has put it in Marxist style, 'the observer transfers into the object the principles of his relation to the object'; as indeed we do when we talk of 'psychiatry' as some entity rather than as the actions of certain individuals in their particular moral and political world.

To understand patterns of psychological distress not simply as biological changes which appear from beyond our awareness until diagnosed, but also as part of meaningful human experience and action – as what we might term cultural patterns – we need to pay some attention to psychiatry's own culture: that is, to the historical origins and politics of its nosologies, to its clinical engagement with its subjects and, indeed, to its very understanding of 'culture'. When psychiatry developed as a medical speciality in late eighteenth-century Europe, physicians recognized that certain of the concerns which (by analogy with physical disease) they examined as sicknesses could appear more commonly in one country or group rather than in another. Psychiatry took up existing speculations on a nation's 'manners' and 'spirit'. In his *Poétique* of 1561, the Italian humanist Julius Scaliger had described the character of his compatriots as 'cunctatores, irrisores, factiosi' (Fumaroli 1996). Britain was identified as a country particularly liable to the *morbus anglicus* (despair and suicide) as a consequence of its climate (cold and wet), its diet (beef) and the pace of its commercial life (fast), all contributing to the vulnerabilities of the national character (melancholic) (Cheyne 1734). Illnesses like melancholia, spleen or neurasthenia were recognized as the cost of accepting new public responsibilities by men of the emerging middle classes in the period of early industrialization and extending political representation. Other sicknesses – hysteria and moral retardation – were rather a distressing inability to accept such responsibility, an outward manifestation of the weaker bodily or moral constitution of European criminals and women, or of slaves and other subdominant or colonized subjects, when they were threatened with the possibility of similar obligations (Brigham 1832). Mental illnesses were characteristic of life in one or other nation or social strata; more immediately to be understood as the manifestation of occupation, age, gender, temperament, habit, bodily constitution and physical environment, as individuals variously conformed to or neglected their immediate obligations; or more generally through some idiom which tried to define those obligations and sentiments, social organization and history, modes of sustenance and technical knowledge, individual character and family life, which together seemed to characterize a particular society: what has become known as its 'culture'.

Along with the Romantic idea of the nation as a distinct entity which demonstrated shared inheritance, language and customs, 'culture' became accepted as a term to place together all those characteristics attributable to living in a particular society, through acquiring which, children, like nursery plants, were cultivated into maturity. 'Culture' as a category was generally placed in opposition to the existing term 'nature'; once referring to the physical world created by divine action, nature now also denoted those features of human life which were found in other living beings – physical form and function, growth and reproduction; or which more specifically were shared with animals – including the passions, sexuality, violence and even such propensities as benevolence and sociality, all natural attributes which could be found in human societies in differing degrees. Maurice and Jean Bloch have suggested that the word 'nature' carries a number of related meanings for contemporary Europe: the archaic and the chronologically presocial; our internal bodily processes; the universal and inevitable order of the organic and inorganic; and (identified and imagined) primitive peoples (Bloch and Bloch 1980). By contrast, the term 'culture' argued for the moral and aesthetic moulding of natural growth, for a precarious social binding of that which was more elemental and basic but which still sought expression in human life. Non-Europeans and European women and children, inaccessible to culture or yet to be cultivated, remained 'in a state of nature' (Michaelis 1814). Donna Harraway has argued in a critique of anthropology (1989, p.13) that in the early industrial period Europeans took as nature 'only the material of nature appropriated, preserved, enslaved, exalted or otherwise made flexible for disposal by culture in the logic of capitalist colonialism'. Culture was thus not only an historical process in time but, like nature, something which could be accumulated to be used and indeed commodified. The more culture, the less significant was nature in human societies: and the converse. As in the earlier Christian schema, nature in herself was in-dependent of willed intention but she could be mastered by man's agency; the development of civilization demonstrated that European men had gradually acquired dominion over nature, both as an industrial resource 'out there', as raw material or slaves, but also in their own bodies: as Francis Bacon put it, in a 'truly masculine birth of time [in which men] would conquer and subdue Nature' (quoted in Easlea 1980, p.247). If they had eventually learnt that they could not control the natural depredations of their bodies' diseases by an act of magical speech or sorcery, or even by divine supplication (John 1550), they could often effect bodily healing through culture's technical power over nature.

The actual relationship between nature and culture – modes of thought taken for concrete entities – was and remains problematic. Different professional disciplines developed to specialize in each: what in Germany became known as the natural and moral sciences. Yet the pervasive notion of an ordered hierarchy within nature – in the eighteenth century the Creator's Great Chain of Being, later an unfolding evolutionary struggle – might place together what we still distinguish as the biological and the moral into a unitary schema: certain races had particularly high rates of one sort of psychological illness or another through their position in the evolutionary chain. If melancholy was the fruit of European civilization's gradual accumulation of culture and self-consciousness, primitive mental illness – a lack of control over natural instinct and impulsivity – was demonstrated by tribal peoples (Madden 1857). Illnesses like Down's mongolism or mass hysteria warned Europeans of degeneration to an earlier and more protean nature (Madden 1857; Morel 1860).

Form and content

Clinical psychiatry developed in the nineteenth-century hospitals of Europe where industrial societies confined those recognized as insane, and the majority of hospitalized patients still remain diagnosed as psychotic – as demonstrating diseases which, if pathological changes in the brain cannot readily be demonstrated, are at least presumed to be present (Schneider 1959), and which reduce responsibility and thus legal accountability. The scientific prestige of hospital medicine, and its identification of an illness which corresponded to what was popularly recognized as insanity and which in the early twentieth century came to be known as schizophrenia, tended to make the predominant understanding of mental illness the medical (e.g. Gaskell 1860). When 'nervous specialists' were called to deal with patterns of distress or unusual behaviour among people who could not be recognized as obviously physically diseased or insane, they were faced with a practical issue of deciding if the patient was responsible for their own symptoms; and whether they were accountable when making a will or giving evidence in a court of law, or if they could accept responsibility for criminal acts or for rearing their children. If members of the upper or middling classes, some disease-like category such as hysteria or nervous prostration (neurasthenia) might be advanced which minimized personal responsibility for the condition itself but not for other actions (e.g. Beard 1881). Doctors in private practice realized that to challenge a patient's own ascription of illness too radically was to lose their client, as sardonically illustrated by Molière and Proust. When deciding accountability for criminal acts where the individual claimed to be ill, doctors might, or might not, hold the prisoner accountable; decisions had to be made as to whether the illness was 'real', caused by physical changes which were independent of the prisoner's awareness and whose actions were unintended – or feigned as they might be among those awaiting trial or sentence. The simulation of insanity under such circumstances might itself be considered an illness, yet not one which provided exculpation for past crimes.

Not every person who was diagnosed as having a particular mental illness reported exactly the same experiences. To deal with variations in the symptoms between individuals, clinical psychiatry still makes a distinction between the essential *pathogenic* determinants of a mental disorder – those biological processes which are held to be necessary and sufficient to cause it – and the *pathoplastic* personal and cultural variations in the pattern. These two are still distinguished in everyday clinical practice by the particularly nineteenth-century German distinction between form and content.[2] To distinguish form from content was once a virtually ubiquitous practice in comparative studies in art history, ethnology, literary criticism or archaeology, indeed in the humanities in general. In these areas it has now been superseded by looser thematic, mimetic or emergent approaches: in part because of the inevitable uncertainty over deciding what was form and what content, together with the problem of justifying whether one or the other was somehow more fundamental, whether (ontologically) in a pattern's historical appearance or in its immediate causation, or (epistemologically) in its observed configuration and scholarly typology. It has been argued that the form/content dichotomy is facilitated by Indo-European subject–predicate syntax, or more specifically that it is characteristic of the scientific method whose advances have been fuelled by the analysis of apparent wholes through the underlying natural properties of their presumed parts, together with an empiricist theory of linguistic realism in which names simply represent distinct entities such as diseases which are already present in the external world (Good and Good 1982; Lewontin, Rose and Kamin 1984; Yap 1974). To which we might add the modern imperative to naturalize experience; so thus hotness, translated into temperature, became something like a natural entity which, like the idea of manic-depression, could easily be rated as a linear scale (Littlewood 1994).

However this may be, the form–content dichotomy continues in psychiatry as a medical proxy for distinguishing the biological from the cultural. It seemed most applicable when abnormal experiences and actions were associated with a recognized and presumably ubiquitous disease such as brain or thyroid tumour, anaemia, or with traumatic and vascular damage to the brain. The hallucinations which were experienced during the delirium of the brain-damaged alcoholic were taken directly to reflect the biological form which could only be expressed through an insignificant content which reflected their particular character and the preoccupations of their society. Thus, looking at persecutory ideas in the West Indies, one study in the 1960s argued that for the local blacks, paranoid suspicions (the form) were directed against relatives and neighbours (content), following local ideas of sorcery in an egalitarian village community, while for the white Creoles, preoccupied with retaining control as a precarious elite, the phantom poisoners were identified among the surrounding black population (Weinstein 1962).

If nature was form and culture content, treatment was to be directed to the underlying biological cause, relatively easy – at least in theory – if it was identified by neuropsychiatrists as an object like a tumour or a bacterium. But to distinguish form from content was problematic in psychiatric illness where there were no evident biological changes, and thus where the distinction had to be made on the basis of the patient's symptoms as presented to the physician. Hallucinations and delusions contrary to shared everyday reality were nearly always regarded as primary and thus biological; their particular themes had even less bearing on the cause (and thus treatment) of the disease than the way patients might understand pain had any significance for ascertaining the origins of the pain. To take an example from the German psychiatrist Emil Kraepelin: that a patient said he was the Kaiser rather than Napoleon (that is, the content) was of little clinical value compared with his delusion of grandiose identification (form). Now this left the shared social world fairly redundant in psychiatric illness as it was observed in the hospital; except inasmuch as a society might facilitate one or other physical cause, as patterns of drinking might encourage alcohol-induced dementia, or local conceptions of risk increased the likelihood of traumatic accidents, or in a less direct way through changes to the physical environment and thus to human biology through genetic selection (as with sickle cell anaemia). If cultural values could thus sometimes cause disease indirectly through transforming nature, they could not cause serious mental illness directly through shared cognitions in the way that Christianity, Islam and popular understandings might still identify erroneous thinking or moral transgressions as the immediate cause of insanity (Littlewood 1993b).

The form–content schema worked fairly smoothly in European mental hospitals where the scope of what counted as clinical observation was limited by the institutional context, but by the beginning of the twentieth century psychiatry began to extend its practice to the peoples of the colonial empires. Many local patterns which suggested novel types of mental illness had been previously recorded by travellers, missionaries and colonial administrators, sometimes indeed as illnesses but often as examples of the criminal perversity of native life or just as picturesque if rather troublesome oddities. Perhaps most notable among these was *amok* (Oxley 1849), a Malay word which has passed into the English language for indiscriminate and apparently unmotivated violence against others. In one of the first discussions of the problems of comparing psychiatric illness across societies, Kraepelin (1904), after a trip to Java during which he collected accounts of amoks and also observed hospitalized patients, suggested that the characteristic symptoms of a particular mental illness – those which one could find everywhere in the world – were the essential pathogenic ones which directly reflected its physical cause. Yet, as he noted, 'reliable comparison is of course only possible if we are able to draw clear distinctions between identifiable illnesses'. This proved difficult given the variety of local patterns together with the intention, which Kraepelin enthusiastically shared, to fit them into the restricted number of categories already identified in European hospitals.

Eugen Bleuler, the Swiss psychiatrist who coined the term 'schizophrenia', argued that those symptoms by which we can distinguish this illness from other patterns directly reflect the underlying biological process

(Bleuler 1911). This coalesced with Kraepelin's idea that the characteristic features are the universal ones, to produce the still current model which may be described as something like a nest of Russian dolls: the unique biological determinants are surrounded by a confusing series of cultural and idiosyncratic envelopes which have to be picked away in diagnosis to reveal the real disease.[3] As Kraepelin's pupil Karl Birnbaum (1923) put it, these pathoplastic envelopes give 'content, colouring and contour to individual illnesses whose basic form and character have already been biologically established'. Wittgenstein (1958) critically likened the same sort of approach in the psychological sciences to our picking away the leaves of an artichoke in a hopeless attempt to uncover some real artichoke, on the assumption that, to use the anthropologist Clifford Geertz's (1986) sarcastic aphorism, 'culture is icing, biology cake...difference is shallow, likeness deep'. The medical observer was to focus on those symptoms which seem distinguishing and characteristic, and thus biologically determining: in fact such symptoms are notably elusive in psychiatry where anxiety, irritation, insomnia, anorexia, depression, self-doubt and suicidal preoccupations are common to virtually all identified illnesses, and which themselves shade into everyday experience. Common features have then tended to be ignored, more by an act of faith in the Kraepelin–Birnbaum model than through an empirical consideration of all the available evidence. Thus the statistical attempt to define key features favoured by epidemiologists in the 1990s results in circular and quite varied arguments about categorization and universality. Psychiatric illnesses have not been shown to form neatly bounded monothetic categories, so multivariate analysis of a multitude of possible symptoms produces rather different types of classification, depending on whether one includes or omits shared symptoms, and indeed on what is to count as a symptom.[4]

The local understandings of illness which a society shared were ignored by colonial doctors who, as in Europe, restricted themselves to examination of those admitted to prison or later to the psychiatric hospital (Fisher 1985; McCulloch 1994). When faced with patients from a society or minority group with which they are unfamiliar, British and American psychiatrists still complain of the culturally exotic factors which obscure the elusive disease process. With European patients in a predominantly European society they have fewer problems in finding universal categories because 'culture' is always there, tacit, to be implicitly omitted in what counted as the clinical assessment, for, being fairly uniform, it does not contribute to variability between patients. Indeed, any differences within the shared social context of western patterns, say between women and men, have been ignored until recently in favour of biological or bio-psychological aetiologies to explain variation. We tend to ignore the cultural contribution to agoraphobia ('a woman's place is in the home') or drug overdoses (the over-representation of women as patients in doctor-directed advertisements for psychiatric medication). There could not seem anything immediately 'cultural' in those patterns identified more commonly in the west – eating disorders, panic reactions, phobias, self-harm, shoplifting or exhibitionism. These could be presumed to be worldwide patterns. Socially appropriate ways of experiencing and demonstrating distress, like everyday notions of personhood and responsibility, have not been as causal, for what appeared as a constant could not explain a variable like illness. Ignoring the full range of symptoms across societies and their relationship to the patients' own beliefs and expectations and to the medical context did not seem inappropriate for practice within apparently homogeneous societies, because there doctor–patient interactions and the process of diagnosis were already significant and taken for granted aspects of daily life: diagnostic decisions were followed by generally accepted patterns of social response – by medication, hospital admission and on occasion suspension of civil rights.

IMPERIAL PSYCHIATRY

It was when they took their diagnostic systems to their colonies at the beginning of the twentieth century that psychiatrists first recognized these difficulties. Dysphoric moods and unusual actions were locally recognized in Africa or Asia, not necessarily as something recalling a physical illness but often as part of totally different patterns of social classification and order – as spirit possession or rituals of mourning, or in the course of initiation, sorcery and warfare. Those patterns that recalled the psychoses of the west seemed generally recognized as unwelcome but not always as akin to sickness (Rivers 1924). Yet, when colonial doctors turned to writing reports and academic communications, local understandings of self and illness which might now seem to us as analogous to psychiatric theories were described, not as self-contained, meaningful and functional conceptions in themselves, but rather as inadequate approximations to western scientific knowledge. At times however, the understandings of small-scale rural societies, like the more recognizably medical practices of India and China, cut dramatically across European experience. The anthropologist Charles Seligman (1929), who had trained as a doctor, reported that there seemed to have been nothing in New Guinea before European contact which could be said to resemble schizophrenia: as cases analogous to schizophrenia have been later identified by psychiatrists, he has been criticized for what is known as 'the Seligman error' – missing a universal illness because local understandings and social response did not allow it to appear objectivized through social extrusion as in a western hospital but rather incorporated it into some shared institution where it lay unremarked by the medical observer. Similarly, Amerindian and circum-polar patterns of healing, religious inspiration and leadership, in which election to the shamanic role might be signalled by a sudden illness, accident or other troubling experience, were said to mask schizophrenia (Devereux 1956).

Patterns like amok or *piblokto* ('artic hysteria') were initially taken as rather odd – generally simpler – variants of the psychiatric disorders described in Europe. Mental illness in Java, said Kraepelin, showed 'broadly the same clinical picture as we see in our country... The overall similarity far outweighed the deviant features'. Individuals locally regarded as amoks were thus really demonstrating epilepsy or perhaps catatonic schizophrenia (Kraepelin 1904). But what were to be taken as these 'deviant features', and what was being compared with what?: presumably the form of the illness, the basis for categorization of the pattern as some clinical entity. If one looked, for instance, at a Malay patient who had a false belief that she was persecuted by her neighbours, then her delusion was the form, and the neighbours provided the content, but the persecution seemed variously one or the other. That she was deluded is important for arguing that she is mentally ill; the neighbours are of no diagnostic significance, but that her delusions were persecutory could be or not, depending on the selected illness. The assumptions made by Kraepelin in his studies in Java remain the dominant paradigms in comparative psychiatry: how similar do patterns have to be before we can say that we are talking about the same pattern? How do we distinguish between those features which appear to be generally the same from those which vary? And what are our units of categorization going to be when deciding sameness and difference, normality and pathology? Does something like 'depression' occur everywhere? Or perhaps just a more general experience like 'distress'? There are similar problems in comparing social institutions such as 'marriage' or 'religion'.

Psychiatric textbooks have generally argued that locally recognized patterns like amok are 'not new diagnostic entities: they are in fact similar to those already known in the West' (Kiev 1972). This equivalence has often been extraordinarily optimistic. To take one pattern which attracted comment because of its exotic salience, *windigo*, the 'cannibal-compulsion' syndrome of the North American Ojibwa and Inuit, was locally described as an individual becoming possessed by a cannibalistic vampire and who then attacked other people in an attempt to devour them. Windigo was identified by psychiatrists confidently but variously with patterns as disparate as depression, schizophrenia, hysteria and anxiety. Similarly, amok was explained not only as the local understanding of epilepsy or schizophrenia, but as malaria, syphilis, cannabis psychosis, sunstroke, mania, hysteria, depression, disinhibited aggression and anxiety (Kiev 1972). *Latahs*, women of the Malay peninsula who uttered obscene remarks when startled and who parodied the speech and actions of others apparently without intent (O'Brien 1883), were identified as demonstrating a 'psychosis [or] hysteria, arctic hysteria, reactive psychosis, startle reaction, fright neurosis, hysterical psychosis [or] hypnoid state' (Kiev 1972). Identifying symptoms rather than the local context meant that amok and latah have generally been regarded not as autonomous cultural institutions, but simply as erroneous Malay explanations which shaped of a single universal disease, although psychiatric observers disagreed radically as to which disease this might be. The extent to which such patterns could be fitted into a universal schema depended on how far the medical observer was prepared to stretch a known psychiatric category, and thus on their preferred theoretical model. By the 1970s, Weston La Barre and Georges Devereux, psychoanalysts who were much less attached to purely biomedical arguments, had gone further in including as instances of schizophrenia a wide variety of local institutions – possession states, shamanism, prophecy, millennial religions and indeed, for La Barre, social change in general. They argued not just that schizophrenia might typically appear in these social institutions but that the institutions exemplified schizophrenic experiences (Littlewood 1993b): everyday culture in non-western societies – ideas of selfhood and agency, creativity, religious experience – could be understood, as it were, as insanity spread out thin.

If psychiatrists of the colonial period remained puzzled about the cultural encrustations they saw adhering to the essential symptoms, they could be struck by the opposite: 'barrenness of the clinical picture... In more primitive culture schizophrenia is 'a poor imitation of European forms" (cited by Yap 1951). Culturally obscured, or simply a primitive form, in neither did culture determine anything but rather acted as a sort of indeterminant soup which passively filled in or distorted the biological matrix. And 'culture' itself could be a proxy for 'race'. Categorizations of illness, medical or popular, are adjacent to other social classifications – to those of character, ethnicity, gender, the natural world and historical experience – on which they draw and which they plagiarize. The distinction, and indeed opposition, between form and content had depended on a fairly clear distinction between universal biology and the variant culture which constrained it, yet by the end of the nineteenth century descriptive psychiatry was increasingly influenced by social Darwinism's idea of racial biology in which the biological, the psychological, the social and the moral were all considered as one.

Kraepelin (1904) explained the unusual symptomatology of mental illness among the Javanese as an aspect of their 'lower stage of intellectual development'. Variations in what doctors called the 'presentation' of illness to them in different societies were attributed until recently not just to particular historical and political experiences (as we might have expected from the 'pathoplastic' model), but to the existence of a fairly uniform primitive mentality (more nature than culture) which was shared with European children and the 'retarded', and which generates novel variants: 'hyperidic states', 'catastrophic reactions', 'malignant anxiety', 'simple responses available to psychologically disorganised individuals' and 'primitive reactions corresponding to outbursts of psychopathic persons in developed countries' (Kiev 1972). Biology, the form of the illness, so far from being universal, was like culture, on a developmental spectrum: indeed on the same line for culture simply reflected 'underlying biology. Not altogether unrelated physiological explanations have attributed *piblokto* ('artic hysteria') and *kayak angst* to the undeveloped mind reflecting on 'the stillness and the sense of impending doom that are so characteristic of the Arctic climate' (Kiev 1972).

This denial of the social sources of psychological illness, together with the assumption that symptoms observed in Europe were somehow more real and less obfuscated by local values, led to the common argument that depression did not yet occur in non-Europeans for its essential western characteristic of self-blame was not observed (Carothers 1953). The absence of depression was sometimes directly attributed to a less evolved brain (Vint 1932), an idea which of course had implications when considering the possibility of independence for colonial Africa under African leadership (Carothers 1954). Guilty self-accusations of the type found in clinical depression in the west were in fact identified in colonial Africa in the 1930s, not by psychiatrists in the colonial hospitals but by an anthropologist looking at the distribution of shrines (Field 1960). Reactions which recall western depression are now frequently described in small-scale, non-industrialized communities but the issue depends, not just on the frequency with which people with less socially disturbing problems come to the hospital to be treated, and thus studied, or on medical failure to empathize, or on a rather cursory epidemiology based on colonial hospital statistics, but on what one means by 'depression'. Is it something like the misery which we might identify in various situations of loss or bereavement, or the pattern of rather physical experiences such as loss of interest, waking up early and poor appetite, which are recognized as clinical depression, or else some more specific sentiment of Judaeo-Christian guilt and a wish to die? Greater psychiatric familiarity with the experience of personal distress in the former colonies has suggested that depression may be a variant of widespread patterns of what we might term dysphoric mood which in depression is represented through a particularly western moral psychology which assumes an autonomous self as the invariant locus of experience, memory and agency. When looking across societies, a more common experience of everyday distress than-'depression' (which figures a phenomenological sinking downwards of the once active self into an inertia for which we remain responsible), may be one of depletion and the loss of something essential which has been taken out of the self – a pattern well glossed in various Latin American idioms of 'soul loss' (Shweder 1985).

CULTURE-BOUND SYNDROMES

In the 1950s, following revulsion against academic German psychiatry's 'eugenics' under the Nazis, the social and medical sciences gradually discarded the idea of biological evolution as an explanation of differences of experience and action between contemporary societies. All societies were now recognized as having 'a culture' in similar ways, and biological differences between groups as a whole – that between men and women still excepted – could not explain their different types of mental illness. The recognition that many non-western illnesses could no longer be subsumed as primitive forms of real categories led comparative psychiatry (or as it was now called, cultural psychiatry) to propose a new category. Patterns like amok and latah, which recalled psychological illnesses in Europe yet were unclassifiable, came to be known as 'culture-bound syndromes' (Yap 1951, 1974). They were usually episodic and dramatic reactions, limited to a particular society where they were locally identified as distinct patterns of action very different from those of everyday life; and which, we might now note, had been of colonial concern because they were bizarre, outrageous or frankly troublesome. Less dramatic patterns of distress – personal withdrawal from shared activities, troubling thoughts, chronic pain, bereavement, despondency – which did not come to the attention of the colonial administration or police were ignored until the development of medical anthropology in the 1980s.

A large number of such 'culture-bound' illnesses have now been catalogued (e.g. Simons and Hughes 1985) as distinctive and consistent patterns, transmitted anew to each generation in a continuing cultural tradition, and which are taken as closely related to a society's distinctive understanding of self and its prescribed norms.[5] Thus, however high the incidence of reactions like grief or terror might be in war-torn communities, they were not regarded as culture specific unless they continued in some consistently recognizable form in successive generations as part of an enduring identity. What exactly was it that was 'bound' in culture-bound syndromes? There is a continuing debate as to what the category refers: usually restricted to a pattern found only in the society in question and which symbolizes and represents fundamental local concerns, on occasion it has been applied to apparently universal illnesses which are shaped, distinguished and treated in a local content (on the changing ideas see Lee 1996; Littlewood and Lipsedge 1987; Ritenbaugh 1982). Thus one might include *kifafa*, *malkadi* and *moth madness*, locally recognized patterns in

Tanzania, Trinidad and among the Navaho which closely recall the medical description of epilepsy (Littlewood 1993b; Neutra, Levy and Parker 1977). A locally recognized reaction in New Guinea, *kuru*, was however once regarded as a culture-bound syndrome akin to hysteria, but no longer, given the likely role of a slow virus identified in its aetiology (which has made it even more exotic through recognition that it could be transmitted through cannibalism). Patterns like kuru or the restricted abilities of senescence, or such apparently motivated patterns as homicide and rape, the deliria of malnutrition or alcohol intoxication, or the use of other psychoactive substances have certainly been regarded as characteristic of a particular society but are seldom described as 'culture bound' because they appear potentially available in any society or else do not immediately recall European 'mental illness'. Yet, if these patterns persisted – like the alcohol abuse, *anomic depression* and suicide consequent on the relocation of Native Americans onto reservations – they were taken as manifestations of 'American Indian culture', ignoring the political relationship between colonizer and native, and thus the context of the psychiatric observation. 'New illnesses' identified by more sophisticated epidemiological techniques in urban populations or through the expansion of psychiatric observation to a wider population have been termed 'culture-change' or 'acculturation illnesses' exemplified by the *brain-fag syndrome* identified in West African students (Prince 1960).

CONFLICT AND RESISTANCE

If these patterns were distinguished as 'culture bound' only in that they occurred in (other) cultures, how then did culture lead to illness? Did 'culture' mean simply shared conceptualizations so that the psychiatrist could identify local concerns and sentiments either in the type of person who was vulnerable, or else in the actual symptoms which represented the culture in a way that recalled seventeenth- and eighteenth-century ideas of a national character? Or could 'culture' be located in social and biological stressors which occurred in a particular society but were not necessarily recognized by it? And anyway how could such illness be clearly distinguished from the social patterns in which it was embedded? A later question, reserved for the late 1980s, was how to deal with illnesses such as eating disorders which were apparently only to be found in European societies (Lee 1996; Littlewood 1992, 1993c).

In part, the continuing problem of 'culture' for psychiatrists lay in its double-edged connotations. Culture was a valued commodity, that constraint on nature which distinguished human from animal, educated European from primitive, and which often referred to 'high culture' alone (Williams 1958). Yet, for western psychiatrists establishing their discipline as a medical speciality, 'culture' remained secondary to scientific biological reality. As frank biological racism became disreputable after World War II, and the unitary idiom of 'development' separated out into the distinct fields of child psychology, economics and technology, the psychological differences between European and non-European could again be perceived only in rather uncertain 'cultural' terms: as a medical proxy for the other's 'difference' (or even for the lingering idea of biological 'race') and which still emersed the individual in some undifferentiated other, now less their biological level than their way of life. As medicine had little idea of how to deal with 'culture', it drew on other disciplines, particularly psychoanalysis and social anthropology, both of which claimed to be able to relate the interests of medicine to the experienced social world in a more empirical and humanistic way than had evolutionary eugenics. Cultural psychiatrists now generally held appointments in western university departments, away from the poorly funded and intellectually marginal concerns of colonial psychiatry which still remained close to popular western ideas of race. Psychoanalysts and anthropologists interested in providing a 'cultural psychiatry' of local patterns in British Africa based on intensive fieldwork in local communities were seldom interested in examining hospital statistics, unlike the epidemiologists associated with the World Health Organization who until recently have preferred to stick with the presumed biomedical universals, and thus with the form–content idioms of hospital psychiatry.

Particularly in the USA where a strong inclination towards psycho-analysis was apparent in medicine and the social sciences from the 1930s, psychiatrists emphasized the similarity of local illnesses to the 'modal personality' which an individual developed in their particular culture. The affected person was now suffering less from something recalling a medical disease with culture tacked on so much as demonstrating in an exaggerated form those psychological conflicts established in the course of childhood socialization. So *windigo* (the Ojibwa cannibal compulsion psychosis) was interpreted as a local preoccupation with food in a hostile environment, fuelled by residues of infantile resentment at the mother for the early weaning necessitated by the scarcity of food. After an indulgent childhood, the young boy was precipitated into early adulthood by brutal tests of self-reliance and encouraged to fast to attain ultrahuman powers. Dependence on his parents was replaced by a precarious dependence on spirits which encouraged solitary self-reliance in hunting. The mother, feared and hated for her violent rejection of her son, returned to possess him in the form of the windigo (Parker 1960).

Psychoanalytically orientated anthropologists proposed that any culture was a dynamic compromise between conflicting interests – ecological, physiological, between self and others, between parents and children, men and women. Symptoms, dreams, religious symbols and social institutions were all to be taken as aspects of the same conflicts (Seligman 1928). Was the European observer now to take the locally identified illness as the expression of such conflicts in unconscious motivations: as a society's symptoms? Or, given the incorporation of personal conflicts into local institutions, was the 'illness' to be considered as a type of collective adjustment, indeed as a sort of healing? Psychoanalysis, developed out of practical therapeutic concerns rather than a concern with diagnosis, still argued that one could distinguish problem, causation and treatment, but differed as to how to go about it. Devereux, perhaps the most sophisticated psychoanalytical anthropologist, eventually proposed that institutions like shamanism (which had often been taken as employing altered states of consciousness to facilitate something akin to western psychotherapy (Janet 1926) were themselves the expression of psychological disturbances in what he called the 'ethnic unconscious': disturbances which could then be enhanced by a society to produce 'ethnic psychoses' as he called these pathological institutions (Devereux 1970). Criticizing the historian Edwin Ackernecht (1943, p.31) who had argued for a clear distinction between cultural meaning and pathological terminology, Devereux (1956, p.24) argued that the local healing of unconscious social conflicts simply exacerbated them: 'there exist societies so enmeshed in a vicious circle that everything they do to save themselves only causes them to sink deeper into the quicksand'. The British biological psychiatrist William Sargant, who argued that religious ecstasy and spirit possession were a type of brainwashing, emphasized more sympathetically the cathartic function of culture-specific patterns which allowed the individual, when in a state of dissociated consciousness, to express otherwise socially forbidden inclinations in a non-threatening and relatively sanctioned manner – as if they were half-way between an 'illness' and its 'treatment' (Sargant 1973). Like Devereux, he still regarded it as all distinctly unhealthy. Alternatively, Weston La Barre, Ari Kiev and Thomas Scheff took the cathartic expression of hidden desires as a resolution rather than an exacerbation of cultural conflicts – as something closer to healing.

This all gets rather circular and, like hospital psychiatry, ignores local conceptions of healing in favour of western ideas of normality and illness. Paralleling the earlier idea of non-western pathologies as masked or incomplete forms, non-western healing was now taken as an incomplete form of psychoanalytical therapy (Frank 1961; Kiev 1964). What remained constant in all of this was the conviction, however muted, that something approximating to medical categories was still the appropriate way to frame the question; and that these provided universal criteria by which one could agree that certain patterns were justifiably termed dysfunctional or maladaptive (Doi 1971). On rare occasions analysts carried out formal psychoanalysis with their African and Amerindian informants (Devereux 1951; Sachs 1937), even if they presumed western ideals of psychological development and maturity to be universally valid. Few of the classic culture-bound syndromes were not at some time explained as the projection of unconscious fantasies and thwarted incestuous wishes, as the consequences of traumatic weaning, or simply as the overwhelming existential anxiety of tribal societies which followed from their unsophisticated psychology (e.g. Roheim 1950).

Eliding the conventional distinction between pathology as an individual phenomenon and treatment as a social response, the cost was, as Ackernecht had warned, 'the wholesale pathologisation of cultures' (Ackernecht 1943). Equivalence between modal personality, personal symptoms and social structure led to an interpretation of small-scale communities as paranoid, obsessive or whatever – even if the implication of these terms was evidently less 'strong' than the clinical usage from which they derived (e.g. Benedict 1935; Lambo 1955). During and after World War II, American psychoanalysts were funded to delineate the 'cultural' psychopathologies of enemy nations (Benedict 1946). Psychoanalysis still subscribed to those positivist ideals of the late nineteenth century which had sought an understanding of human society whose ultimate justification would be in science, not religion. Like the French neurologists under whom he had studied, Freud had explained the medieval persecution of Europe's witches on the grounds that they had really been suffering from mental illness, and psychoanalysts like Devereux took with them the assumption that spirit possession was a type of hysteria as they turned to look at non-European cultures.

The universality of the Oedipus complex in matrilineal (mother-descended) societies was a matter of particular interest (following Malinowski 1927); not unlike the hospital psychiatrist Kraepelin, the psychoanalysts took a European pattern for which theories had been elaborated as the basic form which other societies then manifested as masked or incomplete. If they attempted a more value-free comparative approach and one based on fieldwork with informants rather than on hospitalized patients, psychoanalysts still placed a particular primacy on patterns described in their bourgeois European patients which, in frequent disregard of the ethnographic data, they then identified in other societies. They tended to the evolutionary idioms of late nineteenth-century psychiatry, if in a less biologized way, arguing developmental parallels between archaic ancestor, contemporary primitive, child and neurotic, all as early or arrested forms characterized by an infantile psychology of 'psychic omnipotence' trailing behind the advancing line of mature rationality. Nor, with rare exceptions (Sachs 1937), was colonial power of much interest, whether as the rather unusual site for their psychoanalytical observations, or − occasional comments on the perils for the whites apart (Jung 1930) − as itself pathogenic for the local population (cf. Fanon 1952; Loudon 1959; Mannoni 1950).

More recently, local illnesses have been regarded by psychiatrists influenced by anthropology less as diseases or unconscious conflicts than as particularly salient everyday sensibilities, values and idioms of distress (Kleinman 1988): as with the Hindu *suchi-bar* ('purity mania') and the related *ascetic syndrome*, or the Taiwanese *shen k'uei* and Japanese *taijin kyofusho* ('interpersonal phobia'). If these had been termed pathological or mal-adaptive by western psychiatry, it was because normative institutions − Brahmanical obligations to avoid certain foods and preserve bodily purity, or Japanese expectations of self-restraint and the avoidance of inappropriate familiarity − were taken too enthusiastically by certain individuals, resulting in anxieties or interpersonal problems which could be recognized as disproportionate both in the local context and by psychiatric observers. Or alternatively, recalling the psychoanalytical view, the patterns represent in the individual a conflict or contradiction between the local institutions themselves: thus it has been argued that the continuing antagonism between the values of sexuality and asceticism in India generates the 'purity syndromes' (Malhotra and Wig 1975). Or else, as Sargant had argued, personal conflicts are expressed in limited contravention of role-specific norms in fairly standardized situations, and that it is these contraventions which had been identified, correctly or otherwise, as pathologies. It has been suggested that all cultures have such loopholes which are themselves 'socially reinforced and have the same structural characteristics as other behavioural norms in the system'; and that at least in the case of latah and amok, we should employ a less medical term than 'syndrome': perhaps something like 'stylised expressive traditional behaviours' for those deviant patterns which are fairly standardized and limited in time, but which, while they certainly contravene everyday behaviour, are somehow culturally condoned to allow the expression of apparently repressed but not uncommon sentiments (Carr 1978).

This does push the psychiatrist's normative question back even further, but if deviance (or pathology) is sometimes locally condoned or even encouraged, what is the frame by which one should term it deviant?: the lingering western presumption of pathology, or some local 'don't do this but if you must, do it this way'? As with the earlier colonial psychiatry, the idea of 'a culture' has however remained one which is fairly homogeneous, with values and social order accepted in the same way by all members: a model which followed the idea of a tightly bounded society once prompted by colonial officers and anthropologists, and which ignored any unequal distribution of knowledge and power, of local contestation or global change (Littlewood 1984, 1995).

THE LIMITS OF CULTURAL PSYCHIATRY

Hospital psychiatrists and those inclined to psychoanalysis both argued for unitary theories of the phenomena once observed by missionaires, army doctors and colonial administrators, even if they disagreed as to what any such unity comprised: universally recognizable disease entity, exaggeration of norm, cultural conflict, sanctioned rejection of the norm or even therapeutic response. Social anthropologists have objected that their error was to use a medical grid which inevitably objectifed social action as disease entity. Rather, one should start by simply describing a society in its own terms, for societies are not traditional residues of some nearly forgotten past which is passing away but always constitute themselves anew in their chosen memories and actions. If the term 'culture-bound syndrome' is to retain value only as a concept of local sickness, whether or not psychiatry recognizes it as akin to western disease, what then is to count as a 'concept of sickness'? Social scientists, however, are hardly immune from comparing one society with another to obtain regularities and general patterns, and in order to do that, they too define analogous domains in each – whether those of social structure, kinship, religion or sickness. These domains derive from western experience. Each society easily comes to be read as aggregates of such areas of comparison which become reified as the components of a society with structured and causal relationship to each other (Littlewood 1991). The comparative problem is hardly unique to medicine. As the British anthropologist Edward Evans-Pritchard is said to have observed, 'If social anthropology is anything, it is a comparative discipline – and that is impossible.' It is not that psychiatry's inevitable grid, pathology, is necessarily inappropriate for comparing what looks to the European like 'suffering' or 'madness' in different societies, but pathology is just one possible grid and one which carries with it a particular set of assumptions about normality and abnormality which explicitly ignores consideration of power and of the context of observation; and of what it observes, and how 'observation' shapes it.

The evolutionary schema did offer one sort of comparison by relating societies (or illnesses) as states of transformation along a historical spectrum driven by certain processes. Few anthropologists, some sociobiologists, Freudians and Marxists perhaps excepted, would now subscribe to the idea of unilinear human development through which local institutions and actions are to be understood as determined by underlying processes, whether those of evolutionary selection or of the relations of production. While it is still argued that the insights offered by psychoanalysts may provide a useful perspective when trying to understand psychological experience in non-European societies (e.g. Doi 1971; Kakar 1978), others have argued that Freud's followers have little to contribute to the critical or social sciences for they offer a moralized version of common-sense western assumptions about the inevitability of European rationality with entrepreneurial autonomy as 'health' or 'adaptation' (Littlewood 1993a). On the whole, with the exception of a few psychoanalytically orientated anthropologists such as Melford Spiro and Gananath Obeyesekere, the ethnographic monographs written by anthropologists now place little emphasis on the early childhood experiences which the psychoanalysts had argued were significant in generating culture. They take particular patterns of childrearing as the manifestation rather than the cause of social knowledge.[6]

The assumption that non-Europeans thought is less rational has been superseded by recognition that all societies employ both deductive and inductive logic, both concrete and abstract reasoning, but that they do so within limits which are determined by their own interests. Societies differ psychologically not in their capabilities but in their modes of thought – through cognitions and categorizations of space and time, the sexes and the natural world, their understandings of causality and invidia, and which are encoded in their systems of symbols particularly language. What was once regarded as primitive (magical) thinking on the origins of sickness or misfortune appears now as a focus on the moral 'why' rather than the technical 'how', for societies differ in the focus of their immediate interests and practised knowledge. Indeed, in terms of the everyday understanding of sickness, western medicine has been argued to be less efficacious through its emphasis on the proximate mechanisms of misfortune, leaving the individual with chronic or serious illness little help in answering 'why me?' (Kleinman 1988). In the case of severe mental illness, psychiatry remains unable to offer its patients any understanding, technical or moral, in terms of everyday cultural knowledge.

To recognize some other's pattern as 'cultural' was to assume a privileged perspective on, whether colonial hubris or academic analysis. (As Pascal had put it, we have truth but they have customs.) By the mid-1980s, culture-specific illnesses were recognized as psychiatry's 'twilight zone' (Hughes 1985), 'what other people have, not us' (Hahn 1985). Medical interest in isolated and disembodied exotic patterns was seen to have directed attention from more immediate questions of economic development, poverty, exploitation or nutrition, besides providing yet another justification of the otherness of non-Europeans, and one which ignored the role of western medicine in once facilitating imperial expansion or now in the global marketing of pharmaceutical drugs.

How relevant was psychiatry to imperialism? Both developed at a similar period. Both shared certain modes of reasoning: we might note affinities between the scientific objectification of illness experience as disease and the objectification of others as chattel slaves or as colonial manpower. Both argued for an absence of personal responsibility among patients or non-Europeans. The extent, however, to which any elaborated set of ideas which one might term 'imperial psychiatry' provided an ideological justification of colonialism in British Africa or India is debatable: in a recent review I have argued that the evidence is meagre (Littlewood 1993a; cf. McCulloch 1994): segregated facilities, of course (Ernst 1991; Lugard 1929); prejudice and neglect, yes; but hardly practicable medical ideologies of racial or cultural inferiority.[7] (Indeed, we might more plausibly argue the case of contemporary psychiatric practice in Britain.) While colonial doctors were quite tangential to the making of Colonial Office policy (and were themselves rather 'marginal' individuals within British or colonial society: McCulloch 1994), in the francophone colonies and in Haiti, local psychiatrists developed radical critiques of European domination to argue for a distinct 'African identity' against the white settlers (Fanon 1952; Mars 1946).[8] Ethnographers like W. H. R. Rivers (1926) and Bronislaw Malinowski (1927), aspects of whose work developed into what was to become medical anthropology, while they relied on missionary evidence and colonial office support, did not significantly influence British policy in Africa or elsewhere (Goody 1995). If colonial diseases were of any political interest to the colonial metropolis, the concerns were not about madness but about the acute infections which threatened to deprive the administration of its labour force (Lyons 1992), or the psychological health of the Europeans (Ernst 1991; Littlewood 1985).

Contemporary anthropologists have proposed that all illnesses may be said to be 'culture bound' in that the human response to illness is always socially determined, while biology can never be taken in independence from human action. The classic 'cultural' syndromes remain as titillating relief in the margins of British psychiatric textbooks in the 1990s. Often the hearsay repetition of previous descriptions, travellers' tales and missionary anxieties, frequently in their most bizarre form, they distort local significance and context in providing a voyeuristic image of the other. The windigo cannibal-compulsion has now been recognized as psychiatric folklore, a 'near mythical syndrome' with perhaps three reported instances and one which has never been observed by Europeans (Neutra et al. 1977). Similar doubts have been cast on the evidence for *voodoo death* ('pointing the bone') in which awareness that one had been ensorcered apparently precipitated sudden death through 'a fatal spirit of despondency' (Jarves 1872, cited by Mauss 1926; Eastwell 1982). Psychiatrists concerned with establishing basic mental health services in post-colonial Africa and Asia have deplored the endless collecting of novel syndromes 'by a host of short-term visitors [producing] a wealth of data about some strange ritual of an obscure tribe, analysed with style and erudition, but without comment on general trends particularly as they relate to the more mundane aspects of clinical psychiatry' (German 1972; cf. De Jong 1987). For those concerned with establishing basic medical services and providing humane treatment in situations of poverty and exploitation, debates on the uniqueness of suffering appear otiose.

Yet 'culture-bound syndromes' represent salient instances of a particular community's dilemmas, as extreme if sometimes debatable representations of human distress in its distinctive milieu. To essentialize such social dramas as medical diseases in independence of everyday meanings or other experiences of distress, or in independence of the political context of our observation, is to render them exotic curiosities. To ignore them altogether is to render human adversity bland and familiar, to affirm that the European's experience alone is true, and thus to naturalize the patterns of western illness itself, to affirm them as transcending our intentions, as necessary and immutable.

NOTES

1. This chapter first appeared in the *International Journal of Social Psychiatry* (1996), volume 42, pp.245–265.

2. For example Birnbaum 1923, Schneider 1959. But on the way apparently reversing Kant's characterization of *form* as subjective ordering, *content* as the physical material: a distinction that goes back to Aristotle's distinction between form and matter in his *Metaphysics*. Without examining the nineteenth-century German philosophical and psychiatric texts in detail it is unclear how this happened, but I would suggest something like this: (i) Kant had argued against the British sensationalists in his *Critique of Pure Reason* that perception must involve our subjective ordering of the external natural world to produce the world as our mind can grasp it (that is, as 'phenomenon'). That aspect of our phenomenal world which seemed most evidently subjectively ordered (as opposed to that more evidently produced through immediate sensation of the world but which our minds still ordered) Kant termed 'form'. (ii) German phenomenological studies of psychopathology then became restricted through immediate neuropsychiatric interests to the categorization of the more unusual subjective orderings which were characteristic of the insane (rather than in the total lived subjectivity of any individual in the world); this form became objectified nosologically as various discrete experiences – the 'phenomena' to be examined in psychiatric inquiry (presumably because hallucinations and delusions had no external reference in the consensual world). (iii) By the late nineteenth century, neuropsychiatry began to divide between the neurologists who emphasized observable anatomical structure and the psychiatrists who were stuck with insanity where there were no observable one-to-one correspondences between lesion and illness but only altered functioning and experience; as a residual medical area, psychiatry remains happier talking of 'mental illness' than 'mental disease'. The more evidently subjective process of generating radically new form (for there was nothing

out there which the insane mind ordered except in the case of illusions) became elided with its scientifically more promising (if, for the psychiatrists, only presumed) structuring – altered biology; while that remaining external material which was consensually given and which the mind, insane or otherwise, ordered became clinically residual as simply shared content. By contrast, the generally more radical French 'science de l'homme', as described by Williams (1994), placed greater emphasis on the environmental and social causation of psychopathology; even if (through Broca's biologization of culture) it yielded not dissimilar racist theories by the end of the nineteenth century. It would not be inappropriate to see the French tradition as having contributed most evidently to theories of neuroses in the dominant Anglo-American psychiatry of the 1970s to 1990s, German medicine as providing the clinical schemata for psychoses. In all three, however, there is repeated oscillation between (and conflation of) what may be distinguished as the biological and the moral.

3. Young (1993, p.4) has suggested that this model recalls nineteenth-century 'positivism' in which the chemical makes possible the biological, the biological the social. While it may appear as excessively concrete – and, when pressed, academic social psychiatrists agree that psychiatric illnesses are not entities but rather observed concurrences (Wing 1978) – something very like this, I would argue, is the clinical psychiatrist's naïve realism (to use our customary term for the epistemology of scientists).

4. It is perhaps only for schizophrenia that psychiatrists can argue for any characteristic symptoms at all; the 'first-rank' symptoms described by the younger Schneider. Yet they are found in only a half of identified schizophrenic patients in Britain. The form–content (pathogenic–pathoplastic) model in cultural psychiatry, like its associated 'category fallacy' (Kleinman 1988) which presumes the European core symptoms everywhere, does seem to produce useful conclusions where there is evidence of invariant biological change which may be said to 'determine' behaviour and experience in a unique way such that they do not seem to occur without it. Examples would be delirium tremens and possibly Gilles de la Tourette's syndrome (although behaviours recalling Tourette's are found with other types of brain lesions and in anxiety, and in the experimentally induced hyperstartle response and in social institutions such as latah which encourages hyperstartling).

The World Health Organization's International Pilot Study of Schizophrenia (IPSS) produced evidence in the 1970s that a core schizophrenic pattern can be identified in widely differing societies. What it did not show was the extent of the cultural contribution to the illness, supposedly one of the intentions of the study (Kleinman 1988); emphasis on the core group, which was shown to have comparable rates across cultures, ignored the cases at the edges where there was a much greater difference in rates: a three-fold difference between Denmark and India for a 'broad' category of schizophrenia similar to that actually used in psychiatric practice. The core symptoms of schizophrenia thus appeared to be a *manifestation* of an underlying disease process; taking a wider category of schizophrenia suggests alternatively that schizophrenic symptoms might also be understood as *a response* to a variety of insults, whether neurological or social. Examining stable societies rather than groups of refugees or communities in the midst of civil upheavals emphasizes intrapersonal biological differences in the aetiology of schizophrenia. (Analogous to the way that it is when studying affluent societies that genetic associations appear more salient when looking at differences in height, for we have already minimized one possible environmental source of variation.) Nevertheless, the similarity of core symptoms and rates found in the IPSS argues that we are unlikely to be able to explain all instances of schizophrenia by a more cultural and political understanding as was assumed by anthropologists like Gregory Bateson and by the British anti-psychiatrists of the 1960s.

Cultural considerations of the IPSS results have been limited to the prognosis of an illness taken as primarily biological: vague generalizations about industrialization and schizophrenia (Cooper and Sartorius 1977), or possible correlations with unemployment in capitalist economies (Warner 1985), or differences in relatives' responses to a person with the illness (Leff *et al.* 1987). While the latter suggests that the response which predicts a poor prognosis in Britain has a similar predictive value when 'translated' to India, this conclusion avoids the problem that one British measure, 'overinvolvement', tended to be generally rated less commonly in the Indian context. Nor can we assume that social responses which make for a poor prognosis within a society are those which necessarily differentiate prognosis between societies.

5. By the 1990s, they were acknowledged in the American Psychiatric Association's fourth *Diagnostic and Statistical Manual* (on whose cultural deliberations see Littlewood 1992).

6. A partial reaction may be found however in the work of Rodney Needham, Christina Torrens, Pascal Boyer, Mark Johnson and C.D. Laughlin who have argued against a purely conventional understanding of shared cognitions. The extent to which 'culture' and 'nature' may be said to represent not actually existing entities but rather reified modes of thought (Littlewood 1993b) is beyond the scope of a brief historical survey. Yet we might wonder if the fashionable demedicalization of illness in favour of a cultural understanding is not perhaps a final privileging of western 'culture' over 'nature'.

7. The anthropologist Edward Evans-Pritchard, for example, was commissioned to examine the role of prophets in inciting anti-British resistance among the Nuer of the Sudan. In his text we can note that on a couple of occasions he refers to some of them as 'psychotic' but this is nowhere developed as any sort of racial or medical theory (Evans-Pritchard 1940): on the contrary. By contrast, in the USA, psychiatry was deployed extensively during the nineteenth and twentieth centuries to justify what we may term the internal colonization of Amerindians and African-Americans (Haller 1970). Maurice Lipsedge and I (1982) have argued that this was not simply because of the greater influence of medicine in the USA. In the early stages of imperial expansion, domination is explicitly economic or military, and any necessary justification rests simply on evident technical or administrative superiority, sometimes manifest destiny, or the historical requirements of civilization; only when dominated peoples threaten to achieve some sort of equality do apologies appear couched in a discourse on pathology or biological inferiority.

To an extent we may argue that Europe prepared to abandon her colonies before equality threatened (except in Kenya, Algeria and the French Caribbean: see Carothers 1954; Fanon 1952; Vint 1932), and before colonial administrations had established much beyond a basic mental hospital. (Space prevents consideration here of the case of South Africa (Littlewood 1993a).) In North America, arguments in favour of the emancipation of slaves appeared by the time of Independence to be countered by medical justifications for continued servitude which invoked such novel diseases as *drapetomania* (the impulse to escape) (Brigham 1832) or even, as argued by Benjamin Rush, that African origin was itself an attenuated disease. Among Native Americans, for whom collective political action became impossible as they were dispersed on reservations, twentieth-century administrators and medical officers developed increasingly individual psychological – and thence psychopathological – explanations to explain their high rates of suicide, alcoholism and failure to participate in national life.

8. Why the English–French difference? Perhaps because French colonialism favoured a model of cultural assimilation, the English arguing for segregation (Taguieff 1988).

REFERENCES

Ackernecht, E. (1943) 'Psychopathology, primitive medicine and primitive culture.' *Bulletin of the History of Medicine 14*, 30–68.

Beard, G.M. (1881) *American Nervousness: Its Causes and Consequences.* New York: Putnam.

Benedict, R. (1935) *Patterns of Culture.* London: Routledge and Kegan Paul.

Benedict, R. (1946) *The Chrysanthemum and the Sword: Patterns of Japanese Culture.* Boston: Houghton Mifflin.

Birnbaum, K. (1923) 'Der Aufbau der Psychosen.' Translated as 'The making of a psychosis.' In S.R. Hirsch, and M. Shepherd (eds) (1974) *Themes and Variation in European Psychiatry.* Bristol: Wright.

Bleuler, E. (1911) *Dementia Praecox.* New York: International Universities Press.

Bloch, M. and Bloch, J. (1980) 'Women and the dialectics of nature.' In C. MacCormack and M. Strathern (eds) *Nature, Culture, Gender.* Cambridge: Cambridge University Press.

Bourdieu, P. (1977) *Outline of a Theory of Practice.* Cambridge: Cambridge University Press.

Brigham, A. (1832) *Remarks on the Influence of Mental Cultivation upon Health.* Hartford NY: Huntingdon.

Carothers, J.C. (1953) *The African Mind in Health and Disease.* Geneva: World Health Organisation.

Carothers, J.C. (1954) *The Psychology of Mau Mau.* Nairobi: Government Printers.

Carr, J.E. (1978) 'Ethno-behaviourism and the culture-bound syndromes: the case of amok.' *Culture, Medicine and Psychiatry 2*, 269–293.

Cheyne, G. (1734) *The English Malady.* In V. Skultans (1979) *English Madness: Ideas on Insanity 1580–1890.* London: Routledge and Kegan Paul.

Cooper, J.E. and Sartorius, N. (1977) 'Cultural and temporal variation in schizophrenia: a speculation on the importance of industrialisation.' *British Journal of Psychiatry 130*, 50–55.

De Jong, J.T.V.M. (1987) *A Descent Into African Psychiatry.* Amsterdam: Royal Tropical Institute.

Devereux, G. (1951) *Reality and Dream: Psychotherapy of a Plains Indian.* New York: International Universities Press.

Devereux, G. (1956) 'The normal and abnormal: the key problem in psychiatric anthropology.' Reprinted, translated in G. Devereux (1970) *Essais d'Ethnopsychiatrie Generale.* Paris: Gallimard.

Devereux, G. (1970) *Essais d'Ethnopsychiatrie Generale.* Paris: Gallimard.

Doi, T. (1971) *Amae no Kozo.* [The anatomy of dependence.] Tokyo: Kodansha.

Easlea, B. (1980) *Witch Hunting, Magic and the New Philosphy: An Introduction to the Debates of the Scientific Revolution 1450–1750.* Brighton: Harvester.

Eastwell, H.D. (1982) 'Voodoo death and the mechanism for the despatch of the dying in East Arnhem.' *American Anthropologist 84,* 5–18.

Ernst, W. (1991) *Mad Tales From The Raj: The European Insane in British India.* London: Routledge.

Evans-Pritchard, E.E. (1940) *The Nuer.* Oxford: Oxford University Press.

Fanon, F. (1952) *Peau Noir, Masques Noirs.* Paris: Seuil.

Field, M.J. (1960) *Search For Security: An Ethno-Psychiatric Study of Rural Ghana.* London: Faber and Faber.

Fisher, L.E. (1985) *Colonial Madness: Mental Health in the Barbadian Social Order.* New Brunswick NJ: Rutgers University Press.

Frank, J.D. (1961) *Persuasion and Healing: A Comparative Study of Psychotherapy.* New York: Schocken.

Fumaroli, M. (1996) 'A Scottish Voltaire: John Barclay and the character of nations.' *Times Literary Supplement,* 19 January, 16–17.

Gaskell, S. (1860) 'On the wont of better provisions for the labouring and middle classes when attacked or threatened with insanity.' *Journal of Mental Science 6,* 321–327.

Geertz, C. (1986) 'Anti-anti-relativism.' *American Anthropologist 86,* 263–278.

German, G.A. (1972) 'Aspects of clinical psychiatry in sub-Saharan Africa.' *British Journal of Psychiatry 121,* 461–479.

Good, B.J. and Good, M.-J. D. (1982) 'Towards a meaning-centred analysis of popular illness categories.' In A. Marsella and G.M. White (eds) *Cultural Conceptions of Mental Health and Therapy.* Dordrecht: Reidel.

Goody, J. (1995) *The Expansive Moment: Anthropology in Britain and Africa 1918–1970.* Cambridge: Cambridge University Press.

Hahn, R.A. (1985) 'Culture-bound syndromes unbound.' *Social Science and Medicine 21,* 165–180.

Haller, J.S. (1970) 'The physician versus the Negro: medical and anthropological concepts of race in the nineteenth century.' *Bulletin of the History of Medicine 44,* 154–167.

Harraway, D. (1989) *Primate Visions: Gender, Race and Nature in the World of Modern Science.* New York: Routledge.

Hughes, C.C. (1985) 'Culture-bound or construct-bound?' In R.C. Simons and C.C. Hughes (eds) *The Culture-Bound Syndromes: Folk Illnesses of Psychiatric and Anthropological Interest.* Dordrecht: Reidel.

Janet, P. (1926) (Trans.) *Psychological Healing.* London: Allen and Unwin.

John XX1, Pope (1550) 'Folk remedies against madness.' Trans. in R. Hunter and I. MacAlpine (eds) *Three Hundred Years of Psychiatry 1535–1860.* London: Oxford University Press.

Jung, C.G. (1930) 'Your Negroid and Indian behaviour.' *Forum 83,* 193–199.

Kakar, S. (1978) *The Inner World: A Psychoanalytical Study of Childhood and Society in India*. Delhi: Oxford University Press.

Kiev, A. (1964) 'The study of folk psychiatry.' In A. Kiev (ed) *Magic, Faith and Healing: Studies in Primitive Psychiatry Today*. New York: Free Press.

Kiev, A. (1972) *Transcultural Psychiatry*. Harmondsworth: Penguin.

Kleinman, A. (1988) *Rethinking Psychiatry: From Cultural Category to Personal Experience*. New York: Free Press.

Kraepelin, E. (1904) 'Vergleichende Psychiatrie.' Translated as 'Comparative psychiatry', in S.R. Hirsch and M. Shepherd (eds) (1974) *Themes and Variation in European Psychiatry*. Bristol: Wright.

La Barre, W. (1970) *The Ghost Dance: Origins of Religion*. London: Allen and Unwin.

Lambo, T.A. (1955) 'The role of cultural factors in paranoid psychoses among the Yoruba tribe.' *Journal of Mental Science 101*, 239–266.

Lee, S. (1996) 'Reconsidering the status of anorexia nervosa as a western culture-bound syndrome.' *Social Science and Medicine 42*, 21–34.

Leff, J., Short, A., Bedi, H., Mennon, D.K., Kuipers, L., Korten, H., Ernberg, G., Day, R., Sartorius, N. and Jablensky, H. (1987) 'Influence of relatives' expressed emotion on the course of schizophrenia in Chandigarh.' *British Journal of Psychiatry 151*, 166–173.

Lewontin, R.C., Rose, S. and Kamin, L.J. (1984) *Not In Our Genes: Biology, Ideology and Human Nature*. New York: Pantheon.

Littlewood, R. (1984) 'La migration des syndromes liés à la culture.' *Psychopathologie Africaine 20*, 1, 5–16.

Littlewood, R. (1985) 'Jungle madness: some observations on expatriate psychopathology.' *International Journal of Social Psychiatry 31*, 3, 194–197.

Littlewood, R. (1991) 'Against pathology: the new psychiatry and its critics.' *British Journal of Psychiatry 159*, 696–702.

Littlewood, R. (1992) 'DSM-IV and culture: is the classification intentionally valid?' *Psychiatric Bulletin 16*, 257–261.

Littlewood, R. (1993a) 'Ideology, camouflage or contingency?: racism in British psychiatry.' *Transcultural Psychiatric Research Review 30*, 243–290.

Littlewood, R. (1993b) *Pathology and Identity: The Work of Mother Earth in Trinidad*. Cambridge: Cambridge University Press.

Littlewood, R. (1993c) 'Culture-bound syndromes: cultural comments.' In J.E. Mezzich, A. Kleinman, H. Fabrega and D. Parron (eds) *Working Papers for the DSM-IV Cultural Committee*. New York: American Psychiatric Press.

Littlewood, R. (1994) 'Verticality as the idiom for mood and disorder: a note on an eighteenth-century representation.' *British Medical Anthropology Review 2*, 1, 44–48.

Littlewood, R. (1995) 'Psychopathology and personal agency: modernity, culture change and eating disorders in South Asian societies.' *British Journal of Medical Psychology 68*, 45–63.

Littlewood, R. and Lipsedge, M. (1982) *Aliens and Alienists: Ethnic Minorities and Psychiatry*. Harmondsworth: Penguin.

Littlewood, R. and Lipsedge, M. (1987) 'The butterfly and the serpent.' *Culture, Medicine and Psychiatry 11*, 289–335.

Loudon, J. (1959) 'Psychogenic disorder and social conflict among the Zulu.' In M.K. Opler (ed) *Culture and Mental Health.* New York: Macmillan.

Lugard, F.D. (1929) *The Dual Mandate in British Tropical Africa.* Edinburgh: Blackwood.

Lyons, M. (1992) *The Colonial Disease: A Social History of Sleeping Sickness in Northern Zaire 1900–1940.* Cambridge: Cambridge University Press.

McCulloch, J. (1994) *Colonial Psychiatry and the African Mind.* Cambridge: Cambridge University Press.

Madden, R.R. (1857) *Phantasmata Or Illusions and Fanaticisms of Protean Forms Productive of Great Evils.* London: Newby.

Malhotra, H.K. and Wig, T. (1975) 'Dhat syndrome: a culture-bound sex neurosis.' *Archives of Sexual Behaviour 4*, 519–528.

Malinowski, B. (1927) *Sex and Repression in Savage Society.* London: Routledge.

Mannoni, O. (1950) *Psychologie de la Colonisation.* Paris: Seuil.

Mars, L. (1946) *La Lutte Contra La Folie.* Port-au-Prince: Imprimerie de l'Etat.

Mauss, M. (1926) 'A definition of the collective suggestion of the idea of death.' Translated in M. Mauss *Sociology and Psychology* (1979) London: Routledge and Kegan Paul.

Michaelis, J.D. (1814) *Commentaries on the Law of Moses.* London: Rivington.

Morel, B.A. (1860) *Traité Des Maladies Mentales.* Paris: Masson.

Neutra, R., Levy, J.E. and Parker, D. (1977) 'Cultural expectations versus reality in Navaho seizure patterns and sick roles.' *Culture, Medicine and Psychiatry 1*, 255–275.

O'Brien, H.A. (1883) 'Latah.' *Journal of the Royal Asiatic Society (Straits Branch) 11*, 143–153.

Oxley, T. (1849) 'Malay amoks.' *Journal of the Indian Archipelago and Eastern Asia 3*, 532–533.

Parker, S. (1960) 'The windigo psychosis.' *American Anthropologist 62*, 602–655.

Prince, R. (1960) 'The "brain fag" syndrome in Nigerian students.' *Journal of Mental Science 106*, 559–570.

Ritenbaugh, C. (1982) 'Obesity as a culture-bound syndrome.' *Culture, Medicine and Psychiatry 6*, 347–364.

Rivers, W.H.R. (1924) *Magic, Medicine and Religion.* London: Kegan Paul, Trench and Trubner.

Roheim, G. (1950) *Psychoanalysis and Anthropology: Culture, Personality and the Unconscious.* New York: International Universities Press.

Sachs, W. (1937) *Black Hamlet.* London: Bles.

Sargant, W. (1973) *The Mind Possessed: From Ecstasy to Exorcism.* London: Heinemann.

Schneider, K. (1959) *Clinical Psychopathology*, 5th edn. Trans. M.W. Hamilton. New York: Grune and Stratton.

Seligman, C.G. (1928) 'The unconscious in relation to anthropology.' *British Journal of Psychology 18*, 373–387.

Seligman, C.G. (1929) 'Sex, temperament, conflict and psychosis in a Stone Age population.' *British Journal of Medical Psychology 9*, 187–228.

Shweder, R.A. (1985) 'Menstrual pollution, soul loss and the comparative study of emotions.' In A. Kleinman and B. Good (eds) *Culture and Depression.* Berkeley: California University Press.

Simons, R.C. and Hughes, C.C. (eds) (1985) *The Culture-Bound Syndromes: Folk Illnesses of Psychiatric and Anthropological Interest.* Dordrecht: Reidel.

Taguieff, P.A. (1988) *La Force du Prejugé: Essais sur le Racism et ses Doubles.* Paris: La Decouverte.

Vint, F.W. (1932) 'A preliminary note on the cell content of the prefrontal cortex of the East African native.' *East African Medical Journal 9*, 30–55.

Warner, R. (1985) *Recovery From Schizophrenia: Psychiatry and Political Economy.* New York: Routledge and Kegan Paul.

Weinstein, E. (1962) *Cultural Aspects of Delusion.* New York: Free Press.

Williams, E.A. (1994) *The Physical and the Moral: Anthropology, Physiology and Philosophical Medicine in France 1750–1850.* Cambridge: Cambridge University Press.

Williams, R. (1958) *Culture and Society 1780–1950.* London: Chatto and Windus.

Wing, J.K. (1978) *Reasoning About Madness.* Oxford: Oxford University Press.

Wittgenstein, L. (1958) *Philosophical Investigations.* Oxford: Blackwell.

Yap, P.M. (1951) 'Mental diseases peculiar to certain cultures.' *Journal of Mental Science 97*, 313–337.

Yap, P.M. (1974) *Comparative Psychiatry: A Theoretical Framework.* Toronto: Toronto University Press.

Young, A. (1993) 'Making facts and marking time in psychiatric research: an essay on the anthropology of scientific knowledge.' Unpublished ms.

3

Remembering and Forgetting

Anthropology and Psychiatry:
The Changing Relationship

Vieda Skultans

Those who are incapable of a science, write its history, discuss its methods or criticise its scope. Marcel Mauss (1979, p.10)

I propose in this chapter to look at the sources of solidarity and difference between anthropology and psychiatry. Historically there is more uniting than dividing the two disciplines. Differences are of recent origin and relate to the more radical role that anthropology has assumed towards memory and other psychological processes. This turn in anthropology is in line with post-modernist trends and leaves psychiatry outside. I want to explore the nature of this bifurcation by focusing on memory. Until relatively recently memory was the preserve of psychologists and psychiatrists. Its appropriation by social anthropologists and its very differently perceived status and function serve to highlight the nature of the rift that is opening up between the two disciplines.

Anthropologists bury their ancestors – and especially the unwanted ones – deep. But then like certain New Guinea tribespeople they feel called upon ritually to exhume them; the deeper the burial, the more fun the exhumation. I propose to look at some of anthropology's ancestors and kinship ties and to examine how and why its psychological relatives came to be unwanted.

But first, let us return to the similarities. Anthropology and psychiatry are children of the Enlightenment project: the optimistic commitment to human reason and its powers of penetrating and dispersing unreason. Nineteenth-century evolutionary anthropologists and psychiatrists were within this tradition. They were united by a certain evangelical interest in the primitive. Tylor's view of cultures was hierarchical, but like Tory self-perceptions ultimately democratic in the long run (1958). This contrasts with the early divisive view of culture of Levy-Bruhl (1966). Civilization lay within the grasp of all peoples who joined the evolutionary master narrative. Freud's view of the conscious replacing the unconscious – where id was, ego shall be – is in this same tradition. Indeed, psychoanalytic theory succeeds in fusing individual and evolutionary time. The indebtedness was mutual. Nineteenth-century and early twentieth-century anthropologists borrowed ideas from contemporary psychologists and psychiatrists to explain primitive beliefs and rituals. Conversely psychiatrists made free use of anthropological writings for their own ends. Thus, Malinowski made much use of Freud's ideas, while Freud himself relied heavily on (highly suspect and speculative) anthropology (Stocking 1986).

Anthropology has been defined as the study of the other. Roland Littlewood and Maurice Lipsedge (1997) in their justly celebrated book *Aliens and Alienists* draw our attention to the shared preoccupations of psychiatrists and anthropologists in this respect. Anthropology started life as the study of the exotic, providing Victorian man with a reverse image of himself and the barbaric conditions he had left behind. Psychiatry as an institutionalized set of practices is associated with the enlightenment and the elevation of reason. Its object, the madman, provides the reverse image of man's most highly valued characteristic – reason.

There are other issues which draw the two disciplines together. The Socratic precept 'Know thyself' has long been a core ingredient of psychoanalytic and psychotherapeutic practice. More recently this injunction has been adopted by some anthropological circles as orthodoxy. The impersonal voice and the timeless present of earlier ethnographic studies concealed interests that had little bearing on the scientific study of mankind. Tense and person, it is argued, create the spurious illusion of objectivity and moral impartiality, at the same time allowing the anthropologist to get away with unexamined prejudices. Such unreflexive practices promote the projection of stereotypes which in turn shape and sustain the anthropologist's own fragile identity. The emergence of a critical self-awareness has put the anthropologist under the microscopic gaze of professional peers. If an anthropological monograph does not contain a personal or autobiographical statement of the author's position and involvement in her research it is sure to be extracted by her critics. If we follow this road, we may end by asking: are we really studying ourselves? Has our preoccupation with our own involvement in the production of research come to interfere with our ability to recognize differences between others as Barth suggests (1996)? Or have anthropologists learnt from psychiatrists that self- knowledge contributes both to the ways in which we glean knowledge from others and how we subsequently represent it. My own view is that self-awareness and ethnography are mutually enriching. In Bakhtin's words, 'The listener becomes the speaker' – but this very audibility of the silent listener promotes clarity and understanding (1986: 68). Ethnography is thus not negated but affirmed.

These issues of voice and the construction of knowledge bear on a related field of importance for both psychiatry and anthropology. I refer to the psychoanalytic theories of normal human development and pathology. One of Freud's greatest achievements was to break down the division between the normal and the pathological. The abnormal or pathological does not inhabit a separate order of reality: it is merely a specific elaboration of it. We can describe Freud's achievement either as pathologizing the normal or as normalizing the pathological depending upon our interests and perspective. The paradigm shift entailed by such a perspective has, I believe, influenced anthropological thought. The idea that anthropology is par excellence the study of the other, and that other is constructed as an alter ego and that anthropology is ultimately, therefore, the study of oneself belongs to a unifying vision of humankind.

Psychoanalysis, as we all know, is the talking cure. Patients suffer from unsatisfactory stories of the past and the aim of psychoanalysis is to construct a coherent and satisfying account of the past from the fragments of reminiscences. Freud was involved with reconstructing the fragmentary past at the same time as Durkheim was developing the idea of anomie. Psycho-analysis and talking therapies dealt with narratives long before they were of any anthropological interest. Meanwhile, anthropologists, particularly those investigating violence, are acknowledging that lack of coherence can make us ill. The present anthropological and sociological interest in narrative owes much to its ancestor discipline.

For both disciplines the emergence of narrative brings into sharp focus problems of truth and verification. Where does truth lie? On the surface or, as Popper thought, at the bottom of a well? Do language and narrative open a window on the self and the past or do they create their own densely opaque meanings? We might even argue, following in the footsteps of Freud and more recently of Foucault, that language hides rather than reveals (not, of course, an implication of Popper's view of truth). Language never says exactly what it means. The fascination of narrative is that it both reaches out to reality and in the process creates a new social and personal reality which obscures it. Or does this argument, as Roland Littlewood suggested in an earlier symposium, presuppose an artificial distinction between form and content? We may think we are dealing with an artichoke and working our way towards its precious heart, when in fact what we are left with is the humble onion.

Narrative theory, so central to recent theoretical debate in anthropology, suggests that truth lies in every phrase and gesture if only we are skilful and attentive listeners. Narrative form is not merely the gilt on the gingerbread but carries substantive meanings. This approach is surely heavily indebted to the psychoanalytic emphasis on meaning and its unifying role – as well, of course, as drawing upon linguistic and literary theory. One of Freud's principal achievements was to draw in seemingly odd and 'irrational' phenomena – dreams, slips of the tongue, involuntary behaviours – and show them to be potent carriers of meaning.

So far I have suggested that psychoanalysis and anthropology have a number of areas of common theoretical concern. The dual training and more importantly the continued professional involvement of several of the early ancestors of our two disciplines bear witness to their harmonious co-existence. As Adam Kuper has pointed out, 'For the first twenty years of the century British Anthropology was very largely in the hands of psychologists and physiologists' (1991, p.132). Charles Seligman, William Halse Rivers Rivers and A.C. Haddon are examples. 'Other leading psychologists – including Bartlett and McDougall – were active for a while in anthropological research' (ibid.). Although none of them made tremendous advances towards the integration of the two disciplines or, indeed, to theory at all, they promoted a respectful and harmonious co-existence. If anything, priority was given to the explanatory powers of psychology over those of sociology and anthropology. Indeed, Rivers considered sociology to be a descriptive and psychology an explanatory discipline: 'To me, as to most students of the subject, the final aim of the study of society is the explanation of social behaviour in terms of psychology' (1916, p.2). This is not, of course, a view that Durkheim would have endorsed particularly when applied to primitive society: 'It may be said, and with special force where societies devoid of all written records are concerned, that the chief instrument for the study of past history is a knowledge of psychology; that only through the knowledge of man's mental processes can we hope to reconstruct the past, so that the study of these mental processes should be our first care' (Rivers 1916, p.3). Seligman acknowledged the importance of Freud's theories to his own understanding of the dreams of 'non-European and especially the non-European races' (1924, p.186). Even Marcel Mauss, Durkheim's nephew, felt no embarrassment about acknowledging his indebtedness to psychology. In his essay on sociology and psychology he admitted: 'You know how to get the best out of us' (1979, p.2) and 'our analysis of the facts of collective consciousness can indeed speak no other language than your own' (p.12). It is thus ironic that Rodney Needham's famous structuralist onslaught on psychologism *Structure and Sentiment* is dedicated to Marcel Mauss (1962). These are not views which anthropologists, psychologists or indeed psychiatrists would echo today. What has happened in the meantime?

Far later these views came to be regarded as heresy. Adam Kuper argues that the divergence in thought came about not because of the influence of the Durkheimian paradigm in anthropology but because of 'political considerations, having to do with the professionalization of British psychology' (1991, p.132). The result was a 'sharp recoil' of each from the other.

However, the recoil was not as sharp or as clean cut as Kuper suggests. Radcliffe-Brown, of course, had no truck with psychological explanation but Malinowski's fieldwork was heavily influenced by psychoanalysis. Despite the well-known disagreements over the universality of Oedipus complex, Malinowski was a revisionist Freudian. Instincts or needs, in particular libido, were central to Malinowski's 'functionalism' and, indeed, to his experience of fieldwork, as his diary was to reveal. Malinowski did not challenge Freud's instinct theory outright but made the modest proposal that culture modified the expression of instinct and should, therefore, be taken into account. He did, however, persist in the belief that ultimate explanations rested with psychology. This theoretical allegiance is expressed in his review of the Group Mind: 'McDougall was one of the first clearly to appreciate that in problems of social belief, custom and behaviour it is sentiment and instinct which play a paramount part' (Malinowski 1921, p.107).

Psychoanalysis is a theory of memory, or rather of forgetting. Indeed W.H.R. Rivers singled out active forgetting 'as the distinctive feature of Freud's system' (1917, p.913) More recently Ian Hacking has put this more memorably: 'One feature of the modern sensibility is dazzling in its implausibility: the idea that what has been forgotten is what forms our character, our personality, our soul' (1996, p.70). For Hacking the sciences of memory emerging in the nineteenth century enabled society to acquire knowledge, to expose and to discipline the soul. Proceeding hand in hand with anatomo-politics of the human body and bio-politics of human populations, memoro-politics facilitated the shaping of large populations. 'The soul has been a way of internalising the social order, of putting into myself those very virtues and cruelties that enable my society to survive' (1996, p.73). Forgotten events offer more opportunity for the social reshaping of the past than those still remembered. Hacking's argument draws its power from his ideas on the indeterminacy of the past. By indeterminacy he means not only that we change our perspectives on the past but that indeterminacy is intrinsic to all human action. Any act can be presented under any number of descriptions:

When new descriptions become available, when they come into circulation, or even when they become the sorts of things that it is all right to say, to think, then there are new things to choose to do. When new intentions become open to me, because new descriptions, new concepts, become available to me. I live in a new world of opportunities. (Hacking 1996, p.236)

This type of argument illuminates the development of psychiatric diagnostic categories, in that new angles on human behaviour are discovered through new forms of description. Hacking focuses on multiple personality disorder which 'provided a new way to be an unhappy person' (p.236).

Hacking is a philosopher whose *Rewriting the Soul* is very influential among anthropologists, including Allan Young. Young's book (1996), as its subtitle *Inventing Post Traumatic Stress Disorder* suggests, is about the creation of diagnostic categories and medical knowledge. I must here, albeit apologetically, summarize this theoretically provocative and scholarly book in a few lines. Young argues that PTSD is a way of medicalizing the past. Such medicalization and sanitization of the past enables collective traumas such as, for example, war to be translated into individual problems, thereby alleviating collective responsibility and guilt. Kleinman's articles (1982, 1994) and book *Writing at the Margins* also have as one of their central themes the translation of collective violence into individual illness (1997). Now I do not wish to challenge the reality of such processes of medicalization. The astonishing expansion of the history of medicine provides ample evidence for such processes at work. I merely want to suggest that anthropology also has an interest in colonizing the past. It may be that in documenting the processes of medicalization and the politicization of memory anthropology is seeking to expand its own empire. But to whom does the past belong? Whose empire is it anyway?

If psychoanalysis is a theory of forgetting, as Timpanaro suggests in *The Freudian Slip*, it does not account for the positive aspects of memory (1976). Why we remember is as important a question as why we forget? On this question anthropologists have much to tell us. Maurice Halbwachs published *The Collective Memory* in 1950. It lay dormant for some decades and has belatedly achieved the status of a classic. Halbwachs argues that although we may regard memory as quintessentially private it is, in fact, thoroughly social. Both the quality of experience and memory are determined by the frameworks given by society. Society directs our attention to some aspects of the past and not others. It is because social frameworks are not yet in place that we remember so little of our childhoods. Halbwachs captures the essentially social nature of memory with the phrase 'We are never alone'. There are, of course, purely personal aspects of memory, but Halbwachs was surely right in questioning the dichotomy between a private world of memory and a public world of experience and perception. *The Collective Memory* has set in motion a series of anthropological and historical studies of memory. These studies pursue a number of different issues, most being a variation on a presentist theme – the idea that narrative and memory tell us more about the present than the past.

Elizabeth Tonkin has developed a powerful argument about genre in narrative along these lines. A 'genre' in the sense in which Tonkin uses the term 'provides a mode or code for people's transmission of experience, and, as well, by its own transmission, maintains a version of the past which people can use for their own ends' (1995, p.114). Thus each recollection, be it an oral recitation or a publication, sets up a resonance with the personal experience of its listeners and readers as well as influencing later writers. The genre I am most familiar with is that of testimony, drawn from my study of Latvian memories of collectivization, deportation and exile. In common with all testimonies, these accounts are statements of social as much as of personal identity. In Latvia this genre focuses on the narrative development of a common ethnic identity. The hero of the story is the Latvian nation, and national character ensures survival. The narrative 'I' is sometimes fused with Latvian culture heroes (Skultans 1996, 1998).

I described anthropological approaches to memory as presentist: versions of the past depend upon the narrators present experience. However, the situation is yet more complex and its complexity escapes a straightforward presentist position. The testimonies I encountered are given in the present tense. They refer to experiences that have not yet been processed and laid to rest. Past experience of dispossession and dislocation is trapped in an arbitrary and capricious present which makes separation from them difficult and ensures their continued hold over the imagination. As Valentine Daniel writes so insightfully of the Tamils of Sri Lanka: 'When the present looms large in this manner, both memory and hope become either emaciated or bloated. In either case, it is the present that determines the past, making the past a mere simulacrum of the present' (1996, pp.106–107).

However, for philosophers from Augustine onwards the present has been the most perplexing aspect of time. We may be able to focus on the past and the future, but the present is more inscrutable and escapes our grasp in the very act of focusing on it. Extremes of experience, both joy and terror, transform the present. The presence of violence expands the present so that it has us in its grasp. Thus testimonies about past experience enable the testifier to escape both the past and the present and move towards the future. It is not so much the nature of the present which releases, as the hope and mapping out of a future which violence and the caprice of the present have erased.

Stories of the past therefore relate as much to the future as they do to the past. The programmatic statements of the Latvian Oral History Project make this point quite explicitly, by linking life histories with the quest for a common ethnic identity. Particular versions of the past give a desired shape to the future. Bakhtin's arresting claim that the listener becomes the speaker is at work here (1986, p.68). Listeners and speakers unite in the production of tales of destiny. Thus memory is shaped by the contexts in which it is told and the futures which communities plan for themselves. In focusing on the future – on the imaginative mapping out of the unknown – I am able to single out the specifically anthropological contribution to our under-standing of the life of the mind.

Commemorative practices play an important role in the shaping of memory. Through commemorative ritual and architecture, the writing of children's history books and the retelling of stories within the family, a special kind of light is directed at a particular area of the past leaving other areas in darkness. Paul Connerton (1989) in *How Societies Remember* argues that social memory (by which I mean the shared social aspect of individual memory) and the memory of groups depend upon public commemorative practices. A prohibition on commemoration would, therefore, pose a threat to social memory. Connerton writes: 'What is horrifying in totalitarian regimes is not only the violation of human dignity but the fear that there might remain nobody who would ever again properly bear witness to the past' (1989, p.15). However, this account of social memory does not explain the persistence of oppositional memory in the Baltic countries under Soviet rule. Commemorative practices were strictly censored and even within the family references to the past were for the most part suppressed. Yet individual memory in Latvia survived without the support of public commemoration. How long it could have continued to survive is another question. Do memories have a sell-by date, as Cathy Merridale so aptly asks (1996)? Or does their recycling depend upon a transition from the interior life of an individual (never, of course, entirely pure) to the public realm of ritual commemoration?

Public acknowledgement and commemoration of a past relate to questions about the audience and its readiness to listen. That audience may be the society or group of which the individual is a member or it may be the academic community which chooses to listen now but not at an earlier time. I have in mind here Arthur Kleinman's earlier work on somatization, neurasthenia and depression in China (1982). Kleinman's fieldwork was carried out in the wake of the cultural revolution when many of his patients and their families must have been suffering devastating consequences of dispossession, displacement and the assault on their identity which these constituted. He must have had first-hand experience of this and yet there is hardly a suggestion of such experiences in his books. His approach to neurasthenia using quasi-clinical classificatory categories of pain and unhappiness makes it difficult to get a sense of the subjective meanings of illness for patients. I have only been able to find one narrative that connects in any way with the historical memory of the cultural revolution. It is 'case 4' of a 52-year-old woman who together with her husband and children had been subjected to political harassment and oppression. Here Kleinman offers us a paraphrase of this woman's spoken narrative:

> Suppose, she said, you were looking at the ground, you were climbing a mountain and the mountain was very steep and difficult to climb. To the right and to the left you could see people falling off the mountainside. Holding onto your neck and back were several family members so that if you fell so would they. For twenty years you climbed this mountain with your eyes fixed on the handholds and footholds. You neither looked back nor ahead. Finally you reached the top of the mountain. Perhaps this is the first time you have looked backward and seen how much you have endured, how difficult your life and your family's situation has been, how blighted your hopes... She ended by asking me if this was not a good enough reason to become depressed. (Kleinman 1982, p.169)

I have quoted this at length because I feel it highlights a dimension missing from the rest of his earlier work. This case does not suggest an unwillingness to confront painful emotions. The paradox of Kleinman's position is that he attributes behaviour to his patients which he himself exemplifies. The theme of this early work is the inability of the Chinese to recognize and disclose painful emotions and their translation and perception of psychological distress as bodily symptoms. Kleinman's more recent writing on the ways in which the effects of state-induced violence and mass brutality are represented as individual weakness and vulnerability had to wait until the break-up of the Soviet Union and the public revelations about the extent of Communist violence before making an appearance in print in the 1990s.

I mention Kleinman not because I wish to make him a public scapegoat but because his case illustrates some important theoretical issues about active listening. The psychiatrists among our readers will be more familiar with this art. To anthropologists and others it is highly perplexing. Reception theorists tell us that it is easier to write a book than to read it. Similarly we could say that it is easier to talk than to listen. The art of active reconstruction lies with the reader or listener and is a highly complex and mysterious process. As my example indicates, it depends not only upon the qualities of the listener but also upon the social context and political climate in which they find themselves. Hacking's concept of semantic contagion or leaking is relevant here: the idea that our renaming of an experience has repercussions on the way in which we reassess the rest of our experience. Why is it that we are now more ready to hear the voices of victims of torture? Of sexually abused children? Those voices were surely there before but we were not ready to listen. Perhaps we were too busy paying attention to a different set of voices. So it is with Arthur Kleinman. Is he now remembering the faint voices of his Chinese patients across two decades, or is he listening to the more powerful and louder voices of his academic colleagues? I will leave you to look for the answers.

Paul Connerton reminds us that each beginning, each act of forgetting involves recollection and preserves a memory of the old order (1989, p.13). We might also say that remembering depends upon forgetting. So it is that memory and forgetting depend upon each other.

What does this brief review of the anthropological interest in memory tell us? Early anthropologists looked to psychoanalysis for an understanding of culture. Theories of memory and forgetting provided the meeting ground between the instinctual life of individuals and their culture. The recent work on memory attributes a more radical role to culture in the shaping of memory. The shape of memory may tell us how knowledge is constructed, but it does not tell us about the past. At this point I return to my original problem about the bifurcation of the two disciplines over the issue of memory.

Despite the recent interest in false memory psychiatry still holds to the Enlightenment project: it assumes there is a set of facts. False memory points away from the facts, true memory towards it. Anthropology has for the most part (with notable exceptions) abandoned the Enlightenment project. Memory is not studied as a road to truth but because it provides us with lessons in what Hacking describes as 'that overtilled country' (1996, p.257) of the social construction of meanings.

Let me finish by returning again to Mauss. Our debt is great and I do not think we shall ever repay it. 'Perhaps we will only ever reward you with new usurpations' (1979, p.19).

REFERENCES

Bakhtin, M.M. (1986) *Speech Genres and Other Late Essays*. Austin: University of Texas Press.

Barth, F. (1996) Paper delivered at the Edinburgh Bicentennial Anthropology Celebrations, October.

Connerton, P. (1989) *How Societies Remember*. Cambridge: Cambridge University Press.

Daniel, E.V. (1996) *Charred Lullabies*. Princeton: Princeton University Press.

Hacking, I. (1996) *Rewriting the Soul Multiple Personality and the Sciences of Memory*. Princeton: Princeton University Press.

Halbwachs, M. (1981/1950) *The Collective Memory*. New York and Cambridge: Harper Row.

Kleinman, A. (1982) 'Neurasthenia and depression: a study of somatization and culture in China.' *Culture, Medicine and Psychiatry 6*, 117–190.

Kleinman, A. (1997) *Writing at the Margins*. Berkeley: University of California Press.

Kleinman, A. and Kleinman, J. (1994) 'How bodies remember: social memory and bodily experience of criticism, resistance and delegitimation following China's cultural revolution.' *New Literary History 25*, 707–723.

Kuper, A. (1991) 'Anthropologists and the history of anthropology.' *Critique of Anthropology 11*, 2, 125–142.

Levy-Bruhl, L. (1966) *How Natives Think*. New York: Washington Press.

Littlewood, R. and Lipsedge, M. (1997) *Aliens and Alienists*, 3rd edn. London: Routledge.

Malinowski, B. (1921) 'Review of McDougall's group mind.' *Man 21*, 106–109.

Mauss, M. (1979) *Sociology and Psychology*. Trans. Ben Brewster. London: Routledge and Kegan Paul.

Merridale, C. (1996) 'Death and memory in Modern Russia.' *History Workshop Journal 42*, 1–18.

Needham, R. (1962) *Structure and Sentiment: A Test Case in Anthropology*. Chicago: University of Chicago Press.

Rivers, W.H.R. (1916) 'Sociology and psychology.' *Sociological Review 9*, 1–16.

Rivers, W.H.R. (1917) 'Freud's psychology of the unconscious.' *The Lancet*, 913–914.

Seligman, C.G. (1924) 'A note on dreams.' *Journal of Royal Anthropological Institute 23*, 186–188.

Skultans, V. (1996) 'Looking for a subject. Latvian memory and narrative.' *History of the Human Sciences 9*, 4, 65–80.

Skultans, V. (1998) *The Testimony of Lives. Narrative and Memory in Post-Soviet Latvia*. London: Routledge.

Stocking, G.W. (ed) (1986) 'Malinowski's encounter with Freudian psychoanalysis.' In G.W. Stocking (ed) *Malinowski, Rivers Benedict and Others Essays on Culture and Personality*. Madison: University of Wisconsin Press.

Timpanaro, S. (1976) *The Freudian Slip: Psychoanalysis and Textual Criticism*. London: NLB.

Tonkin, E. (1995) *Narrating Our Pasts. The Social Construction of Oral History*. Cambridge: Cambridge University Press.

Tylor, E.B. (1958) *The Origins of Culture*. New York: Harper Row.

Young, A. (1996) *The Harmony of Illusions. Inventing Post Traumatic Stress Disorder*. Princeton: Princeton University Press.

4

Narrative and Method in the Anthropology of Medicine

John Campbell

This chapter queries the significance of personal narrative and seeks to remind us of the value of other research methods which yield richer interpretations. The emphasis on narrative can be traced to the influence of postmodernism and this relationship is explored in the first part in which I set out the key propositions underpinning postmodernist approaches to narrative.

I then outline two accounts in medical anthropology based upon narrative – the first based primarily on the accounts provided by patients of their illness, the second based upon psychiatrists' accounts and interpretations of multiple personality disorder. I conclude that narrative data is unable to shoulder the burden of analysis and interpretation because such analyses tend to background social structure and action in favour of culture and rhetoric. Second, I do not believe that anthropological studies of medicine can afford to remain at the level of discourse/narrative because 'good' research must situate its subject carefully in the wider political economy of which it is a part, and because medical anthropology must be able to engage with the problems of measurement and verification with biomedicine and psychiatry. Finally, it seems to be that the search for understanding cannot be limited to a literal reading of narratives, whether of patients or medical practitioners, any more than we can afford not to grasp the meaning contained in the cultural classification schemes which shape social beliefs about the body and its engagement with the world.

Finally, it strikes me that there exists in medical anthropology an unresolved tension which needs to be acknowledged: namely the very different concerns, methods and indeed frames of reference underpinning psychological and anthropological research. I therefore conclude on a note of caution about the supposed complementarity of the two approaches, and in particular the ease with which individuals trained in both disciplines shift their disciplinary 'hats' without, it seems to me, addressing the contradictory theoretical positions contained in each approach.

A POSTMODERN TAKE ON MEANING

The 'interpretative turn' arose out of debates in mainstream anthropology in the 1960s. The volume by Rabinow and Sullivan (1987) brought together many seminal essays and sought to establish the basis for 'an interpretative social science'. The editors argue that their approach might function as a 'successor paradigm' to positivist enquiry which, in their view, is unable to deliver on its promise of providing an objective account of the world. In its pursuit of meaning through the analysis of culture, postmodern anthropology rejected 'paradigmatic' social science – namely logical positivism, functionalism, Marxism, structuralism – and causal explanation. However, apart from the rejection of 'science', it is far from clear what the evidential basis for their own accounts might be.

For example, while decrying the deductive character of science with its search for agreement over a shared explanatory paradigm – rejected because such a model is 'fundamentally wrong' about the nature of the human world – postmodernists are nevertheless left with the need to establish and agree methods which might guide cultural analysis (i.e. of 'language, symbol, institutions'; Rabinow and Sullivan 1987, pp.5–6). While basic postulates about the task of interpretation represent interesting jumping off points for research, they do not constitute a sufficient guide to cultural analysis such that any two interpretative accounts might usefully be compared against one another or against the positivist accounts they are meant to supplant.

For example, Rabinow and Sullivan (1987) identify a number of postulates which they see as definitive of this approach:

1. 'The web of meaning constitutes human existence to such an extent that it cannot ever be meaningfully reduced to constitutively prior speech acts, dyadic relations, or any predefined elements' (p.6).

2. 'Meaning exists for a subject in a situation; it is about something; and it constitutes part of a field: there are no simple elements of meaning' (p.7).

3. Inasmuch as humans 'are fundamentally self-interpreting and self-defining, living always in a cultural environment, inside a "web of signification we ourselves have spun"', then it follows that culture 'does not present itself neutrally or with one voice'. In short, 'there is no privileged position, no absolute perspective, no final recounting' (pp.7–8).

As Rabinow and Sullivan note, among the difficulties which arise from this position is that there are 'no verification procedures', that is to say no means by which one interpretation might, by logic, argument or evidence supplant any other interpretation. In short, no means exist by which the field of cultural hermeneutics (the name given this approach) might advance (pp.8–9).[1]

Despite the production of numerous postmodernist ethnographies and the general impact of postmodernism on anthropology, it appears that the majority of practitioners have not felt a pressing need to address the problem of verification. What seems to have occurred instead is for hermeneutic analysis to focus primarily on styles of textual production/writing in the analysis of identity, a focus which is prefigured in the emphasis given to 'discourse' and 'the text' as a subject of ethnographic enquiry. Discourse provides the entry point for analysis in as much as it is 'public and fixed, in one form or another,[2] [it] is therefore freed from the motivations and subjectivity of the author, it is in public, it is intersubjective and therefore open to interpretation' (Rabinow and Sullivan 1987, p.13). In short, since social discourse is in the public domain and forms the basis of shared meaning, its various cultural manifestations provide the proper object of anthropological analysis, particularly since the discipline is noted for detailed, in-depth, micro-level social observation.

It follows that one way of clarifying the meaning(s) which inheres in discourse is to write it down in the form of a text which fixes one 'reading' of the meaning involved in social communication. As it happens, anthropologists produce texts in the form of ethnographic accounts. The principal criteria for evaluating ethnography relate to the manner in which the dialogic nature of communication and social interaction are reported, the inclusion of the anthropologist as part of the picture and the necessity of foregrounding cultural analysis in a wider political economy; thus taking into account the impact of external forces on local subjectivities (e.g. by recognizing a plurality of voices or positioned narratives).

In the words of Marcus and Fisher, the 'problem of the moment' for anthropology is to come to terms with the crisis of representation in the social sciences by turning away from empiricism and addressing problems arising from the task of representing cultural and social realities in narrative form (1986, p.15). For these writers, the need is for a 'jeweler's eye-view' of the world achieved by exploring 'innovative ways of describing at a microscopic level' the processes involved in moments of profound social change such as are now occurring. This, rather than a concern with theory, they argue, is the task of ethnography. As such, ethnographic writing takes two distinct forms (pp.43–44): first, the attempt to find ways of effectively describing 'how ethnographic subjects are implicated in broader processes of historical political economy' (a task which the writers feel is well under way); second, a concern with how cultural difference is to be represented in ethnography (i.e. experimentation with new textual means to represent our subjects' experience).

Issues of cultural identity come to the fore because postmodernists insist that the present, as a time of rapid social change, should be the subject of enquiry because experimentation in ethnographic writing is a 'self-conscious' act, and because 'the modernist problem in historical and social scientific research is foregrounded specifically as one of identity formation, "the question of who, or what controls and defines the identity of individuals, social groups, nations and cultures"' (Marcus 1992, p.311).

In particular, the concern is with emergent identities which arise out of the integration of local and global forces. Put somewhat differently, identity is the problem for investigation precisely because the impact of external forces on locales, regions and communities does not result in cultural anhilation by the centre. Diversity not uniformity is the product of increasing levels of globalization, and this is important for anthropologists to grasp because contemporary cultural forms are incomplete or 'unfinished'. We cannot, postmodernists argue, know what the end result of social change will be but we can be certain that contemporary forms arise out of a process of accommodation and resistance between the individual experience of domination and the desire for autonomy and stability.

It is for this reason that Marcus (1992, pp.314–f.) and other post-modernists insist on the need to rethink the mode of realist ethnography by challenging assumptions about spatial tropes of community, of time and voice or perspective (including the perspective of the anthropologist who shares the experience of modernity and at least some identities with his/her subjects). Yet again the emphasis is placed on experimenting with forms of textual representation, and the analysis of social action is de-emphasized in favour of examining 'categories, metaphors, and rhetorics embodied in the accounts that informants give of their cultures to ethnographers' (Marcus and Fischer 1986, p.47). This reorientation in anthropology derives from the belief of interpretative anthropologists that 'theory building...is a...function of devising textual strategies that modify past conventions of ethno-graphic writing', thereby drawing attention to epistemological questions about 'representing cultural differences across cultural boundaries' (Marcus and Fischer 1986, pp.67–68).

Marcus and Fischer's assessment of experimental ethnography makes it clear not only that a variety of forms exist, but that some forms have proved to be more effective in exploring cultural difference because of the balance struck in acknowledging the presence/role of the ethnographer and other cultural voices in the construction of the text.[3]

The problems arising out of a rejection of 'science' and the difficulty this poses for verifying and assessing accounts based primarily upon narrative can perhaps be illustrated by reference to Ochs and Capps review of research on narration. They remind us not only of its importance, structure and organization in other cultures but also of the enormity of the task which confronts any attempt to record and explain narrative (1996).

To begin with, not only are there many forms of narrative – including verbalized, visualized and embodied ways of framing and sequencing events (real and imagined) – there is also a wide range of genres and combinations with different communicative modes (eg. visual representation, gesture, facial expression and physical activity which in turn can be combined in various ways with talk, song and writing). Furthermore, narratives are *versions* of reality not objective accounts. When narratives are analysed they display characteristic modes of construction and telling which may invoke a variety of experiences that – through their use of time/temporality – reveal a multiplicity of selves constructed for public performance. In short, 'narrative thinking emphasizes the structuring of events in terms of a human calculus of actions, thoughts, and feelings', the telling of which allows the narrator to recast troubling experiences by adopting conventions which normalize and resolve discrepancies (Och and Capps 1996, p.26). Thus coherence and stability rather than disruption and resistance would tend to be the dominant tropes.

Interestingly, Chamberlain (forthcoming) provides a very different perspective on the construction and articulation of narrative and the problems this presents for analysis. She notes that the standard method of collecting narrative is dialogic, that is through a one-to-one interview between researcher and respondent which structures and shapes the narrative form and the metaphors employed; even the choice of genre is influenced by the interview process. This form of elicitation produces accounts whose coherence, internal structure, and focus on individual experience are taken by researchers to be 'realist' accounts (i.e. they conform to formal narrative structures familiar to the researcher).

However, Chamberlain points out that in many cultures this form of elicitation would result in a distorted understanding. This is because memory and the forms in which it is recalled are fundamentally social and elicited and continuously reshaped as part of wider processes of social and cultural production which produce accounts of a more surreal and less recognizably 'realist' nature (to the outsider). In particular, she argues forcefully that Barbadian women 'may have a plural sense of self, fashioned by the roles they perform and their positionings as intermediaries in their lineage'. In contrast, Barbadian male narrative tends to stress individual autonomy and progress. Male and female accounts tend to exhibit different narrative forms, with the former complying more closely to an outsider's understanding and appreciation of what constitutes a 'realist' account. At issue is the effect which a research method may have on the narrative elicited, important differences between the narratives of men and women, and the complexity of the task involved in analysing this type of information.

NARRATIVE IN MEDICAL ANTHROPOLOGY

Moving from general considerations to specific examples, I turn to two different but well-known studies in medical anthropology in which narrative assumes an extraordinarily important evidential role, namely Arthur Kleinman's *The Illness Narratives* (1988) and Roland Littlewood's paper (1996) 'Reason and necessity in the specification of the multiple self'.

At one level, *The Illness Narrative* could be read primarily as an attempt to influence medical practitioners to listen more carefully to how patients, their families and members of their social network 'perceive, live with, and respond to symptoms and disability'; a process in which illness is viewed specifically as 'the lived experience of monitoring bodily processes such as respiratory wheezes, abdominal cramps' etc. (1988, pp.3–4). Kleinman's chief concern is with patients who suffer chronic disorder – cancer, terminal illnesses, etc. – about which patients and medical practitioners possess quite different understandings.

Kleinman argues that patients/subjects employ local cultural idioms to talk about their experience of illness which reflect locally shared understandings; what he calls 'standardized truths' or symbolic codes which express how they construe their social world, themselves and their bodies. Medical practitioners, on the other hand, employ a biomedical model of disease which they use to interpret patient narratives into 'symptoms' which conform to their understanding of illness as defined by a 'disease nosology' or scientific classification scheme.

Kleinman's argument, based in part on cross-cultural comparison and individual case histories, is that practitioners fail to understand the 'meanings of illness' conveyed to them by patients and their families in terms expressive of the experience of chronic suffering; such meanings are disregarded and/or misinterpreted by practitioners. Thus patient narratives are ego centred and focused centrally on bodily processes which are minutely monitored and linked intimately to presumed life transitions and the patient's personal identity. A key component of these narratives is their focus on the experience of pain and dysfunction – and associated self-diagnoses – their emotional tenor and their preoccupation with the present. Life experience is framed by a narrative of suffering which preoccupies sufferers of chronic illness.

Though Kleinman speaks of the need for practitioners to acquire 'an ethnographic appreciation of their context of relationships, the nature of their referents, and the history of how they are experienced', the book is overwhelmingly concerned with the apparent misinterpretation taking place between patient and practitioner (p.18).[4] Even so, one would expect a more critical treatment of patient narratives. The possibilities include an assessment of verbal narratives and their link to other communicative modes as well as to cultural understandings of self and body, and an explanation of how the different contexts in which practitioners obtain information from patients influence the narratives provided.

Perhaps the key to appreciating North American illness narratives lies not so much with the cultural significance of society-wide[5] disorders – today cancer, heart disease and HIV – as with the experience of confronting an all powerful medical bureaucracy which, on the one hand, medicalizes illness and, on the other, excludes growing numbers of people from access to treatment. While Kleinman does raise the issue of the medical bureaucracy, the problem of its impact on individual well-being or on patient accounts is not explored in any depth, in part because he focuses on a specific form of patient–practitioner discourse.

While a focus on the explanatory models employed by patients and practitioners allows the anthropologist to bracket the definition of disease – i.e. its status as a real, natural phenomenon – to study culture and meaning in medical settings, this approach is not without its problems and critics. Perhaps the fundamental problem, as noted by Rhodes, is the tendency to reify illness as somehow 'natural' through an implicit acceptance of biomedical assumptions about the human body and the uncritical use of the very categories of illness/disease which should be investigated (1990). A more fundamental critique would be to argue that this approach fails to call into question 'the material premises of biomedicine', namely issues of power (Scheper-Hughes 1990, p.191). This latter concern ranges from examining the power of medicine to define and control the patient's body to medicine's ability to legitimate and reproduce itself through the conversion of its economic capital into a symbolic capital capable of obtaining public compliance with biomedical interests (Bourdieu 1990).

If we contrast *The Illness Narrative* with Roland Littlewood's (1996) paper on 'double consciousness' or multiple personality disorder (MPD), we are reminded that narrative has different functions and operates at several levels, and that the category of 'medical practitioner' needs to be disaggregated and carefully analysed. This latter task is important not merely to contrast the different methods and understandings which underpin biomedicine – including differences between primary health care, psychoanalysis, psychology and psychiatry – but also to assess the massive influence which biomedicine has had on western culture and politics.

Littlewood takes as his subject the question of whether a specific form of illness can be seen as a metaphor about society: is an illness, he asks, 'somehow characteristic of the particular society in which it is found' (1996, p.1). Medicine is implicated in this question because he is concerned to demonstrate that if a specific illness has social significance then it must have a wider application. It must constitute a 'behavioural syndrome appearing in widely differing cultures [which] takes on local meanings so completely that it appears uniquely suited to articulate important dimensions of each local culture, as though it had sprung naturally from that environment' (Littewood 1996, p.1, quoting Good and Good 1992, p.257).

Such instances of psycho-pathology, like *latah* in Java, are culture specific in that they represent a disorder which is an elaboration of a 'locally identified biological phenomenon' (p.2). However, American psychiatry is at odds about whether MPD is 'a true disease entity' ('is it real') or whether it is 'a kind of behaviour worked up between doctor and patient' (e.g. elicited by the specific form of treatment and as such a collection of symptoms for which there is no agreed organic basis; Hacking 1995, pp.11–12). Rather than address this controversy, Littlewood initially brackets the nature of MPD as a disease and turns instead to the huge rise in its diagnosis in the USA which he seeks to explain by contrasting the interplay of institutional (i.e. experts and practitioners) and lay interests (personalistic interpretations) regarding its recognition and diagnosis.

The first section of Littlewood's paper reviews the history of 'double consciousness' (which he takes to be identical to MPD), the nineteenth-century diagnostic term used to categorize a complex of symptoms (hysteria, catalepsy, somnambulism, fugue and trance states, mediumship and spirit possession, demonic possession, visions and dreams, etc; p.4).[6] It is important to note that the disorders associated with double consciousness were widely disputed at the time, and that most of the symptoms were elicited by a wide range of lay persons (mediums, spiritists, fortune tellers, etc.) and doctors using hypnotic techniques (at that time psychology was not a university subject, nor was psychiatry a professional calling).

Then, as now, patients conformed to a common 'prototype'; they were young and female, and their cases initially came to the awareness of medical practitioners through referral by family members. As Littlewood notes, the interpretation (then as now), appears to have:

> started from the assumption that in the general run of things there is a single bounded and volitional self which shares a biography with the body which gives rise to it, reflecting and directing in turn the experiences of this body, with a characteristic and enduring identity of personal compartments,

responses, habits, sentiments, abilities and memories all of which are experienced, and perceived by others, as hanging together. But this hanging together becomes unstuck. (Littlewood 1996, p.7)

The controversy over the status and cause of 'double consciousness' is best understood in terms of the social values and sense of history specific to the Victorian era and which relate directly to intense debates among psychologists of the day (Ellenberger 1970, Chap. 3). The growing influence of the therapeutic method and the shift away from hypnosis parallelled the rise of Freudian models of the mind and new ways of thinking about mental disorder; increasingly biological explanations bowed to explorations of the unconscious psyche. Whether due to the rise of psychodynamic theory or not, there occurred a marked decline in the diagnosis of double consciousness such that by 1910 it 'suddenly disappears from the medical literature' (Littlewood 1996, p.10).

In the paper's third section Littlewood shifts the focus to anthropological interpretations of 'possession' which, he alludes, have 'commonly been regarded by anthropologists as akin to double consciousness' (p.12). Given the extent of the controversy of what double consciousness/MPD is, and the fact that relatively few anthropologists are trained in psychiatry, this is an extraordinary statement, particularly in its assumption that psychology and anthropology share common understandings of this complex phenomenon. In any event, Littlewood's principal anthropological 'model' is a functionalism that was uninformed by psychiatry and is now largely defunct in the face of recent attempts to contextualize possession behaviour and beliefs in order to explore its instrumental and expressive dimensions (eg. Boddy 1989, 1994).

The paper then shifts back to the 'return' of MPD in the 1970s and reviews literature regarding its authenticity, its (presumed) link to child abuse, and the rise of a new 'movement'[7] of lay and medical persons who seek to establish the diagnosis and its etiology (i.e. the International Society for the Study of Multiple Personality and Dissociation). At this point Littlewood suggests the implausibility of certain evidence brought forward in support of MPD, adding that in his view 'the reality' of MPD has gone unquestioned (p.20). Having initially rejected an investigation of the 'biological' basis of MPD, the paper is not well placed to turn to this question, particularly given its failure to critically analyse the medical literature. In any event such an analysis would require access to patient records and substantively new research to be able to make such an assessment. Since neither option is pursued, it seems clear that the ontological status of MPD as a 'disease' cannot be addressed.[8] In any event, is not the task of anthropology precisely to contextualize and explain the variety of statements made rather than to dismiss them out of hand?

Littlewood cites the interest of philosophers 'like Hacking' in MPD as a basis for supporting theories of the mind, ideas which could have implications for the role of memory and personal identity (p.21). Interestingly, Hacking himself refuses to accept that MPD 'tells us anything *direct* about the mind' at all, nor can rival interpretations of MPD do anything more than *purport* a link between dissociation and a theory of mind (and personhood; 1995, p.222, his emphasis). Hacking's reasoning on this is salutary. He reminds us of the power of ideas/concepts – he uses the term 'semantic contagion' – which, over time, may infuse the way we use language to think about ourselves and our society. The net effect of semantic contagion could well be – we cannot know for certain without careful analysis – a confusion in our thinking which mixes present understandings with a 'redescription' of the past which redefines, reinterprets and refeels the past, in the process investing certain events with an intentionality, significance and meaning that did not exist at the time (Hacking 1995, p17).

In any event, Littlewood proceeds to a discussion of 'multiplicity and modernity', with the latter term taken as an unproblematic link between two 'epidemics' of multiple personality separated by 60 years, two continents and quite different sets of social values and cultural understandings (Victorian Europe and the contemporary USA; p.22). To the question 'why multiplicity?', Littlewood disingenuously argues that Americans are more susceptible to multiplicity because, as a 'psychologised society' in which personal achievement underwrites identity, globalization has undermined a 'linear or determinist theory, whether as prose, progress or biography, in favour of fragmented, multiple, iterative and creolised' constructions of self and society (pp.25, 29). The link from modernity via creolization to 'disease' in the form of MPD is, Littlewood argues, provided by the relationship between patient and therapist and the latter's need to maintain the 'integrity' of patient accounts which result in the elaboration of 'a mutually agreeable script' which forms the basis for a 'paradigmatic new illness' (p.31). The illness, rather than the conditions which generate it, becomes 'an index of cultural life', a culture specific illness.

At this point we have come full circle: having set out to discover whether MPD is a culture-specific illness, Littlewood has argued that 'modernity' has established the conditions for lay persons and aspiring therapists to create a discourse which, once validated by medicine, becomes a 'disease' symptomatic of contemporary America.

If we turn to the issue of narrative in contemporary anthropological analysis, the most important criticism of Littlewood is that he fails to interrogate the different accounts about MPD, a failure which stems in part from a dichotomy which contrasts lay and institutional interests. The variety of interests involved, including but not limited to 'therapists' who employ different therapeutic techniques, indicates a need to carefully evaluate medical and lay claims. Ideally, what is required is a careful analysis of the clinical records therapists keep on their patients, an examination of the potential impact of therapeutic methods (and the therapeutic context) on the production of patient narratives, and a careful contextual analysis of 'medical' and personalistic explanations.[9]

In addition, as Hacking makes clear with respect to 'recovered memory' and MPD, we should not take patient narratives at their face value (1995, p.118). The veracity of all narratives must be questioned, not only because of the ramifications which recovered memory has for familial relations (given the contested link between child sexual abuse and MPD), but also because the lay public unproblematically uses a language informed by popular psychology to communicate personal distress. Inasmuch as the etiology of MPD is widely believed to be caused by childhood sexual abuse, the evidence for which comes from memories recovered decades after alleged incident(s), the accounts provided by patients must be independently corroborated and greater attention needs to be given to the underlying meaning of such narratives.

It seems to me that the questions raised by the study of biomedicine generally, and MPD specifically, are quite different for psychiatrists than for anthropologists. Psychiatrists, regardless of their position on MPD, are confronted by patients in obvious distress who narrate their personal story in a language infused with local 'cultural' understandings and with a 'medical' language which they believe to be relevant to their diagnosis. In effect, and given the emphasis on causation in lay language use, patients actively assist in the medicalization of their illness. Given the politics of the MPD movement and its emphasis on self-diagnosis, we should expect that lay persons will have internalized what remains to be proven, namely the link between child abuse and MPD (but also the unitary nature and organic basis of MPD). For this reason, diagnosis requires careful attention to the language used by the patient and a careful elicitation of the patient's history (including past therapeutic diagnosis and treatment).

For the anthropologist the concern is to 'treat what people believe to be true as if it were true' as the first step in anthropological practice (Chapman, Mcdonald and Tonkin 1989, p.10). The failure to adopt the axiom of cultural relativism undermines the rationality of other people and it substitutes the ethnocentric bias of the observer for explanation. This situation arises because 'other people's truths are contained in their own classification and understandings, and...our own culture offers no self-evidently privileged standard of verity' (Chapman et al. 1989, p.10).

This axiom applies especially to research on one's own society where the values and beliefs of the dominant social group, informed by its own classificatory understandings of difference and otherness,[10] shape its members perception of cultural difference (e.g. as being deviant, abnormal, or simply weird and not to be taken seriously).

The anthropologist's simultaneous concern is to grasp the meaning of observed behaviour, values and informant accounts. With respect to possession, Boddy's review of recent work makes it clear how research has moved away from reductionist, naturalizing approaches which emphasize the instrumentalist use of beliefs by 'disadvantaged' groups and how, in earlier functionalist accounts, possession signalled social pathology. Increasingly the emphasis is to understand the wider social, cultural and aesthetic significance of possession beliefs and practices. For this reason, 'because the body is both the existential ground of belief and the locus of engagement with the spirit world, it is not surprising that possession is often expressed in physical terms, as somatic change or illness' (Boddy 1994, p.411).

The key to the new ethnographic research on possession lies in its attempt to grasp the different levels and modes by and through which cultural meaning is communicated and experienced. Thus, in addition to the three parties – a self, other humans and external powers – implicated in possession, the cultural logic implicit in the moral discourse about possession and social relationships also needs to be addressed (Boddy 1994, p.422). In part through mimesis, such codes build upon understandings of the body (its docility, wilfulness, etc) as well as upon other forms of knowledge and ways of knowing to construct a discourse which at different times may challenge or reinforce the social order. At its most basic, the meaning encoded in possession behaviour and belief tells us something about dominant social codes as well as about subordinate or subcultural assertions of power and identity, but only if they are properly contextualized and if we attend to culturally specific constructions of the body (Lock 1993).

'TRUTH', METHOD AND MEANING

In discussing the work of Kleinman and Littlewood I hope to have provided reasonable justification for my doubts about analyses based primarily upon narrative. Kleinman's book is based on patient narratives supplied directly to him as a clinician or through anthropological fieldwork. Littlewood, on the other hand, bases his analysis primarily upon secondary accounts of the illness provided by psychiatrists, that is to say accounts concerned with the ontological status of MPD; patient narratives which provide the basis for all claims about MPD are not examined. Whatever the 'truth' about an illness, MPD included, it remains the case that accounts which fail to take seriously the culture, beliefs and behaviour of the individuals presenting with an illness cannot adequately address its cultural significance.

I have outlined some of the questions which these studies raise for the analysis of patient–practitioner relations and the nature of illness/disease. However what remains is to remind anthropologists about the value of other research methods which can produce both a stronger evidential basis for analysing illness and a more context-replete account. The simple fact is that the anthropology of medicine need not stake its reputation upon the use of personal narrative. Indeed it must employ other methods if it wishes to say anything useful about biomedical practice and the cultural etiology of illness.

Apropos of the tension between anthropological and psychiatric research, Margaret Mead long ago observed that:

> Anthropologists depend primarily on multi-sensory observation of inter-active groups, with their own position, towards them and among them, fully specified. Psychoanalysis depends upon private dyadic relation-ships, in a setting primarily defined as having a therapeutic goal, in which the interchange is verbal, the paralinguistic materials are primarily in the auditory mode (hesitations, repetitions, pauses, emphases) and the inter-action, although complex...are still linear in type. (Mead 1979, p.45)

Because of the difficulty of accurately reconstructing either the therapeutic or the anthropological record in a manner which provides a complete record of actual events, it is difficult for anthropologists and psychoanalysts to have full access to each other's research. Note taking apart, the limitations of verbal accounts are based on texts and the analysis of words/verbal communication (reflecting a potential bias on one communicative mode, problems of translation, and the ability adequately to communicate verbally). This emphasis has led in part to the adoption of various projective and objective tests from which specific conclusions about the 'characteristics of unconscious thinking' were drawn (though their methodological impli-cations were not fully explored). Mead (1979) and Bateson (1973) also experimented with film and still photography to provide a source of material that was independent of words which could be analysed by others.[11]

As Paul reminds us, a long-standing technique used by psychoanalytically trained anthropologists is the clinical method which produces 'the equivalent of an ethnographic interview'. With due regard to the problems which may arise from countertransference, it is possible to avoid 'treatment of interview data as a fixed text...an error of which Freud himself was guilty, as when he treated Dora's dreams as "holy writ"' (1989, p.180).

While the focus of a clinical interview is an individual, it is often necessary to examine the impact of the wider cultural context in shaping patient experience, for example, in the meaning of dreams or the analysis of cultural symbols used to express aspects of personal identity, conflict, fantasy, illness, etc. The psychoanalytic techniques used to undertake this analysis often draw heavily upon anthropology and cross-cultural analysis (Paul 1989; Stein

1990). If we step back from a concern with the diagnosis of individual pathology, as Bateson has done in relation to schizophrenia, it is possible to examine the nature and etiology of a disease in terms of broader social processes and interaction, in this case social learning and a breakdown in communication were shown to have contributed to schizophrenia (Bateson 1973, part II).

Sampling, linked to in-depth interviews and participant observation, are of course the bread and butter of anthropological fieldwork and it is worth reiterating their value in terms of triangulating and verifying findings from any one method and in terms of ensuring that findings are representative of a population and not the artifact of poorly designed research. Pelto and Pelto (1990), for example, set out the rationale for a holistic study of illness/disease which allows one to contextualize interview data, verify the nature and composition of the wider population from which specific information is drawn and, if necessary, verify by direct observation accounts of practitioner–patient interaction. To draw attention to but one example where holistic analysis can provide insights into medical diagnosis, research in the UK and elsewhere is demonstrating the link between society-wide beliefs about 'normality' and the diagnosis of 'mental handicap'. As Jenkins comments, the question of who defines what is 'normal' is intimately linked not only to biomedical/ institutional interests, in terms of promoting a particular policy, but to broader social norms and values which remain largely unquestioned (1993).

I began this chapter with a discussion of the influence of postmodernism on anthropology,[12] and in particular the growing emphasis on the analysis of narrative. Using two studies in medical anthropology as general examples, I have argued that narrative data is unable to shoulder the burden of analysis and interpretation for three reasons. First, analyses which rely upon narrative tend to background social structure and action in favour of culture and rhetoric. Second, given the concern of this chapter with illness and suffering, I do not believe that anthropological studies of medicine can afford to remain at the level of discourse/narrative. Not only must such studies be situated in an appreciation of the wider political economy, they must be able to engage with the problem of measurement and verification with biomedicine and psychiatry. Finally, the search for understanding obviously cannot be limited to a literal reading of patient or medical practitioner narrative/accounts any more than we can afford not to grasp the meaning contained in cultural classification schemes which shape beliefs about the body and its engagement with the (human and spirit) world.

Finally, it strikes me that there exists in medical anthropology an unresolved problem which needs to be acknowledged: namely the very different concerns, methods and indeed frames of reference for psychological and anthropological research. Skultans' observation that 'the fact that any one individual is capable of wearing two hats does not remove the fact that those two hats sit on top of contradictory theoretical positions' sums up my unease about research which attempts to combine anthropological and psychiatric perspectives (1991, p.15). I am only aware of one attempt to address this contradiction, namely the work of anthropologist and psycho-analyst George Devereux who explored the complementarity of the two disciplines in his book *Ethnopsychanalyse Complementarariste* (1972). As summarized by Hook, Devereux devised thirteen theorems intended to help coordinate interdisciplinary work which, he believed, should be conducted separately and not simultaneously because each type of enquiry, each discipline, employed different frames of reference to explain behaviour. According to Hook:

> The total interdependence of sociological and of psychological data (both created out of the same raw facts) assures the absolute autonomy of both the psychological and sociological discourse. No psychology, however perfect, can permit the formulation of sociological laws, nor can sociology extended to its extreme limits ever arrive at a formulation of psychological laws. (Hook 1979, p.4)

Furthermore: 'Every attempt at explanation within a single frame of reference is subject to the law of diminishing returns. Explanation pushed too far…destroys or explains away the phenomenon it seeks to study.' Devereux devised his theorems to address claims that one explanation necessarily excluded another. However, I would add a further caveat: significant differences between anthropology and psychiatry require that each be carefully theorized and fully researched independently before switching to a different frame of reference. A failure to pay due attention to disciplinary concerns regarding theory and method could easily produce a retrograde throwback of naive and muddled thinking rather than new and significant insight into the contemporary world.

NOTES

1. The authors quote Rabinow on this dilemma, namely that hermeneutic analysis is 'caught in a circle' – 'Ultimately a good explanation is one that makes sense of behavior. But to agree on what makes sense necessitates consensus; what makes sense is a function of one's own readings; and these in turn are based on the kind of sense one understands' (Rabinow 1977, p.14 quoted in Rabinow and Sullivan 1987, p.8).

2. While obviously attempting to allow the broadest interpretation, this formulation of discourse leaves many questions unanswered as to exactly what is being intersubjectively interpreted, by whom, and what the role of the anthropologist in this process is. While some of these questions are addressed by others (eg. Marcus and Fischer 1986, Chap.3), they are seen largely as matters of textual production.

3. See Marcus and Fischer's discussion of the treatment of life histories (1987, pp.57–59). More specifically, 'the promise of ethnographies of the person is traded off at a cost – they tend to elide or background the established ethnographic function' of description at the expense of too much introspection by, and twaddle about, the ethnographer (p.67).

4. Since '80 percent of diagnoses in primary care result from the history alone, anamnesis (the account the physician assembles from the patient's story) is crucial' (Kleinman 1988, p.17), this emphasis is not too surprising.

5. It is important to note that while some medical disorders affect large sections of society, there nonetheless exists a range of responses depending upon ethnic, class, gender and age differences which would result in a variety of illness narratives, a factor which does not seem to have been considered by Kleinman.

6. Much of this is discussed in Ellenberger's history of psychiatry in which the author attempts to set the various theories and practices into their historical and social context, including the development of new ideas about mind and personality which entailed a repudiation of earlier ideas about double consciousness as some now understand it (1970, Chap. 3).

7. In discussing the ISSMPandD and its apparent self-promotion of MPD, Littlewood forgets that the rise of double consciousness in the nineteenth century followed a very similar course through the work of spiritualists, the popular press and fiction (Ellenberger 1970, pp.158–170).

8. Hacking makes it clear that very interesting research is being conducted on these issues and that the American psychiatric community has not completely caved in to personalistic explanation (1995, Chaps. 6–7).

9. Basic but fundamental questions would include looking at the importance of the class, age, race and gender of those diagnosed as suffering from MPD. Here again, Hacking's discussion of the importance of gender to MPD, including the gendered identity of the patient's alters, provides a fascinating picture about the etiology of MPD (1995, Chap.5).

10. As Skultans has argued, 'ethnocentrism has been as much a feature of anthropological as of psychiatric thought', particularly when examining the analyst's own society (1991, p.11).

11. The attempt to taperecord clinical sessions provided a text, but transcription eliminated the paralinguistic dimension and the element of countertransference through which the clinician gained insight into the patient (Mead 1979, pp.47–48).

12. Spiro provides a more fundamental critique of postmodernist anthropology with which I fully subscribe (1998), while Bowlin and Stromberg argue against both postmodern and 'realist' claims about 'truth' and cultural representation by examining the problem of communication among social groups (1997).

REFERENCES

Bateson, G. (1973) *Steps to an Ecology of Mind.* London: Paladin.

Boddy, J. (1989) *Wombs and Alien Spirits: Women, Men and the Zar Cult in Northern Sudan.* Madison: University of Wisconsin.

Boddy, J. (1994) 'Spirit possession revisited: beyond instrumentality.' *Annual Review of Anthropology 23*, 407–434.

Bourdieu, P. (1990) *The Logic of Practice.* Cambridge: Polity Press.

Bowlin, J. and Stromberg, P. (1997) 'Representation and reality in the study of culture.' *American Anthropologist 99*, 1, 123–134.

Chamberlain, M. (forthcoming) 'The global self: narratives of Caribbean migrant women.' In T. Gosslett and P. Summerfield (eds) *The Autobiographical Urge.* London: Routledge.

Chapman, M., McDonald, M. and Tonkin, E. (1989) 'Introduction.' M. Chapman, M. McDonald and E. Tonkin *History and Ethnicity.* London: Routledge, pp.1–21.

Devereux, G. (1972) *Ethnopsychanalyse Complementariste.* Paris: Flammarion.

Ellenberger, H. (1970) *The Discovery of the Unconscious: The History and Evolution of Dynamic Psychiatry.* New York: Basic Books.

Good, V. and Good, M.-J. (1992) 'The comparative study of Graeco-Islamic medicine: the integration of medical knowledge into local symbolic contexts.' In C. Leslie and A. Young (eds) *Paths to Asian Medical Knowledge.* Berkeley: University of California Press.

Hacking, I. (1995) *Rewriting the Soul: Multiple Personality and the Sciences of Memory.* Princeton: Princeton University Press.

Hook, R.H. (1978) 'Introduction.' In R.H. Hook *Fantasy and Symbol.* London: Academic Press, pp.1–10.

Jenkins, R. (1993) 'Incompetence and learning difficulties.' *Anthropology Today 9*, 3, 16–20.

Kleinman, A. (1988) *The Illness Narratives.* New York: Basic Books.

Littlewood, R. (1996) 'Reason and necessity in the specification of the multiple self.' London: Royal Anthropological Institute. Occasional Paper 43.

Lock, M. (1993) 'Cultivating the body: anthropology and epistemologies of bodily practice and knowledge.' *Annual Review of Anthropology 22*, 133–155.

Marcus, G. (1992) 'Past, present and emergent identities: requirements for ethnographies of late twentieth century modernity worldwide.' In S. Lash and J. Friedman (eds) *Modernity and Identity.* Oxford: Blackwell.

Marcus, G. and Fischer, M. (1986) *Anthropology as Cultural Critique: An Experimental Moment in the Human Sciences.* Chicago: University of Chicago Press.

Mead, M. (1979) 'The influence of methods of observation on theory, with particular reference to the work of George Devereux and Margaret Lowenfeld.' In R. Hook (ed) *Fantasy and Symbol.* London: Academic Press, pp.43–54.

Ochs, E. and Capps, L. (1996) 'Narrating the self.' *Annual Review of Anthropology 25*, 19–43.

Paul, R. (1989) 'Psychoanalytic anthropology.' *Annual Review of Anthropology 18*, 177–202.

Pelto, P. and Pelto, G. (1990) 'Field methods in medical anthropology.' In T. Johnson and C. Sargent (eds) *Medical Anthropology: A Handbook of Theory and Method?* New York/Connecticut/London: Greenwood Press.

Rabinow, P. (1977) *Reflections on Fieldwork in Morocco.* Los Angeles: University of California Press.

Rabinow, P. and Sullivan,W.M. (eds) (1987a) *Interpretative Social Science. A Second Look.* Berkeley: University of California Press.

Rabinow, P. and Sullivan, W.M. (1987b) 'The interpretive turn.' In P. Rabinow and W.M. Sullivan (eds) *Interpretative Social Science. A Second Look.* Berkeley: University of California Press, pp.1–30.

Rhodes, L. (1990) 'Studying biomedicine as a cultural system.' In T. Johnson and C. Sargent (eds) *Medical Anthropology: A Handbook of Theory and Method?* New York/Connecticut/London: Greenwood Press.

Scheper-Hughes, N. (1990) 'Three propositions for a critically applied medical anthropology.' *Social Science and Medicine 30,* 2, 189–197.

Skultans, V. (1991) 'Anthropology and psychiatry: the uneasy alliance.' *Transcultural Psychiatric Research Review 28,* 5–24.

Spiro, M. (1998) 'Postmodernist anthropology, subjectivity, and science: a modernist critique.' *Comparative Studies in Society and History 38,* 759–780.

Stein, H. (1990) 'Psychoanalytic perspectives.' In T. Johnson and C. Sargent (eds) *Medical Anthropology. A Handbook of Theory and Method?* New York/Connecticut/London: Greenwood Press.

5

Anthropology and Psychiatry

Two of a Kind but Where is the Other?

Els van Dongen[1]

> We never grasp the human individual – what he signifies –
> except in a delusive way:
> humanity always contradicts itself;
> it goes suddenly from goodness to base cruelty,
> from extreme modesty to extreme immodesty,
> from the most attractive appearance
> to the most odious. (Bataille 1993, p.21)

Every time that I start a new study in the field of psychiatry, one of the first questions which comes to the foreground is what will be the 'use' of your study? This question cannot be answered so easily, because there are many ways in which anthropology might study a certain psychiatric field. For example, we can make a distinction between the anthropology *of* psychiatry and the anthropology *in* psychiatry. The anthropology of psychiatry studies psychiatry as a cultural subsystem which deals with matters of abnormality in a society. The anthropology in psychiatry should generate knowledge which can be used in psychiatric practices. The distinction between 'in' and 'of' caused many debates on the usefulness and applicability of anthropology. Should anthropology remain an independent science or should it become an applied science? What exactly is anthropology's contribution to the well-being of people? How can anthropology contribute to a better, culturally sensitive mental health care? I feel that these debates on anthropology's relevance for psychiatry and its contribution to the knowledge of humankind show a tendency to pass over a fundamental similarity between psychiatry and anthropology. Both disciplines have their roots in the same culture and show a remarkably common historical development.

In this chapter I discuss this cultural foundation of anthropology and psychiatry. Both disciplines assume that one of the possibilities to understand the Other is reflection, an activity which has common moral, epistemological and political aspects. The activity of reflection is rooted in western cultures. I will show that both sciences actively construct and reproduce the Other by transformation of the Other's behaviour and words into their familiar symbolic categories; an activity that alienates the Other of himself or herself. Ethnographic material will show that the transformations made by therapists and the anthropologist have the same effects: both disciplines exclude the Other from the process of interpretation. This is untenable because the Others increasingly are able to challenge the traditional roles of anthropologists and psychiatrists as experts and authorities on their cultures. I argue that to overcome the problem of 'onesidedness' of interpretations, the Other should be involved in the debate.

The idea that cultures are bounded wholes and can be described and explained by anthropologists to inform psychiatrists of the background of their clients, is undermined by processes of the world's heterogenization and fragmentation. Societies become multicultural and ethnically fragmented. I plea for a more dynamic concept of culture and an awareness that – for a great part – culture is constituted in interaction between psychiatrist– anthropologist and client. Therefore, anthropologists should work on different levels. I will discuss these levels.

ANTHROPOLOGY AND PSYCHIATRY AS CULTURAL SCIENCES

Recent thoughts in anthropology and psychiatry have attacked some of the fundamental assumptions entertained by anthropologists and psychiatrists about the nature of understandings of health and illness in the cultures they study and in which they work. Both disciplines claimed that they represent the 'native's' point of view and that they gave an emic or phenomenological account of human suffering in different cultures. One of the common anthropological criticisms of psychiatry is that the latter claims to have developed a theory of the human mind which has a biological foundation and could be universally applicable. Anthropologists argue that this theory, which is based on the Cartesian body–mind dualism, is only applicable in western societies (see Scheper-Hughes and Lock 1987). However, anthropology speaks about western and non-western cultures as if the two are opposite entities. Insufficient knowledge about one's own culture and the assumption that concepts and illness theories of western psychiatry were universally transferable contributed to this duality. There might be some broad similarities in western cultures, but to speak of non-western cultures as if they are broadly similar too would be a bad thing. The distinction between 'the west and the rest' barely makes sense in the present world, in which processes of globalization and fragmentation wipe out old cultural boundaries and establish new ones.

Psychiatry and anthropology are confronted by the effects of those processes with great intensity. Both disciplines share the awareness that if one wishes to study the Other in a comparative way, this study should be free of ethnocentrism and medicocentrism and should also focus on understanding – verstehen – of the Other. The will to understand the Other is a difficult matter. Of course, psychiatrists and anthropologists have the will to understand, but can they? Is it possible to know what is fundamentally different from one's own insights and understandings? This question is difficult to answer. One of the conditions is that it is necessary to reflect critically on one's own culture and to know its peculiarities and limits. Both disciplines have their own techniques for such a reflection. One of the techniques is countertransference. Countertransference is a well-known technique in psychiatry that enables the psychiatrist to reflect on his or her own emotions, values and norms, which are at the core of culture. It is not my intention to enter the debate of how the term 'countertransference' should be understood. In this chapter I refer to the 'totalistic' position (Kernberg 1975, p.52): the therapist's total emotional conscious and unconscious reactions to the Other. In the Netherlands, psychiatrists use the concept in this broad sense within the context of therapeutic interpretations. Anthropology has a similar technique. The anthropological response to the recognition of the 'politics of positionality and location' (Moore 1996, p.2) was the questioning of the interpretative authority of the anthropologist and the focus on writing rather than on fieldwork. More recently, countertransference is seen as a technique which can also serve critical anthropological reflection, especially in the fieldwork situation and co-operation between psychiatry and anthropology (cf. Good et al. 1982; Tobin 1986). The idea is that emotional reactions are markers of tension between the person and society and as such might offer knowledge about appreciation of the world, others, ourselves and our position in the world.

However, countertransference and questioning of interpretative authorities are cultural activities, which are based upon a particular concept of the person and upon particular beliefs about thinking. In psychiatry as well as in anthropology particular emphasis is given to the role of the psychiatrist/anthropologist and the influence of his or her own emotional sociocultural framework on the knowledge produced. However, in anthropology attention is not only paid to fieldwork, but also to the specific means through which knowledge is produced during the fieldwork and given shape in anthropological texts. This reflexive practice in anthropology is more clear cut than in psychiatry. In many ethnographies, reflexivity is an essential part of the publication. Anthropology has had a 'boom' of fundamental self-scrutiny and reflexivity, which has not only epistemological aspects, but also moral and political ones (Crick 1982, p.15). These aspects are inseparable and also mean some danger, precisely because epistemological, moral and political aspects are intertwined. By carefully studying these dangers one might discover the cultural basis of anthropology and psychiatry. Both psychiatrists and anthropologists are dependent on the willingness of their 'informants' to provide access to their lives (cf. Geertz 1973, p.20).

Another dilemma is that the cultural or personal reality (which, of course, is a cultural reality too) which the anthropologist or psychiatrist is trying to analyse does not present itself as a whole, but in bits and pieces. Both dilemmas mean that the knowledge is always incomplete and tentative. It implies that both anthropologist and psychiatrist do not simply record the informants' interpretations, but in fact actively construct them. This activity demands a great deal of imagination and understanding (*verstehen*). This in turn implies that the informants' interpretation is screened by the interpretative framework of the anthropologist or psychiatrist and involves a significant amount of speculation. Both psychiatrists and anthropologists are their own 'research instruments'. This means that frameworks and speculations are mixtures of lay cultural and professionalized (which are also cultural of course) views, and that those views are always contestable.

It is acknowledged that the 'construction of reality' by anthropology and psychiatry is a culturally informed practice, based on western epistemologies and conceptions of society and the person. The bridge between anthropology and psychiatry traditionally was the Cartesian dualism of biology with its reified notions of the mechanistic body on the one hand, and psychology with its equally mechanistic and reified mind on the other hand (Scheper-Hughes 1992, p.221). Beliefs and practices are historically constructed and reveal understandings about life, illness, person, experience, values and meanings. Although many medical anthropologists note that psychiatry (and biomedicine) is a form of ethnomedicine (Gaines 1992) and others plea for an integrated notion of the 'mindful body' (Scheper-Hughes and Lock 1987) and embodiment (Csordas 1990), disease is still treated as an '*individual's* cultural and idiosyncratic experience of socially devalued states of being' (Nichter 1992, p.xii; italics mine). This view is based on a fundamentally western notion of individualism, which permeates psychiatric theories and practices as well as anthropological ones. This notion is a reification and a delusion in which only science believes.

In a sense, psychiatry and anthropology too can be seen as moral systems, because while many researchers accept that culture shapes human behaviour, it is often assumed – implicitly or explicitly – that abnormality is acultural and normality is cultural. There is, for example, a widespread belief that schizophrenic people live 'outside normal reality'. Anthropology and psychiatry have their explanations of why this is so (cf. Van Dongen 1994). Anthropology might focus on sociocultural and personal contexts of people, while psychiatry focuses on behaviour, thought disorders, speech disorders, etc., but both disciplines study the idiom of distress as a deviant idiom.

Thus, anthropology and psychiatry seem to have a lot in common, including their awareness of their cultural basis. This awareness is reflected in an activity shared by both disciplines: reflexivity. It is thought that reflection is a necessary activity, because 'data' are produced in the fieldwork or in the therapeutic session. What knowledge produces reflection? Of course, it produces personal and situational knowledge when one reflects on the interaction and the encounter, either clinical or in the field. Questions are appropriate such as: By what process was the knowledge in the interaction obtained? Which problems in the interactions can be found? What were my reactions, emotional and interactional? This kind of reflection makes psychiatry and anthropology both 'cultural', because it reflects on the activities of the individual, in this case the anthropologist or the psychiatrist, who are 'cultural beings'.

Individualism is believed to be a main characteristic of western cultures. Another important characteristic of western cultures, especially northern European and North American cultures, is 'progress' or 'development' and 'change'. It is believed that by thinking about oneself, one will obtain deeper knowledge about oneself and thus be able to change and improve one's way of being. The reflection enlarges the knowledge of the psychiatrist or anthropologist, but ignores the possible need of the Other (the client or the informant) who also might wish to have deeper insight into what is happening in the interaction. Often, reflexive practices are not dialogical. Besides, reflexivity also has some dangers.

One of the dangers of self-reflexivity is that it might become counter-productive. Anthropologists or psychiatrists could focus so much on them-selves and the conditions of the interaction with the Other that those aspects of the sociocultural world which are important in the lives of their informants could be neglected. This is precisely what happens in the well- known anthropological belief that the study of the Other will lead to self-knowledge and self-understanding, which in turn are based on the traditional western 'know thyself'. Another danger is that reflexivity over-states the degree to which conditions of interaction and knowledge are related. Personal factors and specific events influence the interaction, but this influence need not be overestimated. It could strengthen uncertainty and self-doubt too much. The result might be 'a retreat from a consideration of the power relations in which knowledge is constituted toward an egocentric and nihilistic celebration of the ethnographer or psychiatrist as author, creator and consumer of the Other' (Pollier and Roseberry 1989, p.246). This Other might serve the interests of the researcher.[2] One might ask if it is necessary to 'reflect on reflection'.

Making the Other implies involvement in an arena in which morality and moral claims are contested and difference is constructed (Van Dongen 1998, p.279). In the next section of this chapter I will show how the Other is included in the symbolic domains of psychiatry and anthropology.

THE OTHER IN THE SYMBOLIC DOMAINS OF PSYCHIATRY AND ANTHROPOLOGY

Both psychiatry and anthropology claim an interest in the 'native point of view'. It is important to have an emic perspective on the individual's illness in order to pursue a culturally sensitive therapy or a cultural account, the ethnography or monography. However, the very incorporation of the illness narratives into the idiom of psychiatry or anthropology makes nonsense of emic claims (cf. Obeyesekere 1990, p.220).

In psychiatry, the illness narratives of patients are transformed through psychiatric nomenclature and classification. Through the formulation and reformulation of the worldwide classification system DSM there is a strong belief that people present symptoms which can be categorized. The idea is that the categorization is neutral, distanced and free of values and emotions. However, analyses of formal diagnostic systems show that categories are based on cultural models (Gaines *et al.* 1992; Young 1991). On this level, a debate about cultural permeations is still going on between anthropology and psychiatry. Moral claims and contestation gradually become clear. It takes time to study them.

On the level of clinical practice formal systems seem less important. My research findings (Van Dongen 1994) suggest that the formal diagnosis and classification of people in a psychiatric clinic is 'no big deal'. When I studied an acute admission ward in 1989, I found that psychiatrists and other therapists used the formal classification systems in a loose way. After a first enquiry the patient was given the number of the DSM (Diagnostic and Statistical Manual) in his file. Psychiatrists admitted that 'having' formal diagnosis was 'easy' when the patient was transferred to another clinic or when they had to talk with colleagues, but in clinical practice they were less concerned about formal terminology and more concerned about their relationships with patients. In the words of one psychiatrist: 'Diagnosis is a matter of five minutes, but I will have to work with people.' Within clinical practice great emphasis is on people's behaviour, which is an indicator of their sanity or insanity and the nature and seriousness of their illness. This behaviour is not judged through formal categories, but through experience-near models, based on experiences of daily clinical practices. In their descriptions of people diagnosed as psychotic or schizophrenic, therapists use metaphoric language and signify behaviour in moral terms. Some examples: 'He pulls me into his world'; 'I feel irritation and animosity'; 'she is impulsive'; 'he cracks jokes about the therapy to avoid me'. Also in conversations with patients, therapists transform the former's self-presentations into moral categories, which are important in our culture. To make this clear, I describe the case of a young woman who is formally diagnosed as having a 'schizoaffective disorder'.

Dora suffers from repeated cycles of psychoses and instability in relationships and her sense of self-worth. Her life is a sequence of failed relationships, abuse and misuse by others and wandering from a very young age. But she has not given up looking for a place in society. She feels powerless against forces which escape her control. She feels sorry for the suffering and sadness of others and puts a lot of energy into other people. Then she forgets herself and feels as if she does not exist, as if she is swallowed by others. This in turn gives her feelings of being misused and loneliness. She 'takes others too much to heart'. However, she thinks she is strong enough to take up her life again after 'the dip'. She keeps thinking and hoping that 'everything will be okay in the future'. Her story is a rhetoric of suffering, full of metaphors of involvement and compassion. This story is transformed by therapists into a story of a life with a 'handicap'. Her experiences are reformulated into qualities with which she has to live. 'Taking others too much to the heart' is reformulated into 'sensitivity' and 'handicap'. Dora's claim that her self is related to others is represented by the therapist's claim that her sensitivity is an intrapsychic quality. The transformation 'de-mythologizes' the rhetoric of suffering into another more individualized myth. The transformation is ontological: it tells people how they should be in the world.

The hegemonic ideology of individualism is contested by patients all the time. It is hard for people to accept an individual responsibility for a state of being which also has social origins. The effect of transformation and resistance is 'the struggle for reality' between psychiatrists and patients (Van Dongen 1994). This struggle means time-taking conversations about the 'truth' of the patient's life and often results in strong emotional reactions of both. These reactions are reflected upon by psychiatrists and other staff members during team meetings. In one of my studies of an acute psychiatric clinic I focused on the way a psychiatric team talked about patients during team meetings. The talk of the staff members was very emotional and full of metaphors. An analysis of the metaphors used showed that contacts with clients were seen as war or business. The metaphors were mainly used to express the emotions of nurses and therapists. They used war metaphors like: 'He thinks that he is the general' or 'The undermining and the sabotage of the therapy' when the relationships with their clients were very unstable and tense. They used business metaphors like 'Let's formulate a contract' or 'I cannot sell this to that patient' when they felt that patients were not co-operating and keeping to the contract which was made at the start of the treatment (Van Dongen 1991).

However, the clinical transformations are not malicious intentions, nor are they signs of innocence. They are a token of psychiatry's powerlessness, although this powerlessness is not the same as that of the sick people. To put this in the words of a psychiatrist, while we were talking about the social origins of psychological problems: 'I too think it is an outrage. But what if I tell this to a patient? I think I will let him down and his problem too. That I end up in the gutter with him. I will cheat on him, because I complain with him. He hopes I will have the power to bring about change, while I don't have any. That is not going to get him anywhere.'

In my study of interactions between patients and therapists it is shown that therapists are often powerless during those interactions when patients refuse to attune to the conversations and the transformations made by the therapists (Van Dongen 1994). When patients keep silent, when they fantasize about their future or when they intentionally violate conversation rules, therapists have little possibility of breaking through this defence or resistance. In my opinion, the professional psychiatric transformations 'trivialize the experience of their subjects, and even perhaps render them more difficult to work through' (Kleinman and Kleinman 1991, p.275).

However, medical anthropology has the same dilemma. Its transformation of human suffering and experience into oppression, resistance, disempowerment, conflicts and the symbolic domains of a given culture is of the same order as psychiatric transformations (cf. Kleinman and Kleinman 1991). Its relativistic and cultural point of view also individualizes. One might even wonder if and in what sense interpretation and therefore signification are ethnocentric activities. On the level of fieldwork – just as in psychiatry's clinical practice – in encounters with research participants[3] the anthropologist uses his or her experience-near models, which are based on experiences in the daily lives of people and him/herself. The anthropologist too makes moral claims, which are contested by research participants. I will make this clear with an example of my own fieldwork in the closed ward of a mental hospital.[4]

On my first day on the ward I was introduced to a woman in her thirties. She listened to my explanation of my presence on the ward. She invited me to her room with the words: 'I will tell you my story.' Of course, I felt good; on my first day a story without begging. I was too naive. However, I had to make a round first to introduce myself to all the patients and nurses. When I told her that I was invited into the woman's room, a member of the staff said to me: 'She is quite a thing, but go and see for yourself.' I entered her room and during the next few hours the woman told me her life story, repeatedly assuring me that she was very well able to take responsibility for herself. This idea of responsibility for self and autonomy turned out to be very meaningful in the months to come. It was the central moral claim over which staff members and the woman were struggling. However, that very first day I had the impression that the woman was indeed capable of managing her own life. I felt that the staff were too protective, so I too made a moral claim.

After a couple of weeks, during which I was often unwillingly drawn into this moral debate, I began to feel manipulated. It happened that when I came out of the staff office after a conversation with a nurse on a different topic, I was persuaded to go with the woman into her room to hear 'the truth' about the ward and her situation. It also happened that the woman asked me in public, that is in the living room where we had coffee or tea together with all the patients, what I thought about the behaviour of certain staff members. She broke her promise not to drink alcohol. When we went into town to buy some clothes she sneaked into the toilet of the restaurant where we were drinking tea to swallow half a bottle of gin. I became less convinced of my own silent claim that the staff were over-protective. The question of whose side I was on was put forward by patients as well as by staff members.

Sometimes I became irritated by the manipulation and the awareness that I was entangled in all kind of arguments, controversies and discussions and the pressure to explain my point of view on moral matters. I came to ask myself: if psychiatry was 'abnormalizing' people with its diagnoses and classifications, how was anthropology 'normalizing' people with its symbolic analyses and cultural explanations? If psychiatry was thought to formalize the 'exclusion of people' and thus disempower them, was anthropology not formalizing the 'inclusion of people', because it places people back into culture again by writing about madness and its cultural dimensions? Would this not mean that anthropology also disempowers people, because sometimes people need to be different in order to communicate their suffering as a social consequence? What good would this mean? Sometimes illness is the only remedy against the evil and bad sides of health and life.

Despite all efforts to de-metaphorize mental illness into 'disease', matters of mental health and sickness are moral matters, because they are closely connected to moral issues related to normality and abnormality. They also are closely connected to people's life review. Therefore, reflection is an important activity,[5] but it reaches beyond individual or personal matters. Anthropologists and psychiatrists should ask themselves questions such as: Which events, stories or answers do I define as odd, relevant, interesting, stupid, because I have a particular cultural (or professional) perspective, and which events, stories or answers do the 'informants' define as odd, etc.? And why?

These questions are already important within cross-cultural psychiatry. In the interaction between psychiatrists and people who come from different cultural backgrounds, it is obvious that both are confronted with different ways of thinking, believing and doing. The ways in which psychiatrists act upon such differences are manifold. In general there is a willingness to develop culturally sensitive knowledge and therapies,[6] but it is also possible that culture is used as an excuse for a failing therapy (Van Dijk 1998).[7] However, developing cultural sensitivity and cultural knowledge is hampered by onesidedness: it is the psychiatrist who obtains such knowledge through intensive training, not the patient. We are creating the Other again, even if we reflect on why we experience the other as 'strange'. If we define culture as knowledge of values, norms and cultural competence (cf. Cox, this volume), it becomes obvious that both psychiatrist and patient should develop such sensitivity and knowledge of each other's culture.

My research findings (Van Dongen 1994) suggest that much of the work on the interaction between psychiatrist and patient is precisely about the struggle of both to find out what the other believes to be true or normal. The patient is disadvantaged because the relationship between the two is unequal in the sense that the moral order of the therapist need not be under scrutiny. It is the patient's order which is negotiated and reflected upon. The therapist's reflection is done elsewhere: in supervision sessions or within multi-disciplinary team meetings. I have many examples of taped conversations of therapists and schizophrenic patients in which the patient tries to check what the therapist thinks of the former's ideas, beliefs, values or norms. I found three possible interaction techniques among therapists to deal with these kinds of questions: abstinence, probing if the patient can answer the question him/herself and telling the patient how they think or believe immediately followed by a 'move' towards the patient's world. These kinds of reactions are not due to indifference on the part of therapists. They are based upon everyday beliefs about conversational and cultural values like respect for the uniqueness of people, respect for privacy, respect for 'freedom of thinking', respect for autonomy.[8] However, these values can be viewed differently by people and could be used as an excuse for not having any answers. They create a contradiction. On the one hand the therapist has to break the normal rules, because the patient has to be healed; on the other hand these rules are to be respected because people cannot be forced to adopt other values and thoughts. But it means that sometimes the patient is individualized and left alone without opportunities to explore the moral order, which is problematic in our fragmented world. I would say that this contradiction belongs to the core of our culture, of every culture. Cultural values and meanings are always ambivalent and can be used in different ways, depending on the context and situation.

In fact anthropology has a similar rule. A relativistic point of view, so strongly promoted and insisted upon in anthropology, is of great worth. It might prevent us from being ethnocentric or medicocentric, for example. The consequences of this point of view could be the same as those of silence on moral questions of the therapists. Some anthropologists are of the opinion that they should not make any (evaluative) statement about what their research participants tell them. This principle is based on the same cultural values mentioned earlier. I believe that anthropologists are sometimes forced to make such statements when they are engaged intensively in daily fieldwork. I remember my dilemma when one of the men on the locked ward told me a story about 'fucking a goat'. He told me extensively what he did before he was admitted to the mental hospital and asked me what I thought about it. I felt a strong resistance to tell him that this was repulsive to me, because I knew how guilty he felt about his behaviour. But a deeper self-reflection also revealed that I felt this reluctance for another reason: if I made any comment I would deny 'personal freedom', a concept which entered into Dutch society in the 1960s and 1970s and has been valued since then. I felt how strong this idea was. Who was I to tell him what was wrong and what was good? And to be honest, I also came to the conclusion that when I made any moral comment I would not hear his stories anymore. In the end I told him that I did not favour this kind of sexuality and did not understand it very well.

It is clear that the Other is incorporated in the symbolic domains of both psychiatry and anthropology. On this level, the answer to how anthropology can contribute to a culturally sensitive psychiatry can be answered by saying that anthropology could place self-evident daily clinical practice in another light, so that one can reflect upon such practice. Or that anthropology can provide useful knowledge about cultural practices and beliefs of the Other. Of course, the latter is important. There are many examples in which the behaviour of people with a different cultural background is explained by resistance or unwillingness, while it becomes obvious after anthropological research that through lack of knowledge one makes serious mistakes.

I remember a case in one of the Dutch academic hospitals. An important Muslim leader had died. The nurses wanted to prepare the body, but the alarmed Muslim community came to the hospital. When they heard what the nurses were doing they were outraged because the leader's body had to be prepared in a manner proper to his status and position. The nurses locked themselves into their office because they felt threatened by what they thought was the aggressiveness of the community members. Knowledge about death and dying rituals in Muslim society would have prevented this conflict. Cultural knowledge is important and might lead to a better and more sensitive approach to patients. However, this is an individualizing approach in which writing mini-ethnographies is a useful activity. It will improve individual situations, but would it benefit society in the long term?

Providing knowledge for reflecting upon self-evident practices is useful, as I argued earlier. One has to realise that anthropological knowledge in this sense is 'good to think with', but one might wonder if it makes any substantial changes or a move towards a mental health care system which is tuned to people's needs in very different economic, social and cultural circumstances. Such a scientific practice would only bridge the troubled waters between the disciplines. I am aware of the difficulties raised by a more extended anthropological practice in which psychiatry, anthropology and patients are involved. In *Strangers on Terra Cognita: Authors of the Other in a Mental Hospital* (Van Dongen 1998) I concluded that the heart of anthropology's enterprise is 'grasping the other's world and suffering and passing this on to others again'. This conclusion was based on the difficulty of having psychotic and schizophrenic patients involved in a debate on the research results. The conclusion seemed very unsatisfying to me. However, anthropological research on psychiatric practices might draw the attention of patient associations and groups of patients (and their family members) or of governmental organisations.[9] In the next section I will discuss these relationships.

BETWEEN THEORY AND PRACTICE: THE POSITION OF ANTHROPOLOGISTS IN THE WORLD OF MENTAL HEALTH

The anthropologist often looks at himself or herself as an intermediary between patients and healers or between patients and health policymakers. When one works in a mental health setting one has to be ready to compromise and negotiate. As a consequence attention is directed almost exclusively to patients without critically studying psychiatrists and other mental health personnel. If one wants to study the latter too, one will often experience resistance and uneasiness. When I entered the field of the mental hospital for the second time, to study interactions between therapists and nurses on the one hand and patients on the other, I had to explain at length to the former why I wanted to include them. Many objections were made by staff members. I also know from colleagues and students that it takes a lot of effort and tact to enter the 'doctor's world'.[10] Another problem for the anthropologist might be that one wants to know the 'usefulness' of the research results in psychiatric practice. Often this is hard to explain, because one never knows what data will be obtained beforehand. Connecting theory to practice is difficult because it is hard to explain that nothing is so practical as a good theory.

The role of the anthropologist in the fabric of mental health is ambiguous. Must the anthropologist aim at improvement of communication between psychiatrist and patient and 'make' people more culturally sensitive? Then, what is meant by culture: the culture of the patient or the culture of both, the psychiatrist and the patient? If the latter is intended, how does one have to define culture? The cultures of the patient and therapist are not bundles of values, norms and customs brought to the therapeutic sessions together with the psychiatric illness. Culture is a 'meaning-generating context' (Van Dijk 1998, p.250). This dynamic concept emphasizes the importance of culture as a therapeutic tool, because it gives meaning to images which both have of themselves and each other, the social context, their relationships and their ideas about acting. The concept also takes into account the creation of reality in therapeutic sessions. It will make room for changes in thinking about health and illness under the influence of a much broader context than the individual (Van Dijk 1998, p.250).

What would the role of anthropology be in this case? Scheper-Hughes (1990) made three propositions:

1. The medical system should only be engaged in medical work. All other problems should be studied by other disciplines.

2. Attention needs to be paid to alternative ways of healing.

3. Medical practices have to become radicalized; one has to acknowledge that people's tragic experiences are experiences with the world.

For Scheper-Hughes an anthropologist should be a trickster, a playful personality who could break through the social control of psychiatry, and also a kind of shaman. However, social control is not the only thing at stake in mental health care. I do agree with the idea that symptoms of mental illness are related to what happens in society. The many people who suffer from depression, psychosis, schizophrenia, trauma, etc. are an indictment of society. Mental illness can also be seen as a silent resistance to the struggle for meaning between people, healers, politicians and many others, as well as anthropologists. Therefore, anthropology should study the play of values, norms, meanings and beliefs. I see anthropology's contribution to mental health on different levels.

On the level of psychiatry's clinical practices anthropology can provide cultural knowledge for therapists as well as patients. The many misunderstandings in clinical practice make clear that this knowledge is necessary.

However, this knowledge needs to be about the culture in which the people actually live and should be transferred to all: therapists and clients or patients. It would have been better if the nurses in the academic hospital had known what the customs were when a Muslim leader dies; but it would have been even better if the Muslim community had known the hospital rules and customs in cases of patient death.

Anthropological analyses can reveal the work with culture in psychiatric practices. Values and norms which are at the core of culture get their significance and meaning in daily practice. For example, hopelessness has clinical importance because it is linked with depression and suicide. Therefore its opposite, hope, plays an important role in therapies and interaction between psychiatrists and patients. Hope has individual and social dimensions. Having hope to get healthy means that a person has the will to overcome the illness by his or her own strength. Hope gives people power to overcome suffering. It should be clear that this dimension of hope is closely linked to values of individualism and autonomy. However, hope also has a social dimension when it is the core of interactions within a mental hospital. Anthropological analysis shows that it has different meanings and functions for staff members and patients, which change when the situation changes. Such knowledge shows that hope does not always have the favourable effects we believe it has.[11] It also shows that values, norms and rules are negotiated. This knowledge might be used for reflection on practice, but also for discussion with patients on how to improve interaction and to assess their needs.

Anthropological analysis can describe the context – social, economic and political – in which the psychiatrists and patients work. The anthropologist is an intermediary between governmental institutions and the public on the one hand and health institutions on the other.

It is ironical that most psychiatrists do have clear insights into the social conditions which can lead to lifelong invalidation of psychiatric symptoms (Shay 1994), but feel that they cannot do much with this knowledge in everyday practice. Anthropological studies might direct attention to this issue. It has been suggested that every adult within a culture accepts its moral principles and the normative expectations of society and that 'abnormality' challenges this 'normality', thereby disorienting people (cf. Richters 1995).[12] According to Richters this is one of the reasons for avoiding listening to sufferers' stories and wishing to forget them. Anthropologists and psychiatrists can work together and promote a public attitude that shows concern about conditions which create psychic distress.

One of the main tasks of anthropology is to provide insight into the work of a fragmented world by in-depth ethnographic studies of the social construction of 'facts' and meaning and to highlight the social processes within psychiatry. This cannot be done solely by a description of the cultural basis of psychiatry, or of the rituals and symbolisms of psychiatric practices, nor by a description of the patients' culture. Such anthropological concepts as ritual, rites, myths and symbols can be usefully applied, but more important are the social dimensions of those concepts and the ways in which people use and experience them subjectively. Globalization, fundamentalism, racism, urbanization, homelessness, unemployment and the transformation of family relationships – important characteristics of a fragmented world – are concerns directly related to anthropology (Ahmed and Shore 1995, p.33) and to the people themselves; but they should also belong to the concerns of psychiatry, because they are implicated in the development of many illnesses.

SOME FINAL REMARKS

We have seen that psychiatry and anthropology share their cultural basis. Both disciplines use reflection as a means to avoid ethnocentrism and medicocentrism and to gain a better understanding of the Other. This reflexivity is a culturally determined activity, because it is based upon a particular concept of the person and upon particular beliefs about human thinking. Reflexivity has epistemological, moral and political aspects. Anthropology and psychiatry are moral systems because they study the idiom of distress as deviant and the illness itself as an individually experienced state of being. An important danger of reflexivity is that it can exclude the Other. The result might be that the Other serves the interests of the anthropologist or the psychiatrist and that his or her needs will not be met.

Anthropology and psychiatry transform human suffering into their symbolic domains. The people often are disadvantaged because the relationship between the anthropologist and the Other, or between the psychiatrist and the Other, are unequal in the sense that the moral order of the anthropologist and psychiatrist is not under scrutiny.

Both anthropologists and psychiatrists might individualize people's suffering, while their illness might also have social determinants. These determinants should be the concern of all who are involved in mental health care.

During the years that I worked as an anthropologist in the field of psychiatry I came across many debates and controversies between the two disciplines of psychiatry and anthropology. From a certain viewpoint the disciplines are opposed, although they have much more in common than usually is assumed (see also Skultans, this volume). While anthropology has to struggle to show its relevance for humankind[13] – especially in the field of sickness and suffering – psychiatry developed into an important health science and system of health care.[14] This view on the relevance of both sciences can be related to the debate on universalism versus relativism and the discussion about processes of medicalization and psychologization of human suffering, but also to the apparent controversy between theory and practice.

The controversies between anthropology and psychiatry are complicated by internal debates. Both have theories and ideas of how the world should be organized and controversies with their colleagues. In this sense, they share the contentious nature of all scholars. Of course, it is true that psychiatry is a western science that can be studied as a cultural (sub)system by anthropology (cf. Gaines 1984), but one might be puzzled as to how anthropology is not a western science (the discipline came into being in Europe) and therefore also can be studied as a cultural system. The relationship between the two disciplines has received different characterizations: 'an uneasy alliance' (Skultans 1991); a 'folie-à-deux' (De Jong 1991) or a 'quatre mains' (Van Dongen 1992). No matter how the relationship is described, the two have to cooperate and to reconsider their theories and methods in the light (or darkness) of modern times, because they will have to cope with the complexity of the consequences of a 'brave new world',[15] which causes suffering in so many populations. Therefore, I suggest that the debates and discussions between psychiatry and anthropology have to be extended to the people with whom psychiatry and anthropology are concerned.

However, we have to be careful that the encounter between the cultures of anthropology, psychiatry and the people do not become similar to those which existed in colonial times between administrators, anthropologists and natives (cf. Frankenberg 1995), when anthropologists provided the knowledge to the administrators and were able to speak for and about people who could not speak for themselves. Anthropological research in psychiatric settings must mean 'doing with people' rather than to 'act on people'. Anthropology can bring the different parties in the field of mental health together. This also means that anthropological research results should be discussed with all research participants: psychiatrists and people, so that a dialectic process and reflection can be guaranteed.[16] This also means that anthropology and psychiatry have to take sides. The problem here could be the moral dimension of taking sides. How to overcome the reluctance to this dimension is perhaps a problem in complex situations of the modern world. Reflection, awareness of the subjectivity of people and a dynamic concept of culture can be of help. Psychiatrists are already 'moral explorers' in their interaction with their patients. However, they should make their explorations more public, so that people will be aware of their viewpoints. If anthropology succeeds in describing and analysing how culture as a set of values, norms, customs and rules get its reality in psychiatric interaction, the moral exploration might also become less silent. I end with Frankenberg's words: 'Many voices are perhaps the right replacement of forked tongues' (1995, p.129).

NOTES

1. Els van Dongen is a medical anthropologist and staff member of the Medical Anthropology Unit of the University of Amsterdam. Address: Oudezijds Achterburgwal 185, 1012 DK Amsterdam, Netherlands. email: vandongen@pscw.uva.nl. She wishes to express her gratitude to Vieda Skultans and John Cox for their patience and encouragment.

2. Those interests might be served in a nostalgic and a paternalistic scientific way. Nichter (1992: xiv–xvi) discusses both ways in his introduction to *Anthropological Approaches to the Study of Ethnomedicine* and concludes that these representations and transformations should also be a focus of science.

3. I prefer to speak of research participants instead of 'informants', 'respondents', 'interviewees', 'natives', etc., because I consider the Other as the co-author of the ethnography.

4. I discussed this case in an article from a different perspective (Van Dongen 1998, p.285): the argument was about moral claims and power.

5. Self-reflexivity is inherent to modern societies (Giddens 1994). Thus one could have serious questions about the cultural dimension of this activity. This means that we should be very reflexive (critical) about reflection.

6. In the Netherlands, as well as in many other countries, anthropologists are requested to provide cultural knowledge for psychiatrists through courses, seminars and lectures. Anthropologists are able to do so, but when asked for advice on more practical matters like interaction, they will hesitate to do so immediately because they are often not educated as applied scientists or feel that they need in-depth research before giving any recommendations.

7. If culture is seen as a static concept (the values, norms and customs people *have*), it fails to take into account the flexibility of people and might result in false expectations regarding the outcome of the therapy. It conceals other causes of illness, like the socio-economic situation of migrants which results in feelings of unwellness.

8. See, for example, Grice (1975) who argues that conversations are based upon cooperation and politeness.

9. I was invited to take part in the group of COMPRO, an Amsterdam association of patients, therapists and others who have expertise in the field of care for psychotic people. This association is engaged in improving the skills and autonomy of psychotic patients in formal health-care systems. But I was also invited to take part in scientific expert meetings on subjective (meaning the patients') experiences of mental illness and mental health care. This double position of the anthropologist makes him or her an intermediary between, on the one hand, psychiatry and clients, and on the other between psychiatry and other disciplines (anthropology). I am also involved in the scientific board of a research project on the elderly in one of the bigger cities of the Netherlands, which is financed by the government. This makes the anthropologist an intermediary between health sciences and policymakers.

10. This process of getting permission to enter the medical field also belongs to fieldwork. Going to all the procedures – from ethical committees via boards of hospitals or other health institutions to individual doctors or psychiatrists and patients

– teaches the anthropologist about the power relationships, interests, politics and problems which are important background knowledge for the ethnography. When I was trying to obtain permission from the teams in the different units of the mental hospital, one therapist refused directly, saying that he considered this research of no value to him. Through gossip I learned that this therapist had refused because there were some problems with the hospital board. This taught me that refusal or cooperation with the reseacher can have different meanings, which sometimes have nothing to do with the research. Of course, this is often the case with patients too. They have interests and problems with therapists and sometimes assume that the anthropologist can do something about it.

11. In an article about 'work with hope' in wards for chronic schizophrenic people, I suggest that this work could lead to chronic conditions and require much effort because the staff only use a single meaning of hope (getting better) while the patients also use another meaning: hope of a better life after death, hope of forming a community within the ward (Van Dongen 1998).

12. Richters speaks about trauma stories in this case. However, I believe that many other psychic afflictions have the same effect on people.

13. Anthropology's marginal position among sciences could be explained by processes of globalization and fragmentation of human cultures, which make it extremely difficult to study human cultures as a whole and to compare different cultures.

14. In the Netherlands it is believed that psychiatry replaced religion and psychiatrists replaced priests. On an international level, psychiatry (western) has an important place within local health systems and recently started to play an important role in the care of people traumatized by violence, war, disasters, etc.

15. I refer to Aldous Huxley's novel *Brave New World* (1932) in which the author sketches a technically and psychologically perfect world in which everything can be controlled by medical science. Huxley contrasts this world with the man who remained human and dashed against the wall of soullessness and confirmism of the brave new world.

16. I have already discussed this dialectic and reflection in an earlier article (Van Dongen 1998).

REFERENCES

Ahmed, A. and Shore, C. (1995) 'Is anthropology relevant to the contemporary world?' In A. Ahmed and C. Shore (eds) *The Future of Anthropology. Its Relevance to the Contemporary World*. London: Athlone, pp.12–46.

Bataille, G. (1993) *The Accursed Domain*, vols. 2 and 3. New York: Zone Books.

Crick, M. (1982) *Anthropological Field Research, Meaning Creation and Knowledge Construction. Semantic Anthropology*. London: Academic Press.

Csordas, T. (1990) 'Embodiment as a paradigm for anthropology.' *Ethos 18*, 5–47.

De Jong, J. (1991) 'De "folie à-deux" tussen antropologen en psychiaters: enkele punten van overeenkomst in het zieleleven van psychiaters en antropologen.' *Medische Antropologie 3*, 122–128.

Frankenberg, R. (1995) 'Learning from AIDS: the future of anthropology.' In A. Ahmed and C. Shore (eds) *The Future of Anthropology: Its Relevance for the Contemporary World*. London: Athlone, pp.110–134.

Gaines, A. (1984) *Cultural Definitions, Behavior and the Person in American Psychiatry, Cultural Conceptions of Mental Health and Therapy*. Dordrecht: Reidel.

Gaines, A.E. (1992) *Ethnopsychiatry*. Albany: State University of New York Press.

Geertz, C. (1973) *The Interpretation of Culture*. New York: Basic Books.

Giddens, A. (1976) *New Rules of Sociological Methods*. New York: Basic Books.

Giddens, A. (1994) *Beyond Left and Right. The Future of Radical Politics*. Cambridge: Polity Press.

Good, B. *et al.* (1982) 'Reflexivity and countertransference in a psychiatric cultural consultation clinic.' *Culture, Medicine and Psychiatry 6*, 281–303.

Grice, H. (1975) 'Logic and conversation.' In P. Cole and J. Morgan (eds) *Syntax and Semantics, Vol. 3 Speech Acts*. New York: Academic Press.

Kernberg, O. (1975) *Borderline Conditions and Pathological Narcissism*. New York: Jason Aronson.

Kleinman, A. and Kleinman, J. (1991) 'Suffering and its professional transformation. Toward an ethnography of interpersonal experience.' *Culture, Medicine and Psychiatry 15*, 275–302.

Moore, H. (1996) *The Changing Nature of Anthropological Knowledge: An Introduction. The Future of Anthropological Knowledge*. London: Routledge.

Nichter, M. (ed) (1992) *Anthropological Approaches to the Study of Ethnomedicine*. Philadelphia: Gordon and Breach.

Obeyesekere, G. (1990) *The Work of Culture. Symbolic Transformation in Psychoanalysis and Anthropology*. Chicago: University of Chicago Press.

Pollier, N. and Roseberry, W. (1989) 'Triste tropes: postmodern anthropologists encounter the other and discover themselves.' *Economy and Society 18*, 245–264.

Richters, A. (1995) 'Posttraumatische stress-stoornsi, een feministisch-antropologisch onderzoek.' In J. Baars and D. Kal (eds) *Het uitzicht van Sysyfus*. Groningen: Wolters-Noordhoff, pp.175–199.

Scheper-Hughes, N. (1990) 'Three propositions for a critical applied medical anthropology.' *Social Science and Medicine 30*, 189–199.

Scheper-Hughes, N. (1992) 'Hungry bodies, medicine, and the state, toward a critical psychological anthropology.' In T. Schwartz and G. White (eds) *New Directions in Psychological Anthropology*. Cambrige: Cambridge University Press, pp.221–251.

Scheper-Hughes, N. and Lock, M. (1987) 'The mindful body: a prolegomenon to future work in medical anthropology.' *Medical Anthropology Quarterly 1*, 1, 6–41.

Shay, J. (1994) *Achilles in Vietnam. Combat Trauma and the Undoing of Character*. New York: Atheneum.

Skultans, V. (1991) 'Anthropology and psychiatry: the uneasy alliance.' *Transcultural Psychiatric Research Review 28*, 5–25.

Tobin, J.J. (1986) '(Counter)transference and failure in intercultural therapy.' *Ethos 14*, 120–144.

Van Dijk, R. (1998) 'Culture as excuse. The failures of health care to migrants in the Netherlands.' In S.V.D. Geest and A. Rienks (eds) *The Art of Medical Anthropology. Readings*. Amsterdam: Het Spinhuis, pp.243–251.

Van Dongen, E. (1991) 'Oorlog en zakendoen. Over het gebruick van metaforen in teambesprekingen in een psychiatrisch institut.' *Tijdschrift voor Psychiatrie 33*, 2, 138–145.

Van Dongen, E. (1992) 'Folie à-deux of quatre mains? Een commentaar op de pathologische visie van De Jong op de relatie tussen antropologie en psychiatrie.' *Medische Antropologie 4*, 87–92.

Van Dongen, E. (1994) *Zwervers, Knutselaars, strategen. Gesprekken met psychotische mensen.* Amsterdam: Thesis Publishers.

Van Dongen, E. (1998) 'Strangers on terra cognita: authors of the Other in a mental hospital.' *Anthropology and Medicine 5*, 279–293.

Van Dongen, E. (1998) '"I wish a happy end." Hope in the lives of chronic schizophrenic patients.' *Anthropology and Medicine 5*, 169–192.

Young, A. (1991) 'Emil Kraepelin and the origins of American psychiatric diagnosis.' In B. Pfleiderer and G. Bibeau (eds) *Anthropologies of Medicine.* Braunschweig: Vieweg and Sohn Verlagsgesellschaft, pp.175–185.

PART 2

Clinical Approaches

6

Social Anthropology and the Practice of Public Health Medicine

Jane Jackson

INTRODUCTION

Most medical students nowadays get a brief introduction to social anthropology through books such as Helman's *Culture, Health and Illness* (1984). Psychiatrists, psychologists and other mental health professionals find much of interest in transcultural psychiatry and other aspects of anthropological research. Doctors wanting to specialize in public health medicine, however, find little about the subject in among the epidemiology, statistics, medical sociology, management theory, politics, economics and health service planning on their reading lists.

This is a pity, because if anthropology is the study of humans in society and the ways in which they interact with each other and with their environment, and if medicine involves the science and meanings of health as well as ill health – then all doctors should be concerned with the social structure of human groups and how people in different societies cope with or try to prevent illness, disease and disability. Public health doctors in particular are responsible for determining the health and health needs of specific populations and have an important role in the planning and provision of appropriate and acceptable care for all sections of society within these populations. For this to be successful, it is important to understand the views of local people about health and how to deal with ill health; to find out how these concepts vary across different sections of the population; and consequently how best to organize and deliver effective health services for them.

TRAINING

What persuades a student to choose a career in social anthropology, in psychiatry or in public health? I was once told that most social anthropologists had undergone some major discontinuity in their lives which subconsciously moved them towards working in this field. Is this a spurious finding, a myth? It was certainly true of us as postgraduate course members in Oxford thirty years ago. Did it make us more flexible, open minded and understanding? Perhaps we were free floating in limbo, unsure of our own roots but keen to peer into other people's lives and examine the way they were coping. Maybe some of us just wanted an excuse to run away to warmer climes and bluer seas for a while.

There is an argument that novelists can only write fully and faithfully of experiences they have been through themselves. Others would say that these can be conjured up by writers blessed with rich imaginations. Is there a parallel argument about psychiatrists who spend their lives delving into other people's disordered actions and listening to their disturbed ideas and explanations? Are these specialists more effective if they too have suffered some degree of mental distress? Are they settling other people's problems and their own as well?

And what of public health physicians? Here we have a group of people who, in Britain anyway, have worked first in other branches of medicine before opting for public health. Are they control freaks, wanting to sort out population problems at one remove rather than remaining intimately involved in investigating and treating the concerns of individual people?

I was fortunate enough to train in social anthropology while working in general practice and hospital medicine in Oxford. It was particularly inspiring to hear from Evans-Pritchard himself about his fieldwork among the Azande (1937) and his efforts to see life through their eyes and on their terms. It was valuable to learn that *how* misfortunes such as injury or illness came about could be obvious and easy to explain but that *why* it happened (and therefore what ought to be done about it) was capable of very different explanations depending on the particular society involved.

I undertook fieldwork alongside hospital medicine in the Caribbean as a member of a research team in St Vincent and Barbados under the leadership of Fernando Henriques and Sheila Patterson, focusing especially on how factors such as social class and ethnic origin were reflected in the society. This increasing interest in populations and different cultures and socio-economic opportunities led to my career shift into public health medicine and eventually to work in London's East End.

There has been a move (nominally anyway) from social medicine first to community medicine and then to public health in recent years and the specialty is now regaining some of its potential for active involvement in promoting health and effecting change in health service delivery. Many social anthropologists too have moved from academe into more practical if more contentious fields of work, advising on developmental projects around the world. Lewis (1976) writes:

> The use of anthropology in development has a more practical, a theoretical ring, disturbing to professional purists. The latter tend to regard 'applied anthropology' with suspicion and embarrassment, the sort of activity likely to appeal to the least academically able. In fact, however, those who are attracted to applied work are often academically highly qualified, radical activists who are not prepared to sit tight and ignore pressing social and political problems in their own and other countries and who find the aims of anthropological advocacy and 'action anthropology' inspiring. (Lewis 1976, p.376)

Some of them may be specializing in medical anthropology, studying human behaviour in relation to health, illness and the delivery of care within different societies. They can be found working in such fields as public health, epidemiology, social geography, psychiatry, botany, community planning and development, botany or genetics. They detect some of the effects of environment, ecology and social structure upon people's health and apply their findings to promote useful changes in health or health behaviour or in the organization of health care. They can often explain why certain programmes designed to improve local health care have been unsuccessful or why compliance is poor, and can advise on how to encourage increased take-up among the indigenous population.

John Orley (1970) as a psychiatrist and anthropologist in East Africa enquired into local beliefs about epilepsy and madness among the Baganda people. His close involvement with them and understanding of their concerns was then used to help practitioners and planners. A senior academic explained:

> He has come to think in Luganda and has taught us to try to think as our patients do. He has made vital contributions to our knowledge of how the Baganda approach illness, how they classify it, what there is in it that they fear, and, perhaps most important of all, how they communicate their discomforts. (Foreword)

Though very clearly not in the same league, I hope to show how some understanding of social and medical anthropology has helped me in my work, using some anthropological concerns and a few of the main tasks of public health medicine as examples.

TASKS OF PUBLIC HEALTH MEDICINE
Assessing health and health-care needs

At least I have learnt to guard against making hasty generalizations about people. On my return from the Caribbean I was concerned to hear assumptions made so glibly in Britain about incoming West Indian families, their purported lack of structure and the so-called 'shadowy father figure', regardless of individual circumstances and without consideration of important factors such as class, ethnicity, education, income or religion. I had found in St Vincent that upper-class and (especially) middle-class families conformed rather strictly to 'western' ideals of monogamous mating of young adults formalized by the sanctions of the Christian church; with nuclear families; and households which tended to be dominated by the male. Divorce and remarriage was acceptable among upper-class people but occurred very rarely among those in the middle class. Most lower-class households on the island, as in other parts of the Caribbean at the time, showed instead diverse parental and mating patterns and variations in domestic life along with a general commitment to the idea of monogamy.

Certainly some low-income couples did marry early, had small nuclear families with little emphasis on extended kin, and had stable households. What was unusual was that alongside these were many other quite acceptable relationships and domestic groupings made possible by the open and flexible society and the independence of women as well as men. The slight increase in prestige offered by marriage among poorer people might not be sufficient to compensate a woman for the loss of her independence or the fear of being tied to a man forever – because the marriage bond was considered to be unbreakable and led to loss of power for the wife.

It would be rare nowadays to find a society consisting of separate sections along rigidly defined lines according to features such as class, colour or religion. Nearly always there are people who cannot be precisely categorized, who cross the borders, who succeed in gaining in status or who do not conform to the particular group in some way. In any case, however much people within certain groups have their own mores, attitudes and opinions, they are still likely to share some opportunities, facilities and problems with the rest of the population. This makes it imperative that public health physicians and others who plan and organize services do not assume that all members of a population or group run their lives in a similar way and hold the same attitudes and opinions. Similarly, Leach (1961) argues that anthropologists should not compete in capturing, categorizing and pinning out societies or sections of society like butterflies, but rather seek to understand and explain what goes on in society and how societies work. He suggests that social anthropologists 'are like the medieval Ptolemaic astronomers; we spend our time trying to fit the facts of the objective world into the framework of a set of concepts which have been developed *a priori* instead of from observation' (p.26).

Anthropologists are taught to be careful about making generalizations about groups within society, but their findings can still be dangerous if used injudiciously and indiscriminately as 'proof' of certain aspects about a particular section of the population. Thus Mayer (1960) is careful to describe how the apparent rigidity of the Indian caste system was actually breached as individuals manoeuvred and managed their lives; for example, Brahmins remained extremely strict vegetarians while low caste people such as labourers ate eggs and meat. Douglas (1966) notes that to touch excrement in that society was to be defiled and so Hindus might be expected to be: 'controlled and secretive about the act of defecation. It comes as a considerable shock to read that slack disregard is their normal attitude... caste pollution represents only what it claims to be. It is a symbolic system, based on the image of the body, whose primary concern is the ordering of a social hierarchy' (pp.124–125).

In Newham where I worked for many years, it was found that Indian families who moved to Britain from East Africa tended to retain much stricter rules of behaviour (about permitted food, for example) than those who had come to this country more recently directly from the subcontinent. Among all groups in the population, as elsewhere, factors such as social class, age and gender affected attitudes towards health and welfare systems. An anthropologist can explore and explain many important aspects of these systems, for example, the subtle interrelationships between patient and practitioner in terms of economic and other forms of exchange.

Methods of working

One of the main areas of public health work is the measurement of health status in the local population, and the extent to which health services adequately fill the health needs. This community diagnosis requires gathering, collating and analysing a wide range of information from a vast number of sources, some of it statistical and relatively hard (if often out of date and limited), some of it extremely soft and subjective. Comparisons are made with findings in other districts and reviewed against research literature before advice is given as to where and what improvements might be made. Such advice tends to be more acceptable if it is based on reasonably rigorous quantitative research, but it is now recognized that qualitative methods of enquiry into aspects such as practitioners' and patients' attitudes, beliefs and preferences are important. However, these qualitative methods are still seen as particularly useful for tackling research questions which cannot easily be answered by experimental methods (Green and Britten 1998) rather than being a necessary part of all health-related studies. Public health research is often limited in scope and depth in any case because of the need to provide rapid superficial information and advice gained by 'quick and dirty' methods about a multitude of services.

A psychiatrist or psychologist gathers, collates and analyses information and the results of tests gained directly from the patient and adds some data indirectly from family, staff members and others; compares these against norms for the particular population, age group or other relevant section of society; forms a diagnosis; considers and advises on options for treatment; records the process; undertakes therapy in a variety of forms; and reviews the outcome. Public health work might be seen as not too different from that of a clinician but on a larger and more nebulous scale, with results of advice and 'treatment' slow to appear and rarely due to the efforts of one person alone.

Traditionally, social anthropologists seek out as much information as possible about 'their' societies through participant observation, immersing themselves in the local setting, learning the language, checking and re-checking details with local respondents about how local people order their world and their concepts and actions. This information has to be considered and analysed in relation to the wider body of anthropological works and compared with other cultures so that the definitive description or eth-nography with its theoretical basis can be written. It is a difficult but fascinating task needing empathy, understanding and analytical skills. Thus, being 'unable to use tests, questionnaires, polls, experiments, and the like, in human communities where they were guests and where western instruments of "objectivity" were inappropriate, anthropologists have fallen back on human powers to learn, understand and communicate' (Keesing 1981, p.5).

Lewis (1976) suggests that social anthropology has strong links with history, sociology and comparative religions. Because it is so involved in observing and interpreting interrelationships and interpersonal transactions within a society:

> Study of the forces animating community life inevitably brings us very close to psychiatry and social psychology where the roles people play are also of critical importance...to define mental alienation and abnormality, the psychiatrist must first know what is normal, accepted and socially approved. (Lewis 1976, pp.21, 23)

Kleinman (1981) argues for the development of cross-cultural studies to link medicine and psychiatry and medical and psychiatric anthropology. In his work on different health-care systems he shows that the internal structures are roughly the same though the content varies, and that health beliefs, behaviours and related actions, like the systems, are 'cultural constructions, shaped distinctly in different societies and in different social structural settings within those societies' (p.38). His own structural model has proved useful in the analysis of local systems of health-related behaviour.

He describes three social arenas in which ill health is experienced and reacted to:

1. The popular arena, encompassing beliefs, choices and decisions, roles, relationships, interaction settings and institutions. These can be for the individual, the family or the wider networks and community.

2. The professional arena, consisting of professional scientific medicine and indigenous healing traditions which have been professionalized.

3. The folk arena, with its non-professional healing specialists.

A very large proportion of sickness is managed within the popular arena and this is where most decisions are made about when to seek help, whom to consult, whether the remedy is successful or whether alternatives are required.

Public health physicians charged with the responsibility for assessing the level of need for mental health care services in a particular population must keep all three arenas in mind though often information is limited about two of them. Most effort goes into exploring common data sources about services used in the professional arena (such as statistics on psychiatric outpatients and inpatients, social services residential and day care service users, or community mental health staff caseloads).

Little may be known about people in distress who do not use services. Certainly much more information is required about what goes on in the popular arena, such as the relevance of family or social networks; current beliefs about mental disorders; or how effective the local options are. There are several research instruments which can be used to detect and measure symptoms in a population (such as the General Health Questionnaire) but it is much more difficult to assess psychological well-being and positive health. 'At present, in terms of public mental health, we can say how ill a population is and how illness is distributed within it, but it is difficult to say how well it is' (Bartlett and Coles 1998, p.294).

National statistics can be used to give very general estimates of need but it is essential to check these against local findings and any research about mental health in different communities within the population. The 1993–4 survey of psychiatric morbidity (Meltzer et al. 1995) among people living at home can provide useful comparisons. It shows the wide variation in prevalence of mental disorders in relation to factors such as gender and social class. Thus, for example, men in Social Class I had half the rate for neurotic disorders (60 per 1000) compared with other men. Twice as many women as men said they had anxiety and depression (94 and 54 per 1000 respectively). Drug dependency rates were twice as high in men than women (27 per 1000 in men compared with 14 per 1000 for the women).

Service use rates also vary widely. For example, in Newham, a district of about 230,000 in East London, the standardized hospitalization rate for mental illness was close to the national average of 462.3 per 100,000 people in the 1989–90 Health Service Indicators. There was a huge variation in rates at that time across the North East Thames Region from the lowest of 199.3 per 100,000 in Mid Essex to the enormously high rate of 1064.1 per 100,000 in Bloomsbury. If the statistics were to be believed (a separate matter altogether) this begged all sorts of questions on, for example, urban/rural variation; accessibility, availability and responsiveness of statutory services and alternative options; general practitioners' expertise and confidence; and psychiatrists' opinions and practices – to say nothing of what was happening in the hugely important popular and folk arenas.

These figures might suggest that the population of Newham was similar in general to the national average and that access to hospital care was reasonably in line with this. In fact, the borough is the most materially deprived local authority area in England and there are many people who suffer multiple disadvantage (Griffiths 1994; Newham Health Authority 1992). It has an unusually young population, is markedly multicultural, has high unemployment rates and long-term sickness levels. Housing needs are high, with many households being overcrowded or lacking basic amenities. Staffing levels in community and hospital mental health care are low.

In 1990 a survey of patients entering the acute psychiatric admission ward in Newham (Robin 1991) found that people of African/Caribbean background were over-represented while those of Asian origin were fewer than expected. The latter also seemed less likely than the indigenous population to contact their GPs or other statutory services for help with mental health problems, though this was not formally tested in the district at the time. Findings elsewhere in Britain appear to show a mixed picture (Rack 1982). It is important in any case to enquire more deeply into the local situation. How do members of different cultural backgrounds define and view mental health problems in themselves or others? How do they cope and what makes them decide to seek help? Do their concepts and actions vary with factors such as age, ethnic origin, gender or social status? We must encourage further research and make better use of the findings.

In summary, public health physicians, psychiatrists and anthropologists differ in the scope, aims and methods of their work. Psychiatrists of whatever persuasion use their acquired knowledge, clinical skills and judgement in diagnosing and treating patients deemed by them to have mental health problems. Though more often working nowadays in multi-disciplinary teams and sharing a greater degree of responsibility for individual patient care with other mental health staff (through the Care Programme Approach), most still interact with single patients on a one-to-one basis, needing to recognize the context in which their patients live and enquiring into their health-related beliefs and behaviours. Their expertise and status help to shape professional and public perceptions of mental disorders and how they should be managed within a health-care system.

Public health physicians view mental health services as part of the whole range of health-care provision for perhaps half a million people in their area. They compare information about the supply and use of services against national norms and local data to estimate levels of need for different types of health care. They must balance the needs of mentally ill or disabled people against competing needs of others in the population. They act as change agents, working with professional staff, patients' groups, voluntary agencies and management to make services more appropriate and responsive.

An anthropologist undertaking in-depth mental health research in a section of the population (maybe 200 people) will place them within the context of the society, including its social structure, formal and informal networks, economic, religious and many other aspects so as to:

- understand better their concepts about mental distress, their health-seeking behaviour and the various options for care;
- see how these may be affected by factors such as family background, education or status.

Such information, if carefully sought and skilfully presented, can be of great value to public health and mental health staff in their attempts to develop and improve the service. Local examples of such benefits were: clearer information about informal and folk arenas in mental health care, including the importance of different religious groups and their support systems; better understanding of the multiplex, demanding and often competing roles which had to be played by staff while living in on duty for 24 hours at a time in group homes for people with learning difficulties; and recognition that certain women of Asian origin who were in need of mental health support could be helped effectively by attending a 'sewing circle' when a more overt form of psychiatric input would have been unacceptable.

Detection of mental ill health

Helman (1984) describes how definitions of normality vary across the world, being based on shared beliefs within each cultural group as to how people should behave – as might be appropriate in relation to their age or other factors. There is a spectrum between what is regarded as 'normal' and 'abnormal' behaviour in each society, while abnormal behaviour may be seen as 'controlled' as in religious trances, or else 'possessed', 'uncontrolled', 'mad' or 'bad'.

Some types of unusual behaviour are readily defined as evidence of mental illness wherever they occur. Edgerton (1966) undertook valuable anthropological research into the way psychotic symptoms were viewed and dealt with in four East African societies. He excluded respondents who had been significantly influenced by European culture, yet found there was broad agreement across the four tribal groups about certain behaviours (such as going naked, talking nonsense, or violent acts) occurring without obvious reason, that would be considered as equivalent to a diagnosis of psychosis. These were similar to the behaviours seen among patients admitted to the European-directed East African mental hospitals at the time. However, the tribes differed in their ideas about causation and the effectiveness of therapy: Kamba and Hehe tribespeople tended to think that the condition was due to supernatural or magical causes and that drugs and magic could lead to cure, at least temporarily; those from Sebei and Pokot tribes thought that the illness was contracted for no reason and had little confidence that any of their range of treatments would be successful.

Edgerton shows that the recognition of psychosis in these societies involved:

> Considerable interpretation and negotiation in order to determine the 'reason' why an action occurred, and consequently, what person, group, or supernatural force is to be held responsible, as well as to determine the kinds of compensatory actions required...psychosis is recognized, defined, and responded to through a process of interpersonal negotiation and jural consideration scarcely less complex than that which obtains in modern Western societies. (Landy 1977, p.366)

Littlewood and Lipsedge (1997) describe how mentally ill people with an ethnic minority background may have delusions couched in the terms of that culture but tend to use the symbols and vocabulary of the dominant culture so that their problems can be recognized and addressed. Where unusually high rates for schizophrenia were found in London among people of black African/Caribbean descent, they consider it was partly due to misdiagnosis by white psychiatrists. 'The practice of psychiatry continually redefines and controls social reality for the community. Whatever the empirical justification, the frequent diagnosis in black patients of schizophrenia (bizarre, irrational, outside) and the infrequent diagnosis of depression (acceptable, understandable, inside) validates the stereotypes' (p.251).

It can be argued that symptomatology and the way in which it is reflected in diagnosis may be similar across the world for certain psychotic illnesses, such as delirium tremens, but not for disorders in which the meaning and expression of mental distress are culture bound, such as severe depression. Within British communities rates for the detection of depression vary as Brown and Harris (1979) found in their study of adult women in London. They were higher among those with particular 'vulnerability' factors (lack of husband or boyfriend; loss of mother while under eleven years of age; having three or more children under fourteen at home; and/or unemployment). The opposite of these offered a degree of 'invulnerability' to depression. Unfortunately the possession of any of these factors made it more difficult for the affected women to attend their general practitioners and therefore also less likely to be diagnosed or referred for specialist psychiatric care.

There has been increasing concern about the low rates of detection of depression among Asian families in Britain, especially as their suicide risks are higher than average. Jacob *et al.* (1998) interviewed women of Indian descent in a West London general practice where the GPs were of the same ethnic group. Among other instruments they used the Short Explanatory Model Interview. One-third of the women were found to have some degree of psychiatric morbidity (a similar prevalence to other British populations) but only half of these had mentioned all their concerns to their GP and were less likely to be diagnosed. It appeared that many women did not perceive their emotional distress as something for which medical treatment was appropriate, but were ready to divulge it when asked direct questions. The researchers conclude that because the models diverged between doctor and patient a treatment plan needed to be worked out which was acceptable and made sense to both.

Improved compliance is gained by trying to understand and ally the models held by practitioner and patient. Geertz (1960) describes 'tjotjog' or fittingness and its importance in Java in relation to divination and healing by the local dukun. If the dukun, however skilful, and patient did not tjotjog the patient would remain sick, so he would go on trying different dukuns and/or western-trained doctors until he was cured.

Currer (1986) interviewed a small sample of Pathan mothers who had migrated to Britain from the North West Frontier of Pakistan. They were very strict Muslims, and it was thought possible that levels of depression would be particularly high among these very secluded women in purdah. In fact, however, they took little responsibility for the occurrence of illness because they viewed life, health and happiness as all in the hands of God and so had to be accepted. It was important, though, to behave correctly in the face of illness and on all other social occasions. There was little outlet for distress but in any case the women tended to be protected from stressful situations. There was the characteristic somatization of mental illness, and treatment would be sought for problems such as headaches or lack of sleep which otherwise would affect their responsibilities in the home. Access to GPs was limited and women might be treated through their husbands. Illness and distress were under-reported or might be missed or misdiagnosed, but Currer considers that seclusion and isolation did not seem to give rise to higher than expected levels of depression.

Fernando (1995) explains that integration, balance and harmony are important components in eastern thinking about mental health, for individuals, their families and the wider community, while in the west greater emphasis is laid on other aspects such as self-sufficiency, efficiency and individual autonomy. Thus insights from anthropology and transcultural psychiatry are valuable in determining what constitutes mental health and health problems in a multicultural population. Other important factors which shape public and private perceptions and experience of mental disorders, such as family background and socio-economic status, must receive equal attention.

Reviewing the quality of care

Just like anthropologists, public health physicians have 'their' own populations. Their responsibilities are wider, however, as they not only have to examine and assess the health needs of a very large number of people but must also participate in management to ensure that means are found (and effectively used) to alter and improve health care and ultimately, health status. Anthropologists can, if they wish, pick up their bags and steal away from the community they have studied. They can go home and read, write up field notes, publish their findings and become experts in their area in a much more genteel and academic way. This action is denied to public health doctors. Anthropological insights can, however, provide powerful fuel for change.

Forty years ago Goffman's anthropological study of patients and staff in a hospital in Washington DC led to his seminal work *Asylums* (1961). Much earlier work by Van Gennep (1908) and others had described the transition rites which mark the passage from one significant situation in life to another. Thus initiation rites are followed by separation and segregation into an insubstantial limbo, after which more rites attend the person's re-emergence and social acceptance as a new member of the society imbued with changed status.

Rites of passage are familiar enough in everyday life, but Goffman shows how powerfully they worked in the mental hospitals and other 'total institutions' of his day. Admission procedures depersonalized and separated the patient from his ordinary roles and home environment; he was required to provide intimate details which could be shared among staff; his own face-saving manoeuvres were used as evidence against him; the regimentation and lack of privacy, the over-intrusiveness on one hand or complete disinterest on the other, all added to the 'mortification' process. Goffman describes how people tried to cope by learning the house rules and finding out which actions led to punishment and which to rewards and privileges. They got by in different ways: withdrawing, being intransigent, by showing some degree of acceptance, or by becoming wholly converted into the staff's idea of the perfect patient. Most people seemed to play the system to some extent, though, and presented different pictures of themselves as necessary. The staff also were locked into the same system and found their own ways of dealing with it.

This came home to me very vividly when setting up the Oxfordshire Mental Handicap Register (Elliott, Jackson and Graves 1981). There were people and staff in some long-stay mental institution wards who had become bound into a quite separate and limited way of life and work and showed little enthusiasm for change. These units were in contrast to others where much more effort had been made to encourage patients to learn or renew skills and gain respect in their own right. Staff learnt to take large pleasure in even small achievements by the patients and this exchange of 'gifts' led to mutual satisfaction.

Jones's description of 'Ward 99' (1975) is a severe indictment of the worst type of institutional care found in Britain in the not so distant past. Senior staff opted out and junior nurses withdrew from emotional contact and endured their three-month assignment there; patients were seen as insensitive, unable to discriminate or be taught anything; the ward was commonly referred to as 'the farmyard' and staff felt justified in eating the patients' food both as a perk and as compensation for working there. She describes the 'back ward syndrome' in which the staff's concept of the patients and their potential for development was low, and the ward, 'acquires a separate image as 'low-grade' or 'severely subnormal' or 'difficult' or simply 'bad'; and once it is so defined, the image is self-reinforcing' (p.106). There was also a lack of specific techniques for treatment; staff adopted a parental role; patients were expected to do as they were told when they were told to do it so there was no opportunity for learning; there was a lack of interaction between patients; staff had no motivation and shirked work which could be left for others; and there was a general poverty of human relationships with nurses keeping a social distance from patients, between patients and from each other. Routine was seen as absolutely essential. Anything which upset routines such as an attempt to change methods of feeding or which involved other professional staff or volunteers was opposed. Jones suggests that the only way to improve the situation besides minimizing many of the routine procedures would be to introduce new technology such as behaviour modification, new skills derived from occupational therapists and others, and ensure that staff activities had specific and positive objectives for the patients.

Barrett (1996) describes the back wards in a large state psychiatric hospital in Australia which were 'like living museums where people were still performing the same functions they would have carried out prior to the 'therapeutic revolution', whereas in the front wards staff kept abreast of the latest developments in psychiatric practice' (p.36). Patients diagnosed by psychiatrists as acute received progressive treatment, but those deemed chronic appeared to be 'less interesting, less frequently seen, and less valued' (p.32). Nursing staff in the back wards tried hard to achieve rehabilitation goals and even one successful transfer of a patient to a community hostel was seen as a tremendous achievement. Interestingly, while doctors decided whether patients were to be treated in front or back wards, nurses decided (on the basis of perceived dangerousness) which patients should be in open or closed wards.

In any district there is still likely to be a back ward or residential home where people receive less than ideal care. In acute general wards too there are often long-stay patients whose needs are overlooked or who are poorly treated. Bliss (1998) describes how the quality of acute hospital care for old people has been affected by the pressure on beds and the shortage of nurses who rush from one crisis to another and 'are so poorly trained, so pre-occupied with medicolegal documentation, so lumbered with technological procedures, so bewildered by the concept of "rehabilitation" instead of care.' An old person who has been put out of bed into a chair from 8 am might feel dizzy later and feel pressure pain in her buttocks, slide down and fall to the floor but would then be returned immediately to the chair. Bliss comments that such treatment, 'almost universal in general and elderly medical and orthopaedic wards today, in any other setting would be classed as torture' (p.153).

Jones (1988) is concerned that the positive moves to improve the lives of people with mental illness and learning difficulties and promote greater opportunities for them through 'normalization' and community care came at a time when the wider society was tending to abandon its liberal and humanitarian values and adhere instead to the profit motive.

Scull (1993) describes some of the ill effects of poorly supported community care, but recognizes that the presence of asylums in the past made it easy to remove many difficult and disturbing people from society and also affected to what degree other people were willing to put up with those who were disruptive or very dependent. Jones (1988) explains that once mentally ill people were supposed to be the same as everyone else it became possible to ignore their problems and explain bizarre behaviour as awkward or criminal or wicked. Chronic patients discharged from hospital would be expected to cope with life with no extra help; as long as they had a roof over their heads and a little money their very real needs could be discounted.

On the other hand, when strong efforts have been made to ease the transition from institutional care and people are well supported, the change can be very beneficial. Murphy (1991) describes how she visited ex-patients from an old long-stay ward who she remembered as 'a seriously disturbed, difficult group of people, peculiarly dressed in assorted hospital garb, behaving in an irksome and irritating manner'. After long rehabilitation they had moved into sheltered flats in a Victorian terrace in Newham, supported by staff. They were transformed; though 'still shy and inarticulate...they clearly took pride and delight in their new home. They were better dressed and seemed less "peculiar" in their behaviour'. Many had begun to go to pubs and shops nearby. She found it 'a most convincing demonstration that the most severely mentally disturbed people have a capacity for developing a better quality of life if they are provided with the right environment and skilled help' (pp.22–23).

Anthropology teaches us that individuals or groups who do not conform to the society's norms may be seen as marginal and of little account or, like witch doctors or special sects, can have very great power. Douglas (1966) describes how societies accommodate and deal with such aberrant people, whether by exclusion, indifference, respect or exaltation. Institutions too can be beyond the pale in some sense, as seen above. When proposing a new service for people who were unusual, stigmatized, perceived as upsetting the system or dangerous, I found it useful to try to raise their image and make the service appear in some degree 'magical'; thus, for example, when planning a new semi-secure ward in 1980 I suggested it should be called instead a Psychiatric Intensive Care Unit (mirroring high status acute teaching hospital units for medicine and surgery nearby) and recommended that it should provide very high quality treatment and care, be closely involved with good academic and research work, and offer excellent and much needed training courses to a range of people who would benefit from and later transfer such specially acquired and respected skills elsewhere.

Public health doctors are involved in planning and improving services, so need to find ways of measuring their quality. Øvretveit (1992) emphasizes the importance of reviewing quality in three different dimensions, using the viewpoints of the client, the professional staff and the service. This may be more difficult in relation to mental health care as people may be unwilling or unable to say what they think. One useful method is for staff to trace a randomly selected client's career through the service, trying to judge it from the person's point of view and thus providing better insight into the part the staff themselves have played in the process.

Miller and Gwynne (1972) have described life in several residential institutions for people with chronic illness or disability. The organization of these places varied markedly from units run on a 'warehouse' model of care in which the main task was seen to be the prolongation of physical life through good medical and nursing care, to those run on a 'horticultural' model in which the primary task was to develop those capacities and drives which were unfulfilled in the residents. In the warehouse model people remained very dependent and were expected to fit in with the staff's concept of good and correct treatment. The horticultural model meant that people were encouraged to greater independence. However, the authors pointed out that in fact a more flexible and sensitive model was required to allow very disabled people to exercise choice, having the opportunity either to rest and be relatively dependent or be more active and independent, recognizing their own desires and capabilities at the particular time.

An important finding was that in the units at that time death was the only outcome for the residents; also, because they were cut off from normal life and isolated, they suffered social death well before physical death. In most traditional societies on the other hand social death follows physical death in an orderly way, surrounded by relevant rituals which serve to draw the community together and comfort the bereaved.

Anthropologists and medical sociologists have provided powerful evidence of how easy it is to banish people who are disturbing, difficult or heavily dependent to somewhere out of sight and out of mind, and how hard it may be for staff to counter this attitude. Public health physicians need to do all they can to help everyone involved in mental health care, so that this one-time Cinderella service can be seen as a positive and much respected source of good in the society.

The outsiders

Social anthropologists have much to offer when considering the situation of individuals or groups who are to some degree seen by others as outside the system. This may be because of some stigmatizing characteristic such as disfigurement or because they are members of an unusual or non-conforming section of society; they may be ignored altogether if 'socially dead'. Goffman (1968) describes their 'moral careers' by which they learn about their plight and go through similar personal adjustments in their changing conception of self:

> Stigma involves not so much a set of concrete individuals who can be separated into two piles, the stigmatized and the normal, as a pervasive two-role social process in which every individual participates in both roles, at least in some connexions and in some phases of life. The normal and the stigmatized are not persons but rather perspectives... The lifelong attributes of a particular individual may cause him to be type-cast; he may have to play the stigmatized role in almost all of his social situations...However, his particular stigmatizing attributes do not determine the nature of the two roles...merely the frequency of his playing a particular one of them. (Goffman 1968, p.163)

Goffman also shows how an individual might manage his stigma and the discomfort it causes him and others. He considers the position of people who are discreditable but not yet discredited and how they manage the situation. Should they tell or not; lie or not; and who to, when and where? The ex-mental patient whose background is unknown to others has a problem, 'not that he must face prejudice himself, but rather that he must face unwitting acceptance by individuals who are prejudiced' (p.58) against people who are mentally ill.

Rack (1982) suggests that mental disorder is viewed with extra concern among those groups in the population who believe strongly in supernatural forces because:

> Any unexplained affliction (especially anything sinister like madness) gives rise to the suspicion that its victim is an unfortunate person – not merely in the sense that his illness is a misfortune, but with a deeper apprehension that fortune (or something) is not on his side. It is prudent to avoid becoming too closely involved with such a person, or with his family. (Rack 1982, p.174)

Douglas (1982) uses 'grid-group' analysis to place societies in different categories depending on whether interrelationships between group members appeared to be strong or weak, and whether the behaviour and actions of individuals were constrained or not. Where there were strong group ties and weak opportunities for individuality she suggests that the sick role would be accepted and well supported; blame would be attached to those who were unsympathetic; and everyone would be concerned to seek out causes and responsibility for ill health. On the other hand, where society favoured the individual and group loyalties were weak, people would be unable to use the sick role to muster support and would try to keep fit and hide their ills. Care of the sick then became a problem because the emphasis on self-reliance would not require family members to sacrifice their own lives to support them. One solution in that case might be for affected individuals to join up with others in a similar predicament (for example, suffering the same disorder or disability) and so become strong together as a group.

There are many instances in any population of people who are at once stigmatized, disadvantaged and vulnerable. Some, however, are able to exert a degree of power because of their individuality, their adherence to a high status group or their activities. Thus poverty need not detract from skill in the arts. Someone recovering from mental illness can be a forceful advocate and adviser to service planners. A young person with learning difficulties can play a full part in the workplace or college.

In health-care systems some individuals and groups are relatively low in status yet manage to achieve some degree of power. Professional hierarchies are obvious in hospital, though less evident now in primary care or mental health services where the emphasis is on teamwork and greater autonomy of staff from different disciplines. Doctors may have less overall power but still carry ultimate responsibility, and an increasing bureaucratic burden makes the work less attractive. Generalists tend to have less kudos than specialists though their broader view and knowledge is invaluable; many therefore build up interest and expertise in particular areas.

Psychiatry itself can appear to be rather low in the district's pecking order with regard to resource allocation, especially when its base is physically separated (out of mind again) from other local NHS sites. However, the psychiatric profession also exerts strong influence on public perceptions of deviant behaviour and how it should be managed so that psychiatrists 'and other social control experts for that matter, negotiate reality on behalf of the rest of society. Theirs is preeminently a moral enterprise, involved with the creation and application of social meanings to particular segments of everyday life' (Scull 1993, p.391).

While there will be individual mental health experts and academic staff with prestige and power in the district, it is often necessary to raise the profile of the service in the hopes of getting more equitable treatment in the fight for resources and a better deal for patients and staff. Powerful allies may be sought to strengthen the argument. Anthropology teaches us that very few societies nowadays have a static social structure and this is doubtless true for groups within each society too. Leach (1954) gives an intriguing account of communities apparently in cyclical change between those where power happened to be derived through kinship and those where power was gained through rank, the driving force for change being provided by individuals competing for power. The neighbouring populations of Shans and Kachins differed markedly in their political structure, yet they could perceive themselves as members of both groups. This meant that they could be seen to hold different status positions in several social systems at the same time. People tried to manipulate the systems to their own advantage, and Leach suggests that when a considerable number of them or 'collectivity' changed in response to a powerful individual then the structure of the local society altered too. Given a push by some charismatic or forceful person, 'big man' or group, perhaps one day the status and resources of the more collaborative mental health services will do a Leach and rise as those of the distinctly hierarchical acute general hospital sector diminish.

Health promotion

An important area of public health work is the promotion of health in the population and the prevention of ill health, described by Landy (1977) as the 'attempt by a society to control the behavior of its members for what the reigning groups and belief systems define as the welfare of the community as a whole' (p.231). In traditional societies this is likely to include efforts to control those spiritual and cosmic forces which are believed to affect people's health and welfare.

Attempts to introduce new practices into any society will only be effective if they are seen as relevant and congruent with local concepts and customs. Cassel (1957) describes the effects of introducing new foods into the diets of Zulu mothers and infants in an attempt to reduce the very high levels of severe malnutrition. Families took rapidly to growing and eating green vegetables but there were strong and deep-seated cultural prohibitions on women drinking milk, especially if they were menstruating, or if the milk came from cows belonging to members of the same kin group. Powdered milk offered along with assurances that it did not come from cows belonging to Bantu people was readily accepted.

It is now recognized that if health promotion is to be successful then greater understanding is needed about the concepts, beliefs and actions of groups within a community and how these fit into the whole society. There is also increasing acceptance that qualitative approaches are relevant and necessary. Faltermaier (1997) for example, states:

> The urgent need for new approaches in health practices, in particular the ongoing challenge of finding more effective strategies of disease pre-vention and health promotion, requires more individually based and contextualized knowledge; qualitative methods could be a way of achieving this. (Faltermaier 1997, p.357)

Chapman and Lupton (1994) list many of the barriers put up against public health goals, including political philosophies which emphasize economic outcomes and devalue the importance of health; political and bureaucratic unwillingness to provide regulation and laws which would promote health; marketing of unsafe products; and problems such as sexism and racism as expressed in people's values and behaviour. They describe some of the ways in which public health advocacy (lobbying) could be successful but note that research so far has focused mainly on relatively trivial interventions rather than on those which would have much wider significance and affect many more people. Among the many skills which they see as necessary for the advocate are 'political science, the sociology of mass communications, the symbolic role of politics in the structuring of media and political discourses on health issues, and networking techniques'. They must learn to adopt 'opportunist, responsive, imaginative, flexible, dramatic, and above all newsworthy tactics' (p.16). Quite a list, indeed.

They quote the fable of the people who fall into a river from an overhanging cliff. Very costly rescue and resuscitation is provided and applauded, though a safety fence might have prevented many deaths from drowning. The fable adds, however, that:

Fences can be ugly, that they disrupt views, and that as dull, static and unchanging objects they don't attract the same acumen as bright shiny ambulances or dramatic rescue routines. Above all, a fence does its job when *nothing* happens, while rescue services are frequently defined as successful when they are merely busy. The opening of a fence provides one photo opportunity for a politician; dramatic rescues can provide dozens. (Chapman and Lupton 1994, p.8)

Besides the familiar ways of trying to prevent mental ill health, such as providing a wide range of information and support services through the statutory, alternative and voluntary agencies, it is important to deal with the views and attitudes of local people. Byrne (1997) shows how stigma related to mental illness is an ongoing source of distress for patients, their families and their wider networks. In relation to the patient it can mean that illness is not disclosed or only presented after long delay; there is a greater likelihood of co-morbidity; treatment may be refused or compliance may be low; the psychiatric label can make the initial symptoms worse; rehabilitation efforts fail so that the illness becomes chronic and relapsing; there is an increased risk of becoming homeless, unemployed and isolated; and suicide is more likely. He describes the common negative psychiatric stereotypes presented in the media and writes:

No section of either mental health professionals or patient support groups can alone effect a major and enduring change in public perceptions. A coordinated approach is required, with a common policy and strategy. National campaigns of health promotion through all media should coincide with legislation to discourage discrimination and promote greater equality. Local initiatives seem the best way forward, with specific outcome measures ...that could be used to record reductions in the overall effects of stigma. (Byrne 1997, p.621)

Planning and development of services

Reliable information is needed about the aims and objectives of a service, its strengths and weaknesses and overall quality. Are there similar statutory or voluntary agencies already operating in the area? Does the service fulfil its purpose and if not, what changes are needed? Are these changes major or minor, and would they be feasible given the available resources? Would such service changes be appropriate and acceptable to service users, staff and the public? Will expenditure of time, effort and finances on this service be to the detriment of others as worthy? Who will do the work and come up with the plan?

These are just a few of the questions which need to be addressed by those responsible for managing the district's resources (or those to whom the resources have been devolved). Anthropological research can help to show where there is a mismatch between the services offered and used. Ineichen (1989) in his study of services for people with dementia finds that there were problems in the detection and diagnosis of patients due to disinterest among mostly rather passive general practitioners. Good nursing and social services, when provided, allowed many people with quite severe dementia to live at home for long periods. However, having studied the 'dementia careers' of some of the patients he found that half had refused services which staff had considered to be appropriate to their needs.

Collaboration and teamwork is essential in mental health care. In hospital and more particularly within community mental health teams it may not be clear between doctors, nurses, social workers and professional managers as to who holds the major share of power, who has to carry the ultimate burden of responsibility and who holds the key to unlock the resources. This may lead to confusion, disillusionment, unfair expectations and opportunities for opting out and so can be a source of much frustration, anxiety and anger. Tyrer (1998) seeks much greater coordination and integration of community and hospital services including common training of staff who should share the same philosophy of care; careful testing of proposed reorganization and service changes is also needed before they are set in policy. He comments wryly that recent reforms which came about as a result of the new financial imperatives have actually failed because of the same market forces – that is, they have not paid. Anthropologists could have much to say about political actions which promote social change but which may fail to achieve the original aims.

Anthropologists can also analyse and explain the complex interactions between people as they take part in planning teams, battling and bartering their way towards a solution. Organizational issues are intriguing, whether concerning individuals, their multiplex roles and their reciprocal actions, or in the management of the office, hospital unit or practice. How plans are translated into action in health service development is an important question for research both in Britain and abroad; examples from poorer countries where mental health needs and problems are starker are given by Desjarlais *et al.* (1995).

The involvement of psychiatrists and other specialists in the organization and management of their service is essential, though most of their work is with individual patients. Public health physicians, by contrast, only rarely treat patients directly but are very involved in management issues in the hope of improving the population's health status and health services. While they all must cope with dilemmas about needs and demands, priorities for action and how best to use the facilities and resources available, the public health doctor has a much wider responsibility to the whole population (rather than just, for example, to those people who have mental health problems) and must also maintain and improve health in general, working with environmental health staff and others in local authority departments to protect the public.

The Director of Public Health in each authority has the privilege of making and publishing independent statements about the health needs of the population and advising how these may be tackled. A good opportunity to do this is through the annual public health report which may be quite hard-hitting and effective. Most however (including my own over a number of years in Newham) were reasonably strong on supplying information about the population and its needs but mealy-mouthed in advising what therefore should be done to improve matters. Little use was made of qualitative research by anthropologists and others apart from publicizing the findings of local small-scale studies. Results were not presented in a broader social context though this could have helped readers to understand how relevant sections of the population thought about their health, its meaning to them and how they would cope with ill health. Public health reports are sometimes now included in health authorities' annual reports which focus mainly on commissioning and finance, so providing even less opportunity to impart valuable qualitative information about the population to whom they are responsible.

Public health roles

Pity the poor public health physician who must wear so many hats and fight so many corners. Among the multiplex roles are: epidemiologist/social scientist/statistician; advocate; prophet; entrepreneur; go-between; manager; team leader; judge; academic; teacher/trainer; and agent of social control. Some of these roles may be difficult but very rewarding. Being an entrepreneur is tricky but fun. According to Lewis (1976): 'The successful entrepreneur brings together goods, services and people in a happy and mutually satisfying conjunction, so far as possible on his own terms…this job applies with embarrassing accuracy to the social anthropologist' (p.232).

A go-between, on the other hand, holds an uncomfortable place between two individuals or groups, knowing much about each of them and therefore not fully trusted by either. It can be an essential role, perhaps in trying to get two intransigent consultants to work together, chairing a prickly multidisciplinary group, or translating governmental or managerial imperatives into workable guidelines acceptable to initially hostile staff. Goffman (1959) states, 'as an individual, the go-between's activity is bizarre, untenable, and undignified, vacillating as it does from one set of appearances and loyalties to another. As a constituent part of two teams, the go-between's vacillation is quite understandable' (p.149).

In public health work the giving of advice, treatment and support to individual patients and receiving their positive 'strokes' are missing, as are the sometimes urgent and pressing anxieties about accuracy and appropriateness of diagnosis and care (though some of the public health decisions which have to be taken in fields such as communicable disease control can have very wide and problematic consequences, of course). Just occasionally, however, I was called upon to judge whether to invoke special public health orders regarding the removal to hospital or a residential home of an old person who was deemed in urgent need of physical care and attention but who adamantly refused to accept any.

In a random sample of very old people living at home we found that 70 per cent were socially isolated. About 12 per cent had moderate or severe dementia and a similar proportion suffered from depression, but there was no apparent association between the two findings. A very large proportion of them all (84 per cent) said they were satisfied with life in general and most were coping well alone or with some help. Alongside these were a few people who raised anxieties among neighbours and staff. Such a one was Mrs R, a widow aged 78, who was very dirty and unkempt with long strands of hair, six layers of clothes and bare swollen feet; her small terraced house was dirty with the sparsely furnished rooms and staircase covered in feathers long after her bad-tempered little dog had torn up all the pillows and cushions. She had stopped accepting help and her neighbours were becoming increasingly worried about her appearance, her night wandering and her antagonism. Her garden was a rubbish heap and harboured rats and spreading weeds. The general consensus locally was that she should be taken out of her home into care, but she was lucid and not mentally disturbed and simply refused to move or accept help of any kind.

This picture is reminiscent of the description of women accused of witchcraft in England centuries ago. Many were poor and isolated widows whose position in society was uncertain and described by Scot (1584, in Parrinder 1958) as 'women which are commonly old, lame, blear-eyed, pale, foul, and full of wrinkles... These miserable wretches are so odious unto all their neighbours, and so feared, as few offend them' (p.61). Doubtless many of these unfortunate people also suffered from physical disabilities such as deafness or arthritis and were prone to paranoia or obsessional neurosis. Certainly they were marginal beings, upsetting and dangerous.

Nowadays there are many scapegoats – the government, the housing department, the immigrant, to name but a few. The society is less cohesive, and eccentric and frail people may be ignored more easily, yet it is surprising how much neighbourly support is provided to people who are vulnerable. If behaviour becomes too bizarre or threatening, however, then the call goes out for something to be done about the situation. An underlying fear, perhaps, is that a similar fate may await the rest of us and we do not like confronting it. How much more comfortable to tidy the problem person away to hospital or residential care against her will.

I felt like the person with the ducking stool testing the old person's case. When those accused of witchcraft underwent the swimming ordeal they ended up dead whether apparently guilty or innocent. Was the old, cantankerous, independent old lady of today to suffer social death by being forced into institutional care or remain at home, isolated, neglected, antagonistic and friendless? Fortunately these cases were few and far between and it was nearly always possible to solve the complex problems and find some way of providing acceptable help.

While the role of judge and agent of control may be uncomfortable, there are many aspects of public health medicine which are interesting, intellectually challenging and fulfilling. It is rarely – probably never – possible to claim that innovations or improvements in the population's health or health services are exclusively due to one person and my watchwords remained, 'It's amazing what you can achieve if you don't mind who takes the credit.' There is a great opportunity to work in a constructive way alongside a wide range of people from different disciplines and agencies who have a whole variety of skills and expertise.

The status of the public health physician varies depending on the context of work. Thus in the medical hierarchy public health medicine is seen as relatively weak, but in fact there are situations in which considerable power can be wielded. These include the public health powers in relation to control of infection and involvement in the management and allocation of resources. Thus there is the opportunity to initiate change despite being regarded by some of our professional peers as marginal and of little account.

Malinowski (1922) described the way in which the status of important members of the Western Pacific community was raised by the exchange of valuable objects and Lewis (1976), commenting on this, writes:

> Prestige and power *within* one's own community are enhanced by successful confrontations with equals *outside* it… A leader's internal position is delicately linked to the respect he enjoys in the company of peers outside his own group. If the outside world takes him seriously, so, sooner or later, will his local followers. Similarly, academics 'display' their brilliant erudition in fierce intellectual 'exchanges' in seminars and conferences, and in learned 'debates' in scholarly journals. (Lewis 1976, p.204)

When considering the role and status of people working in the public health field, it is not the power and prestige of individuals which is important but rather how through them energies may be harnessed to develop the best possible health-care services for local people. We want the caring professions to provide services which are appropriate, responsive and effective, and which are accepted as such by people in need and the public at large. We want patients and practitioners to 'tjotjog'. We want planners to learn about how people cope with health problems in the popular, professional and folk arenas.

It would be great if a new Malinowski dropped in and undertook an intensive study of the local population in a district such as Newham. This would give information and explanation about the social structure of the society; the ideas people hold about life and death, health and ill health, and how these vary in relation to aspects such as culture, class or religious background; where power lies and how it can be used to improve health services; in-groups and out-groups; institutional care; the effects of rapid social change, and much else.

Patently, this extensive and intensive type of research is not going to happen and the most that can be expected in any district is the collection, collation and use of a disparate array of small local studies and comparative data from elsewhere. Given that public health physicians are usefully placed to influence the scope and quality of service provision, any anthropological insights will be helpful if they explain how people think and act in relation to health and health care. 'Commitment to improving the world is no substitute for understanding it' writes Keesing (1981), and:

> If we do not have the power to see beneath the surface of things, to see processes rather than symptoms, to see whole systems rather than separate parts, then our individual efforts and energies will be dissipated; our voices will add to the confusion that surrounds us. (Keesing 1981, p.497)

REFERENCES

Bartlett, C.J. and Coles, E.C. (1998) 'Psychological health and well-being: why and how should public health specialists measure it? Part 2: stress, subjective well-being and overall conclusions.' *Journal of Public Health Medicine 20*, 3, 288–294.

Barrett, R.J. (1996) *The Psychiatric Team and the Social Definition of Schizophrenia.* Cambridge: Cambridge University Press.

Bliss, M. (1998)'Technological medicine and the elderly: who cares?' *Journal of the Royal Society of Medicine 91*, 152–153.

Brown, G.W. and Harris, T. (1979) *Social Origins of Depression.* London: Tavistock.

Byrne, P. (1997) 'Psychiatric stigma: past, passing and to come.' *Journal of the Royal Society of Medicine 90*, 618–621.

Cassel, J. (1957) 'Social and cultural implications of food and food habits.' *American Journal of Public Health 47*, 732–740.

Chapman, S. and Lupton, D. (1994) *The Fight for Public Health.* London: British Medical Journal Publishing Group.

Currer, C. (1986) 'Concepts of mental well- and ill-being: the case of Pathan mothers in Britain.' In C. Currer and M. Stacey (eds) *Concepts of Health, Illness and Disease.* Oxford: Berg.

Desjarlais, R., Eisenberg, L., Good, B. and Kleinman, A. (1995) *World Mental Health Problems and Priorities in Low-income Countries.* Oxford: Oxford University Press.

Douglas, M. (1966) *Purity and Danger.* London: Routledge and Kegan Paul.

Douglas, M. (1982) *In the Active Voice.* London: Routledge and Kegan Paul.

Edgerton, R.B. (1966) 'Conceptions of psychosis in four East African societies.' *American Anthropologist 68,* 408–442.

Elliott, D., Jackson, J.M. and Graves, J.P. (1981) 'The Oxfordshire mental handicap register.' *British Medical Journal 282,* 789–792.

Evans-Pritchard, E.E. (1937) *Witchcraft, Oracles and Magic among the Azande.* Oxford: Oxford University Press.

Faltermaier, T. (1997) "Why public health research needs qualitative approaches.' *European Journal of Public Health 7,* 357–363.

Fernando, S. (1995) 'Social realities and mental health.' In S. Fernando (ed) *Mental Health in a Multi-Ethnic Society.* London: Routledge.

Geertz, C. (1960) 'The religion of Java.' New York: Free Press.

Goffman, E. (1959) *The Presentation of Self in Everyday Life.* New York: Anchor.

Goffman, E. (1961) *Asylums.* Harmondsworth: Penguin.

Goffman, E. (1968) *Stigma.* Harmondsworth: Penguin.

Green, J. and Britten, N. (1998) 'Qualitative research and evidence based medicine.' *British Medical Journal 316,* 1230–1232.

Griffiths, S. (1994) *Poverty on Your Doorstep.* London Borough of Newham Poverty Profile.

Helman, C. (1984) *Culture, Health and Illness.* Bristol: Wright PSG.

Ineichen, B. (1989) *Senile Dementia.* London: Chapman and Hall.

Jacob, K.S., Bhugra, D., Lloyd, K.R. and Mann, A.H. (1998) 'Common mental disorders, explanatory models and consultation behaviour among Indian women living in the UK.' *Journal of the Royal Society of Medicine 91,* 66–71.

Jones, K. (1975) *Opening the Door.* London: Routledge and Kegan Paul.

Jones, K. (1988) *Experience in Mental Health.* London: Sage.

Keesing, R.M. (1981) *Cultural Anthropology. A Contemporary Perspective,* 2nd edn. New York: CBS College Publishing.

Kleinman, A. (1981) *Patients and Healers in the Context of Culture.* Berkeley: University of California.

Landy, D. (ed) (1977) *Culture, Disease and Healing.* London: Macmillan.

Leach, E.R. (1954) *Political Systems of Highland Burma.* London.

Leach, E.R. (1961) *Rethinking Anthropology.* London: Athlone.

Lewis, I.M. (1976) *Social Anthropology in Perspective.* Cambridge: Cambridge University Press.

Littlewood, R. and Lipsedge, M. (1997) *Aliens and Alienists.* London: Routledge.

Malinowski, B. (1922) *Argonauts of the Western Pacific*. London: Routledge and
    Kegan Paul.

Mayer, A.C. (1960) *Caste and Kinship in Central India*. London: Routledge and
    Kegan Paul.

Meltzer, H., Gill, B., Pettigrew, M. and Hinds, K. (1995) *The Prevalence of
    Psychiatric Morbidity Among Adults Living in Private Households*. London:
    OPCS/HMSO.

Miller, E.J. and Gwynne, G.V. (1972) *A Life Apart*. London: Tavistock.

Murphy, E. (1991) *After the Asylums*. London: Faber and Faber.

Newham Public Health Department (1992) *Health and Health Care in Newham*.
    London: Newham Health Authority.

Orley, J.H. (1970) *Culture and Mental Illness*. Nairobi: East African Publishing
    House.

Øvretveit, J. (1992) *Health Service Quality*. Oxford: Blackwell.

Rack, P. (1982) *Race, Culture, and Mental Disorder*. London: Tavistock.

Scot, R. (1584) 'The discoverie of witchcraft. London.' In G. Parrinder (1965)
    Witchcraft: European and African. London: Faber and Faber.

Robin, E.C. (1991) *A Study of the Views of Newham Residents with Severe Mental Health
    Problems on their Needs for Care in the Community*. London: Newham Public Health
    Department.

Scull, A. (1993) *The Most Solitary of Afflictions. Madness and Society in England
    1700–1900*. London: Yale University Press.

Tyrer, P. (1998) 'Cost-effective or profligate community psychiatry?' *British Journal
    of Psychiatry 172*, 1–3.

Van Gennep, A. (1960/1908) *Rites of Passage*. London: Routledge and Kegan Paul.

7

The Implications of an Anthropology of Religion for Psychiatric Practice

Simon Dein

RELIGIOUS ISSUES FOR PSYCHIATRISTS

This chapter examines a number of issues in religion and psychiatry. What diagnostic problems occur in those who are religious? Does being religious enhance mental health? How should psychiatrists deal with religious and existential issues in their practices? How do religious issues relate to psychotherapy? How can anthropology illuminate the problems of religious beliefs for the practice of psychiatry?

For many psychiatrists the word religion has a number of negative associations: "irrationality, outdated and dependency forming", a view which derives from Freud (1966) who saw religion as a "universal obsessional neurosis". According to a number of studies (Lukoff 1992; Larson 1986; Peck 1992) traditionally psychiatry has under-emphasized religious issues and the topic of religion plays little part in psychiatric training. In fact psychiatric training may be selected by people of a lower level of religiosity than the background population (Larson and Larson 1991; Rubenstein 1994). The Danish theologian Hans Kung refers to religion as "psychiatry's last taboo". Larson (1986) found in a study of four psychiatric journals that only 2.5 included religious variables, more often than not the psycho-pathological uses of religion by patients.

Why this aversion to religious issues? First, as biological and psycho-logical explanations of mental illness are elucidated, religious explanations are rendered superfluous (Neelman and Persaud 1995). Second, following the legacy of Freud there is an assumption that religion is linked with negative attitudes such as dependency and guilt. Brody (1990) points out that through its premature "biologism" contemporary psychiatry overlooks essential knowledge about the cultural basis of behaviour.

There is a religiosity gap between clinicians and their patients with both Kroll and Sheehan (1981) and Neelman and Lewis (1994) pointing out that psychiatrists are often far less religious than their patients and the consequent misunderstandings which may ensue. In their 1981 study Kroll and Sheehan found that the religious beliefs of mental health patients are nearly identical to those of the general population. Both the general public and psychiatric patients report themselves to be more religious than psychiatrists and to attend church more frequently than mental health professionals. Over half of psychiatrists reported that they attended church rarely or never (APA Task Force 1975) and only 18 per cent of psychologists agreed that they attended organized religion. This should be compared to the fact that one-third of the general population considers religion to be the most important dimension of their life and another third considers it very important (Gallup 1985). Although psychiatrists and psychologists may not practice organized religion, they may consider spiritual understandings of the universe important (Bergin and Jensen 1990) with the implication that "there may be a reservoir of spiritual interests among therapists that is often unexpressed due to the secular framework of professional education and practice (p.3). There is inadequate training of psychiatrists and psychologists in religious issues even though, as Barnhouse (1986) points out, "Sex and Religion are, in some form, universal components of human experience." Psychiatrists who know very little about religion would do well to study it. Similarly Shafranske and Malony (1990), in a survey of members of the American Psychological Association, reported that 83 per cent of members rarely discusses religious issues in training. A 1975 APA task force in religion and psychiatry indicated that half of psychiatrists surveyed described themselves as agnostics compared to 1.5 per cent of the general population. Why should psychiatric trainees receive training in religious issues? This chapter argues that an understanding of religion is necessary both in terms of differential diagnosis and patient management.

Although religious issues have been under-emphasized in psychiatry there is some evidence that religion actually promotes better mental health, although the field of religion and mental health is fraught with difficulty (Dein 1996). In perhaps the most comprehensive study to date, Batson Schoenrade and Ventis (1993) listed the findings from 57 different studies that provide empirical evidence of the relation between religion and mental health. They conclude: "Except among clergy, religious involvement is positively correlated with absence of mental illness." Similarly other studies point to the fact that religion appears to enhance psychological well-being in the non-mentally ill (Bergin 1983; Witter et al. 1985). However, those specific religious factors relating to mental health remain to be elucidated. In relation to mystical experience, a number of therapists have viewed these as a sign of health (James 1961; Jung 1973) and studies have found that those reporting mystical experiences scored lower on psychopathology scales and higher on measures of psychological well-being than controls (Hood 1976; Spanos and Moretti 1988). There is some suggestion that those people who have a near-death experience may have an increased appreciation for life, self-acceptance and concern for others (Ring 1984). They may develop new insights into life and no longer fear death. Many claim to have mystical experiences such as feeling at one with the universe.

RELIGION AND DIFFERENTIAL DIAGNOSIS

It may be difficult to differentiate religious beliefs and experience from psychiatric conditions. Below are two case studies which the author encountered in his own clinical practice where the differential diagnosis remained in doubt. It is obviously necessary to differentiate between religious states which may be normal and mental illness which may require treatment. Without an understanding of religious issues, religious patients may be misdiagnosed as having a mental illness and treated inappropriately sometimes with drugs which may have severe side effects. However, the opposite is also true. If the patient's experiences are misdiagnosed as being purely religious, a treatable illness may be missed and suffering may be prolonged. Similarly spiritual or mystical experience may become pathologized even though these experiences are common in the general population (Spilka *et al.* 1985).

Case 1

Miss A is a 25-year-old Nigerian student who came to Britain six months prior to her admission. As far as we could gather she had no previous psychiatric or drug history in Nigeria. Her background was uneventful. She came to London to study but while living there joined a Pentecostalist church. Over the next six months her level of religiosity increased and she spent much of her time proselytizing. For about two weeks prior to her admission she hardly slept, going around the streets of London telling people to 'come to the Lord' and how they would be saved by doing this. According to friends, for a week prior to admission she was neglecting herself, her level of activity had increased and she was stopping numerous people in the street to give them this information. On the day of her admission she became so excited that she jumped onto the back of a moving lorry and was arrested after this and brought to casualty on a Section 136. At that time her mental state was such that she was severely neglected, had lost some weight and spoke incoherently. Her level of activity was also increased. When questioned by the admitting doctor she said she was a 'sister of Christ'. He wrote down incorrectly that she claimed to be 'the sister of Christ', implying that she had a grandiose delusion. She was administered 100 mg of oral Largactil and settled down rapidly and fell asleep.

When she was questioned the following morning she admitted that she had been rather 'over the top'. She told us that she felt she had a mission to spread the word of Christ to other people but she realized that what she did was wrong. For the next couple of days she remained settled on the ward and was due to be discharged the following day. While discussing her on the ward round her diagnosis remained in doubt. It is possible she had an affective disorder (perhaps a mixed affective state) or a brief reactive psychosis. However, the following night she jumped from a window three flights up and killed herself. Until this day we are uncertain of the circumstances which led to this. At no time did she exhibit any signs suggestive of a depressive disorder. It is possible that she was auditory hallucinated and a voice told her to jump. It is often difficult to make a formal psychiatric diagnosis in people who go around the streets in a very excited way proselytizing. Some of these do suffer from a formal functional disorder such as hypomania or schizophrenia. They may hold grandiose delusions believing that they are messianic or have some special religious purpose.

Case 2

A 30-year-old lady from Trinidad was admitted to the ward with a two-week history of extreme agitation. She stated she had been a victim of Obeah, a form of witchcraft which was inflicted upon her by an unrequited lover. She told us that on account of this a spirit had entered through her vagina and was devouring her intestines. She was agitated and could not sleep; she had also lost a significant amount of weight over the prior two weeks. While she was on the ward she held firmly to this belief. We enlisted the help of a traditional healer who attempted to exorcize this spirit to no avail. She remained severely agitated and was given benzodiazepines which slowly settled her down. We considered the use of neuroleptic medication for her, but were uncertain whether she was psychotic or not. This case presents a good example of an instance where in fact it is very difficult to differentiate cultural factors from illness.

Why is it so important to diagnose a religious state? A religious problem may be dealt with by a religious person. Although there has been relatively little work done on the use of pastors in psychiatric units, many of our own patients have asked to see priests, imams or rabbis. We would recommend that all patients with a religious problem should be seen by a religious person. Beyond this it is often difficult without the help of a member of the person's own religious group to decide how much of this is illness and how much is religious. In both the examples given above we asked a member of the Church to come up to give an opinion and in both instances they stated they felt that this was illness and not normal religious state.

Without an understanding of a patient's religious background it is often impossible to know the significance of religious phenomenology. I would argue that psychiatric trainees should have at least some knowledge of a patient's religious background. I have been positively struck by the absence of such knowledge in psychiatric trainees working among ethnic minority patients such as Afro-Caribbeans and Asians. I would suggest that psychiatric trainees may benefit from attending church services and reading about patients' religious background.

PATIENTS PRESENTING WITH RELIGIOUS ISSUES

Lukoff *et al.* (1992) point out that the DSM IV is not sensitive to the religious and spiritual dimensions of problems that become the focus of psychiatric treatment. They recommend a Z code category for the 4th edition of the DSM published in 1993. They talk of psychoreligious problems or experiences that a person finds troubling or distressing which involve the beliefs and practices of an organized church or religious institution. They include loss of religious faith, conversion to a new faith and intensification of adherence to religious practices and orthodoxy.

Religious problems often involve conflicts over questions of faith and doctrine. These should generally be resolved by clergy or a religious counsellor who may typically not have training in psychotherapy (Young and Griffin 1989). However, some of these problems may be resolved through psychotherapy and members of the American Psychological Association reported that at least one in six of their clients presented issues that involve religion or spirituality (Shafranske and Malony 1990). As an example, patients may present to psychotherapists who have recently intensified their adherence to religious practices and orthodoxy. The psychotherapist may need to determine the potential conflicts existing between the former and current lifestyle, beliefs and attitudes (Spero 1987).

In some instances a patient may present to a psychiatrist with a number of religious issues within the context of psychiatric illness. These often need to be addressed by a religious person and it is often within the province of a psychiatrist to deal with them. For example, a 50-year-old Roman Catholic man was admitted to a psychiatric ward as severely depressed. He had been low in mood for about two months and ruminated how bad he had been. Apart from having biological symptoms, early morning waking and loss of appetite with some weight loss, he was preoccupied with the fact that he had let God down. He had vowed to attend church on two consecutive occasions but had not and felt very guilty about this. He thought he deserved to be punished. He recurrently stated that God would no longer be able to help him and he was better off dead. In fact he began to believe that he was already entering the gates of hell.

From a diagnostic point of view it appears that this man has a severe depressive illness with delusions of guilt. However, this is markedly coloured by religious content. Although he did slowly recover with high doses of antidepressant medication, when he was better he reported how useful it was for him to discuss the matter with a priest. As a psychiatrist we are often unable to empathize and to understand patients' religious concerns.

It may be that patients have religious issues which they want to discuss. It may not just be part of their illness, but they may believe that some religious misdemeanour has led to the occurrence of the illness and feel guilty about this. It is useful to discuss the matter with a clergyman who may come up and see the patient. Beyond this, patients admitted to psychiatric hospital may have religious needs, such as the need to pray and perform rituals.

The patient can be helped in this respect by enlisting a religious person to come to the ward. However, this does cause problems with the other patients and it is useful to allocate a separate space where the patient may perform this ritual. Many psychiatric patients desire to see clergy. In fact, a recent study shows that 'clergy are as likely as mental health professionals to be sought out by individuals from the community who have serious psychiatric disorders' (Larson *et al.* 1988).

PSYCHIATRY AND EXISTENTIAL DILEMMAS

Patients presenting to psychiatrists may be attempting to grapple predominantly with existential crises such as meaning in their lives and the fact that one day they may die. These are issues which are not easily addressed by psychiatrists and may be better addressed by clergymen.

For example, a 40-year-old man who suffered with a bipolar affective disorder came to outpatients one day. Although his mood was very stable on lithium carbonate he asked the following question, 'Doctor, why have I suffered all of these years? Why was I born to suffer? I know I won't live for ever, it seems strange that we are born to suffer and to die.' This man was Jewish in origin, although not practising his religion currently. I listened to him carefully and it seemed to me that he was very tormented by many of these issues. I asked whether he wanted to speak to a local rabbi which he readily agreed to do.

I would argue that without a religious framework it is difficult to understand many of these existential dilemmas. In a recent paper editorial by King and Dein (1999) the authors point out that many patients have strong spiritual beliefs. In his paper Sims (1994) argues that 'psychiatrists have too often concentrated exclusively upon the mental and ignored, to the extent of denying its possibility, a spiritual dimension'. Although Sims argues that spirituality relates to finding meaning in one's life, we posit that the term spirituality refers to both the belief and experience in a higher power which is 'cut off' and treated as sacred. This may be difficult to 'quantify'. A number of studies are beginning to indicate that spiritual belief may be a useful way of coping at times of crisis (Littlewood and Dein 1995). There is good evidence that both religion and spiritual belief may be common coping mechanisms at times of sickness (Dein and Stygal 1997). This is especially the case when it is serious or life threatening such as cancer. Spilka *et al.* (1983) suggest that in life-threatening illness the use of religion as a coping mechanism improves the psychological prognosis. There has as yet been relatively little work done on the way that psychiatric patients use religion and spirituality as a framework for coping with their illness. When we talk about these terms we differentiate religiosity which is the outward framework of a religious belief from spirituality which is a belief in a higher power. I argue that we may want to attempt to strengthen this spiritual belief in an endeavour to help patients cope with this illness and in fact referral to a clergyman may be useful to this extent.

RELIGION AND PSYCHOTHERAPY

Religious patients present a number of 'problems' for psychotherapists (Peteet 1981). These include resistance to treatments and rejection of modern psychiatry, struggle with characteristic conflicts especially guilt and particular countertransference issues. Ethical issues arise in relation to the therapist's attempt to stimulate independent thinking. Psychology is considered suspect and heretical, challenging the existence of God and ridiculing the dogma and codes of behaviour. Greenberg and Witztum (1991) suggest a number of practical guidelines for working with strictly religious patients. First, there should be cooperation with the patient's spiritual mentor to reduce resistance. Second, the therapist must examine his or her own religious attitudes to modify countertransference feelings. The therapist should acquire knowledge of the patient's religion to facilitate interviewing, and to help distinguish belief from delusion and ritual from compulsion. Witztum *et al.* (1990) described therapeutic work among Bratslav Hasidum, emphasizing how a basic understanding of the patient's terminology and beliefs is necessary to direct their intervention accordingly. They utilize a therapy which is couched using the symbols and metaphors that have meaning within the cultural religious context. They make the point that the therapist should avoid a religious debate and should leave the persuasion to a religious authority such as a rabbi.

So what do we conclude in this chapter in relation to the training of psychiatrists? We have first to point out that psychiatrists who are religious may run into conflict with patients who are not. In this respect we may need guidelines regarding possible conflict between psychiatrists' religious commitments and psychiatric practice as the APA published in 1977. A number of authors have made suggestions regarding: training (Sims 1994); diagnosis and treatment of religious patients (Beit-Hallahmi 1975; Beit-Hallahmi and Argyle 1977; Bronner 1964; Greenberg 1987; Greenberg and Witztum 1991; Lovinger 1984; Lukoff *et al.* 1992; Peteet 1981; Smith and Handelman 1990; Waldfolgel and Wolpe 1993; Witztum et al. 1990). Larson *et al.* (1988) have suggested collaborative consultations between mental health practitioners and pastoral counsellors and ministers. It may be that clergymen need to talk to doctors about religious issues and there may be a reciprocal dialogue with doctors teaching clergymen about mental illness issues. There should be cross-referrals such that clergymen may refer their clients to doctors and doctors may refer them to clergymen. In this respect I myself have been asked to teach on pastoral counselling programmes for clergymen. An attempt should be made to formulate a 'bio-psychosocial/spiritual' psychiatry (Peck 1992) where psychiatric trainees incorporate religious issues into their psychiatric practices.

ANTHROPOLOGY OF RELIGION

The study of religion is part of the staple diet of anthropologists, although there has been much debate as to the definition of religion (Klass 1995). The defining feature is often a belief in spiritual beings, although this is not the case for all systems which are traditionally called religious, e.g. Buddhism. I would prefer to use the term ultimate reality in place of spiritual beings, i.e. religion relates to a belief in ultimate reality. This ultimate reality is set apart from the mundane earthly reality and is treated as 'sacred'. Religious rites allow a person to enter this sacred reality and for a time to transform their mundane existence and to transcend their earthly troubles. This ultimate reality is seen as perfect, moral and eternal.

Ritual is characteristic of all religious systems. Again, there is debate over its definition, although most anthropologists agree that it is a form of repetitive behaviour that does not have direct instrumental effect and often has an element of symbolic communication. It often communicates a culture's key values. Rituals can be divided up into three types: calendrical rituals, rites of passage and rituals of misfortune.

Calendrical rituals celebrate changes in the cosmic cycle linking worldly events to events in the cosmic cycle. Examples include harvest festivals such as the Passover in the Jewish tradition. This is not just a commemoration but a symbolic re-enactment of the Jewish Exodus from Egypt. It is associated with a celebration meal and prayer.

In many societies changes in the life cycle such as pregnancy, birth, menarche, weddings and funerals are highly ritualized. Van Gennep (1965), who coined the term rites of passage, argued that these ceremonies consist of three phases: separation, transition and incorporation. During the transition phase the person is considered to be in a highly ambiguous state and may be seen as polluted or dangerous and in need of measures to protect them. For instance, a woman in labour is considered a danger to others due to pollution. She is in the transitional state between pregnancy and being a mother.

At times of misfortune ritual may be used both as a form of diagnosis and of treatment, especially of illness. In many societies sickness is presumed to be caused by a breach of a taboo and may be remedied by a ritualized offering to the gods which may involve sacrifice. Among the Merina of Madagascar misfortune is attributed to breach of the taboo resulting in the displeasure of the ancestors. It is because of them that misfortune occurs and to redress this a ritual is held whereby a bull is sacrificed and prayers are offered to the ancestors. (Bloch 1992).

Although many functions have been attributed to ritual, such as the control of the unknown and the restoration of group cohesion, I would argue that what all rituals do is to reorder ordinary experience and put the participant in touch with the sacred reality. His or her experience of the world is transformed. A well-known example of ritual in western culture is that of the Holy Communion. In the mid-1960s the Christian ecumenical council in Rome reaffirmed the significance of the Eucharist (Holy Communion).

The Eucharist – a Greek word for thanksgiving – is associated with the 'breaking of bread' and is a memorial ritual to recall the Hebrew Passover and the Last Supper. It also embraces the notion of sacrifice – the loss of one's life for a cause is considered as the supreme sacrifice. Christians do not simply remember but experience the living Christ. The bread and wine in the Eucharist ceremony convey the presence of Christ (Abbott 1966):

> The renewal in the Eucharist of the Covenant between the Lord and man draws the faithful into the compelling love of Christ and sets them afire. From the liturgy, therefore, and especially from the Eucharist, as from a fountain, grace is channelled into us and the sanctification (that is, making holy) of men in Christ and the glorification of God, to which all the activities of the church are directed as towards their goal, and most powerfully achieved. (Abbott 1966, p.207)

During Holy Communion participants are born anew by breaking the bread or the wafer. The priest does not simply remember the last supper of Jesus or express his good wishes, rather he symbolically repeats an action that began with God's action through which people will be transformed. During Mass the participant becomes part of Christ's sacrifice.

REFERENCES

Abbott, W. (ed.) (1966) *Documents of Vatican II*. Trans. J. Gallagher. New York: Guilford Press, p.143.

APA Task Force (1975) *Psychiatrists' Viewpoints on Religion and their Services to Religious Institutions and the Ministry*. Washington DC: American Psychiatric Association.

Barnhouse, R.T. (1986) 'How to evaluate patients' religious ideation.' In L. Robinson (ed.) *Psychiatry and Religion: Overlapping Concerns*. Washington DC: American Psychiatric Press.

Beit-Hallahmi, B. (1975) 'Encountering orthodox religion in psychotherapy.' *Psychotherapy: Theory, Research and Practice 12*, 357–359.

Beit-Hallahmi, B. and Argyle, M. (1977) 'Religious ideas and psychiatric disorders.' *International Journal of Social Psychiatry 23*, 26–30.

Batson, C.D., Schoenrade, P. and Ventis, W.L. (1993) *Religion and the Individual. A Social–Psychological Perspective*. New York: Oxford University Press.

Bergin, A.E. (1983) 'Religiosity and mental health: a critical re-evaluation and meta-analysis.' *Professional Psychology: Research and Practice 14*, 2, 170–184.

Bergin, A.E. and Jensen, J. (1990) 'Religiosity of psychotherapists: a national survey.' *Psychotherapy 27*.

Bloch, M. (1992) *From Prey into Hunter: The Politics of Religious Experience*. Cambridge; Cambridge University Press.

Brody, E.B. (1990) 'The new biological determinism in sociocultural context.' *Australian Journal of Psychiatry 24*, 464–469.

Bronner, A. (1964) 'Psychotherapy with religious patients: review of literature.' *American Journal of Psychotherapy 18*, 475–487.

Brown, L.B. (1994) *Religion, Personality and Mental Health*. New York: Springer-Verlag.

Dein, S. (1996) 'Religion and mental health.' *British Medical Anthropology Review 3*, 2, 40–49.

Dein, S. and Stygal, J. (1997) 'Does being religious help or hinder coping with chronic illness: a critical literature review.' *Palliative Medicine 11* 291–298.

Freud, S. (1966) 'Obsessive actions and religious practices.' In J. Strachey (ed. and trans.) *The Standard Edition of the Complete Psychological Works of Sigmund Freud*, vol. 1. London: Hogarth Press.

Gallup, G. (1985) 'Fifty years of Gallup surveys on religion.' *The Gallup Threshold of Death*. Gallup Pole Report No: 236. Princeton: Gallup Organization Review of Religious Research.

Greenberg, D. (1987) 'The behavioural treatment of religious compulsions.' *Journal of Psychology and Judaism 11*, 41–47.

Greenberg, D. and Witztum, E. (1991) 'Problems in the treatment of religious patients.' *American Journal of Psychotherapy 45*, 554–565.

Hood, R.W. (1976) 'Conceptual criticisms of regressive explanations of mysticism.' *Review of Religious Research 17*, 179–188.

James, W. (1961) *The Varieties of Religious Experience*. New York: Macmillan.

Jung, C.G. (1973) *Psychology and Religion.* Princeton NJ: Princeton University Press.

King, M. and Dein, S. (1999) 'The spiritual variable in psychiatry.' *Psychological Medicine 28,* 1259–1262.

Klass, M. (1995) *Ordered Universes – Approaches to the Anthropology of Religion.* Boulder: Westview Press.

Kroll, J. and Sheehan, W. (1981) 'Religious beliefs and practices among 52 psychiatric inpatients in Minnesota.' *American Journal of Psychiatry 146,* 67–72.

Larson, D.B. (1986) 'Systematic analysis of research on religious variables in four major psychiatric journals 1978–1982.' *American Journal of Psychiatry 143,* 329–334.

Larson, D.B. and Larson, S.S. (1991) 'Religious commitment and health.' *Second Opinion,* 27–40.

Larson, D.B. *et al.* (1988) 'The couch and the cloth: the need for linkage.' *Hospital and Community Psychiatry 39,* 1064–1069.

Littlewood, R. and Dein, S. (1995) 'The effectiveness of words: religion and healing among the Lubavitch of Stamford Hill.' *Culture Medicine and Psychiatry 19,* 339–383.

Lovinger, R.J. (1984) *Working with Religious Issues in Therapy.* New York: Jason Aronson.

Lukoff, D. and Turner, R. (1992) 'Toward a more culturally sensitive DSM-IV: psychoreligious and psychospiritual problems.' *Journal of Nervous and Mental Disease 180,* 673–682.

Neelman, J. and Lewis, G. (1994) 'Religious identity and comfort beliefs in three groups of psychiatric patients and a group of medical controls.' *International Journal of Social Psychiatry 40,* 2, 124–134.

Neelman, J. and Persaud, R. (1995) 'Why do psychiatrists neglect religion?' *British Journal of Medical Psychology 68,* 169–178.

Peck, M.S. (1992) 'Biopsychosocialspiritual psychiatry: what is psychiatry to do about spirituality?' Paper presented at 148th Annual Meeting, American Psychiatric Association, Washington DC, May.

Peteet, J.R. (1981) 'Issues in the treatment of religious patients.' *American Journal of Psychotherapy 35,* 559–564.

Ring, K. (1984) *Heading Toward Omega: In Search of Meaning of the Near-Death Experience.* New York: William Morrow.

Rubenstein, G. (1994) 'Political attitudes and religiosity levels of Israeli psychotherapy practitioners and students.' *American Journal of Psychotherapy 48,* 441–454.

Shafranske, E. and Malony, H.N. (1990) 'Clinical psychologists' religious and spiritual orientations and their practice of psychotherapy.' *Psychotherapy 27,* 72–78.

Sims, A. (1994) '"Psyche" – spirit as well as mind?' *British Journal of Psychiatry 165,* 441–446.

Smith, J.H. and Handelman, S.A. (1990) *The Psychology of Religion: An Empirical Approach.* Englewood NJ: Prentice Hall.

Spanos, N.P. and Moretti, P. (1988) 'Correlates of mystical and diabolical experiences in a sample of female university students.' *Journal of the Scientific Study of Religion 27*, 105–116.

Spero, M.H. (1986) *Handbook of Psychotherapy and Jewish Ethics.* New York: Feldheim.

Spero, M.H. (1987) 'Identity and individuality in the nouveau-religious patient. Theoretical and clinical aspects.' *Psychiatry 50*, 55–71.

Spilka, B., Spangler, J.D. and Nelson, C.B. (1983) 'Spiritual support in life threatening illness.' *Journal of Religion and Health 22*, 98–104.

Spilka, B., Shaver, P. and Kilpatrick, L.A. (1985) 'A general attribution theory for the psychology of religion.' *Journal of the Scientific Study of Religion 22*, 43–49.

Van Gennep, A. (1908/1965) *The Rites of Passage.* London: Routledge and Kegan Paul.

Waldfogel, S. and Wolpe, P.R. (1993) 'Using awareness of religious factors to enhance interventions in consultation-liaison psychiatry.' *Hospital and Community Psychiatry 44*, 473–477.

Witter, R.A., Stock, W.A. and Okun, M.A. (1985) 'Religion and subjective well-being in adulthood: a quantitative synthesis.' *Review of Religious Research 26*, 332–341.

Witztum, E. and Greenberg, D. (1990) '"A very narrow bridge": diagnosis and management of mental illness among Bratslav Hasidim.' *Psychotherapy 27*, 124–131.

Young, J.L. and Griffin, E.E. (1989) 'The development and practice of pastoral counselling.' *Hospital Community Psychiatry 40*, 271–276.

8

Establishing Cultural Competency for Mental Health Professionals

Maureen H. Fitzgerald

Establishing cultural competency among health professionals is about more than developing an awareness that culture is an issue in health, illness and health care. It is about more than recognizing oneself and others as cultural beings. It is about developing the ability to identify and challenge one's cultural assumptions, one's values and beliefs. It is about developing empathy and 'connected knowledge' (Belenky *et al.* 1986), the ability to see the world through another's eyes or, at the very least, to recognize that others may view the world through different cultural lenses. It is about the ability to analyse and respond to the 'cultural scenes' (Spradley and McCurdy 1972) and 'social dramas' (Turner 1974) of everyday life in ways that are culturally and psychologically meaningful for all the people involved – client and health professional alike. It is about becoming critical and reflective thinkers (Dewey 1933; Kitchener and King 1990) and the ability to turn such thinking into praxis. It is about providing meaningful, satisfying and competent care.

Although many address cultural issues in professional practice or the understanding of social dramas in terms of conflict and crisis and problem situations, cultural competency is more about avoiding problems and crisis situations. It is about making 'sense out of experience, to give it form and order' (Geertz 1973, p.140). It is about understanding 'how people define situations and how they go about coming to terms with them' (Geertz 1973, p.141). It is about developing the ability to 'see' a situation from multiple perspectives and, if necessary, to reconcile them. It is about developing multiple potential interpretations and using critical reflective thinking to choose which alternatives are most likely to provide effective strategies for care. It is about using such understandings to become more competent and effective professionals.

This chapter explores some concepts and approaches that can be used to develop a more culturally competent mental health workforce. These have been refined within the context of the Intercultural Interaction Project at the University of Sydney.[1] As this chapter uses the concept of cultural competency in a particular way, I begin by exploring it in more detail.

CULTURAL COMPETENCY

The term cultural competency first made a serious appearance in relation to health professionals in the 1980s in an American Psychological Association commissioned position paper by Sue *et al.* (1982). The term became ubiquitous in the health professional literature in the 1990s. Elsewhere I have suggested that this term became popular for at least two reasons:

> First, it came into use to fit with a cultural movement towards something called 'workplace competencies'. It was an attempt to put this aspect of practice into a conceptual framework that was consistent with other ways of talking about good professional practice. Second, and perhaps more importantly, I think it came into use because of the problems with the concepts of 'cultural sensitivity' and 'culturally relevant', the terms of the 1980s…I think the concept of cultural competency came into use as a way to encompass these two concepts, to make clear that the two must be intimately intertwined. (Fitzgerald 1996, p.1)

The concept of cultural competency can be considered from at least three different, but related, perspectives: culture specific, intercultural, or culture general (e.g. Kim 1991; Lustig and Koester 1996). This chapter focuses on culture general competency as it is more compatible with the way competency is currently being used in the workplace or professional competency approach to the education and evaluation of health professionals. Thus, cultural competency in this sense is not about developing culture specific competency, although it may contribute to this type of competency, and it is not only about intercultural competency, although it may contribute to it as well.

Culture specific competency

Culture specific competency relates to the ability to 'participate in the everyday web of social relationships, even if at a limited or reduced level' (Marshall 1996, p.250), of a particular social group. It means possessing a 'social intelligence inside' and being able to express or communicate that intelligence in meaningful ways (Marshall 1996, p.252). It means having sufficient cultural knowledge, reasonable 'mental blueprints for culturally appropriate behavior' (Clement 1982, p.195) to 'pass' (Goffman 1959, 1963) as an insider, as a real or fictive member, of a particular cultural group. In this sense of the term, cultural competency is more in line with the way it is used in ethnoscience and, therefore, 'culturally patterned behaviour and artifacts are but epiphenomena of this competence' (Clement 1982, p.194).

To have insufficient cultural knowledge or to be unable to express that one possesses such knowledge is to be culturally incompetent and situates the person as an outsider, an impaired or disabled person, or even as a non-person (e.g. Armstrong and Fitzgerald 1996; Fitzgerald and Armstrong 1993; Ingstad and Whyte 1995; Marsella and White 1982–4; Marshall 1996). To be viewed as culturally incompetent, or even to believe that one is viewed as culturally incompetent (Fitzgerald 1995; Fitzgerald and Paterson 1995), can have a profound effect on a person's concept of self and their behaviour. In mental health, culture specific competency is more often related to evaluations of a person's mental status, by oneself or others, to determine whether or not a person is mentally ill or incompetent.

This type of cultural competency involves an extensive period of socialization. Few health professionals have the time, opportunity or skills to develop this kind of cultural competency in more than one or two cultures. Furthermore, few health professionals work in monocultural or bicultural settings. Most health professionals need to be able to work with people from very diverse cultures and they must be able to work with the diversity within each cultural group. Therefore, a focus on culture specific training or competency has limited utility in most modern health-care contexts.

This does not mean that culture specific information is unimportant, but possessing bits and pieces of decontextualized knowledge of the kind clinicians and students often request (information on 'beliefs and practices', diet, holidays, and so on) rarely leads to culturally competent care. This 'cookbook' approach often leads to culturally incompetent behaviour, stereotyping and inflexible approaches to care. Such requests demonstrate a lack of understanding of the concept of culture or, at best, a simplistic materialist concept (e.g. Avruch and Black 1991, 1993; Fitzgerald and Mullavey-O'Byrne 1995, 1996; Fitzgerald et al. 1997b). In fact, requests for information of the 'cookbook' variety can be viewed as evidence of a fairly low level of culture general competency.

Perhaps more important, this 'cookbook' approach to social interactions and the provision of services leads to specific expectations. When these expectations are not realized, these 'disconfirmed expectancies' (Brislin et al. 1986; Fitzgerald et al. 1997b; Mullavey-O'Byrne 1994) can lead to a sense of cultural dissonance and dissatisfaction and a lack of ability to deconstruct or interpret the situation in a way that leads to satisfying solutions and strategies for care. Disconfirmed expectancies are often the foundation for the kind of 'critical incidents' (see below) professionals share with us in interviews associated with the Intercultural Interaction Project and the kinds of critical incidents we use in our training programmes.

Intercultural competency

The concept of intercultural competency is widely used in the culture and communication and the multicultural or transcultural counselling literature. It was developed to address issues associated with the growing awareness that most health professionals work in multicultural settings where they often interact with people from cultures which are distinctively different from their own. It addressed the need for an awareness of and sensitivity to cultural differences. When the term cultural competency is used in the health professional literature, the author generally means intercultural competency. Intercultural competency is essentially the same as culture general competency, but it emphasizes working across cultures rather than treating all health professional interactions as cultural, even multicultural (Fitzgerald 1992). In culture general competency the principles, knowledge, skills, etc. associated with intercultural competency are treated as applicable to all interactions, whether or not there are obvious cultural differences. With the growing recognition that culture influences all aspects of health, illness, and health care, and that all people are cultural beings, culture general competency appears a more appropriate term; one that might help people move away from an 'us and them' mentality.

CULTURE GENERAL COMPETENCY

Culture general competency is more of a context-bound, practice-based awareness, knowledge, attitude and skills concept (e.g. Cope *et al.* 1997). The culture general competent professional does not assume (or simulate) another cultural identity, but performs in a way that indicates the professional recognizes and values cultural differences and the potential implications of culture (as a general concept) on everyone's illness and clinical experiences at both the macro and micro level. The person demonstrates the ability to use a range of knowledge and skills (especially communication and problem-solving skills) to understand and address cultural issues in practice in a way that results in an outcome that is satisfying (or at least acceptable) to everyone involved.

Culture general competency is about the ability to function in the ambiguous, dynamic, open-ended interactions common to therapy situations for which no adequate cultural blueprint exists; and to do so with a reasonable level of comfort. It is about being able to understand and interpret these events, whether or not they involve people from 'different' cultures, as 'cultural scenes' (Spradley and McCurdy 1972) or 'social dramas' (Turner

1974), and to do so from multiple perspectives. There is a recognition that culture influences everyone's perceptions, interpretations and evaluations of the situation. Then, if some action is necessary, they act in an informed, culturally and psychologically sensitive, appropriate, non-judgemental, meaningful way. Furthermore, culturally competent professionals demonstrate that they can use their analyses and analyses of the results of any action taken to develop flexible adaptive strategies that allow them more effectively to respond to similar situations in the future.

Borrowing from Geertz (1973), these people demonstrate they can use cultural knowledge, cultural resources and reflective thought or directive reasoning to make sense of, to interpret, their experiences and the experiences of others. They can identify the relevant features of the situation to give it meaning and form. In other words, they can use their knowledge and skills to transform both common and perplexing situations into ones that make sense, into ones that are clear, coherent and harmonious (Geertz 1973). Culturally competent people try to achieve something more in line with Geertz's (1973) 'thick description', they try to develop an understanding of content and context (or structure), at both the micro and macro level, and use it as a basis for action.

Reflective judgement and cultural competency

Reflective thinking leading to reflective judgement appears to be an important aspect of culture competency; in fact, it may be more critical than some other aspects, like possessing specific knowledge or having a particular kind of attitude towards specific groups of people. Based on the work of Dewey (1933), Kitchener and King (1990, p.160) define a reflective thinker:

> As someone who is aware that a problematic situation exists and is able to bring critical judgement to bear on the problem...a reflective thinker understands that there is real uncertainty about how a problem may best be solved, yet is still able to offer judgement about the problem that brings some kind of closure to it. This judgement...is based on criteria such as evaluation of evidence, consideration of expert opinion, adequacy of argument, and implications of the proposed solution.

Brookfield (1990) notes that the critical reflective thinker can:

- identify the assumptions that underlie his or her thoughts and actions;
- evaluate the accuracy and validity of these assumptions;
- as necessary, reconstitute these assumptions.

In other words, they can use the kinds of critical reflective analytical processes anthropologists use to make sense of cultural scenes and social dramas and apply these processes to the events in their everyday life in a beneficial way.

Kitchener and King (1990, p.160) suggest that 'the ability to make reflective judgements is an outcome of a developmental sequence' affected by age, experience and education. Belenky *et al.* (1986) also consider gender as a factor. Reflective thinking and the development of reflective judgement build on previous knowledge and experiences, but do so in an analytically critical way. Therefore, the level of expectation at the undergraduate level is not as high compared to that of more mature health professionals. Kitchener and colleagues have suggested seven developmental stages for reflective judgement. People at the lowest levels believe knowledge is certain and absolute and beliefs are based on personal uncritical observation. Moving across the stages beliefs about knowledge move from knowledge is certain to knowledge is uncertain to knowledge is relative but some interpretations have greater 'truth' than others. At each stage different strategies for obtaining and evaluating information are involved. There is a transition from a reliance on personal observation and experience to a reliance on 'experts' where expert information is accepted as 'truth' to a broad range of enquiry and information accumulation strategies where the information is critically assessed in terms of its validity and usefulness.

Although their work is based on western, reasonably well educated populations, Kitchener and King's (1990) reflective judgement model has some utility for understanding cultural competency. There appear to be important similarities in the developmental processes associated with both; in fact, the two appear to be intimately related (see below and Edwards 1999). At each level there are epistemological assumptions about the nature of knowledge and the ability and willingness to engage in information evaluation, enquiry and analytical processes, including the evaluation and analysis of profession specific knowledge. In terms of cultural competency these equate with ethnocentrism at the lowest level to cultural awareness to cultural particularism to increasing degrees of cultural competency. This developmental sequence should be considered in developing programmes to enhance cultural competency as the same learning strategy can have a very different effect at different levels.

Finding ways to establish or enhance cultural competency in health professionals, helping them progressively to move to higher levels, presents interesting challenges. Many cultural competency programmes can be personally and professionally confronting. They challenge people's concepts of self and their core personal and professional cultural values. If people do not feel culturally and psychologically 'safe', challenged but safe, such programmes can lead to more firmly entrenched ethnocentrism and cultural stereotypes. Equally disastrous, they can lead to avoiding situations where culture is obviously an issue and missing the cultural issues in situations where culture is not marked.

In our work, my colleagues and I have developed several approaches to enhancing cultural competency and reflective thinking among both student and graduate health professionals. One strategy revolves around analyses of critical incidents as reported by health professionals and clients and their families. Another involves participation in research projects addressing cultural issues relevant to professional practice. In some cases, we combine these two approaches and address both content and process issues. The examples presented below both revolve around critical incidents so I begin by introducing critical incidents as we use the concept.

CRITICAL INCIDENTS

Using an adaptation of Brislin's (Brislin *et al.* 1986; Brislin and Yoshida 1994) critical incident concept, critical incidents can be defined as distinct occurrences or events which involve two or more people; they are neither inherently negative nor positive, they are merely distinct occurrences or events which require some attention, action or explanation; they are sit-uations for which there is a need to attach meaning (Fitzgerald *et al.* 1997a, 1997b; Fitzgerald and Paterson 1995; Mullavey-O'Byrne and Fitzgerald 1995). Critical incidents are 'social dramas' (Turner 1974) and can be viewed as 'units of aharmonic or disharmonic process' (Turner 1974, p.37). Like Turner for social dramas, Sue and Sue (1990, p.245) suggest critical incidents represent 'an area of *conflict* of cultures, values, standards, or goals', but they do not necessarily arise out of conflict situations. In our work, the conflict, if this is the appropriate term, is more often associated with 'disconfirmed expectancies' (Brislin *et al.* 1986; Fitzgerald *et al.* 1997b; Mullavey-O'Byrne 1994): the event or social drama did not 'play out' in quite the way the respondent or narrator anticipated. It may have had a result viewed as negative; one that may have evoked a disquieting state of emotional arousal (e.g. frustration, anxiety, a sense of having lost control). However, just as often, the result was viewed as positive − there was a better than expected result. In both cases there is a need for explanation, a need to attach meaning. Often it seems people tell a particular story as a way better to understand an event in their lives.

The critical incident approach is, to a large degree, based on the idea that we communicate, try to understand, problem solve and often teach using stories or narratives (Brody 1987). We use narratives to give coherence and meaning to distinctive events. 'The plot lines, core metaphors, and rhetorical devices that structure...narrative are drawn from cultural and personal models for arranging in meaningful ways and for effectively communicating those meanings' (Kleinman 1988, p.49). Furthermore, as Kleinman and others point out, narratives can 'shape and even create experience' (Kleinman 1988, p.49). We construct and reconstruct our human experiences when we relive them through narrative. We can use this reconstruction process to help people develop alternative narratives and alternative meanings for critical incidents, to help people see the incident through different lenses.

THE CRITICAL INCIDENT APPROACH
TO CULTURAL COMPETENCY

Critical incidents are commonly used in cultural competency training (e.g. Brislin *et al.* 1986; Sue and Sue 1990) to foster critical thinking and transformative learning (Brookfield 1990; Edwards 1999). Transformative learning or perspective transformation is a process that involves the use of reflective thinking to challenge, evaluate and, if necessary, reform people's assumptions, values, beliefs and perspectives on the world (Cranton 1994; Mezirow 1990). The goal is to understand and, if necessary, construct new or alternative cognitive schema that are more effective and satisfying.

The critical incident approach to cultural competency can take on several forms: all involve critical analysis, interpretation and the development of strategies for action. The most common approach is the analysis of specific incidents. Another is to use the ethnographic interview process to collect information on critical incidents where both the process of collecting the information and the reported incident become the focus of analysis. The first approach focuses on content; the second can be used to address process, structure and content; both are designed to promote reflective thinking and the development of reflective judgement.

Critical incidents as triggers to promote reflective thinking

Critical incidents, as training tools, are presented as a form of narrative; thus, although the structure is similar to that of other narratives, there are differences (Fitzgerald *et al.* 1995, p.28). Both begin with a brief introduction to 'situate the set of events in time, place, and context', introduce the primary characters and establish a storyline. The introduction provides essential information and captures interest. In a standard story, narrative, or social drama the action follows a logical sequence that builds to a climax or high point, which is then resolved (e.g. Turner 1974). In critical incidents there are often issues embedded in issues and the storyline does not necessarily follow a smooth logical sequence. The issue, incongruity or conflict is not resolved or the resolution is less than satisfactory or not well understood. Critical incidents can be presented as either narratives with alternative endings or, as we do, as narratives without endings (Fitzgerald *et al.* 1995). Either way they are intentionally left more 'open' so each person has to use their knowledge and skills to interpret the information and reach their own conclusions, along the lines of that suggested by Burke (1991) for the 'new' narrative history.

To be effective, critical incidents need to be relevant to the people involved. They should involve familiar people and situations. Some programmes use hypothetical incidents designed to emphasize a particular point or issue. We use actual events as told to us by one or more of the people involved. We do not simplify the narratives, but present them with all their complexity so they reflect the complexity of real life events. Thus, we try to maintain the 'integrity' of the original, although we may remove some of 'the normal digressions common to everyday discourse' (Fitzgerald et al. 1995, p.28) and add essential contextual information not embedded in the narrative. As a result, these incidents have validity in the sense that they 'ring true' to others, both in terms of the incident and in the telling. Obviously, as Geertz (1973, 1983) notes, this process involves some interpretation so the final product is on the order of a second or third level of interpretation. As a result, we have inevitably reconstructed the event to some extent, but our aim is to maintain integrity from the narrator's point of view and still present a smooth, coherent, stand-alone story.

The analysis of personally experienced critical incidents can also be used (e.g. Brookfield 1990). My experiences suggest this approach should be used with caution early in training and with those at the early stages of reflective judgement or cultural competency, and should probably only be used by a facilitator with good counselling skills. Early on it is better to use incidents to which people can relate, but where there is no personal investment. As noted earlier, such training must take place in a culturally and psychologically safe environment or it may encourage exactly the opposite of what is intended.

Critical incidents can be presented using various media, for example, print, video and verbal narration, storytelling or performance. The most effective approach involves using several media (even within a single session), as each appears to address different learning needs. For example, in a recent study by Edwards (1999) print appeared to be more effective for developing cognitive empathy and video affective empathy. Edwards' study suggests that some media may be more appropriate at particular levels of competency or for particular purposes.

The usual approach is to present a critical incident followed by guided discussion. Allowing people initially to discuss the incident in small groups (3–5 people) is generally more effective than beginning with large group discussions. Once people have become comfortable with the analytical process, and if they feel culturally and psychologically safe, larger group discussions can be effective. Whether in small or large groups, the facilitator needs to facilitate and guide the discussion by asking critical questions or providing information or means of obtaining additional relevant information.[2]

The purpose of the guided discussion, which may or may not involve a set of structured questions, is to assist movement from superficial or thin description (quick and easy, often stereotypical answers) to interpretation or thick description that allows the identification of multiple explanations for the event as it occurred. This involves consideration of all the information provided and determination of what is or is not important for the analysis. 'These potential explanations undergo further analyses and exploration to determine whether or not they are reasonable. Unreasonable explanations or interpretations are rejected with explanation, reasonable explanations provide the foundation for developing strategies for action' (Fitzgerald *et al.* 1995, p.29). This guided, analytical discussion is important. If learners are not pushed to engage in deep reflective thinking, to look for alternative explanations and critically evaluate them, to identify strategies that would help them interpret the situation, there is a risk that the sessions will reinforce cultural stereotypes or superficial analyses.

Finally, especially with experienced professionals and those who personally relate to the incident, there is a need to 'debrief', to resolve any personal issues and to be sure they have moved from sympathetic responses to empathic ones. Obviously, such programmes require culturally competent and skilled facilitators.

CRITICAL INCIDENT RESEARCH PROCESS TO PROMOTE REFLECTIVE THINKING

Analyses of print and video critical incidents are commonly used in cultural competency workshops and as classroom exercises. With this approach, research as a form of enquiry learning is introduced as a way to obtain and evaluate the evidence needed critically to analyse and interpret the critical incidents and design and evaluate strategies for action.

A more explicit collaborative enquiry, experiential, research approach can also be incorporated into cultural competency programmes to enhance learning (Mullavey-O'Byrne and Fitzgerald 1994). This approach involves participatory research (De Koning and Martin 1996; Graves 1992; Van Willigen 1986; Whyte 1991) as the basis for transformative learning and the development of reflective thinking. The experiential learning approach, again based on the work of Dewey, is designed more fully to engage people in the learning process, to help them learn how to examine and process information, to help them develop their reflective thinking skills and reflective judgement. In this approach, participants, as a group, identify a cultural issue they would like to explore in more depth. They collect the necessary data, generally through critical incident-focused ethnographic interviews, and analyse both the data collection process and the data. Project development and data and process analyses involve guided reflective discussions.

In these projects critical incidents are generally the focus of data collection. The interviews involve either the request for respondents to talk about a situation (a critical incident) in which their thought culture was an issue and/or they are asked to talk about a previously developed critical incident. In this approach, each participant conducts at least one interview and analyses it from both a process and content perspective. These analyses are then shared with and re-analysed by the group (for a more detailed description of this process see Fitzgerald *et al.* 1996). In other words, the process used to analyse critical incidents is also used to analyse aspects of the interview itself.

Reflective judgement and cultural competency revisited

Responses to critical incidents and the process of collecting and analysing them provide insights into the relationship between the development of reflective judgement and cultural competency. In these responses we can see evidence of Kitchener and King's reflective judgement developmental stages and the need to consider them in designing programmes to promote cultural competency. A critical incident from a subject where the participatory research process was a primary focus is particularly informative in this regard (see also Fitzgerald *et al.* 1996, p.110).

This incident occurred during the interview content discussion, one of the last sessions of the subject. A student reported that her respondent related an incident in which the husband had been accused of abusing his wife. This student, and most of her classmates, would not or could not accept that there might be alternative explanations for this situation; for example, that there may have been a misunderstanding on the part of the health professionals involved or that it might even have been a false accusation.[3] An 'expert' had accused the man of abuse, abusive behaviour is always wrong and abuse is against the law; therefore, he must be treated as an abuser. End of story.

When the students were encouraged to apply the analytical process they had been using for other incidents, even if this generated only hypothetical interpretations, many refused to consider alternative explanations. They refused to consider the idea that further investigation into the situation from both the husband and wife's perspective (preferably with an interpreter) should take place before there was any further action. They refused to accept the possibility that even if the situation met contemporary, local criteria for abuse that the husband (and possibly his wife and others in the community) might not share that view, or even that members of their own cultural group might have defined the behaviour differently in the past. Such ideas were considered irrelevant. This was now and this was Australia. It does not matter what might be considered 'OK' elsewhere, if people want to live in Australia they have to live by the rules in Australia.

Similar incidents often arise on this subject and in workshops with graduate health professionals. These incidents always evoke emotional, affective responses in both students and health professionals. However, most students and health professionals recognize that they need more evidence than an accusation before they decide how to respond. They recognize that others might interpret the event in different ways and there is a need to understand and reconcile any other interpretations before they act. They are also often willing to consider the consequences of acting on a false accusation.

This subject is normally an elective, but in this particular year the majority of students were assigned to 'electives' so many did not really want to be in this subject. However, this does not really explain the students' reaction. There was a qualitative difference between this group and those from other years. Upon reflection, for the most part the students in this particular group appeared to be at lower stages of reflective judgement and cultural competency than in other years. Initially they appeared not only less willing, but less able, to engage in critical, reflective thinking. Even at the end of the subject, fewer were willing to consider alternative interpretations for some critical incidents. Although there were notable exceptions, many continued to exhibit absolutist, dualistic thinking of the kind Kitchener and King associate with Stage Two or perhaps Stage Three reflective judgement; stages they suggest are consistent with high school or first year undergraduate students (Bruning, Schraw and Ronning 1995; Kitchener and King 1990). In other years the majority of the students, and the exceptional students in this year, more often responded in ways more consistent with Stage Four and, in some cases, Stage Five. Kitchener and King suggest that Stage Four reasoning is commonly found among final year undergraduate students with Stage Five being more typical of graduate students. Students at the higher levels are often honours students, mature age students, or those with some strong personal motivation for studying cultural issues (e.g. students from migrant backgrounds or those who had fieldwork experiences in culturally complex environments).

Edwards' (1999) analyses of first and fourth year occupational therapy students' responses to print and video critical incidents suggest that the responses of the first year students in her study were consistent with Stage Three with the fourth year students' responses consistent with Stage Four. In my work with health professionals from a variety of disciplines, the responses to critical incidents range from those consistent with Stage Three to those consistent with Stage Six, with most between Stages Four and Five. Higher stage responses appear more common among experienced health professionals with significant experience in multicultural mental health contexts. Again, this is consistent with the work of Kitchener and King.

These findings suggest that, like reflective judgement, cultural competency is very likely age, education and experience related. However, none of these, even in combination, appear sufficient (e.g. Fitzgerald *et al.* 1997, 1997a, 1997b; Pope-Davis, Eliason and Ottavi 1994; Pope-Davis *et al.* 1993; Robison 1996). There is probably also a motivational aspect that involves a willingness to experience and deal with uncertainty in one's interactions (Lustig and Koester 1996). Robison (1996) suggests that people who exhibit cultural competency have a combination of something he calls a 'cultural attitude' and compassion. An emphasis on attitudes can be seen throughout the cultural competency literature.

This material also suggests that programmes to encourage the development of cultural competency must take all of these factors into consideration. People in early stages of cultural competency often require greater guidance and more structured exercises. At every stage, they need to engage in activities that are stimulating and actively encourage reflection thinking.

CONCLUSION

Cultural competency is then a complex concept involving knowledge, attitudes, behaviours, in particular the application of communication and interaction skills, and a way of being with the world and the people around us. Thus, establishing or enhancing this competency must address all of these aspects. No one strategy, even the critical incident approach, can address all of these aspects, although some can address more than one. To some degree, like the anthropologist trying to understand another culture or the person trying to learn another language, one of the best approaches is to learn by immersion. But total immersion without prior cognitive and affective preparation and the knowledge and skills to deal with novel situations can be an emotionally distressful experience; one that can result in negative and unproductive reactions and outcomes. In this chapter I have suggested some approaches revolving around critical incidents that can be used to help people develop knowledge, skills and attitudes that can contribute to the development of culturally competent health professionals. The analysis of critical incidents and becoming involved in research programmes addressing cultural issues can contribute to developing cultural competency. They provide opportunities to do so in situations which are more culturally and psychologically 'safe'. If, however, the knowledge and skills acquired during such exercises cannot be transferred to practice then little has been accomplished. Therefore, there is a need for ongoing training, training based within professional practice. This includes addressing cultural issues (the obvious and the subtle) during client–patient evaluations, case conferences and professional supervision. It requires opportunities for professional reflection on one's professional practice and evaluations of that practice. As health professionals mature with age and experience, they are in a position to become more culturally competent and reflective thinkers, but age, education and experience are obviously not enough. We must also help professionals continuously to engage in high quality, well-designed professional development programmes, to help them regularly revisit culture and its consequences for them, their clients and patients.

Cultural competency is not just about being competent in situations in which culture is an obvious component. It is about being professionally competent and recognizing that culture is a component of all interactions and all health and illnesses situations. Our work with the Intercultural Interaction Project suggests that health professionals who are highly competent in general are often also reasonably culturally competent. These professionals have good interpersonal and communication skills; are good and highly reflective problem solvers; and show a true concern for the people with whom they work. They are resourceful and comfortable working in ambiguous situations because, first, they feel competent to deal with such situations and, second, it is the social dramas of everyday life that make their work exciting and challenging.

NOTES

1. For a detailed description of this project see, for example, Fitzgerald, Mullavey-O'Byrne and Clemson (1997) or Fitzgerald *et al.* (1997a). I am indebted to all the participants in the Intercultural Interaction Project, in particular Colleen Mullavey-O'Byrne, co-director of the Intercultural Interaction Project, and Margot Edwards, for their contributions to the ideas presented in this chapter.

2. The manual in the *Enhancing Cultural Competency Training Package* includes information on some of the key topics which are likely to arise during discussions of the videos in the package, references for further information and resource identification exercises for just this purpose.

3. The first scenario in the *Enhancing Cultural Competency* video depicts just such a situation. In the actual case upon which this scenario is based the husband was accused of abuse based on a misunderstanding, no abuse was involved.

REFERENCES

Armstrong, M.J. and Fitzgerald, M.H. (1996) 'Culture and disability studies: an anthropological perspective.' *Rehabilitation Education 10*, 247–304.

Avruch, K. and Black, P.W. (1991) 'The culture question and conflict resolution.' *Peace and Change 16*, 1, 22–45.

Avruch, K. and Black, P.W. (1993) 'Conflict resolution in intercultural settings: problems and prospects.' In D. Sandole and H. van der Merwe (eds) *Conflict Resolution Theory and Practice: Integration and Application.* Manchester: Manchester University Press, pp.131–145.

Belenky, M.F., Clinchy, B.M., Goldberg, N.R. and Tarule, J.M. (1986) *Women's Way of Knowing: The Development of Self, Voice, and Mind.* New York: Basic Books.

Brislin, R.W. and Yoshida, T. (1994) *Improving Intercultural Interactions: Modules for Cross-Cultural Training Programs.* Thousand Oaks CA: Sage.

Brislin, R.W., Cushner, K., Cherrie, C. and Yong, M. (1986) *Intercultural Interactions: A Practical Guide,* vol. 9. Newbury Park CA: Sage.

Brody, H. (1987) *Stories of Sickness.* New Haven: Yale University Press.

Brookfield, S. (1990) 'Using critical incidents to explore learner's assumptions.' In J. Merziow (ed) *Fostering Critical Reflection in Adulthood: A Guide to Transformative and Emancipatory Learning.* San Francisco: Jossey-Bass, pp.177–193.

Bruning, R.H., Schraw, G.J. and Ronning, R.R. (1995) *Cognitive Psychology and Instruction.* Englewood Cliffs NJ: Prentice Hall.

Burke, P. (1991) 'History of events and the revival of narrative.' In P. Burke (ed) *New Perspectives on Historical Writing.* Oxford: Blackwell, pp.233–248.

Clement, D.C. (1982) 'Samoan folk knowledge of mental disorders.' In A.J. Marsella and G.M. White (eds) *Cultural Conceptions of Mental Health and Therapy.* Dordrecht: Reidel, pp.193–213.

Cope, B., Kalantzis, M., Lo Bianco, J., Lohrey, A., Luke, A., Singh, M.G. and Solomon, N. (1997) *'Cultural understandings' as the Eighth Key Competency.* Sydney: Centre for Workplace Communication and Culture, Occasional Paper 11.

Cranton, P. (1994) *Understanding and Promoting Transformative Learning: A Guide for Educators of Adults.* San Francisco: Jossey-Bass.

De Koning, K. and Martin, M. (eds) (1996) *Participatory Research in Health: Issues and Experiences.* London: Zed Books.

Dewey, J. (1933) *How We Think.* Lexington MA: Heath.

Edwards, M. (1999). *Critical Incidents and Perspective Transformation: A Comparative Media Study.* Unpublished honours thesis. Sydney: University of Sydney.

Fitzgerald, M.H. (1992) 'Multicultural clinical interactions.' *Journal of Rehabilitation,* April/May/June, 1–5.

Fitzgerald, M.H. (1995) 'The Aussie battler: understanding hidden disability behaviour using cultural analogy.' In A. Davison, M.C. Dinh, M.H. Fitzgerald and J.M. Lingard (eds) *Current Topics in Health Science.* Lidcombe: University of Sydney, Faculty of Health Sciences, pp.35–36.

Fitzgerald, M.H. (1996) 'Cultural competency education and training: issues and needs.' Paper presented at the NSW Department of Health Mental Health Education and Training Strategic Planning Day, Sydney, 31 October.

Fitzgerald, M.H. and Armstrong, J. (eds) (1993) *Culture and Disability in the Pacific.* Durham NH: University of New Hampshire, World Rehabilitation Fund.

Fitzgerald, M.H. and Mullavey-O'Byrne, C. (1995) 'Intercultural interactions in rehabilitation.' In A. Davison, M.C. Dinh, M.H. Fitzgerald and J.M. Lingard (eds) *Current Topics in Health Science.* Lidcombe: University of Sydney, Faculty of Health Sciences, pp.37–38.

Fitzgerald, M.H. and Mullavey-O'Byrne, C. (1996) 'Analysis of student definitions of culture.' *Physical and Occupational Therapy in Geriatrics 14,* 1, 67–89.

Fitzgerald, M.H. and Paterson, K. (1995) 'The hidden disability dilemma for the preservation of self.' *Journal of Occupational Science, Australia 2,* 1, 13–21.

Fitzgerald, M.H., Mullavey-O'Byrne, C., Twible, R. and Kinebanian, A. (1995) *Exploring Cultural Diversity: A Workshop Manual for Occupational Therapists.* Sydney: School of Occupational Therapy, University of Sydney, Faculty of Health Sciences.

Fitzgerald, M.H., Mullavey-O'Byrne, C., Clemson, L. and Williamson, P. (1996) *Enhancing Cultural Competency.* Sydney: Transcultural Mental Health Centre.

Fitzgerald, M.H., Robison, S., Clemson, L. and Mullavey-O'Byrne, C. (1997) 'Cultural issues in physiotherapy practice.' (Unpublished manuscript) Sydney: University of Sydney.

Fitzgerald, M.H., Beltran, R., Pennock, J., Williamson, P. and Mullavey-O'Byrne, C. (1997a) *Occupational Therapy, Culture and Mental Health.* Sydney: Transcultural Mental Health Centre.

Fitzgerald, M.H., Mullavey-O'Byrne, C. and Clemson, L. (1997b) 'Cultural issues from practice.' *Australian Occupational Therapy Journal 44,* 1–21.

Geertz, C. (1973) *The Interpretation of Cultures.* New York: Basic Books.

Geertz, C. (1983) 'Thick description: toward an interpretive theory of culture.' In R.M. Emerson (ed) *Contemporary Field Research: A Collection of Readings.* Prospect Heights IL: Waveland Press, pp.37–59.

Goffman, E. (1959) *The Presentation of Self in Everyday Life.* New York: Anchor Books.

Goffman, E. (1963) *Stigma: Notes on the Management of Spoiled Identity.* New York: Simon and Schuster.

Graves, W.H. (1992) 'Participatory research: a partnership among individuals with disabilities, rehabilitation professionals, and rehabilitation researchers.' *Rehabilitation Education 6,* 221–224.

Ingstad, B. and Whyte, S.R. (eds) (1995) *Disability and Culture.* Berkeley: University of California Press.

Kim, Y.Y. (1991) 'Intercultural communication competence.' In S. Ting-Toomey and F. Korzenny (eds) *Cross-Cultural Interpersonal Communication.* Newbury Park CA: Sage, pp.259–275.

Kitchener, K.S. and King, P.M. (1990) 'The reflective judgement model: transforming assumptions about knowing.' In J. Merziow (ed) *Fostering Critical Reflection in Adulthood: A Guide to Transformative and Emancipatory Learning.* San Francisco: Jossey-Bass, pp.159–176.

Kleinman, A. (1988) *The Illness Narratives: Suffering, Healing, and the Human Condition.* New York: Basic Books.

Lustig, M.W. and Koester, J. (1996) *Intercultural Competency: Interpersonal Communication across Culture,* 2nd edn. New York: HarperCollins.

Marsella, A.J. and White, G.M. (eds) (1982–4) *Cultural Conceptions of Mental Health and Therapy.* Dordrecht: Reidel.

Marshall, M. (1996) 'Problematizing impairment: cultural competence in the Carolines.' *Ethnology 35,* 4, 249–263.

Mezirow, J. (ed) (1990) *Fostering Critical Reflection in Adulthood: A Guide to Transformative and Emancipatory Learning.* San Francisco: Jossey-Bass.

Mullavey-O'Byrne, C. (1994) 'Intercultural interactions in welfare work.' In R.W. Brislin and T. Yoshida (eds) *Improving Intercultural Interactions: Modules for Cross-Cultural Training Programs.* Thousand Oak CA: Sage, pp.197–220.

Mullavey-O'Byrne, C. and Fitzgerald, M. (1994) 'Personal development and training: compatibility or conflict?' *Australasian and New Zealand Association for Medical Education (ANZAME) Annual Conference: Compatibility and Conflict: Directions in Health Professional Education.* Newcastle NSW: ANZAME, pp.108–113.

Mullavey-O'Byrne, C. and Fitzgerald, M.H. (1995) 'Disconfirmed expectancies in intercultural interactions.' Paper presented at the Australian Association of Occupational Therapists, 18th Federal and Inaugural Pacific Rim Conference, Hobart, Tasmania, p.159.

Pope-Davis, D.B., Eliason, M. and Ottavi, T. (1994) 'Are nursing students culturally competent? An exploratory investigation.' *Journal of Nursing Education 33,* 1, 31–33.

Pope-Davis, D.B., Prieto, L.R., Whitaker, C.M. and Pope-Davis, S.A. (1993) 'Exploring multicultural competencies of occupational therapists: implications for education and training.' *American Journal of Occupational Therapy 47,* 9, 838–844.

Robison, S. (1996) 'Exposure and education: the impact on the cultural competency of physiotherapists.' Unpublished honours thesis, University of Sydney.

Spradley, J.P. (1979) *The Ethnographic Interview.* New York: Holt, Rinehart, Winston.

Spradley, J.P. and McCurdy, D.W. (1972) *The Cultural Experience: Ethnography in Complex Society.* Chicago: Science Research Associates.

Sue, D., Berbier, J., Durran, A., Feinberg, L., Pedersen, P., Smith, E. and Vasquez-Nuttall, E. (1982). 'Position paper: Cross-cultural counseling competencies.' *The Counseling Psychologist 10,* 45–52.

Sue, D.W. and Sue, D. (1990) *Counseling the Culturally Different: Theory and Practice,* 2nd edn. New York: Wiley.

Turner, V. (1974) *Dramas, Fields, and Metaphors: Symbolic Action in Human Society.* Ithaca: Cornell University Press.

Van Willigen, J. (1986) *Applied Anthropology: An Introduction.* South Hadley MA: Bergin and Garvey.

Whyte, W.F. (ed.) (1991) *Participatory Action Research.* Newbury Park CA: Sage.

9

Cambodian Concepts of Perinatal Mental Disorder

Relevance to Understanding Western Approaches to Perinatal Mental Health

Maurice Eisenbruch

Perinatal disorders of one or another sort have been described in many countries and cultures. The psychiatric evidence would suggest that, no matter which culture, the disorders form similar symptom groups, syndromes and disorders. Kumar (1994) has grouped the postnatal disorders into maternity blues, which do not appear to be related to cultural factors; postnatal depression, which does not seem to vary across cultures; and postpartum psychosis, which has had an unchanging incidence over the last 150 years and which, he argues, is primarily endogenous, in other words, something biologically orchestrated rather than simply a response to the social environment.

The experience and the *meaning* of perinatal disorders will be profoundly shaped by culture. Ethnographic studies can illuminate this meaning, and this chapter is an attempt to understand more by describing the taxonomy, explanatory models and attributions, and traditional means of preventing and treating perinatal disorders in one culture, that of Cambodia. In the same way as some western studies might focus on the theories of psychiatrists, I use as my lens the views of the local Cambodian traditional healers who deal with women after childbirth. This work was carried out in the context of a larger study of traditional healing for communicable and non-communicable diseases affecting Cambodians throughout life.

In response to the need for a screening instrument, Cox and his colleagues developed the Edinburgh Postnatal Depression Scale (EPDS), a ten-item, self-report scale, for use in Scotland (Cox, Holden and Sagovsky 1987). The instrument has since been validated (and, where necessary, translated into local languages) among women from several countries including Australia, Chile, China and Hong Kong, Portugal, Sweden and the United Arab Emirates. The EPDS is the best available benchmark for a 'cross-cultural psychiatric' measuring scale for postnatal depression. One must bear in mind that the EPDS is validated, however, against other western-derived instruments such as the Research Diagnostic Criteria (RDC) or SADS. Given this ethnocentric yardstick, it is possible that women suffering puerperal illness from certain cultural backgrounds, and who show different idioms of perinatal distress, may be overlooked.

How might comparative cultural studies of postnatal depression extend our understanding of changing roles of motherhood? In evolutionary terms, humans, unlike animals, ascribe cultural meaning to pregnancy, which explains why postnatal depression seems to be universal among humans and absent among non-human primates (Cox 1996). Warning against the danger of cultural stereotyping, Kumar (1994) states that there is no research data for or against the theory that postnatal depression is partly the result of traditional rituals being stripped away in developed western societies. 'Western' obstetric practice has not eliminated the rite of passage, but it has replaced one set of rituals with another. Kumar notes, nevertheless, that the third set of rituals, incorporation of the mother back into the society with recognition of her new status, is not usually emphasized. I will show that in rural Cambodian society a semblance of these rituals is maintained.

In a pioneering review of the anthropological context of postpartum depression, Stern and Kruckman (1983) identified common elements in the social structuring of the postpartum period. Arguing in the opposite direction to that taken later by Kumar (1994), they proposed that postpartum depression was a sort of culture-bound syndrome that had to do with the lack of social structuring and social recognition of the role transition for the new mother. Researchers such as Stewart and Jambunathan (1996), in their study of postpartum depression among Hmong women living in the USA, have found that traditional beliefs and practices helped the women to adjust to the postpartum period. It is more difficult to prove, however, that the loss of these rituals leads directly to an increase in postpartum disorders.

Social support is in itself a cultural construction. In a comparative study of the significance of social supports to western depression, the social support network and postnatal mood of Anglo-Celtic women (having mothers and partners, and uninhibited in expression of feelings), Vietnamese refugees (lacking mothers and even partners, and suppressing the expression of personal difficulties), and Arabic migrant women (high in expressing desire for more help) were compared (Stuchbery, Matthey and Barnett 1998). The research highlights the many factors (social structure, culture, religion, effects of migration, reduced access to a community necessary for observance of traditional postpartum rituals, post-trauma) to be disentangled in conducting PND research among immigrants in western countries. The authors warn that lack of 'social support, as an explanatory concept for postnatal depression, cannot be exported with impunity to nonwestern cultures'.

In most non-western societies, childbirth is a rite of passage that continues for a month or more. The mother is given status and exempted from normal work (Cox 1996). In an example of culturally appropriate strategies to reduce the risk of postpartum disorders, public health nurses in Hawaii have integrated the use the local 'talkstory' as a caregiving strategy into the prenatal and postnatal programmes for Asia Pacific Islander ethnic groups (Affonso *et al.* 1996).

While most cross-cultural studies of perinatal disorder have focused on postnatal depression, postpartum psychosis has also been described in various countries. Cox (1979) described a psychosis, known as Amakiro, found among the Baganda of Uganda. Amakiro was ascribed to promiscuity and not using traditional herbal baths during pregnancy; 78 per cent of the women described wanting to eat their babies. Women suffering postpartum psychoses in Kinshasa were found to show 'sharp delirious blasts' compared with western studies (Mampunza *et al.* 1984). Was the difference in symptoms simply cultural shaping of the same psychobiological disorder? Zula and Xhosa obstetric patients developed puerperal psychiatric disorders in which cultural factors contributed to the symptoms (Cheetham, Rzadkowolski and Rataemane 1981).

CULTURAL VIEWPOINTS

Within a strictly psychiatric or psychobiological focus on illness, cultural factors are interpreted as modulating, rather than driving, the aetiology and pathogenesis of disorder. Few studies of perinatal mental disorder measure, let alone explore the meaning, of culturally specific symptoms such as, for example, 'heat in the head', found among Yoruba women of Nigeria (Jinadu and Daramola 1990). In applying western yardsticks of mood and mind, might we be systematically overlooking some local disorders that do not fit the western diagnostic criteria? Social scientists present other facets drawing, for example, upon stress, labelling and feminist models (Thurtle 1995).

If traditional culture protects women against puerperal reactions, does the erosion of traditional rituals and values undermine this protection? From his study of sociocultural aspects of postnatal depression in East Africa, and his review of the evidence that in many non-western countries postpartum rituals are still carried out, Cox (1988) proposed that the absence of routine postpartum rituals (at least in Scotland) increased the likelihood of postnatal depression. Cox (1996) argued that the attenuation of these rituals in industrialized western society might partially explain the existence of postnatal depression. Culture changes and changes in family structure in modern post-industrial society further interrupt the transmission of 'women's knowledge' and may be associated with ambivalence about the maternal role and may result in depression. On the other hand, postnatal depression (PND), as we have seen, is also found in non-industrialized societies.

In contrast to the clinical epidemiological studies, the anthropological research on the puerperium, in considering the *meaning* of a new mother's state within the society and the culture, considers perinatal mental disorders in a different voice. Having carried out clinical ethnographic research in Cambodia for ten years, I was struck by the high prevalence of some sort of puerperal disorders, none of which fitted the western diagnostic criteria for baby blues or postnatal depression. Cambodia, like neighbouring Thailand and Laos, is a Theravadin Buddhist society with strong Hindu influences. Most of the population live in the countryside and depend on rice farming. The western health system, which was never strong in the rural areas, is slowly being rebuilt after the Khmer Rouge regime and the civil war. Childbirth and its complications have been handled by the traditional birth attendant (TBA) along with other types of traditional healer.

Much of the literature on cultural prescriptions affecting the health of a young mother focuses on the period *before* delivery. Much less has been written, however, about the childbed requirements *following* the birth. Many societies such as the Negev Bedouin (Forman *et al.* 1990) and in rural Kenya (Harkness 1987) have instructions for women for a prescribed period of around a month or more after childbirth (Laughlin 1992) and, among societies such as the Yafar of New Guinea, until the child is speaking (Lugina and Sommerfeld 1994). Among the Gusii of Kenya, the lengthy postpartum seclusion is designed to restore the mother's normal reproductive career and permit the baby to survive despite small size at birth (LeVine *et al.* 1994). These concerns seem generally to cover work. The mother may choose – or avoid – particular foods because of their presumed effect on her health, and on that of her breastfeeding child. Childbed in the Andes is a rite of transition during which mother and child bond and sex is proscribed (Burgos-Lingan 1995). There is a gradual resumption of sexual activity – among Nigerian women, the longest mean resumption time occurred for breastfeeding and cultural reasons (Adinma 1996) but, with modernization, the period of abstinence in West Africa is decreasing.

In traditional Chinese culture, the practice of 'doing the month' after confinement is associated with strict food proscriptions (Pillsbury 1978). Marjorie Muecke (1979), in her study of 'wrong menstrual wind illness' in

Northern Thailand, was the first to hint that the postpartum problems after violating the expected prescriptions could give rise to psychosomatic conditions that included indigestion and transient headaches, fainting, difficulty in breathing, palpitations, cold hands and feet, perspiration, pallor and dizziness; and severe episodes with paralysis, loss of consciousness, incoherent talk, disorientation and sensory impairment. Indigenous explanations from healers included smelling noxious odours; eating bad food; sex; and possession by bad spirits. Despite the clear implications for gynaecology, psychosomatic medicine and psychiatry, Muecke's work has not been developed apart from a survey in Cambodia (White 1996), and a clinical case report among Vietnamese refugees (Eisenbruch 1982). Although the nutritional issues are important, my focus is on the psychological meaning and cultural context of such prolonged and disabling symptoms following childbirth.

In the next section, I consider how Cambodian traditional healers and their patients understand and deal with perinatal mental disorders. The two most prevalent indigenous categories of illness will be considered: 'incompatibility illness' ('toah'), which resembles a chronic stress-related somatoform disorder; and 'madness of the puerperal bed of fire' ('ckuət krɑlaa pləəŋ'), which seems to resemble psychosis secondary to an organic puerperal illness.

METHOD

The clinical ethnographic lens of this chapter focused on the cultural meaning of childbirth and afterwards – and so I wanted to observe the healers at work with their patients. In the course of my visits to Cambodia between 1990 and 1999, I took on various roles, as ethnographer and at times as a short-term disciple of certain healers. The sample I studied was remarkable for the number of healers, but also because it was drawn from every province of the country even during the height of the Khmer Rouge insurgency when many areas were inaccessible.

On arrival in an area, we found each practising traditional healer and, for this study, focused on those dealing with women during and after childbirth. Most saw cases within a few months of birth, but healers who treated 'postpartum' conditions at any time (sometimes many years after the delivery) were not excluded. Up to 1999, more than 200 healers knowledgeable or experienced in illnesses affecting women during and after childbirth were selected from my larger sample of 1042 traditional healers (316 female, 726 male) gathered over nine years.

The healers could be categorized broadly into three groups. Lay healers had no training or formal practice, but knew and occasionally applied traditional treatments (3.5 per cent). This group included Buddhist devotees who gravitated to the Buddhist pagodas or 'wats'. Mediums had no formal training but acted as vehicles for healing forces (12.6 per cent). This group included mediums possessed by healing force or power, and known as 'ruup' for the healing power or 'baarea?m əy' (8.9 per cent); by ancestral spirits (1.7 per cent); and by other forces, such as guardian spirits, in the forest (1.9 per cent). Professional healers had been apprenticed and had acquired formal knowledge of healing theory and ritual (84 per cent). This group included the monks, along with their ritual assistants (8.8 per cent); the 'true' professional healers, known as 'kruu' (59.6 per cent) and the traditional birth attendants (TBAs) (15.5 per cent).

We observed the healers and the women after childbirth in the course of ritual treatment. We observed how the healers prepared objects such as amulets or medicaments, and how they tried to help their patient's integration back into the village. After the treatment session was completed, we clarified the healers' rationale and choice in examining, diagnosing and treating the women; the nosology of her illness; and how it mirrors problems in social and economic development. In order to elicit the healers' and women's notions of the physical disorder in the body after childbirth, I showed them crude outlines of the body and invited them to draw what they thought to be the disease process.

ETHNOGRAPHIC FINDINGS

'Incompatibility illness' – Postpartum psychosomatics

The Khmer term 'toah' means 'to be different', 'in conflict', incompatible', or 'to quarrel' and is the name given to the illness affecting a woman after childbirth because of overwork, for example, or the wrong food intake, or premature sexual behaviour with her husband – any of which was 'incompatible' with her postpartum physical state.

Taxonomy

First there is 'incompatibility of the tubules', or 'incompatibility of the uterus', which are probably similar to 'incompatibility of the tubules which hold up the uterus'; 'wrong from working too hard' and 'wrong pounded husked rice' or 'incompatibility from walking on the husks of rice'. 'Incompatibility from rain' and 'incompatibility from frost' also seem to belong to this group. The second group includes 'incompatibility of food eaten', and is divided according to whether the offending food is known – 'incompatibility we know the kind'; or not – 'incompatibility we don't know the kind'. Embedded in this taxon is another pair, both known as 'incompatibility of fright', the first when the woman gets alarmed when people point out the identity of the wrong food she has eaten, and the second when she becomes startled by people. The third group includes 'incompatibility sleeping', for which another name is 'incompatibility head of an eel'.

There is another block of 'incompatibility illness' in which, for the most part, the types are named on the basis of their physical characteristics. Some of these overlap with the acute puerperal illnesses, including the puerperal psychoses, affecting the woman shortly after childbirth – and which have titles like 'incompatibility of "priey" spirits of bed of fire', which may lead to 'madness of confusion' and 'incompatibility of placenta peeling'. In this block there are also several forms of incompatibility illness that are second-stage complications of the three common forms: 'incompatibility of broken or peeling skin' and 'incompatibility of being protracted and dried up', which are probably the forerunners of 'chronic incompatibility', 'ripe and mature incompatibility', and 'serious incompatibility' – a condition that can develop after one pregnancy and overshadow the next. The form known as 'incompatibility of grinding molars' might also be part of this group.

There are other forms. In one group, which included 'incompatibility of headache', 'incompatibility of trembling' and 'incompatibility of thinking', the types reflect the consequences of the woman's worries. In another, there is a cluster that develops when a woman is exposed to noxious fumes and includes 'incompatibility of smell of poison from fumes', or 'incompatibility of burning rubber', or 'incompatibility of fumes from burning wood'. Here the incompatibilities are classified according to whether or not the cause was known: in one, according to the clinical features; and in another, according to the clinical stage.

Incompatibility of uterine tubules, or of working too hard

All the types of illness grouped with 'incompatibility of the tubules of the uterus' were brought about when the mother worked too much during the period after having her baby. The tubules (a hybrid of the western notions of blood vessels, nerves and tendons) were believed to run from the lumbar region of the front of the spinal column down to either the top or the neck of the uterus and from there to the placenta and other tissues. Cambodian healers and at least some of their patients believe the uterus to be suspended in the pelvis by these tubules, which also supply it with blood and nutrients. If bad blood enters the uterus it becomes diseased and if bad blood leaves it the rest of the body becomes diseased. After childbirth the tubules are weak and immature (the Khmer term was 'green unripe tubules'). The mother has to rest from heavy work to allow these tubules to toughen up. If she returns to work too soon the immature tubules cannot take the strain and the uterus is damaged.

This biomechanical folk explanatory model for 'incompatibility of uterine tubules' is perhaps a culturally cryptic allusion to the real social problem. Women are overworked after childbirth, especially in the face of poverty and need. Beyond that, however, Cambodian men are said to be notorious for going after other women while their wives are sexually unavailable from the last trimester of pregnancy until some months after the delivery. Inevitably, in the village, the word gets around and the convalescing young mother discovers her husband's infidelity. Some women became enraged, others sank into despair. Either way, many of these women developed 'incompatibility of the heart' ('toah cet'). The symptoms were the same as those of 'incompatibility of working too hard'.

Medicaments

Women who had overworked needed tonics. Here is an example of a recipe with ingredients comprising the bark of three trees: the 'stopping tree in the mountain', *Barringtonia acutangula*; the tree called 'soft and flexible'; and 'the summit stone' tree. The first ingredient could allude to the birth of Buddha in the mountains – while his mother stood during the birth. In an allusion to this plant's ability to sprout its own offspring (and, by sympathetic magic, the offspring of the mother), this remarkable flower blooms directly from the trunk as well as from the branches – an ideal fertility symbol for a medicinal ingredient.

Incompatibility of food

The second main category of 'incompatibility illness' affecting women after childbirth was 'incompatibility of "camn-y"' (literally, of the dessert). This condition was almost always caused by eating the wrong food, especially when the woman was in poor health to begin with. A poor woman had to eat whatever she could get.

Given that many poor women have little control over their diets, there had to be some escape clause. If a woman had to eat a forbidden fruit, for example, she could get an injection that might protect her. Moreover, she was free to eat during the first days, while she was still on the puerperal 'bed of fire' (see p.214); only afterwards did she need to watch her step.

Fish was singled out, mainly by the TBAs, as the 'chief' of the offending foods, having a stronger effect than pork and causing unstoppable dysentery. The central fish that, when eaten, caused incompatibility illness was a fish similar to a pike.[1] The birds included feral fowl, peacock and a kind of very large duck with a red comb on its head, probably a hybrid, and capable of flying very far. These hybrids were feared not only by pregnant women but also by people who had contracted infections, as it was believed that the bird's flesh would make an ulcer or wound extend in size – the person with poison had the ulcer on the surface; the woman after childbirth had a wounded uterus. This duck was considered by men also to precipitate the emergence of AIDS from the dormant state of 'hidden mango', the indigenous Cambodian category for syphilis (Eisenbruch 1998, 2000). The most notorious animal food was the head of a pig. Beef caused no harm because it contained a 'hot' element and, when eaten, it warmed the woman. The flesh of the water buffalo, on the other hand, contained a 'cold' element that chilled the woman and caused incompatibility illness.

Most of the food taboos come into effect around five days after the delivery. Mothers can maintain their nutritional taboos not because they are pregnant but because they are 'waiting' for the next pregnancy – the taboo against overwork, realistically, is the shortest, lasting a few months. The taboo against sexual relations with the husband is a little longer, up to half a year. But the taboo against the wrong food could continue for a year or more, as it was believed that the danger continued until the woman became pregnant again, from which time the taboos against food were lifted; during the pregnancy, there was nothing to stop a woman eating anything she liked. So 'tradition' does not necessarily contribute to the chronic malnutrition of Cambodian women.

The taboos were interpreted in a particular way by each woman during and after her pregnancy. One avoided a particular sort of fish, one a particular species of banana, another a cucumber, but most continued to eat whatever was available – with the exception of that sort of food. There is little doubt that malnutrition remains a serious problem, but the causes are more likely economic than cultural.

Not long after a woman ate the forbidden food, she developed diarrhoea, or vomited and had a bellyache. Sometimes her jaw became rigid and her mouth closed. Some women lost the sense of taste.

Treatment

To treat 'incompatibility of wrong food', the healer prepared medicaments that included the forbidden ingredient. If a woman had eaten cucumber, the healer included this vegetable, sometimes after it had been grilled, in his ingredients; and, more often than not, he dissolved them in alcohol, a 'hot' liquid that replenished the heat she had lost in the course of the birth.

Parasitic plants (and not merely epiphytic plants that grew on others for physical support) were popular. The term 'knuckle of the crow' literally means the crow that is sent and taken care of for someone; the parasitic plant, like the crow, sprouts on top of the tree to obtain all of its nutrition from that host, co-existing with it but decreasing its chances of survival or reproduction. The special ingredients sometimes included the fork of the sugar palm tree *Arenga pinnata* – the fork was a part of the tree that developed fully after the sugar palm had already borne fruit and was in the process of involution. The sugar palm, hard on the outside but with a soft, juicy interior, takes 25 years to bear its paltry batch of first fruit but after that it remains fertile for decades.

Cambodian healers were pragmatists. If the first line of treatment did not work, or if the woman could not recall what she had eaten wrongly, one healer, for example, would scrape into water the root of a tree having small fruit used as sour spice, *Antidesma diandrum* or *Stilago diandra*, and cold rice water left over from washing the impurities from the rice. In this ritual the healer used a sour ingredient, such as was often used by people to disinfect wounds – the sour root cleaned the wounded uterus – and he used old water filled with impurities washed off the now clean and safe rice: everybody eats rice, but it has to be cleansed and separated from impurities. In the ritual the healer put impurities into the woman to reverse those she inadvertently absorbed when she ate the wrong food and these cancelled them out. Moreover, he used cold water, which runs contrary to the principle of using 'warming medicine' to reverse the coldness the woman might have suffered; the botanical ingredients in themselves were warming agents, but the substitution ritual worked paradoxically, not by providing the warmth that was lacking, but by putting in more of what the woman had done to herself that was wrong. Here is the familiar principle of the 'substitution ritual'. Even if the woman did not know what she had wrongly eaten, the healer could still get hold of it symbolically by preparing medicaments in the same earthenware cooking pot as the offending food had originally been cooked. Earthenware pots, unlike metallic ones, gradually absorb the foodstuffs.

Several healers used as a panacea for 'incompatibility illness' the stomach or the teeth of a wild or forest variety of porcupine. This is because this animal is reputed to eat 'more than one hundred types' of parasitic plant, in other words, they eat anything, anywhere. The healers seek out the bigger porcupine that lives in the forest where it is forced to forage for the parasitic plants. This echoes the familiar separation of safe village from dangerous forest, and the woman for a time was separated her from her compatriots in the village. Normally innocuous foodstuffs, like cucumber, grown in the village, suddenly become dangerous. To cancel out danger, the woman needed something from the wild, returning her body to its healthy 'safe' village status.

Incompatibility of sleeping' – forced sex after childbirth

The third main form of 'incompatibility illness', known as 'incompatibility of sleeping', or literally as 'incompatibility of the way (or place) of sleeping' ('toah dɔmneɛk'), was caused when the husband forced his wife to have sex within several months after she had given birth. Some healers emphasized the physical side of this – the unhealed uterus was damaged by intercourse. For the most part, however, this disorder said as much about the disrupted marital relationship. The healers were not bashful about this condition, as this excerpt from a discussion between myself, the healer and his patient showed:

The healer told the woman why she was sick. Her husband's sexual urge, especially when drunk, made him force himself on her. His penis, no matter what length, pressed hard against her immaturely healed uterus and scratched or blistered the tubules of the uterus. The man did not understand about contagion from outside, which he could transmit to his wife.

The healer explained to us that at the moment of orgasm the uterus swelled and the combined sexual secretions dropped out. If, on the other hand, they stayed inside her, she would have shooting pains in the tubules on the right side of her uterus. Or maybe women like her became ill because during the confinement their husbands had sought their pleasures elsewhere by indulging in the triple vices of drinking, sex and gambling. He accused her of having a lover, but it was he who had disported with a prostitute and put his vulnerable wife in danger from the venereal microbe. The healer explained the notion of the five incarnations of the Buddha, each of whom took care of one sort of the person's body elements. For example, he said, the first incarnation took care of the 12 elements of water and related to the good deeds of the mother, and the second took care of the 21 elements of the earth and related to the good deeds of the father.

In the case of this woman, the healer covered four levels of explanation, starting with the most innocuous, the physical damage to the uterus caused by the thrusting movement of sex. The healer went on to 'infection', which, far from being a neutral cause, showed up the normal behaviour of men impatient for their carnal pleasures even while their wives were confined. The healer focused on the marital problems. Finally, the healer placed these issues on a supernatural and theological level by showing that this form of 'incompatibility' was also about incompatibilities between the conduct of people and the society's moral code exemplified by Buddhism. The healer spoke of the karmic principle and implied that a problem in the conduct of the father towards the mother led to a problem among those Buddhas believed to be responsible for the care of the 12 body elements derived from the mother (as opposed to the 21 derived from the father). The disruption to the woman's uterine tubules by the penis and the healer's line of treatment in restoring the uterine tubes were in this context obvious.

Treatment

The women whose husbands had manhandled them, curiously, seemed to handle therapeutic handling by male healers (Figure 9.1):

In an example, the healer, a male medium, influenced the flow of blood through the women's uterine tubules by touching her on strategic locations along her back, transferring healing power derived from his

Figure 9.1 After the healer told the woman to extend her legs, he moved his fingers from her chest to the small of her back – where the uterine tubules originated

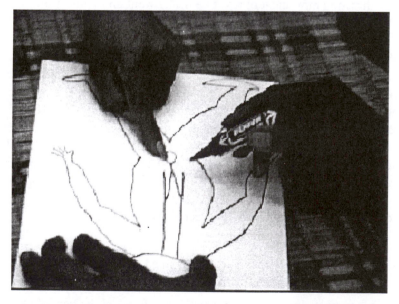

Figure 9.2 Drawing of the tubules flowing from the uterus to kidneys and brain. The healer points out the uterus location where the husband's forced sex after childbirth started disorder in the wife, with symptoms spreading to her brain

former master. The woman told the healer that she had had a headache and a hot and agitated feeling in the head. The healer motioned her to turn with her back facing him again. He placed his fingers between her shoulder blades. Then he moved his left hand to press into her left waist. Holding his hands in this position, he told her she had a problem with the nerves of her heart and her tubules that ran from her uterus to her backbone. Moving both hands to either side of her spine at her waist, he asked her to extend her legs.

This drawing by the medium [Figure 9.2] showed the uterus as a small circle just above the top of the legs.

In this case, the healer has constructed a detailed map of the problem, its causes and its consequences in a way that also makes sense to the woman. The abnormal movements in the tubules of the uterus were designated the way he also knew well, the movements of air in the windpipe and throat. The grumbling sound he likened to the reed instrument's sound produced by the movement of air. As he and the woman seem to share a common under-standing of the goings-on inside her, he satisfies her that he has put the abnormal uterine tubules into place. The husband had put his sexual products into his wife's lower orifice. Now the healer got the wife to put an extract of them into her upper orifice, her mouth; in this way the medicine cancelled out the effects of the violation. Or they got the husband to wash his penis to extract its secretions. In the traditional family the couple sleeps on a woven mat placed on top of the transverse bamboo slats of the bed. Several male healers took the frayed bits of that heavily used old mat, where the couple had intercourse, added pubic hair and burned them, and the woman drank the mixture.

The ingredients could be decoded by understanding the animal allusions. A Cham healer, for example, used the hide of the large fruit-eating bat which, like other animals that 'do their work' at night, is an allusion to the husband who did his 'night work' on his wife. Some Khmer healers made medicine using a species of wasp like the mud dauber, which was burned red, put in water and given to the woman to drink. The wasp spins its nest and provisions its cells with hapless worms, caterpillars or other insects, which are eaten by the wasp larvae, and so the worm 'became' a wasp. In this way Cambodians used to employ an expression 'the child of a wasp' to designate an adopted child. The wasp, like the sick woman, is in the process of nesting, and its nest corresponds to the woman's uterus. The sick woman's uterus needs a tonic and, in this substitution ritual, the healer inserts the 'food' as if the woman herself had become parasitic and could feed on virtually anything.

This particular case has a tragic coda, as we discovered in our follow-up six years later. The healer told us that the woman had contracted 'falling white' (leucorrhoea) as a result of her husband's 'mango illness' (syphilis, but in this case AIDS). Finally she had contracted AIDS from her husband and died.

Incompatibility of puerperal bed of fire

Apart from the three main types of 'incompatibility illness', there are other types. In one case in Ratanakiri province, 'incompatibility of the puerperal bed of fire' started only two or three days after childbirth. The woman's mood became labile, with much singing and crying. She would become very angry and would eat the edge of the floor mat for sleeping, as a sort of prelude to the full-blown 'madness of the puerperal bed of fire'. She could not tolerate the heat of lying anywhere near the bed of fire, the cauldron of water kept simmering postpartum for some days under the slats of her elevated bamboo sleeping platform. The coagulation problem began in the womb and bladder and then travelled to the chest. Untreated, the coagulation could propagate with obstruction of the blood vessels of the heart. The healer showed what had happened in two drawings of the woman (Figures 9.3 and 9.4).

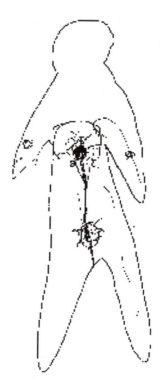

Figure 9.3 Drawing of patient's illness in womb, after forced sex or premature work following childbirth, bad blood rising from uterus to heart and beyond

Figure 9.4 Next phase; illness ascends, carried as 'bad blue blood' from chest to throat, made neck blue

There were two levels of understanding, tubules and body elements. Spirits or bad blood reach the brain and induce the characteristic behaviour symptoms.

Fear or fright incompatibility

All types of 'incompatibility illness' have obvious psychological triggers, often reflecting the woman's powerlessness against her man, her social status and her economic position. The most obvious, perhaps, is the type known as 'fear or fright incompatibility'. Usually the woman with this condition traced the onset to a moment when she had been badly startled. This sort of 'incompatibility illness' is consistent with other states in which the person is shocked. A person startled and frightened, the heart pounding, expresses the feeling that one or more of their 19 souls has temporarily left the body, or they have 'lost the soul'. The soul is safely inside, however, and a moment later the person realizes all is well. If the soul really leaves the body, the state is known as 'reduced soul'.

Some female healers pointed out that a woman might have eaten the forbidden food, say a particular fish, with no apparent bad effects until, one day, she overheard a villager telling another: 'that fish makes women get "toah"'. Immediately she panicked and developed the symptoms of 'incompatibility of fear' as well as 'incompatibility of wrong food'. She is a passive victim – but also partly to blame.

Incompatibility related to walking in rain and on frost

The vulnerability of the freshly healed postpartum woman to the natural elements was shown up in another type of incompatibility in which the woman was vulnerable to water – walking in the rain, or getting wet. This condition was called '"toah" of the headache' when it developed after the woman poured water over her head for the first time after the delivery. In another type, '"toah" of standing on frost', the woman walked over frost on the grass during the first two weeks after childbirth; in rural Cambodia women walked barefoot in the fields and it was believed that the frost could enter through the pores in the skin and ascend. In these situations, the woman was dangerously cooled. One can see the fear of being overcooled by the widespread rural practice of keeping the mother well covered even while she squats on top of the bed of fire.

Incompatibility of inhaling toxic fumes

Pregnant women in Cambodia are discouraged from inhaling fumes and smoke from certain types of wood, believed to include a harmful toxin. The category called 'incompatibility of poison from fumes' or 'incompatibility of rubber' is common in towns, where rubber is burned on the footpaths of towns by those who repair bicycle punctures or who change the rubber soles of shoes. Women after childbirth take pains to avoid these sites. The burning rubber produces fumes that cause 'incompatibility illness' if they enter a woman while she is not yet recovered. The fumes emitted upon burning of the *Pterocarpus cambodiana*, a tree used for building, are commonly thought to cause the same sort of 'incompatibility'.

'Locked jaws'

'Incompatibility of clenched jaws' is of sudden onset and must be treated quickly. The ingredients were prepared as a paste to be poured or scraped into the woman's mouth, which was prised open with a spoon. Ingredients included skink, whose tongue flicks food into its mouth while its jaws remain rigid, like the woman. In this substitution ritual, the woman eating the lizard will acquire its ability to eat food despite her locked jaws and they will unlock.

Chronic forms of incompatibility

When any of these forms of 'incompatibility' (but usually those of the tubules) remain untreated, the illness evolves into a chronic disability called 'ripe incompatibility' or 'serious incompatibility'. Affected women are dehydrated, arms and legs are just skin and bone and the non-functioning tubules are said to become invisible. In 'incompatibility of sex', on the other hand, the peripheral tubules function normally.

Patent tonics

It is apparent that healers and lay folk endeavour to prevent and treat all subtypes of 'incompatibility illness' with medicinal tonics. The healers have a rich pharmacopoeia. Any woman with enough money can buy traditional medicine at the market. Colourful 'package inserts' provide what we might call 'benchmark' knowledge for the masses. One such packet, labelled with the name of the healer, is entitled 'the fangs of a porcupine'. The front of the packet shows a healthy looking mother and baby. Below them are several animals including a snake and a scaly anteater or pangolin, *Manis javanica*. The deer, one of the foods said to cause 'incompatibility of wrong food', appears on the package. The snake has scales and stands for the woman's scaly skin. So does the ambiguous pangolin (also known incorrectly as the scaly anteater); it has scales composed of cemented hairs, as resembles the scaly skin of the woman with incompatibility illness – one is a bit like a cold-blooded fish as well as like a mammal.

Madness of the puerperal bed of fire – Postpartum illness

The previous section on 'incompatibility illness' – the seemingly lifelong state of unwellness that afflicts so many women who have borne children – opened up questions on gender and health and how childbirth defines the social place of the woman. In this section I will focus on acute illness that affects women shortly after delivery. I will consider how the various prescriptions – for delivery of child and placenta, for burying the placenta, for resting over a heated bed, for protecting against blood-hungry spirits – show up the relationship between the woman, the natural world as represented by her body and the supernatural world as represented by the spirits who can attack her and make her acutely ill.

I will consider issues central to the cultural understanding of childbirth and postpartum illness: the importance of the rituals carried out by the woman and her family, usually under the tutelage of the traditional birth attendant; and the place of the traditional healers when something goes wrong after the delivery and, as a result, the woman develops puerperal illness including, sometimes, puerperal psychosis. The focus is on women – the new mother and the TBA (the male healer is not called upon as a routine to assist labour, unless there are complications).

Some broad concepts lie behind these understandings: the question of heat and cold and their impact on the safety of the woman's body; and the place of her body (and that of the neonate) in the cosmos. In countries like Cambodia, the body is defined in a vertical axis, with safety and purity above, danger and demons below. It is also defined in a horizontal and radial axis, with safety in the nearby radius of the village, danger in the far compass of the forest; within this horizontal dimension there are propitious or perilous quadrants (Eisenbruch 1992).

Terminology

Puerperal illness is known literally as 'spirits + square grid + fire' ('priey kralaa plǝǝŋ'). To make sense of the illness, we need to understand each of the three words in this term. The spirits ('priey') affecting the mother with this illness are part of what Ang (1986) terms a continuum of spirit anthropomorphs that resemble human rather than animal forms.[2] The term kralaa signifies the consecrated space or air delimited by magical procedures that the 'kruu' sacralises as the place for the process of delivery, and the 'plǝǝŋ' is the fire or cauldron placed under the bed. Ang defined the 'kralaa plǝǝŋ' as signifying the space where one finds the woman being delivered of her child.

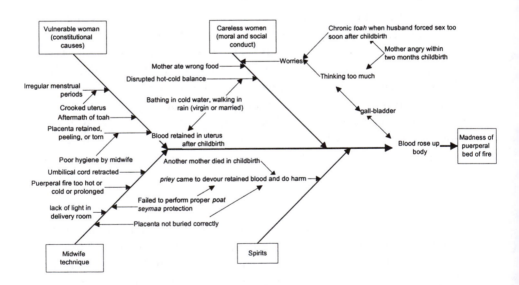

Figure 9.5 Ishizawa cause and effect diagram of puerperal illnesses including puerperal psychosis

Cause

The puerperal illnesses exemplify disorders that arise not from violation of a moral code but from failing to observe a prescribed ritual. In the Cambodian traditional view, puerperal illnesses arose as a result of four factors: a woman who was already vulnerable because of some physical irregularity; who acted carelessly in her own conduct; who was treated badly by the traditional birth attendant or the western-trained midwife; and who happened to fall foul of spirits. I have tried to summarize these factors in an Ishizawa cause and effect diagram (Figure 9.5).

Vulnerable woman

A structural anomaly, such as a crooked uterus, made the woman vulnerable, as it was more likely to retain bad blood. Sometimes the woman had a history of irregular menstrual periods, a sign that she tended to retain blood – menstrual and puerperal.

Incompetent TBA or modern midwife

Given the onerous responsibility placed on the TBA for overseeing the rituals following childbirth (supervising the family to bury the placenta in the correct place and to protect against blood-hungry spirits who could attack mother and child), the male finger of blame was levelled at her if, later, a woman developed puerperal illness.

Not only were some women constitutionally vulnerable, but they could also be at fault for unwitting carelessness with their hot–cold balance. The woman with blood in her uterus was 'unclean' and readily caught illnesses that engendered heat in her body and 'damaged' her arms and legs. In the second type, a woman who had just given birth walked in the rain before all of the blood had dropped out, and the residue made her mentally ill; being hit by the rain caused the remaining blood not to drop. The TBA was at fault for not ensuring that every drop of blood had come out after delivery. Either way, the cold rainwater entered the woman's body, coagulated the blood, cooled the uterus and stopped the completion of the period. To get well, she needed 'hot' medicine to liquefy the blood and let it come out.

Even if the husband had disported himself badly by visiting prostitutes, over-reaction by his wife was her infraction, not his, and she became sick as a result. People in Cambodia used to counsel against anger using ono-matopoeic ditties like this: 'anger wrong, anger and damaged and nasty self, and anger to lose or smash' (*khoh, khooc, khaat*). The ditties reinforced the moral view that there is nothing redeeming about anger. This lay expression is rooted in the Buddhist dhamma, in which anger was one of the three classic roots of evil condition in human existence. The woman who developed puerperal illness, no matter what the provocation caused by her brutish husband, remains responsible for her own angry reactions.

Malicious spirits

In Southeast Asia, women who die in the course of childbirth stand apart in the spirit world, as Tambiah (1970) puts it, 'because of their unfilled and clinging interests in and attachment to life in this world'. This makes them doubly malevolent and, unlike those who die in old age and who 'can act as moral and disciplinary spiritual agents, the youthful on the other hand become capricious ...relatively difficult to control and to immunise, and are removed from the channels of rebirth'. The spirits of those who died prematurely in the course of an accident are known in Thai and in Khmer as 'tai haoɲ'. Those of women who died in childbirth are known in Thai as 'phii prai'.[3] There seem to be three categories in Khmer: someone who died so quickly that they had no time to realize they were dying; someone who died in the forest with no witnesses, and no one found the body within a short time after death; and someone who committed suicide. Women convalescing after childbirth, their defences down, were easy prey for such wandering spirits. Confronted by the sight of another woman successfully giving birth to her child, the spirit of someone who had died in the same act of giving birth would be provoked to an envious rage – why should another survive the transition to motherhood and, moreover, gain the love of a live baby, when she had lost all in the attempt? Well may the wandering spirit be angry, but the woman in confinement, no matter what her circumstances, must avoid taking on these qualities of anger or she, too, becomes vulnerable to ending up sick or dead.

The woman, not being versed in magic, could not see the wily spirit that had entered her without resistance. After all, the spirit had to disguise itself in a ruse to penetrate the magical protective cord that had been set up around the house, so it masqueraded as, say, the woman's husband. If the woman caused her own downfall by being mad at her inconsiderate husband, the circle is completed by her falling for the spirit, in the belief that it was him.

Movement of blood up the body

In one way or another, puerperal illness is thought to be caused by 'bad blood', blood with the wrong colour or consistency. For a while after the childbirth, the mother's uterus and the tubules running from it were 'green', that is, immature. Say there had been a vaginal tear with bleeding and the accumulated bad blood moved around in the vessels around the vagina: normal blood descended to the uterus and mixed with the bad blood encountered there and began to block the vessels. This mixture of bad blood flowed upwards from the uterus and lodged in the front of the brain where it entered the nerve centres, as signalled by the feeling of 'heated agitation'.

Step by step, disruption to the flow of normal blood caused illness. When the blood clotted, there was a local disturbance in the tubules near to and above the uterus and this was associated with puerperal illness. The clot gathered bad blood which, when the clot dissolved, was released and flowed upwards. Usually the blood rose to the brain, where it caused various symptoms and, eventually, psychosis. Most healers believed the bad blood got stuck here or there on its way up to the brain. Bad blood stuck in the chest, for example, made the woman cough; bad blood in the meninges blistered or scratched them and gave the woman headache.

The bad blood also ascended to mask the eyes, which assumed a scary stare, and they affected the face muscles so that the woman looked terrifying, as if possessed by a spirit. It was as if the spirit got into her bad blood so that her view of the world was seen through the spirit's eyes and the spirit looked out through hers – they became one. Spirits or bad blood get to the brain in the tubules from the uterus, to disrupt the brain's elements and induce the symptoms. The puerperal illness is becoming puerperal madness.

Characteristics

Mostly the illness developed two to seven days after the birth when the placenta became either broken or retained, usually not long after the woman got off the bed of fire:

> Three days after being delivered of her third child, a 30-year-old woman developed intense fever. The family called the 'kruu', who instantly recognised the disorder as 'puerperal bed of fire'. This woman could hardly bear the touch of the bedclothes. Extraordinarily for a Cambodian woman, she lay half naked. The newborn lay by her side, of no interest to her, relying for its food on sugar water given by the maternal grand-mother. The 'kruu' performed ritual spraying from the head to the feet, which, he said, was urgently needed to cool her fever. With the help of the family who went off to gather the ingredients, he quickly prepared medicaments. A week later, we followed up. Although her face was somewhat swollen, the patient sat comfortably, suckling her baby. She was dressed normally. She had made almost a full recovery.

This case vignette is typical. The illness usually started with a high fever caused by the bad blood released from the womb. The classic description was that the woman picked at the edge of objects, usually the edge of the mat on which she lay, and tried to eat the fibres. When the woman began to talk deliriously and shout and cry out, people said that it was the spirit talking. This is the point at which the 'illness' turns into the 'madness'. The spirits had entered and made her wild like Rambo and lose consciousness.

The woman's restless behaviour is depicted in Khmer by several terms depending on whether it is directed at objects or at people. She picked restlessly at objects such as the hem of a mat and at people's skin or her own, and snatched and pulled at objects and people. In the second classic sign, she peeled and ate strips off the wall, and tried to climb the walls. She tore her sarong and tried to eat that too. She was offensive, terrifying people by making grotesque faces at them or poking out her tongue. It is worth recalling the popular belief throughout mainland Southeast Asia that some terrifying apparitions of the dead, especially when wracked by thirst, have long tongues that they stick out. In confusion, she might even try to devour her newborn child. Most families knew that the child should be protected from the mother and took steps to find alternative care.

In her state of confusion, the woman could not tolerate any form of heat. She could not stay on the heated bed, even for the shortest while, until a TBA made the blood and the placenta drop down and after that the woman was instantly relieved.

Treatment

The female healers and, to some extent, traditional birth attendants were more involved in such cases than in most other conditions. Although the male healers were excluded from managing 'women's business' in the normal course of events during the days following childbirth, there was not a moment's hesitation in calling in a male healer once a woman developed puerperal psychosis. As was usual, the healers, in treating puerperal illness, attacked the problem on all fronts, carrying out a ritual ensemble.

Pharmacological

Mostly, the healers used medicaments as their main treatment and usually began with them. One set of ingredients was to repel and drive away spirits from the mother and the other to melt the bad blood inside her uterus so that it could come away. Spirits hate dirt. The healer prepared dirt gathered from various repellent substances: scrapings of the cutting board or from the rungs of the stairs to the house; filthy house rags; foamy mud around the house where they throw refuse; bone fragments of incinerated cadavers, gathered around the crematorium in the pagoda; and the penis of a dog. All were dissolved in alcohol (this seems to be the standard solvent for 'hot' medicines used to combat feverish patients), and activated with Pali stanzas, before the woman drank the mixture. In this ritual treatment, the healer has gathered 'old hands' that know all about the day-by-day activities of the human life cycle – what the spirits threaten by attacking the new mother and, implicitly, the new baby. The ingredients are gathered from all geographical corners of the human life cycle: food preparation; the gathering of all kinds of people up and down the stairs, the residue of which knows all kinds of life and people; all manner of refuse from cooking and from the detritus of the bodies of the people who live in the house; the part of the corpse that survives the incinerator and symbolically is the most enduring. As for the penis of the black dog, some believe that the dog has the capacity to see evil forces when its vision is heightened at night, and signals this by its nocturnal howling.

The baying of a dog during the night was a sign that illness had struck the village whence the noise came. The dog can see spirits wandering from house to house to make people sick. The dog howls as a sort of ghost detector. Up to now, many people are said to believe in the magical powers of the tubular parasitic plant and they search in the forest to find one. I heard of some cases of elderly people with poor sight who wished that they could have the eyes of a dog substituted for their weakened eyes. The healer uses the dog's penis, an allusion, perhaps, to the Brahmanic use of the 'penis of Siva' plant used for healing.

Substitution ritual of plant names to dissolve blood and expel spirits

The medicaments formed part of a 'substitution ritual' in which the names of the ingredients had double meanings or were otherwise used in a puzzle to solve the illness. Through the use of these substitution rituals, retained blood was made to dissolve and fall and invading spirits were driven out.

The woman in the case just described got sick after she got off the bed of fire and now the healer 'substituted' for the needed heat by putting scrapings of firewood tree, as medicine, into the woman's body. The substitution may suggest fertility. Once the woman was strong enough to endure the medicaments, the 'kruu' prepared albumin from chick eggs; he also used fish sauce, honey and alcohol. People valued honey because the bee had sucked nectar from the flowers in many places – something that humans lacked the power to do.

Many of the plant ingredients used to treat spirit illnesses are characteristically spiky, which repels the spirits. The same is true of the ingredients used in puerperal illnesses.

Yantra

Yantra, magical designs drawn by the healer, were sometimes directly used to ease labour and to prevent all manner of complications including, it was hoped, puerperal psychosis. Here is the yantra known as '"?aathan" of the birth of the child', stirred into water and given to the woman once her contractions had begun (Figure 9.6).

Unlike most other images of '?aatthan', here there is the image of the immature child crouching underneath a male figure in a familiar posture of protection. It is likened to a fowl roosting over its chicks.

Pali stanzas

As the spirits were so often implicated in the attack on the mother with puerperal illnesses, healers used magical stanzas in efforts to banish them. This kind of magic was also used as a kind of non-invasive technique when medicines would prove dangerous:

Figure 9.6 Yantra of ' ?aatthan' used to facilitate childbirth and in an effort to prevent puerperal madness

The healer 'tied' and expelled the spirit. He applied wax to the top of the woman's forehead, the nape of her neck, and her sternum. He had to tie the thumbs and the big toes. The healer knew that a good-hearted deity might take pity on the bound spirit and, with the best of intentions, untie it and unwittingly undo his efforts. Now he had to be doubly vigilant. The cornered spirit, sensing that the healer was starting to tie up its route of escape, might rush up into the woman's chest to suffocate her. To prevent this disaster, the healer recited a magical stanza, which 'tied' the woman's chest.

Discussion

Childbirth is no bed of roses for Cambodian women who, burdened with overwork, poor nutrition and sexual demands by their husbands, may be vulnerable perinatally to sickness.

The cost of a woman's wrong conduct – somatoform disorders

'Incompatibility illness' is a common enough chronic perinatal illness, which does not quite fit the psychiatric 'big three' – the women are neither depressed nor psychotic. Is it PND masquerading as a chronic somatoform disorder, a Cambodia-specific, culture-bound disorder, or is it a signal that there might be other forms of perinatal disorder hitherto overlooked by psychiatric studies?

In one of the few anthropological–psychiatric reports on postpartum illness, Becker (1998) used ethnographic interviews to explore the social mediation of 'na tadoka ni vasucu', literally 'the flu of childbirth', a postpartum somatic illness among ethnic Fijian women. The syndrome is associated with perceived inferior social supports. More than half the women studied indicated that after childbirth they worried about suffering from an episode of 'na tadoka ni vasucu' and took traditional remedies to ward it off. They believed the illness to be caused by premature overexertion or by stress. The symptoms included headache, backache, heaviness in the head, restlessness, dizziness, cold, fever and anxiety. These are symptoms similar to those found in 'incompatibility illness' among the Cambodians. According to Becker, 'na tadoka ni vasucu' empowers women, using culturally sanctioned symptoms, to gain access to material and emotional resources during a critical time.

The ethnographic findings from Cambodia reveal more about the local logic of perinatal disorders, social conduct and gender relations. A Khmer Rouge TBA, whom I met in a military camp of a breakaway group of Khmer Rouge at O Bai Tap on the Thai border, provided a down-to-earth view of 'incompatibility illness'. Half the cases were 'incompatibility of tubules' because the husbands were away fighting in the jungle for most of the year; 10 per cent were 'incompatibility of forced sex' because a husband far away in the battlefield could not time his short visits home – with life at risk, sex with the wife was not to be postponed. In this enclave, such folk beliefs endured 30 years of Khmer Rouge rule.

With so many foods nominated as forbidden – in various regions, among various families, and with so many escape clauses – it is best to regard the Khmer term 'incompatibility' as a guide rather than an absolute interdiction. Postpartum women in Malay society face the same food restrictions ('pantang'), which Laderman (1983) notes as 'guideposts for behavior, which...have no moral or jural force'. The Cambodian and Malay lists of forbidden foods are similar (cucumbers, watermelon, molluscs, crustaceans and many fish) and have a similar classification of forbidden fish (inconsistent features such as the feral fowl or hybrid ducks, threatening features such as spiky fish, or disturbing eating habits).

The pangolin's scaly features make it – and the woman with incompatibility illness – a bit like a cold-blooded fish as well as like a mammal.

Maybe this shows us why, of all the foods avoided during the puerperium, the fish stands out – who wants to take the risk of eating a scaly-looking fish and turning into a scaly-looking sufferer of 'toah' with peeling skin? Mary Douglas (1966) writes about the pangolin – an armoured placental mammal covered in scales of cemented hairs – as a taboo animal that does not conform to any single category. The pangolin, as a violator of categories in nature, makes the ideal symbolic ingredient in patent medicines for postpartum mothers who, after all, may have no idea which particular category of proscribed behaviour they had violated.

Society offers the woman time out after delivery. On the other hand, the woman who worked too hard – the family was too poor – or who was used as a sexual object – a victim of her husband's insensitivity – fell ill through no fault of her own. Even as the victim, however, she was still responsible – witness the treatments for incompatibility illness caused by forced sex after childbirth. In 'incompatibility of eating the wrong food' – the blame clearly lay with the woman. Virtually every woman in Cambodia knew the interdictions. This is not to say that eating this particular food caused illness; as usual, these explanations are post hoc. The notion that a woman is 'wrong' because of something her husband may have forced her to do is found elsewhere in Southeast Asia. Carol Laderman (1983) describes a similar condition in Malaysia. Whereas in Malaysia the woman threatened the man by her sexual indiscretion, here it is the man who forces sex on his wife – but the illness is her fault. As in Malaysia, she must drink the secretions from his penis. In Malaysia, perinatal disorders are regarded as affecting particular women rather than women as a group. 'Incompatibility illness' among Cambodians, while affecting individuals, was also a problem of the social group. Some healers believed that it could spread from mother to mother and quickly treated any woman suffering from it to nip such propagation in the bud.

The treatment of most sorts of 'incompatibility illness' aims to reverse the disruption. Too much work? Put some shavings of the pestle or staff into her, preferably with alcohol to help restore her lost heat. Eaten the wrong food? Get her to eat some more. She did not know what she had eaten? Never mind, make a symbolic gesture in which a broad spectrum anti-food is eaten and no one need be the wiser about what she had done wrong. Fed up with a sexually demanding husband? Eat a symbolic part of his sexual products. None of these treatments materially changed the woman's social circumstances. She remained poor, having to work, to eat what she could get, to put up with her husband. But she joined a group of women in the village with a socially acceptable label – she was not 'mad' – and they gathered strength as a group. In recent years, I have repeatedly encountered women, often accompanied by their husbands, who arrive at the house of a 'kruu' to seek help for their chronic problems, who come across other women with the same problems. They may have been sick for twenty or more years since childrearing, punctuated by acute episodes that some healers told them were 'magical human interference' illness, but their somatic symptoms grumbled on. Given encouragement, they enthusiastically compare notes and the conversations seemed to help them to gather strength as a group. Even if the healer does not succeed in curing their disabling somatic symptoms, 'incompatibility illness' as a steady state that can continue for life seems to be better than the alternative of personal or family breakdown.

The cost of wrong conduct – puerperal psychosis

The studies of puerperal psychoses in western settings focus on women who have had obstetrically normal deliveries. In developing countries with high maternal morbidity, however, women face other hazards: puerperal infection, complications of malaria or dengue haemorrhagic fever, thromboembolism, malnutrition such as beriberi and eclampsia. Cultural practices sometimes influence complications such as anaemia. Such organic states may give rise to acute confusional states that may resemble acute postpartum psychoses. The indigenous Cambodian taxonomy of puerperal psychosis recognizes this continuity, with 'puerperal bed of fire illness' merging into 'madness of the puerperal bed of fire'. Cambodian explanations for these two illnesses span the organic (a toxin rising from the uterus to the brain) and the supernatural (spirits attacking the mother).

Southeast Asia is a cultural crossroads of Chinese, ayurvedic, Islamic and animistic notions of pregnancy and the puerperium. In the Malay peninsula, for example, coldness equates with health and fertility, heat with disease and sterility (Laderman 1987). As for Cambodia, the reported results demonstrate clearly the emphasis put from within moments of birth on 'getting it right' with the heat imbalances. There is the custom by which the woman remains inactive on her bamboo bed, while cauldrons of steaming water are kept burning beneath her, until the 'kruu' ritually puts it out. This 'roasting' is a custom widespread throughout Southeast Asia (Manderson 1981).

Birth in Southeast Asian societies tends to what Laderman (1983) terms a 'directional system' and, as she noted in the Malay village, was anything but precise. The threat is metaphorically fixed by the location of the placenta, hence the preoccupation with getting it buried quickly and in the right place. Spirits live not only in the nether world but also in particular quadrants. Whereas Laderman found the emphasis in Malaysia to be on the location of the mother during delivery, in rural Cambodia, I found, the emphasis is on where to dispose of the placenta. Cambodians take great care to bury it in the right place as it represents the origin of the child's soul. It is buried in a direction according to the birth date. If it is not buried correctly, the mother may become ill.

In covering the place where they bury the placenta with cactus or spiny plants, especially the plant *Zizyphus cambodiana* because of its hooked spines, the actors symbolically seal off the danger lurking in the earth, in which the placenta has been interred, from the domestic world above the earth, inhabited by the vulnerable new mother and her baby.

The finishing touch of the separation between safe and dangerous is shown by the ritual of surrounding the woman's house with a protective cordon. The term used is a composite of 'encircle' ('poat') and 'limit or boundary' ('səymaa') and is used on a larger scale to consecrate the Buddhist pagoda (Giteau 1969). It separates the sacred from the profane (Ang 1986, p.67) and, as such, reinforces the split between the patient in the safe world of the village and the invading illnesses that inhabit the wild and dangerous forest.

Women in developing countries with high maternal mortality will naturally fear that childbirth is a ticket to death. The treatment, too, seems to recognize the combined effects of organic and psychological disturbance. The perinatal prescriptions in Cambodia – delivery of child and placenta, burying the placenta, resting on a heated bed, protecting against blood-hungry spirits – show up the relationship between the woman, the natural world as represented by her body and the supernatural world as represented by the spirits who can attack her and make her ill.

The clinical picture described by the healers matches that of a delirious mental state caused by an acute organic psychosis, such as one might expect in the wake of a puerperal infection. One would expect that in Cambodia, with its enormous rate of maternal morbidity and mortality, this would be an important health problem. One might argue that puerperal psychosis in Cambodia is secondary rather than a puerperal illness in its own right. Against this view, however, it has to be said that many such cases appear to arise without obvious organic disease. The traditional attributions seem to combine the focus on organic aspects to do with substances rising from the uterine tubules to disrupt the brain, with non-organic aspects that are labelled as 'priey' spirits. The psychological element may be a woman's fear in bearing a child that, like so many others with poor obstetric care, she may die – and join that underworld community of kindred 'priey' spirits; if she lives, she may earn their enmity for having survived what they could not. The treatment, too, seems to recognize the combined effects of organic and psychological disturbance.

One of the symptoms I describe – the woman wanting to eat her baby – may represent method in the madness; Cox (1979) has noted that in Amakiro, a postpartum psychosis in Uganda, the women want to devour their babies, and he proposed that this might represent a repressed though universal fear. An ancient legend, widely known in India, China, Japan and Java, describes the conversion of the demon 'yaksi' Hariti and her husband Pañcika. It is also depicted in iconography in northern Thailand and Cambodia. This female deity, mother of 500, was in the habit of mercilessly devouring babies. The sandstone lintel carvings depict her with long pointed breasts. The Buddha, in an effort to teach her compassion, temporarily deprived her of her youngest child. The grief-stricken Hariti stopped devouring children, but argued that the first precept of Buddhism, not to kill, condemned her and her sons to die of hunger. The Buddha promised that henceforth all his disciples would offer a daily pittance, on condition that she stopped eating babies (Boeles 1968). The fear of babies being eaten is found among other cultures: 'In ancient Arabic folklore…a *ghul* stalked the desert, often in the guise of an attractive woman, trying to distract travelers, and, when successful, killed and ate them. Anglicized as 'ghoul,' the word entered English tradition and was further identified as a grave-robbing creature that feeds on dead bodies and on children' (Britannica 1999).

The disorders described reflect violations of codes popularized in the section of the code of ethics learned until recent times by young people, known generally as 'Various codes' ('cbap psəəŋ psəəŋ'). The codes of conduct to do with work, food and sex, and those described in this chapter to do with the identification of the woman's special status following childbirth, have been well documented. The requisite time for lying over the cauldrons of steaming water which are ritually extinguished by the 'kruu' in the 'tumleak caŋkran', or descent of the fire, was described by Ang (1986, pp.129–130), and by Porée Maspero (1954). The fire is never extinguished by pouring water over it in situ, but the woman quits the spot to resume sleeping in the normal location and the coals are removed bit by bit, to avoid generating steam. I am raising questions about the potential harm that could come of the abandonment of traditional rituals as modern health practices spread further afield from the capital city to the provincial towns and the countryside.

Puerperal women in the natural and supernatural worlds

All of the illnesses affecting women after childbirth epitomize the place of proper conduct in Cambodian society. The threat of illnesses, and of mental disorders in particular, is a potent way to define the limits of proper social behaviour. Observing the codes of conduct, bizarre as they may appear to the western health worker, seems to bolster the psychological status of women. In this chapter there are constant allusions to male and female power relationships, often expressed in the metaphors of treatment: the wife eating her husband's pubic hair, or the yantra with the male parent figure crouching over the baby in what resembles a sort of birthing posture – the latter a gender paradox reminiscent of the cultural reversal of biological facts as in the Old Testament story of Adam giving birth to Eve. Edmund Leach has something to say about this.

The findings show up the relationship between the woman, the natural world as represented by her body, and the supernatural world as represented by the spirits who can attack her and make her ill. These questions have practical implications in countries like Cambodia. If, as I argue, the period surrounding childbirth is a critical moment in the woman's life cycle, one that is still salient after twenty years of the Khmer Rouge and the civil war, we need to pay attention to the effects of introduced changes such as modern health-care programmes. Maternal and child health programmes – some involving efforts to re-educate TBAs in basic hygiene – need to be tuned to the cultural world of the women and their families. The traditional healers can help provide the basic data needed.

ACKNOWLEDGEMENTS

The work was supported by the Australian Research Council and the National Health and Medical Research Council (Australia); and Fondation Fyssen and the Ministry of Higher Education and Research (France). I am grateful to John Cox for inviting me to participate in a postnatal depression research meeting at Stoke on Trent.

NOTES

1. Seafood included the large white clams or mussels ('krum'), the same word as the vulgar term for vagina.
2. The idea of a nocturnal spirit lady constituted of a head and entrails, and associated with childbirth, is widespread in South-East Asia, as reported since the historic records of Skeat in 1860 in Malaya.
3. Tambiah notes that in Thailand when the pregnant woman dies the child inside her turns into a 'phii prai' and consumes her blood. In order to prevent the child from continuing its existence as a dangerous 'phii prai' which could grow up to suck blood from other mothers at childbirth, or from those who bleed a lot after injury, the foetus is removed from the womb and mother and foetus are buried separately.

REFERENCES

Adinma, J.I. (1996) 'Sexual activity during and after pregnancy.' *Advances in Contraception 12*, 1, 53–61.

Affonso, D.D., Mayberry, L., Inaba, A., Matsuno, R. and Robinson, E. (1996) 'Hawaiian-style "talkstory": psychosocial assessment and intervention during and after pregnancy.' *Journal of Obstetric, Gynecological and Neonatal Nursing 9*, 737–742.

Ang, C. (1986) *Les êtres surnaturels dans la religion populaire khmère*. Paris: Cedoreck.

Becker, A.E. (1998) 'Postpartum illness in Fiji: a sociosomatic perspective +AFs-see comments+AF0-.' *Psychosomatic Medicine 4*, 431–438.

Boeles, J.J. (1968) 'The Buddhist tutelary couple Hariti and Pañcika, protectors of children, from a relief at the Khmer sanctuary in Pimai.' *Journal of the Siam Society 61*, 2, 187–205.

Britannica (1999) *Encyclopædia Britannica DVD 1999*. Encyclopædia Britannica.

Burgos-Lingan, M.O. (1995) 'The cultural understanding of childbed in the Andes region; Das kulturelle Verstandnis von Wochenbett im andinen Raum.' *curare 8*, 143–158.

Cheetham, R.W., Rzadkowolski, A. and Rataemane, S. (1981) 'Psychiatric disorders of the puerperium in South African women of Nguni origin. A pilot study.' *South African Medical Journal 13*, 502–506.

Cox, J.L. (1979) 'Amakiro: a Ugandan puerperal psychosis?' *Social Psychiatry 14*, 1, 49–52.

Cox, J.L. (1988) 'Childbirth as a life event: sociocultural aspects of postnatal depression.' *Acta Psychiatrica Scandinavica Supplement*, 75–83.

Cox, J.L. (1996) 'Perinatal mental disorder: a cultural approach.' *International Review of Psychiatry 8*, 1, 9–16.

Cox, J.L., Holden, J.M. and Sagovsky, R. (1987) 'Detection of postnatal depression. Development of the 10-item Edinburgh Postnatal Depression Scale [see comments].' *British Journal of Psychiatry 150*, 782–786.

Douglas, M. (1966) *Purity and Danger: An Analysis of Concepts of Pollution and Taboo*. Oxford: Oxford University Press.

Eisenbruch, M. (1982) '"Wind illness" or somatic depression: a case study in psychiatric anthropology.' *British Journal of Psychiatry 143*, 323–326.

Eisenbruch, M. (1992) 'The ritual space of patients and traditional healers in Cambodia.' *Bulletin de l'École Française d'Extrême-Orient 79*, 2, 283–316.

Eisenbruch, M. (1998) 'Cambodian techniques to prevent failure to thrive, childhood epilepsy, and STD/AIDS in childhood.' *Clinical Child Psychology and Psychiatry 3*, 4, 503–515.

Eisenbruch, M. (2000) 'Femmes, enfants et guérisseurs khmers face au Sida.' In L. Husson and M.-E. Blanc (eds) *Sociétés Asiatiques face au Sida*. Paris: L'Harmattan.

Forman, M.R., Hundt, G.L., Towne, D. and Graubard, B. (1990) 'The forty-day rest period and infant feeding practices among Negev Bedouin Arab women in Israel.' *Medical Anthropology 12*, 2, 207–216.

Giteau, M. (1969) *Le bornage rituel des temples bouddhiques au Cambodge*. Paris: École Française d'Extrême-Orient.

Harkness, S. (1987) 'The cultural mediation of postpartum depression.' *Medical Anthropology Quarterly 1*, 194–209.

Jinadu, M.K. and Daramola, S.M. (1990) 'Emotional changes in pregnancy and early puerperium among the Yoruba women of Nigeria.' *International Journal of Social Psychiatry 36*, 2, 93–98.

Kumar, R. (1994) 'Postnatal mental illness: a transcultural perspective.' *Social Psychiatry and Psychiatric Epidemiology 29*, 6, 250–264.

Laderman, C. (1983) 'Wives and midwives: childbirth and nutrition in rural Malaysia.' Berkeley: University of California Press.

Laderman, C. (1987) 'Destructive heat and cooling prayer: Malay humoralism in pregnancy, childbirth and the postpartum period.' *Social Science and Medicine 25*, 4, 357–365.

Laughlin, C.D. (1992) 'Pre- and peri-natal anthropology: II. The puerperium in cross-cultural perspective.' *Pre and Peri Natal Psychology Journal 7*, 1, 23–60.

LeVine, R.A., Dixon, S., LeVine, S., Richman, A., Leiderman, P.H., Keefer, C.H. and Brazelton, T.B. (1994) *Child Care and Culture: Lessons from Africa*, 10th edn. New York: Cambridge University Press.

Lugina, H.I. and Sommerfeld, D.M. (1994) 'Postpartum concerns: a study of Tanzanian mothers.' *Health Care for Women International 15*, 3, 225–233.

Mampunza, M., Dechef, G., Kinsala, Y., M'Pania, P.M., Mbanzulu, P.N. and Ntudulu, N. (1984) '+AFs-Postpregnancy psychoses in Kinshasa. Various clinical and hormonal aspects+AF0-.' *Acta Psychiatrica Belgica 3*, 284–293.

Manderson, L. (1981) 'Roasting, smoking and dieting in response to birth: Malay confinement in cross-natural perspective.' *Social Science and Medicine 15B*, 4, 509–520.

Muecke, M.A. (1979), 'An explication of "wind illness" in Northern Thailand.' *Culture, Medicine and Psychiatry 3*, 3, 267–300.

Pillsbury, B.L. (1978) '"Doing the month": confinement and convalescence of Chinese women after childbirth.' *Social Science and Medicine 12*, 1B, 11–22.

Porée-Maspero, E. (1954) 'Notes sur les particularités du culte chez les Cambodgiens.' *Bulletin de l'École Française d'Extrême-Orient 44*, 619–641.

Stern, G. and Kruckman, L. (1983) 'Multi-disciplinary perspectives on post-partum depression: an anthropological critique.' *Social Science and Medicine 15*, 1027–1041.

Stewart, S. and Jambunathan, J. (1996) 'Hmong women and postpartum depression.' *Health Care for Women International 17*, 4, 319–330.

Stuchbery, M., Matthey, S. and Barnett, B. (1998) 'Postnatal depression and social supports in Vietnamese, Arabic and Anglo-Celtic mothers.' *Social Psychiatry and Psychiatric Epidemiology 10*, 483–490.

Tambiah, S.J. (1970) *Buddhism and the Spirit Cults in North-east Thailand.* Cambridge: Cambridge University Press.

Thurtle, V. (1995) 'Post-natal depression: the relevance of sociological approaches.' *Journal of Advances in Nursing 3*, 416–424.

White, P.M. (1996) *Crossing the River: Traditional Beliefs and Practices of Khmer Women During Pregnancy, Birth and Puerperium.* Phnom Penh: PACT/JSI.

10

Social Anthropology and Stigma

The Importance for Psychiatry

Gerard Hutchinson and Dinesh Bhugra

Our passion for categorization, life neatly fit into pegs, has led to an unforeseen, paradoxical distress. (Baldwin 1964, p.24)

INTRODUCTION

Any form of classification is said to be superior to chaos (Lévi-Strauss 1966). However, when those resultant categorizations give rise to meanings that allow for definitions of acceptability and normality, in other words, the validation of a social order, those who do not fit are likely to encounter significant distress. When someone is considered socially abnormal, their interaction with the rest of society and indeed their peers is likely to be informed by their deviance rather than their whole personality (Goffman 1963). This then is the purview of stigma, encompassing always the idea of difference as deviance, but implying too a sense of failing, handicap or abnormality. In its most devaluing guise, it provides the basis for prejudice and discrimination and their deleterious consequences. It is, however, essential to remember that we construct categories in order to render the world intelligible. In western society, these categories are usually founded in the notion of dualities or parallel dichotomies. These are important as identities are based on differentiating oneself from others and thus facilitate the formation of social groups as defined by their shared social, biological and cultural identities. Becoming a person or a moral subject is therefore indispensable from belonging to a social group that is constituted by these shared norms and, paradoxically, it is that same generation of cultural belonging which in turn results in the generation of difference between different social groups (Leach 1982). It is not surprising then that stigma is the result when membership of a group is associated with a socially defined handicap that is associated with the inability to bear responsibility for its actions.

DEFINITION

Stigma has been defined as the expectation of a stereotypical and discrediting judgement of oneself by others in a particular context (Brown 1998). This is a development of Goffman's definition (1963) of stigma as the situation arising when an individual, because of some attribute, is disqualified from full social acceptance. There are several negotiable components in the above definitions and as such the concept of stigma is itself negotiable (Porter 1998), primarily in the sense that it is deeply embedded in the sociocultural milieu in which it originates (Kleinman *et al.* 1995). It is also affected by the particular attribute that is being stigmatized so that, for example, when it is one of illness or disease, the negotiation is informed by the nature of the illness and its historical trajectory in that environment.

The experience of stigma therefore refers to a discrediting or discreditable attribute that may result in a spoiled or changed social identity in conjunction with a negative view of self (Goffman 1963). The Greeks originated the word to refer to bodily signs that exposed something unusual and negative about the signifier. The term has evolved to refer more to the connotation than the sign itself. This has led to broader conceptualization of stigma to include:

- a mark that sets an individual apart;
- links that individual to some undesirable characteristic;
- rejection, isolation and/or discrimination against that individual (Jones *et al.* 1984).

It means that the process of stigmatization includes behavioural, cognitive and sociological characteristics which are unseen, of course, in addition to the physical mark or label. By this definition, race, sexual preference, drug abuse, criminal behaviour, mental disorders as well as physical characteristics such as height, facial appearance and blindness are all potentially stigmatizing. In addition, a stigmatizing reaction may not always involve stereotyping, although the marking process is likely to move toward stereotype formation over time in an effort to justify negative affective reactions (Jones *et al.* 1984). There is an undeniable human psychological tendency to set apart those who are different and potentially dangerous in order to preserve self-identity (Gilman 1982). This means that social and psychological stereotypes may be in place just by being reared in a particular culture and, as such, the relationship between stigma and stereotype becomes difficult to disentangle (Devine 1989).

FUNCTION OF STIGMA

When people encounter a target person, their initial categorization is based on whatever information is available about that person. If that information can be used to assign the person to a stigmatized category, then the perceiver will make inferences on the new member based on his previous characterization of that category (Fiske and Neuberg 1990). The reactions of individuals to those with stigma have been shown to be more positive for those with physical origins and worse for those with mental or behavioural origins (Weiner, Perry and Magnusson 1988). Stigma is thereby mediated by emotional reactions that are the result of prejudices developed over time in a particular context (Clausen 1981). Stigma can then affect social networks, social interactions, employment opportunities, self-esteem and quality of life in general, regardless of its origin (Link et al. 1997). The stigmatization process would therefore include cultural induced expectations of rejection, actual experiences of rejection and efforts at coping with the stigma and the accompanying experiences (Link et al. 1989). The experience of stigma in this way calls for a renegotiation of social identity, with the added tension of censoring information and passing (Goffman 1963) in the case of the non-physical stigma, and confrontation with the stereotypes and discrimination associated with the more obvious physical stigma.

The sick are therefore easy targets for stigmatization by the wider society because once they are recognizable or marked, e.g. by hospitalization or contact with medical services, they are easily categorizable and the 'well' can sustain their sense of well-being (Porter 1998). The stigmatization of the afflicted therefore facilitates their restriction to a lesser participation in everyday life and devalues their social and moral worth, allowing society to represent the danger of that particular attribute, i.e. being sick. Diseases themselves are not stigmatizing. What they represent in a particular social context is what contributes to stigma and, as such, is purely a value judgement for that time and place. As diseases change, the society's definition of sickness behaviour and sick roles also changes alongside altered expectations of treatment affecting stigma-related perceptions across different eras and cultures. However, those that are so categorized because of their visibility, e.g. leprosy, tend not to change as significantly as those which are associated with some moral or social deficiency. One longstanding view on the effect of culture has been that the expression of emotional distress in physical or somatic terms is preferable to the psychological and/or social idiom in non-western societies because it is less stigmatizing (Kirmayer 1984). This has been supported by some empirical research (Cheung et al. 1981; Raghuram et al. 1996) and illustrates how stigma can affect both symptom expression and treatment.

Mental illness provides a sound basis to discuss stigma because negative attitudes toward those who are mentally disturbed seem to be held by the general public of most societies (Brodskey 1988; Dasberg 1984; Eker 1989; Green *et al*. 1987; Ng 1997). These negative attitudes, certainly in western societies, are also extended to mental hospitals (Graubert and Alder 1977) and suggest a pervasive stigmatization of the mentally ill. Beliefs and attitudes, however, may not always coincide and previous knowledge about an individual will affect an observer's interpretation of their actions. In this way someone who is already known to belong to a stigmatized group is likely to encounter more negative attitudes than one who is not known (Stiles and Kaplan 1996). This can also serve to control the stigmatizing response, particularly for larger social categories such as race and gender (Rush 1998). Conversely, a cultural knowledge that is strongly rejecting may be quite benign and less stigmatizing in practice (Littlewood 1988).

MENTAL ILLNESS AS STIGMA

The assertion of life-style correctness with emphasis on individual responsibility and control are deeply embedded in the western cultural approach to health (Leichter 1997). This has important consequences for discrimination and stigma and may also serve to augment disparities in health. Mental illness in particular has historically and cross-culturally been viewed in a negative way (Bhugra 1989; Ng 1997) and acceptance of the mentally ill by the wider society remains problematic. In the public mind, it is not thought of as a disease in the same way as physical disorders such as heart disease or cancer (Albrecht, Walker and Levy 1982). A history of mental illness is therefore associated with being discredited, devalued and diminished in social terms. (Townsend and Rakfeldt 1985). It is also one of the peculiar disadvantages of mental illness that official labelling though possibly leading to positive treatment effects can also incur negative stigma effects (Link *et al*. 1997).

The widely held view that the application of a medical model to mental disorder diminishes the stigma may not be entirely true (Mehra and Farina 1997). The tension that is created by not knowing how to negotiate a public disclosure of mental illness is a major challenge and has been identified as one of the difficulties in getting such individuals to accept or continue with treatment (Ben-Noun 1996). Interest in the stigma of mental illness has waxed and waned over the years (Hayward and Bright 1997), but has intensified recently because of the shift in treatment focus toward community care (Bhugra 1989). There has also been renewed interest because of its potential impact on insight and the implications for treatment as well as variations between social groups (Johnson and Orrell 1995).

The sociological idea of stigma is therefore fundamental to an understanding of the status of the mentally ill in western society. Horwitz (1982) sees the use of such labels as madness, craziness and insanity as representing an attempt at social control of mental illness. Two models of mental illness are described, one primarily sociological in which the illness is to be understood as a consequence of social conceptualizations and the other psychiatric in which an autonomous disease process initiates the social response. This means that mental illness has significant biological and social components and the relationship is entirely interactional (Estroff 1982). The label of psychiatric illness when put on by psychiatrists is understood as a natural category almost independent of social contingencies, but this is clearly not so in the social arena (Littlewood 1991). Labelling is powerful as the public have been found to be more tolerant of deviant behaviour when it is not described as a mental illness (Sabin and Mancuso 1970). Psychiatric diagnoses remain relatively fluid and the hazards that are likely to be encountered when inaccurate diagnoses are made must be considered (Witztum *et al.* 1995). However even if the illness was such, what of the perception of the public regarding the mentally ill? Clausen (1981) points out a salient but often neglected fact: societal conceptions of mental illness usually have their basis in observable behaviour which either serve to establish or reinforce the stereotype of the mentally ill. This may be due not only to the manifestations of odd behaviour but also the overt failure to perform their expected social roles once they have engaged with mental health services.

PUBLIC PERCEPTIONS OF STIGMA

In one of the earliest reported studies of lay public perceptions of the mentally ill, Cumming and Cumming (1957) measured attitudes in a rural Canadian town to mental illness. Then they offered residents an educational programme to improve their knowledge about it, but found such a hostile reaction that they were forced to discontinue the programme. This rejection arose out of a proposition put forward by the researchers that anyone in the community could become mentally ill under certain circumstances. Subsequent studies have demonstrated a slight overall shift in the acceptance of the mentally ill (Brockman and D'Arcy 1978) and reviews of this area by Segal (1978), Rabkin (1974, 1981) and Bhugra (1989) have identified that frequency and predictability of behavioural events, particularly those involving violence, visibility in the community (both of mentally ill patients and mental health services), repeated hospitalizations and respondent factors such as age, socio-economic class and educational background (with those of older age and lower education being more intolerant) were important in the attitudes of the public to the mentally ill. There is also the perceived stigma and fear engendered in the clients because of negative public attitudes which serve to increase tensions in communities with mentally ill members.

However, the deviant role associated with the stigma of mental illness is very specific and does not generalize to other socially deviant roles such as criminal behaviour and drug addiction (Skinner et al. 1995). This has remained consistent over time although there are signs that attitudes are becoming less negative. Interestingly, psychiatrists are also seen negatively by the public (Bourne 1978), primarily because they have failed to deliver on the perceived promise of curing the mentally ill with an accompanying lack of any firm scientific basis. We have found that this view is held within the medical profession which feels that there is not a rigorous and consistent method in psychiatry when compared with other medical specialities (Buchanan and Bhugra 1992). This is so and remains pervasive (Jamison 1998), in spite of the fact that many modern biobehavioural treatments for major mental disorders surpass those for the treatment of heart and kidney disease (American Psychiatric Association 1996; Kommana et al. 1997). Views of the public may also vary by gender, as Bhugra and Scott (1989) found when investigating public attitudes to mental illness through a questionnaire circulated to general practice surgery attenders. Male respondents were much more likely to express resistance to the idea of the mentally ill settling in their communities.

Cultural variations

While the universality of mental disorder is acknowledged, Fabrega (1991) described the ways in which there was a difference in the stigmatization of mental illness in non-western societies. The conditions likely to have stigma attached are those which are chronic, irreversible and frequently relapsing, and judged to be the result of spiritual punishment, hereditary and/or constitutional deficits and social/moral transgressions. In some societies there is a tendency to medicalize psychotic type illnesses but generally there is an integrated somatopsychic approach that does not reflect the mind–body dualism which pervades western ideas about mental illness. This underscores the point that our discussion of stigma is primarily from a western perspective and there is a lack of systematic research exploring this issue across different cultures. In non-western societies, the difference in cultural references will also affect the conditions that are deemed stigmatizing as well as the community's response to these conditions. Cross-cultural research in psychiatry has led to a reformulation of the concept of stigma that is embedded in social and cultural processes, and affected by paradigms of power, social structures and appropriate behaviour (Kleinman et al. 1995). In multicultural societies, the range of beliefs and the extent to which mental illness is allied with stigma must be understood in any attempt to make psychiatric practice more meaningful to these communities (Johnson and Orrell 1995).

The historical and ongoing preoccupation with health as a moral imperative in western society may be one means by which the complexity of the stigma label has evolved and why particularly the medical model of mental illness has not diminished significantly the stigma attached to these conditions. It may also endorse the view that local common-sense conceptions of mental illness in any given society shape the practical professional responses more so than explicit psychiatric theory (Townsend 1979). Demographic changes are one mechanism whereby there can be altered perceptions; for example, as a result of migration, there may be a change in the gradient of the stigmatizing response. Younger people may also have different views to their older counterparts or may want to project a more westernized attitude in spite of their cultural background. Bhugra (1994) found some evidence for this in a sample of Indian teenagers who had very positive attitudes toward mental illness and very optimistic views of treatment.

Many people are frightened of mental illness, partly because of ignorance but also because they do not want to contemplate their own vulnerability. It is this denial that allows stigma to thrive and also continually to create 'us and them' categories in society (Heginbotham 1998). This pervasiveness is related to the nature of stereotyping and the prejudices inherent in the society, but will also impact on the cognitive, behavioural and affective lives of both stigmatized and stigmatizer (Crocker, Major and Steele 1998).

Methodology

In general, there are several approaches which have been used to identify the prevailing beliefs about mental illness in a given population. These include:

1. Attitude scales which involve ratings of agreement or disagreement with statements made about the mentally ill. These can then be scored and analysed. Examples are the Community Mental Health Ideology Scale (Baker and Schulberg 1967); the Social Response Questionnaire (Beiser *et al.* 1987); the Community Attitudes to Mental Illness Scale (Taylor and Dear 1981). These scales tend to find mixed community responses calling for both confinement and humane treatment (Hayward and Bright 1997).

2. Semantic differential studies where the subjects are asked to rate qualities of the mentally ill as compared to normal behaviour. This was pioneered by Nunnally (1961) and showed that people regarded the mentally ill as relatively dangerous, unpredictable and worthless.

The scale has been criticized for its low inter-item consistency (Ahmed and Vishwanathan 1984).

3.   Social Distance Scales which measure the degree of social proximity which subjects would be willing to share with the mentally ill. Whatley (1959) found that tendencies to restrict social interaction with the mentally ill was reserved for situations of closeness.

4.   Vignette studies utilize short case reports of mentally ill individuals which are then followed by a variety of questions which elicit attitudes toward these patients (Star 1957). These studies can be combined with others such as the social distance scale (Bhugra 1994; Bhugra and Scott 1989; Kirk 1974; Phillips 1966).

CLIENT PERCEPTIONS

These scales have been used to measure attitudes of the mentally ill themselves toward mental illness with contradictory results (Hayward and Bright 1997). Each individual's perception of stigma is strongly influenced by self-perception (McQueen, Swartz and Perfile 1995). Some have reported attitudes in patients that are just as negative as those of the general public toward other mentally ill people (Backner and Kissinger 1963; Kennard 1974). However they seem to be able to avoid labelling themselves in a stigmatizing way (Quadagno and Antonio 1975). Link (1987) demonstrates that labelling does diminish the self-esteem of the mentally ill, while others suggest that acceptance of the label is a better prognostic sign (Warner et al. 1989). Acceptance of illness is now seen as a valid treatment goal and approaches utilizing this rationale have been encouragingly successful, particularly in the domains of compliance and insight (Kemp et al. 1996).

Although the decades of advocacy have attempted to diminish the degree of stigma for mental illness, its legacy remains and in the words of a former psychiatric patient, 'There is still the feeling that it's somebody's fault if they suffer from a mental illness, so they should stay quiet about it. I was determined to resist this but I came up against the stigma that still sticks to mental illness in the workings if not in the letter of the law' (Shaw 1998). Stigma therefore continues to have enduring effects on people's lives, even after their symptoms or other forms of defined deviant behaviour subside (Link et al. 1997). We can however see that the concept encompasses local or contextual ideas of moral justice, a perceived absence of control and capacity to meet shared obligations, the disability incurred, the presence of violence or dangerousness, and to personal and family shame. How these can be negotiated in the clinical setting with the implications for both the patients and mental health professionals will now be discussed.

STIGMA AND CLINICAL MANAGEMENT

The socialization of someone who is labelled with a mental illness begins with a conception of how their society responds to people with mental illness. This will include an assessment of the extent of rejection they can expect as neighbours, intimates and employees (Link *et al.* 1997). When these are reinforced by actual experiences of rejection, they are more forcefully held (Link and Cullen 1990). Two of the major responses to this state of affairs are secrecy and withdrawal. Secrecy refers to the Goffman (1963) described phenomenon of passing, i.e. concealing the evidence of mental health treatment. This may extend to refusing to attend outpatient appointments or community services lest they be identified. Withdrawal is a means whereby the clients choose themselves to limit interaction with the wider social world to avoid the possibility of rejection. This may occur in refusing to be discharged from hospital or becoming a social recluse. These realities are in some ways independent of the success of treatment but may sometimes impair the efficacy of the therapeutic process. Gove (1982) argues however that the effects of stigma are small and transitory and cites the success of mental health treatments as evidence to support this hypothesis. Before this can be addressed, it is necessary to consider the finding that long-standing deficits in behaviour prior even to the onset and labelling of mental illness create a burden for family and friends and may be the most important determinant of the tenacity of the social stigma (Bean *et al.* 1996). In addition, Weiner *et al.* (1988) have shown that stigma arising out of physical or visible problems incur more sympathy and helping concerns than those that have arisen from mental-behavioural phenomena. Lower self-esteem and negative affect have also been found to be more prevalent in those with concealable stigmas (Frable, Platt and Hoey 1998). With these in mind, two studies have now shown that stigma exerts an independent effect on the maintenance of psychiatric symptoms and that treatment and stigma coexist as a package that is difficult to disentangle (Link *et al.* 1997).

The contrasting views of stigma are really the expressions of the difference between labelling perspective of mental illness and the disease (psychiatric) perspective. In the psychiatric model, the outcome of people with mental illness is solely dependent on the severity of their illness and the effectiveness of their treatment (Lehman, Possidente and Hawker 1986), while the labelling model claims that the devaluation and discrimination created by the label interfere with a broad range of life areas including access to social and economic resources (Link *et al.* 1987, 1989). Rosenfeld (1997), in comparing the effects of the receipt of services with the perception of stigma on the subjective quality of life, found that life satisfaction was highest for those who experienced little stigma and were able to access high quality services, while the reverse held for those experiencing the lowest life satisfaction. This suggests that good psychiatric services in a relatively non-stigmatizing social environment may be sufficient in itself but that the social environment must be extremely supportive. However, when the treatment programme exists within a community that is harsh and hostile to mental illness, treatment alone cannot decrease the stigma (Angermeyer, Link and Majcher-Angermeyer 1987) and consequently life satisfaction is severely compromised.

Interventions must therefore also seek to reduce the stigma within the wider social community for mental illness. Undeniably, people with severe mental illness have impaired social functioning. They have diminished interpersonal skills (Corrigan, Schade and Lieberman 1992) and tend to alienate friends and family, therefore creating a smaller social network (Meeks and Murrell 1994). Rehabilitation strategies allied with appropriate psychopharmacological interventions seek to enhance the behavioural repertoire of the mentally ill so that they are better able to negotiate environmental stresses (Corrigan and Penn 1997; Liberman 1992). However, if they continue to be parodied in the media (Wahl 1995; Jamison 1998), their socio-economic disadvantages are likely to be maintained and opportunities in society will be withheld (Nagler 1994; Riger 1994). How the society unfavourably views mental illness compared to physical illness was demonstrated by Socall and Holtgraves (1992) who, using a vignette study, found that for the same behaviour a psychiatric label led to a more negative evaluation, expectations of a poorer outcome and increased unpredictability when compared with a medical label.

In the employment world, participants in a study preferred to work alone than with a mentally ill person and when it was unavoidable blamed the latter for any perceived inadequacies in joint performance, though task performance was better for those pairs in which a co-worker was viewed as mentally ill (Farina and Ring 1965). It then comes as no surprise that users perceive the public as generally unsympathetic and afraid. This is experienced in a hierarchical sense, with friends being the most sympathetic and the Police Service the least (D. Rose 1996). Users also report that the way they are addressed by professionals affects their sense of being labelled, with a non-significant majority preferring to be called clients rather than patients (Mueser et al. 1996).

COMMUNITY AND FAMILY INVOLVEMENT

It is clearly important to understand the nature of stereotyping and prejudice that informs the views of the public. One factor that impacts on the level of intensity of stigma is the extent to which someone has interacted with mentally disordered people in the past. Individuals who have had few such interpersonal experiences appear to stigmatize to a larger degree than those who have greater acquaintance with mental patients (Farina 1998). It is a common finding that familiarity seems to decrease stigma (Link and Cullen 1986; Penn *et al.* 1994). Huxley (1993) found that those who had encountered the mentally ill on the streets tended to stigmatize them more than those who knew a mentally ill person who attended a clinic, suggesting that personal knowledge of the individual seeking help was destigmatizing. However, slow improvement implying less responsive illness and evidenced by prolonged treatment is associated with more negative attitudes (Ingham 1985). On the contrary, information about post-treatment living arrangements (e.g. supervised care) seems to diminish negative judgements among the lay public (Penn *et al.* 1994).

The family is frequently the first point of contact for the mentally ill individual and they are sometimes also stigmatized as a result of their ill relative. Phelan *et al.* (1998) reported that while relatives did not feel they were being avoided by others because of the hospitalization of their ill relative, half reported concealing the hospitalization. They were more likely to conceal the information if they did not live with the affected relative, if the relative was female and if there were less severe positive symptoms. However, family members with more education and whose relative had experienced an episode of illness within the past six months reported greater avoidance by others. It is also interesting that in the hierarchy described by Rose (1996) above, users rated friends and religious groups above family as agents of sympathy and help.

Family members who effectively cope tend to be females who articulate their needs, actively engage in seeking help and information and have resources that enable them to make efforts to take care of themselves (L. Rose 1996). The evidence also suggests that it is the burden of failed role performances which is most important in the negative attributions of families toward their mentally ill relatives (Bean *et al.* 1996). Studies of expressed emotion have shown that high levels of critical comments are associated with long periods of poor premorbid functioning (MacMillan, Gold and Crow 1986) and greater expressed emotion was found in families where the mentally ill members had shorter employment histories (Barrelet, Pellizzer and Ammann 1988). Although this may also be correlated with severity of illness, only one study has substantiated this (Glynn *et al.* 1990) while two others have not (Miklowitz, Goldstein and Falloon 1983: Vaughn *et al.* 1984). In general nuclear families are said to be less accepting of mental illness than extended families (Lefley 1990) and this is one of the reasons adduced for the better prognosis of schizophrenia in non-western societies (Sartorius *et al.* 1986). Categorizations of illness attributing external causation may also be influential in this respect (Waxler 1979).

Some authors have suggested that public perceptions of stigma are mediated through the perspective of the 'outgroup' homogeneity which allows the development of stereotypes without any need for enquiry into the characteristics of individual members of that outgroup (Judd and Park 1988; Park *et al.* 1992). This allows for the merger of the concepts of stigma and stereotypes and further distances the society from the mentally ill who are represented by their most socially deviant examples in the public mind. Murphy (1976) argues that homogeneous societies in which there are fewer social variables identifiable by their members show greater emotional tolerance. Disruption of that homogeneity, particularly because of people of different ethnicities, is likely to decrease that tolerance. This is similar to how stigma towards ethnic groups is coded by skin colour in white-dominated western societies (Corrigan and Penn 1997). Minority group members can justifiably be seen as doubly stigmatized when they suffer from any stigmatizing disability (Alston, Russo and Miles 1994).

Feelings of stigma in healthy subjects can be engendered by apparently positive social interactions as Schneider *et al.* (1996) illustrated. They found that black subjects in the USA who received unsolicited help from white subjects on an intelligence task reported lower competence based self-esteem and more depressed affect than white subjects in the same situation. No differences in self-esteem were found in those blacks and whites who received no help. Since mental illness is no respecter of persons, being black, poor and mentally ill may well be the most extreme discrimination which western society can impose. It is also easy for people to believe that those who are unfortunate are responsible for their misfortunes, allowing the fortunate to believe they are incapable of falling victim to similar misfortunes (Lerner and Miller 1978). This places the onus of responsibility on the one being stigmatized rather than the stigmatizer to find ways to overcome their problem. It is then not surprising that people of lower social class are less likely to initiate help-seeking from psychiatric services for either themselves or their relatives (Hollingshead and Redlich 1958).

Cross-cultural comparisons of community perceptions suggest that the degree of stigma attached to disabilities is similar, but how the definition of these disabilities arise and their meaning in a social context has not been comprehensively addressed. The understanding of these attitudes in migrant communities would be highly relevant in providing acceptable and accessible mental health services (Ng 1997). Paranoid illness is the most readily recognized mental illness and this seems to apply to different cultures (Erinhosho and Ayonrinde 1978; Parra and Yin-Choeng So 1983). The value placed on the autonomous individual in western culture may accentuate the extrusion of the mentally ill by the community, so there may be something to learn from the cohesive kinship and community network in developing countries (Kirmayer 1989). In these societies as well, the environment for schizophrenic patients has been described as being more supportive with lesser risk of prolonged rejection, isolation, segregation and institutionalization (Cooper and Sartorius 1977); in other words a more benign form of stigma. This is in contrast to western societies where individual responsibility is assigned for mental illness with an effect on the sense of personal identity. Cooper and Sartorius also hypothesize that this difference contributes to the better prognosis for schizophrenia in the developing world. Communities need to develop realistic, humane and sympathetic responses to the mentally ill, taking account of the real hardships and problems encountered by these individuals and provide cohesion and support that is less judgemental.

DEALING WITH STIGMA

It is necessary to devise specific strategies to confront and overcome feelings of stigma as they can influence both entry into and maintenance of treatment (Ben-Noun 1996; Docherty 1997). This fear may also affect the judgement of clinicians, as documented by author William Stryon who was urged by his psychiatrist to resist hospitalization for his mood disorder because of the potential stigma, with almost disastrous consequences. Health professionals may need to address stigma in its own right as a separate and important factor if they are to maximize the well-being of their patients (Link *et al.* 1997). This must be recognized as one of the social factors that needs to be addressed in effecting clinical recovery and also preventing social disability (Kuipers 1996). This is well reflected in the recent campaigns of the Royal College of Psychiatrists to challenge prejudices against mental health disorders and consequently facilitate faster recognition of problems by clients and the medical profession, improved access to care and easier community reintegration (Royal College of Psychiatrists 1998).

A multidisciplinary approach which combines features of both labelling and psychiatric models is essential to obtain positive outcomes (Rosenfeld 1997). The biopsychosocial model is perhaps the most effective paradigm in which to frame a response (Vandiver 1997). The need to address these individual, community and societal factors demands that attitudinal conflicts relating to stigma and stereotyping must be actively confronted and resolved by both mental health professionals and consumers (Manning and Suire 1996). The most basic of these is denial, which must be overcome if interventions are to be successful.

One author (Levy 1993) has suggested the establishment of a specialized service to manage stigma exclusively with the goal of optimizing social function. The approaches fall into two broad categories: information control e.g. disclosure guidance, differential association strategies, methods of framing stigma and other strategies such as confrontation and dissonance induction. Stigma management must also include an evaluation of the experience of the stigmatized in terms of how they understand and interpret their stigmatization; how they feel they should cope with it; and its impact on their well-being, cognitive functioning and interactions with the non-mentally ill world (Crocker et al. 1998). Its salience in their view of themselves must also be assessed to determine the extent to which it should be addressed (Fine and Asch 1995). The specific stigmatizing beliefs should be explored with attention being given to maladaptive views of cause, dangerousness, prognosis or individual responsibility for symptoms. Cognitive-behavioral strategies can then be used to counter these beliefs. Three possible strategies outlined for the protection of self-esteem in stigma are comparison with other members of the group rather than with a non-stigmatized group; the devaluation of things which the individual is not good at; and the attribution of any negative feedback they may receive to belonging to a stigmatized group, rather than to personal faults (Crocker and Major 1989).

Client-centred psychotherapies can also be introduced to inculcate values of unconditional positive regard, warmth and congruence so that the individual can reorient himself in a destigmatized way (Mosher and Burti 1992). A sense of mastery and self-esteem are fundamental goals that protect and enhance the self and contribute to a feeling of well-being (Pearlin et al. 1981). People with severe mental illness must be encouraged to confront their symptoms and accept the limitations they may pose while building independent and quality life (Corrigan and Penn 1997). Mentally ill patients need to be empowered to take control of their lives. Fostering advocacy groups (Chamberlin 1984) and promoting rehabilitation programmes that are run in the community by the patients themselves may also be useful (Chamberlin, Rogers and Sneed 1989).

Since familiarity with the mentally ill may reduce stigma, a controlled community exposure and contact programme can be established. Alternatively, recovered or stabilized individuals can visit community environments to discuss their encounters with mental illness and their need for renewed opportunities (Kommana et al. 1997). Stigma may also be effectively tackled through the mass media. One avenue is the public disclosure of mental illness by celebrities, which has occurred in the USA through individuals such as actress Patty Duke, who has also spent time educating communities about mental illness (Duke and Hochman 1992). Books describing such experiences are also useful in this regard (Wurtzel 1994).

The media can also facilitate widespread public education campaigns and the accepted fact that there are effective pharmacological, psychological and social interventions available. Wolff *et al.* (1996) have demonstrated that a public education programme designed to sensitize residents to the planned opening of a residential facility for the mentally ill was able to change attitudes and behaviour in a positive direction. There is also a need to temper the media's tendency to describe crimes committed by the mentally ill in a way that further raises public antipathy. It has been demonstrated that the impact of violent attacks on public figures by mentally ill individuals serves to increase the level of social distance required by the general public from all mentally ill persons (Angermeyer and Matschinger 1995). Popular images of mental illness by the media have also been identified in the fears of students contemplating fieldwork with psychiatric patients (Lyons and Ziviani 1995). A sympathetic presentation would be more useful, identifying that while a subgroup of mentally ill patients is more likely than the general population to be violent, the vast majority are not (Torrey 1994; Wahl and Lefkowitz 1989). The conflation of mental illness and violence is largely constructed through this means and the use of less pejorative descriptions of the mentally ill would be one helpful step in reversing that perception.

A comprehensive infrastructure of community supports, particularly in the areas of housing and employment, is a bridge to effective social reintegration. However, services must be catered to individual needs rather than a generic provision of supported housing or sheltered work programmes (Shepherd 1998). Governmental support for increased access to jobs, adequate housing and community services will also facilitate this process. Only when the exclusion of people with mental health disabilities is directly addressed with a legislated policy of social inclusion will it be possible to revalue the needs of these individuals in the context of community integration and safety (Heginbotham 1998).

Social and interpersonal skill training for the mentally ill is necessary for them to overcome the impediments to social interaction (Kommana *et al.* 1997). Perceived attractiveness has been shown to improve with improved social skills in schizophrenia (Penn *et al.* 1994). The promotion of positive interactions between the sufferer and others has been shown to reduce the sense of stigma and the stigma itself (Desforges *et al.* 1991). Healthy lifestyle and self-management skills would also be useful in this regard in order to build a sense of self-efficacy and personal worth (Hayward and Bright 1997).

Psychiatrists as the label-ascribing agents in mental illness have a responsibility to interrogate their own attitudes about mental illness and confront the stigma that they may themselves feel. Recruitment of psychiatrists will depend on a positive view of the speciality (Weismann *et al.* 1994) and encouraging medical students to develop positive attitudes toward psychiatry and psychiatric patients is an integral part of that process.

This needs to occur early in medical training (Ney *et al.* 1990) as medical students will reflect the views of the societies from which they come, so psychiatry must be presented early as an attractive, unique and rewarding speciality (Menninger 1994). Psychiatrists must engage their other medical colleagues in constructive mediation to remove the fear of mental illness from within the medical profession, as many doctors feel that admission of their own mental health problems would mean dismissal, revocation of licences and loss of practising privileges (Jamison 1998).

Criteria for involuntary hospitalization, outpatient compliance and follow-up procedures need to be researched in order to placate community fears about psychiatry's capacity to handle patients in the community (Torrey 1994). Advocacy and political campaigning for legislative recognition of the rights of the mentally ill by psychiatrists would also negate the discrimination that those with mental illness encounter. A refocusing of treatment outcomes to include greater life satisfaction and improvements in living standards rather than mere symptom resolution would also be helpful (Sartorius 1998). Emphasis should therefore not be on a diagnostic label but on the management of a particular set of problems with goal setting to generate behaviours that are incompatible with a disabling conception of mental illness. Sontag (1977) has described both the celebration of the confirmation of the organicity of a disease to decrease stigma or the social scapegoating of any disease to explain stigma as intellectually dishonest and undesirable.

The problem of stigma and mental health can then be broadly framed within the management of social diversity in any society. However, this diversity must be seen in the context of the duality that informs the formation of groups. Although the mentally ill remain members of the social groups from which they came, i.e. family or community, they represent a particular kind of deviance which serves to define the appropriate boundaries of expected social behaviour. Tolerance is therefore not a contemplative position, dispensing indulgence to what was and what is, but has to be a dynamic attitude consisting in the foresight, understanding and active promotion of what wants to be (Lévi-Strauss 1973). This allows the continuous review of the duality that informs the identification and treatment of the other. To maintain its stability, society needs a means to certify deviance. The social roles of both those who are entrusted with the responsibility of certification and those who receive this label are therefore guided by the social order and those who exert power over the maintenance of that order. All people experience the world as something given by history rather than something they create. The challenge is to restore to those identified by psychiatry as being mentally ill the sense of personhood so that they can exert the social agency necessary to contribute to redefinitions of normality for the societies where they live. This is to recognize that the ascription of difference to devalued status is based on a scale of evaluation that is itself a product of group identity, but therefore susceptible to change and adaptation. This may be the only way to reform the internalized expectations of rejection associated with being a member of a devalued group.

REFERENCES

Ahmed, S. and Vishwanathan, P. (1984) 'Factor analytical study of Nunnally's scale of popular concepts of mental health.' *Psychology Report 54*, 455–461.

Albrecht, G., Walker, V. and Levy, J. (1982) 'Social distance from the stigmatised: a test of two theories.' *Social Science and Medicine 16*, 1319–1327.

Alston, R.J., Russo, C.J. and Miles, A.S. (1994) 'Brown vs Board of Education and the Americans with Disabilities Act: vistas of equal educational opportunities for African Americans.' *Journal of Negro Education 63*, 3, 349–357.

American Psychiatric Association (1996) *Practice Guidelines.* Washington DC: American Psychiatric Press.

Angermeyer, M.C. and Matschinger, H. (1995) 'Violent attacks on public figures by persons suffering from psychiatric disorders: their effect on the social distance towards the mentally ill.' *European Archives of Psychiatry and Clinical Neuroscience 245*, 2, 159–164.

Angermeyer, M.C., Link, B.G. and Majcher-Angermeyer, A. (1987) 'Stigma perceived by patients attending modern treatment settings: some unanticipated effects of community psychiatry reforms.' *Journal of Nervous and Mental Disease 175*, 4–11.

Backner, B.L. and Kissinger, R.D. (1963) 'Hospitalised patients' attitudes toward mental health professionals and mental patients.' *Journal of Nervous and Mental Disease 136*, 72–75.

Baker, F. and Schulberg, H.C. (1967) 'The development of a community mental health ideology scale.' *Community Mental Health Journal 3*, 216–225.

Baldwin, J. (1964) *Notes of a Native Son.* London: Michael Joseph.

Barrelet, L., Pellizzer, G. and Ammann, L. (1988) 'Family expressed emotion and outcome of schizophrenics: a study in French cultural environment.' *Schweizer Archives of Neurology and Psychiatry 139*, 27–34.

Bean, G., Beiser, M., Zhang-Wong, J. and Iacono, W. (1996) 'Negative labelling of individuals with first episode schizophrenia: the effect of premorbid functioning.' *Schizophrenia Research 22*, 111–118.

Beiser, M., Waxler-Morrison, N., Iacono, W.G., Lyn, T-Y., Fleming, J.A.E. and Husted, J. (1987) 'A measure of the sick label in psychiatric disorder and physical illness.' *Social Science and Medicine 25*, 251–261.

Ben-Noun, L. (1996) 'Characterization of patients refusing professional psychiatric treatment in a primary care clinic.' *Israel Journal of Psychiatry and Related Sciences 33*, 3, 167–174.

Bhugra, D. (1989) 'Attitudes towards mental illness. A review of the literature.' *Acta Psychiatrica Scandinavica 80*, 1–12.

Bhugra, D. (1994) 'Indian teenagers' attitudes towards mental illness.' *British Journal of Clinical and Social Psychiatry 9*, 1, 10–12.

Bhugra, D. and Scott, J. (1989) 'The report of a working party of the fourth Collegiate Trainees Committee. The public image of psychiatry – a pilot study.' *Psychiatric Bulletin 13*, 6, 330–333.

Bourne, P. (1978) 'The psychiatrist's responsibility and the public trust.' *American Journal of Psychiatry 135*, 174–177.

Brockman, J. and D'Arcy, C. (1978) 'Correlates of attitudinal social distance toward the mentally ill: a review and resurvey.' *Social Psychiatry 13*, 69–77.

Brodskey, B. (1988) 'Mental health attitudes and practices of Soviet Jewish immigrants.' *Health and Social Work 13*, 130–136.

Brown, L.M. (1998) 'Ethnic stigma as a contextual experience: a possible selves perspective.' *Personality and Social Psychology Bulletin 24*, 2, 163–172.

Buchanan, A. and Bhugra, D. (1992) 'Attitude of the medical profession to psychiatry.' *Acta Psychiatrica Scandinavica 85*, 1–5.

Chamberlin, J. (1984) 'Speaking for ourselves: an overview of the ex-psychiatric inmates' movement.' *Psychosocial Rehabilitation Journal 3*, 56–63.

Chamberlin, J., Rogers, J.A. and Sneed, C.S. (1989) 'Consumers, families and community support systems.' *Psychosocial Rehabilitation Journal 12*, 93–106.

Cheung, F., Lau, B.W. and Waldman, E. (1981) 'Somatization among Chinese depressives in general practice.' *International Journal of Psychiatry and Medicine 10*, 361–374.

Clausen, J. (1981) 'Stigma and mental disorder. Phenomena and terminology.' *Psychiatry 44*, 287–296.

Cooper, J.E. and Sartorius, N. (1977) 'Cultural and temporal variations in schizophrenia: a speculation on the importance of industrialisation.' *British Journal of Psychiatry 130*, 50–55.

Corrigan, P.W. and Penn, D. (1997) 'Disease and discrimination: two paradigms that describe severe mental illness.' *Journal of Mental Health 6*, 4, 355–366.

Corrigan, P.W., Schade, M.L. and Liberman, R.P. (1992) 'Social skills training.' In R.P. Liberman (ed) *Handbook of Psychiatric Rehabilitation*. New York: Macmillan.

Crocker, J. and Major, B. (1989) 'Social stigma and self esteem: the self protective properties of stigma.' *Psychological Review 96*, 2, 608–630.

Crocker, J., Major, B. and Steele, C. (1998) 'Social stigma.' In D.T. Gilbert and S.T. Fiske (eds) *The Handbook of Social Psychology*, vol. 2, 4th edn. Boston: McGraw-Hill.

Cumming, E. and Cumming, J. (1957) *Closed Ranks: An Experiment in Mental Health Education*. Cambridge MA: Harvard University Press.

Dasberg, H. (1984) 'Local attitudes as a basis for the planning of a community mental health service in Jerusalem.' *Israel Journal of Psychiatry and Related Sciences 21*, 247–265.

Desforges, D.M., Lord, C.G., Ramsey, S.L., Mason, J.A., Van Leeuwen, M.D., West, S.C. and Lepper, M.R. (1991) 'Effects of structured cooperative contact on changing negative attitudes toward stigmatised social groups.' *Journal of Personality and Social Psychology 60*, 531–544.

Devine, P.G. (1989) 'Stereotypes and prejudice: their automatic and controlled components.' *Journal of Personality and Social Psychology 56*, 5–18.

Docherty, J.P. (1997) 'Barriers to the diagnosis of depression in primary care.' *Journal of Clinical Psychiatry 58*, 1, 5–10.

Duke, P. and Hochman, G. (1992) *A Brilliant Madness: Living with Manic Depressive Illness.* New York: Bantam.

Eker, D. (1989) 'Attitudes toward mental illness: recognition, desired social distance, expected burden and negative influence on mental health among Turkish freshmen.' *Social Psychiatry Psychiatric Epidemiology 24*, 146–150.

Erinhosho, O.A. and Ayonrinde, A. (1978) 'A comparative study of opinion and knowledge about mental illness in different societies.' *Psychiatry 41*, 403–410.

Estroff, S.E. (1982) 'Long term psychiatric clients in an American community: some sociocultural factors in chronic mental illness.' In N. Chrisman and T.W. Maretzki (eds) *Clinically Applied Anthropology.* Dordrecht: Reidel.

Fabrega, H. Jr (1991) 'Psychiatric stigma in non Western societies.' *Comprehensive Psychiatry 32*, 534–551.

Farina, A. (1998) 'Stigma.' In K.T. Mueser and N. Tarrier (eds) *Handbook of Social Functioning in Schizophrenia.* Boston: Allyn and Bacon.

Farina, A. and Ring, K. (1965) 'The influence of perceived mental illness on interpersonal relations.' *Journal of Abnormal Psychology 70*, 47–51.

Fine, M. and Asch, A. (1995) 'Disability beyond stigma: social interaction, discrimination and activism.' In N.R. Goldberger and J.B. Veroff (eds) *The Culture and Psychology Reader.* New York: New York University Press.

Fiske, S.T. and Neuberg, S.L. (1990) 'A continuum of impression formation, from category based to individuating processes: influences of information and motivation on attention and interpretation.' *Advances in Experimental Social Psychology 23*, 1–73.

Frable, D.E.S., Platt, L. and Hoey, S. (1998) 'Concealable stigmas and positive self perceptions: feeling better around similar others.' *Journal of Personality and Social Psychology 74*, 4, 909–922.

Gilman, S. (1982) *Disease and Representations: From Madness to AIDS.* Chichester: Wiley.

Glynn, S.M., Randolph, E.T., Eth, S., Paz, G.G., Leong, G.B., Shaner, A.L. and Strachan, A. (1990) 'Patient psychopathology and expressed emotion in schizophrenia.' *British Journal of Psychiatry 157*, 877–880.

Goffman, E. (1963) *Stigma: Notes on the Management of Spoiled Identity.* New Jersey: Prentice Hall.

Gove, W. (1980) 'Labeling mental illness: a critique.' In W. Gove (ed) *Labeling Deviant Behaviour.* Beverly Hills, Sage.

Gove, W. (1982) 'The current status of the labelling theory of mental illness.' In W. Gove (ed) *Deviance and Mental Illness.* Beverly Hills: Sage.

Graubert, J.G. and Adler, L. (1977) 'Cross national comparisons of projected social distances from mental patient related stimuli.' *Perceptual and Motor Skills 44,* 881–882.

Green, D.E., McCormick, I.A., Walkey, F.H. and Taylor, A.J. (1987) 'Community attitudes to mental illness in New Zealand twenty two years on.' *Social Science and Medicine 24,* 417–422.

Hayward, P. and Bright, J.A. (1997) 'Stigma and mental illness: a review and critique.' *Journal of Mental Health-UK 6,* 4, 345–354.

Heginbotham, C. (1998) 'UK mental health policy can alter the stigma of mental illness.' *The Lancet 352,* 1052–1053.

Hollingshead, A.B. and Redlich, F.C. (1958) *Social Class and Mental Illness.* New York: Wiley.

Horwitz, A.V. (1982) *The Social Control of Mental Illness.* New York: Academic Press.

Hudson Jones, A. (1998) 'Mental illness made public: ending the stigma?' *The Lancet 352,* 1060.

Huxley, P. (1993) 'Location and stigma: a survey of community attitudes to mental illness – Part 1. Enlightenment and stigma.' *Journal of Mental Health 2,* 73–80.

Ingham, J. (1985) 'The public image of psychiatry.' *Social Psychiatry 20,* 107–108.

Jamison, K.J. (1998) 'Stigma of manic depression: a psychologist's experience.' *The Lancet 352,* 1053.

Johnson, S. and Orrell, M. (1995) 'Insight and psychosis: a social perspective.' *Psychological Medicine 25,* 3, 515–520.

Jones, E., Farina, A., Hastorf, A., Markus, H., Miller, D. and Scott, R. (1984) *Social Stigma: The Psychology of Marked Relationships.* New York: W.H. Freeman.

Judd, C.M. and Park, B. (1988) 'Outgroup homogeneity: judgements of variability at the individual and group levels.' *Journal of Personality and Social Psychology 54,* 778–788.

Kemp, R., Hayward, P., Applewhaite, G., Everitt, B. and David, A. (1996) 'Compliance therapy in psychotic patients: randomised controlled trial.' *British Medical Journal 3,* 12, 345–349.

Kennard, D. (1974) 'The newly admitted psychiatric patient as seen by self and others.' *British Journal of Medical Psychology 47,* 27–41.

Kirk, S.A. (1974) 'The impact of labeling on rejection of the mentally ill: an experimental study.' *Journal of Health and Social Behaviour 15,* 108–117.

Kirmayer, L.J. (1984) 'Culture, affect and somatization, parts 1 and 2.' *Transcultural Psychiatric Research Review 21,* 159–188, 237–262.

Kirmayer, L. (1989) 'Cultural variations in the response to psychiatric disorder and emotional distress.' *Social Science and Medicine 29,* 327–329.

Kleinman, A., Wang, W.Z., Li, S.C., Cheng, X.M., Dai, X.Y., Li, K.T. and Kleinman, J. (1995) 'The social course of epilepsy: chronic illness as social experience in interior China.' *Social Science and Medicine 40,* 1319–1330.

Kommana, S., Mansfield, M. and Penn, D.L. (1997) 'Dispelling the stigma of schizophrenia.' *Psychiatric Services 48*, 11, 1393–1395.

Kuipers, E. (1996) 'The prevention of social disability in schizophrenia.' In T. Kendrick and A. Tylee (eds) *The Prevention of Mental Illness in Primary Care.* Cambridge: Cambridge University Press.

Leach, E.R. (1982) *Social Anthropology.* London: Fontana.

Lefley, H. (1990) 'Culture and chronic mental illness.' *Hospital and Community Psychiatry 41*, 277–286.

Lehman, A.F., Possidente, S. and Hawker, F. (1986) 'The quality of life of chronic patients in a state hospital and in community residences.' *Hospital and Community Psychiatry 37*, 901–907.

Leichter, H.M. (1997) 'Lifestyle correctness and the new secular morality.' In A.M. Brandt *et al.* (eds) *Morality and Health.* New York: Routledge, pp. 359–378.

Lerner, M.J. and Miller, D.T. (1978) 'Just world research and the attribution process: looking back and ahead.' *Psychological Bulletin 85*, 1030–1051.

Lévi-Strauss, C. (1966) *The Savage Mind.* Chicago: University of Chicago Press.

Lévi-Strauss, C. (1973) *Structural Anthropology 2.* London: Penguin.

Levy, A. (1993) 'Stigma management: a new clinical service.' *Families in Society 74*, 4, 226–231.

Liberman, R.P. (ed) (1992) *Handbook of Psychiatric Rehabilitation.* New York: Macmillan.

Link, B. (1987) 'Understanding labeling effects in the area of mental disorders: an assessment of the effects of expectations of rejection.' *American Sociological Review 52*, 96–112.

Link, B.G. and Cullen, F.T. (1986) 'Contact with the mentally ill and perceptions of how dangerous they are.' *Journal of Health and Social Behaviour 7*, 289–303.

Link, B.G. and Cullen, F.T. (1990) 'The labelling theory of mental disorder: a review of the evidence.' In J. Greenley (ed) *Mental Illness in Social Context.* Greenwich: JAI Press.

Link, B.G., Cullen, F.T., Frank, J. and Wozniak, J.F. (1987) 'The social rejection of former mental patients: understanding why labels matter.' *American Journal of Sociology 92*, 1461–1500.

Link, B.G., Cullen, F.T., Struening, E., Shrout, P.E. and Dohrenwend, B.P. (1989) 'A modified labeling theory approach to mental disorders: an empirical assessment.' *American Sociological Review 54*, 400–423.

Link, B.G., Struening, E.L., Rahav, M., Phelan, Jo-C. and Nuttbrock, L. (1997) 'On stigma and its consequences: evidence from a longitudinal study of men with dual diagnoses of mental illness and substance abuse.' *Journal of Health and Social Behaviour 38*, 177–190.

Littlewood, R. (1988) 'From vice to madness: the semantics of naturalistic and personalistic understandings in Trinidadian local medicine.' *Social Science and Medicine 27*, 2, 129–148.

Littlewood, R.L. (1991) 'Against pathology: the new psychiatry and its critics.' *British Journal of Psychiatry 159*, 696–702.

Lyons, M. and Ziviani, J. (1995) 'Stereotypes, stigma and mental illness: learning from fieldwork experiences.' *American Journal of Occupational Therapy 49*, 10, 1002–1008.

MacMillan, J.F., Gold, A. and Crow, T.J. (1986) 'Expressed emotion and relapse.' *British Journal of Psychiatry 148*, 133–143.

McQueen, A.H., Swartz, L. and Perfile, L.L. (1995) 'Epilepsy and psychosocial adjustment: a selective review.' *South African Journal of Psychology 25*, 4, 207–210.

Manning, S.S. and Suire, B. (1996) 'Consumers as employees in mental health: bridges and roadblocks.' *Psychiatric Services 47*, 9, 939–940, 943.

Meeks, S. and Murrell, S.A. (1994) 'Service providers in the social networks of clients with severe mental illness.' *Schizophrenia Bulletin 20*, 399–406.

Mehta, S. and Farina, A. (1997) 'Is being sick really better? Effect of the disease view of mental disorder on stigma.' *Journal of Social and Clinical Psychology 16*, 4, 405–419.

Menninger, W.W. (1994) 'The future of psychiatry and implications for recruitment.' *Bulletin of the Menninger Clinic 58*, 4, 519–526.

Miklowitz, D.J., Goldstein, M.J. and Falloon, I.R.H. (1983) 'Premorbid and symptomatic characteristics of schizophrenics from families with high and low levels of expressed emotion.' *Journal of Abnormal Psychology 92*, 359–367.

Mosher, L. and Burti, L. (1992) 'Relationships in rehabilitation when technology fails.' *Psychosocial Rehabilitation Journal 15*, 11–17.

Mueser, K.T., Glynn, S.M., Corrigan, P.W. and Baber, W. (1996) 'A survey of preferred terms for users of mental health services.' *Psychiatric Services 47*, 7, 760–761.

Murphy, H.B.M. (1976) Book Review of A.R. Askenasy's Attitudes toward Mental Patients: a study across cultures. *Transcultural Psychiatric Research Review 13*, 49–51.

Nagler, M. (ed) (1994) *Perspectives on Disability.* Palo Alto, CA: Health Markets Research.

Ney, P.G., Tam, W.W.K. and Maurice, W.L. (1990) 'Factors that determine medical student interest in psychiatry.' *Australian and New Zealand Journal of Psychiatry 24*, 65–76.

Ng, C-H. (1997) 'The stigma of mental illness in Asian cultures.' *Australian and New Zealand Journal of Psychiatry 31*, 3, 382–390.

Nunnally, J. (1961) *Popular Conceptions of Mental Health: Their Development and Change.* New York: Holt, Rinhart and Winston.

Park, B., Ryan, C.S. and Judd, C.M. (1992) 'Role of meaningful subgroups in explaining differences in perceived variability for in groups and out groups.' *Journal of Personality and Social Psychology 63*, 533–567.

Parra, F. and So, A.Y. (1983) 'The changing perceptions of mental illness in a Mexican-American community.' *International Journal of Social Psychiatry 29*, 95–100.

Pearlin, L., Menaghan, E., Lieberman, M. and Mullan, J. (1981) 'The stress process.' *Journal of Health and Social Behaviour 22*, 337–356.

Penn, D.L., Guynan, K., Daily, T., Spaulding, D.W., Garbin, C.P. and Sullivan, M. (1994) 'Dispelling the stigma of schizophrenia: what sort of information is best?' *Schizophrenia Bulletin 20*, 567–578.

Phelan, J.C., Bromet, E.J. and Link, B.G. (1998) 'Psychiatric illness and family stigma.' *Schizophrenia Bulletin 24*, 1, 115–126.

Phillips, D.L. (1996) 'Public identification and acceptance of the mentally ill.' *American Journal of Public Health 56*, 755–763.

Porter, R. (1998) 'Can the stigma of mental illness be changed?' *The Lancet 352*, 1049–1050.

Quadagno, J.S. and Antonio, R.J. (1975) 'Labeling theory as an over socialized conception of man: the case of mental illness.' *Sociology and Social Research 60*, 33–45.

Rabkin, J. (1974) 'Public attitudes towards mental illness.' *Schizophrenia Bulletin 10*, 9–21.

Rabkin, J. (1981) 'Public attitudes: new research directions.' *Hospital And Community Psychiatry 32*, 157–159.

Raghuram, R., Weiss, M.G., Channabasavanna, S.M. and Devins, G.M. (1996) 'Stigma, depression and somatization in South India.' *American Journal of Psychiatry 153*, 8, 1043–1049.

Riger, A.L. (1994) 'Beyond ADA: APA's responsibility to disability rights.' *APA Monitor*, December, p.34.

Rose, D. (1996) *Living in the Community*. London: Sainsbury Centre for Mental Health.

Rose, L.E. (1996) 'Families of psychiatric patients: a critical review and future research directions.' *Archives of Psychiatric Nursing 10*, 67–76.

Rosenfeld, S. (1997) 'Labeling mental illness: the effects of received services and perceived stigma on life satisfaction.' *American Sociological Review 62*, 4, 660–672.

Royal College of Psychiatrists (1998) *Mental Disorders: Challenging Prejudice*. London: Royal College of Psychiatry.

Rush, L.L. (1998) 'Affective reactions to multiple social stigmas.' *Journal of Social Psychology 138*, 4, 421–430.

Sabin, T. and Mancuso, J. (1970) 'Failure of a moral enterprise: attitudes of the public towards mental illness.' *Journal of Consulting and Clinical Psychology 35*, 159–173.

Sartorius, N. (1998) 'Stigma: what can psychiatrists do about it?' *The Lancet 352*, 1058–1059.

Sartorius, N., Jablensky, A., Korten, A., Ernberg, G., Naker, M., Cooper, J.E. and Day, R. (1986) 'Early manifestations and first contact incidence of schizophrenia in different societies: a preliminary report on the initial evaluation phase of the WHO Collaborative Study on Determinants of Outcome of Severe Mental Disorders.' *Psychological Medicine 16*, 909–928.

Schneider, M.E., Major, B., Luhtannen, R. and Crocker, J. (1996) 'Social stigma and the potential costs of assumptive help.' *Personality and Social Psychology Bulletin 22*, 2, 201–209.

Segal, S.P. (1978) 'Attitudes among the mentally ill: a review.' *Social Work 23*, 211–217.

Shaw, F. (1998) 'Mistaken identity.' *The Lancet 352*, 1050–1051.

Shepherd, G. (1998) 'Developments in psychosocial rehabilitation for early psychosis.' *International Clinical Psychopharmacology 139*, Supplement 1, S53–S57.

Skinner, L.J., Berry, K.K., Griffith, S. and Byers, B. (1995) 'Generalizability and specificity of the stigma associated with mental illness label: a reconsideration twenty-five years later.' *Journal of Community Psychology 23*, 1, 3–17.

Socall, D.W. and Holtgraves, T. (1992) 'Attitudes toward the mentally ill: the effects of label and beliefs.' *Sociological Quarterly 33*, 435–445.

Sontag, S. (1977) *Illness as Metaphor*. New York: Allen Lane.

Star, S.A. (1957) *The Public's Ideas about Mental Illness*. National Opinion Research Centre, University of Chicago (unpublished).

Stiles, B.L. and Kaplan, H.B. (1996) 'Stigma, deviance and negative social sanctions.' *Social Science Quarterly 77*, 3, 685–696.

Taylor, S.M. and Dear, M.J. (1981) 'Scaling community attitudes toward the mentally ill.' *Schizophrenia Bulletin 7*, 225–240.

Torrey, E.F. (1994) 'Violent behaviour by individuals with serious mental illness.' *Hospital and Community Psychiatry 45*, 7, 653–662.

Townsend, J.M. (1979) 'Stereotypes and mental illness: a comparison with ethnic stereotypes.' *Culture, Medicine and Psychiatry 3*, 205–230.

Townsend, J.M. and Rakfeldt, J. (1985) 'Hospitalisation and first contact mental patients: stigma and changes in self concept.' *Research in Community Mental Health 5*, 269–301.

Vandiver, V.L. (1997) 'Services to the severely and persistently mentally ill.' In T.R. Watkins *et al.* (eds) *Mental Health Policy and Practice Today*. Thousand Oaks: Sage.

Vaughn, C.E., Snyder, K.S. and Jones, S. (1984) 'Family factors in schizophrenia relapse: a California replication of the British research on expressed emotion.' *Archives of General Psychiatry 41*, 1169–1171.

Waxler, N.E. (1979) 'Culture and mental illness.' *Journal of Nervous and Mental Disease 159*, 379–395.

Wahl, O.F. (1995) *Media Madness, Public Images of Mental Health*. New Brunswick, NJ: Rutgers University Press.

Wahl, O.F. and Lefkowitz, J.Y. (1989) 'Impact of a television film on attitudes toward mental illness.' *American Journal of Community Psychology 17*, 521–528.

Warner, R., Taylor, D., Powers, M. and Hyman, J. (1989) 'Acceptance of the mental illness label by psychotic patients: effects on functioning.' *American Journal of Orthopsychiatry 59*, 398–409.

Weismann, S.H., Haynes, R.A., Killian, C.D. and Robinowitz, C. (1994) 'A model to determine the influence of medical school on students' career choices: psychiatry, a case study.' *Academic Medicine 69*, 1, 58–59.

Weiner, B., Perry, R.P.C. and Magnusson, J. (1988) 'An attributional analysis of reactions to stigmas.' *Journal of Personality and Social Psychology 55*, 738–748.

Whatley, C.D. (1959) 'Social attitudes toward discharged mental patients.' *Social Problems 6*, 313–320.

Witztum, E., Margolin, J., Bar-On, R. and Levy, A. (1995) 'Stigma, labelling and psychiatric diagnosis: Origins and outcomes.' *Medicine and Law 14*, 7–8, 659–669.

Wolff, G., Pathare, S., Craig, T. and Leff, J. (1996) 'Public education for community care: a new approach.' *British Journal of Psychiatry 168*, 441–447.

Wurtzel, E. (1994) *Prozac Nation: Young and Depressed in America.* Boston, MA: Houghton and Miffin.

11

Structures of Medical Thought

Professional Dispositions in Practice

Simon Sinclair

In this chapter I wish to show how medical students learn the cultural categorization of the different specialties of medicine (such as Surgery, Medicine and Psychiatry)[1] that they study during their years of clinical training. The chapter is in three parts. There is first a brief introduction. This is followed by some results from my own fieldwork in a London medical school in 1993–4.[2] At that time, the traditional tripartite structure of medical training in England – two preclinical years, three clinical years and, lastly, the year of 'general clinical training' as a House Officer or houseman (known as internship in the USA) – was unaffected by the wave of more recent reforms among medical training, prompted to some extent by the General Medical Council's *Tomorrow's Doctors* (1993). Third, I discuss the similarities and differences between my own work and a famous earlier study of medical training, *Boys in White* (1961) by Becker and his colleagues.

INTRODUCTION

Medical schools are institutions which produce doctors, and their prospectuses and curricula describe how this is done: the school teaches students and tests them, while students must learn what they are taught to pass examinations. An early account, that broadly takes just such a straightforward view of what medical schools say they do is *The Student-Physician* (Merton, Reader and Kendall 1957). It has been pointed out (Bloom 1971, pp.97–99) that this title reflects the view of medical socialization as a relatively orderly transmission of professional knowledge, skills and value to emergent professional colleagues, while that of *Boys in White* implies that students are a more lowly and autonomous body. Here, students are described as developing their own ways of dealing with the system of training to get through medical school any way they can to qualify as doctors. This approach has been strongly criticized by Atkinson (1983, pp.230–231) because of the attention paid to the 'hidden' rather than the 'manifest' curriculum and because of its implied assumption that students are almost in a 'total institution' (see Goffman 1991). But both these studies – and indeed Atkinson's own work (1981) – attend in their different ways to what is taught or how students learn. They do not cover the large areas of students' life which do not apparently have anything to do with either the 'manifest' or the 'hidden' curriculum (games, dramatic performances and Rag Week, for example). In other words, though these researchers have taken different views of medical training, they have tended to focus on what might be called the 'official' aspects (teaching and learning) rather than the 'unofficial' (games and so on).

A framework for integrating these different approaches and including 'unofficial' areas is provided by another well-known analytic concept of Goffman's, the extended metaphor of the social stage (see particularly Goffman 1990). While the institution itself should clearly be seen less in terms of physically bounded space and more in terms of cognitively bounded time, it can also be subdivided into 'frontstage' and 'backstage' of both 'official' and 'unofficial' areas (see Figure 11.1).

	OFFICIAL	UNOFFICIAL	
FRONT STAGE	'Manifest curriculum' Lectures, ward rounds, examinations Merton *et al.* (1957) Atkinson (1981)	Games field (e.g. rugby) Theatrical performances (Christmas pantomime) Rag Week	Lay
			OFFSTAGE
BACK STAGE	'Hidden curriculum' Libraries, wards, students' homes Becker *et al.* (1961)	Preparation for unofficial frontstage activities Students' bar	World

Figure 11.1 The conceptual institution of the medical school (its boundaries indicated by a heavy line), showing its different 'stages' and the various activities that take place on them, with the main location of previous studies. Time is also spent on the non-medical 'offstage'.

Within this institutional framework, how now to chart the transformation of inexperienced medical students to qualified doctors? The way that I have chosen to describe the acquisition of a medical identity makes use of Bourdieu's concept of the 'habitus'. The habitus, 'the durably installed generative principle of regulated improvisations' (Bourdieu 1977, p.78), is composed of the infinitely variable (though organized) sum of collectively created mental and physical manifestations of its constituent 'dispositions', inculcated and embodied in and practised by, individual people. While the dispositions of a distinct group of people are the same, and are expressed in a common habitus, dispositions only direct thought and action and do not determine them: each individual interprets and practises them according to his or her own personal 'style'.

DISPOSITIONS IN MEDICAL TRAINING

Before describing their use as cultural categories, I now hope to show how the practice of medical dispositions (which I indicate by capital letters) may be discerned at the three separate levels of training. A fuller account of this is to be found in my ethnography of medical training (Sinclair 1997).

All applicants to medical school must demonstrate their zealous interest in acquiring the first disposition to be mentioned, medical Status; any doubt or hesitation about taking this step must be hidden, or acceptance to medical school is highly unlikely. Although altruistic motives for deciding on medicine as a career are still common, these too must be dissimulated both in written applications and also at interview. Despite this dissimulation, Idealism is another medical disposition, though it should be remembered that, at this point, it is personally held. On application to medical school, Competition with other applicants is keenly felt; after acceptance, its inverse, that of Cooperation between students, becomes the dominant disposition, as indeed it is in the profession generally (partly because it is within the practice of Cooperation that all other dispositions are learnt, taught and practised).

Preclinically, students are taught uncontentious and factual visible Knowledge – certain, in the language of Sociology – still (at the time of my fieldwork) most frequently in lectures, where the spoken word accompanying a profusion of slides is matched by the lavishly illustrated textbooks read elsewhere, in libraries and at their own desks (computers now also provide equivalent Knowledge). Such Knowledge is collectively available (and may also be acquired by those without even the limited medical Status of preclinical students). Away from the official frontstage settings where Knowledge is taught and tested, work for written preclinical exams is accomplished by the practice of the dispositions of Cooperation and Economy: groups of students work together, on the official backstage of home and in libraries, to establish what needs to be learnt to pass (by circulating copies of previous Multiple Choice Questionnaires, for example) and to help each other out in various ways (such as by interchanging essays between members of the group). But preclinical students also attend the dissecting room and, through the practice of anatomical dissection, there learn the disposition of Experience, which involves not only sight but also touch (and smell and hearing). As they stand round the corpse in almost the only 'hands-on' setting during these two years, they are learning something very different from the Knowledge they are taught as they sit writing in lecture theatres.

Cooperation is also pre-eminent in the communal unofficial activities that so distinguish a medical school, particularly in the preclinical years. The prominence of clubs (particularly sporting ones) and of the large group responsible for the Christmas pantomime indicate the importance of Co-operation in activities on what I have called the unofficial frontstage. Another such group is the Rag, formed for the Economic and Idealistic aim of raising money for charity during Rag Week; here is also found the universe of the disposition of professional Responsibility – public licence – for example, in the sexual and scatological jokes made in the Rag Mag. Public licence is also found more generally in medical students' behaviour on the unofficial backstage – their sometimes heroic scale of drinking is notorious – and the way in which they may escape public sanction for misdemeanours, and indeed sometimes criminal activities, on the simple grounds that they are medical students.

Clinically, students (now on the hospital wards, with ambiguous medical Status indicated by their short white coats) are attached in rotation to 'firms' (hierarchical groups of doctors in one of the specialties of medicine). Here, they are principally taught Experience, a personal acquisition of specialized forms of questions and body techniques to elicit definite positive symptoms and concrete physical signs from patients; the certainty of these findings is stressed. Unlike Knowledge, Experience is limited to those with medical Status, taught orally from privileged access to patients (as it was during the preclinical years from privileged access to dead bodies): no one could learn how to elicit and interpret the findings from a physical examination (with its multisensory aspects of sight, touch, hearing and even smell) from reading a book about it. For the purposes of learning Experience, students are now introduced to another disposition, that of Responsibility: they are granted a temporary and hypothetical Responsibility for patients when they are allotted ownership of patients properly belonging to the firm's consultants. These are mostly, however, what Atkinson (1981, pp.72–91) calls 'cold' patients, those whose diagnosis has been established and whose treatment has already begun. The second aspect of Responsibility, medical action directed at a patient, is usually again only hypothesized verbally: students can by and large only exercise the real action of Responsibility towards the 'hot' patients whom they find in Casualty and on their Obstetric firm.

On ward rounds (the official frontstage for the teaching of Experience), students again learn that the personal Idealism with which they came into medical school should not be displayed. Instead, a professional Idealism, manifest keenness, now in pursuit of Experience and Responsibility, is the disposition most likely to gain the approval of their teachers, although it may excite the contempt of their fellow students away from such settings. For, once again, among themselves, students practise Cooperative Economy (sharing their work out, clerking patients particularly when this is to their advantage, and covering up each other's absence). But Cooperation becomes increasingly tinged with Competition (often expressed as professional Idealism), as students strive for good firm grades to help them maximize their chances of getting the 'house job' they want.

Housemen, at this third level of training, again work within the Co-operative firm (at the lowest rank of the hierarchy) and are delegated Responsibility for the patients owned by the consultants who head the firm (all hospital patients 'belong' to a named consultant). At this level, it is now the practice of Responsibility and the acquisition of further Experience that are most emphasized. The ownership of Responsibility is found in house-men's reference to patients they 'have' or 'had', in distinction to patients they 'saw' (in the disposition of Experience as students). The other aspect of Responsibility, medical action, leads to another form of certainty, based on what happens to patients treated by housemen and their firm. Knowledge is at a discount, despite the houseman's year being described officially as the last stage of medical education and their posts needing the academic approval of the university.

For housemen, the distinction between the official frontstage and back-stage is now even more clearly marked; they need to present professional Idealism on ward rounds, showing (for example) how completely their energies have been expended on getting investigations done and their results ready for the consultant ward round, as this is the setting where consultants assess housemen's performance for the purposes of writing their references for their next job. But away from such formal settings, housemen for the third time practise Economy, now on their own, getting tests done any way they can, for example, by deliberately being Economical with the truth and putting down false information on request forms. These contrasts and conflicts lead both to the irony and black humour that characterizes medical culture and, especially among those whose personal Idealism has persisted, to demoralization and despair. Cooperation is again important, housemen seeing others in the hospital (mostly patients and nurses) principally as whether they are Cooperative or not – that is, whether or not they fall in with what the houseman needs to do in pursuit of Responsibility.

The use of dispositions to categorize medical specialties

In my account, I have indicated how medical students and housemen practise the medical dispositions of Status, Idealism, Cooperation, Competition, Knowledge, Experience, Responsibility and Economy. I will now show in more detail how clinical students use these dispositions to categorize different medical specialties, as they rotate around them in their attachment to firms in their clinical years. Students often see their never-to-be repeated clinical rotation as a privileged glimpse of different specialties, to allow them to see which branch of medicine they might choose and, partly with this in mind, they discuss different specialties among themselves. They are also often taught quite explicitly by a teacher from one clinical specialty how that specialty sees itself and others; this practice by senior doctors emphasizes the general professional nature of dispositions. The segments of the profession, then, are classified and ranked in terms of dispositions, which, as well as being practised, are also found (in accordance with structuralist anthropological theory) as 'good to think with'. In Bourdieu's terms, the taxonomies of the system 'at once divide and unify, legitimating unity in division, that is to say, hierarchy' (1977, p.165).

The way that students are taught to see other specialties often involves what Dingwall (1977) calls 'atrocity stories': this method of categorization by disparagement is used to define both non-professionals and intra-professional segments, and consultants show clinical students the way. As doctors, they disparage non-doctors, such as administrators and managers, about whom adverse comments are frequent; they lack medical Status and have no medical Responsibility for patients. As clinicians, consultants disparage preclinical teachers and academic doctors, again as having no Responsibility; as hospital doctors, they disparage General Practitioners, who have no specialized Knowledge, Experience or Responsibility; and as specialists, they disparage other specialties, in distinction to their own, in line with these other specialties' stereotyped categorization.

So, for example, a consultant ENT (Ear, Nose and Throat) surgeon made a remark in the course of a clinical lecture (often the setting for such comments) about the management of a child with croup: 'The paediatrician may say "Do a Chest X-ray"; and down the cold corridor they [such patients] go, put on the cold lead shield. The kid'll die in X-ray [in the X-ray room]! And if you think radiographers are good at resuscitating children, you're wrong! A lot of children die each year out of ignorance!' The point being made by the ENT surgeon was that paediatricians (in a branch of Medicine) and radiographers (not doctors at all) don't know what they're doing – paediatricians do not have a correct understanding of the Experience gained from physical examination of the child and so, while the request for an X-ray may be based on published Knowledge (and, of course, X-rays and other medical images have much in common with the visible facts of Knowledge), paediatricians do not take the correct Responsible action.

Here we have the elements of the basic professional stereotypes: Surgery scores higher on Responsibility, perhaps higher on Experience, and less on Knowledge than Medicine. Some surgical specialties are culturally held to require even less Knowledge than others, as an orthopaedic surgeon implied in this caricature of his own specialty during a lecture: he asked the audience, 'Why do orthopaedic surgeons have hunched shoulders and flat foreheads?', and then answered his own question, 'Because when you ask them a question, they go [here he shrugged his shoulders to indicate their ignorance] and when you tell them the answer, they go [and he struck his forehead with his right palm, indicating their recognition of the obviousness of the answer]!' In teaching hospitals, Medicine and Surgery broadly share the highest Status, though through different routes, the greater Responsibility of Surgery being matched by the greater Knowledge in Medicine.

Another specialty is of some interest here. For some students, their attachment to an Obstetrics firm is the high point of their clinical years. The reasons for this are not hard to find in terms of the practice of dispositions. When on obstetric wards, students do not have to attend any conflicting lectures of Knowledge, and they may stay with 'their' patients (who are, in Atkinson's terms, clearly 'hot') throughout their labour. Students are at first closely supervised by midwives, but later it is only the delivery which is supervised, the midwife sometimes simply being present with a few words of advice or help: students' medical Status is therefore less ambiguous than it normally is on the wards. During the hours spent with the patient, a close relationship may be established in the practice of Cooperation, when the powerfully physical process of labour allows students full range for the verbal and indeed physical encouragement of Cooperation, as they strain and breathe in sympathy with their patients. Their patients provide not only Experience but, much more importantly, the opportunity for the practice of the action of Responsibility; the aims of the student (in whom, for once, personal and professional Idealism closely overlap) and the woman in labour are effectively identical and usually realized in the safe delivery of a healthy baby.

But it is essential to appreciate that the professional specialty with the lowest Status is Psychiatry. This is vigorously affirmed by other consultants; for example, one physician said, speaking of patients with enuresis, 'It's a *tragedy* when patients like this fall into the hands of the psychiatrists!' Such low Status is confirmed for students by several dispositional factors. The psychiatric 'literature' of Knowledge contains far fewer facts than most specialties, with widely different approaches being taken towards patients' problems (based on the varieties of assumption made about the origins of psychiatric symptoms); Psychiatry is thus short of proper Knowledge. Psychiatric patients tend to score low on the category of Cooperation, often being resistant to being seen by students. Further, the patient's history is not just a straightforward account from the patient, but itself becomes part of the equivalent of the physical examination, although this yields no proper Experience in the form of concrete and objectively verifiable pathology. And students find that psychiatrists lack Responsibility for their patients in terms of both ownership and action: not only are there 'multidisciplinary teams' including many non-doctors, but a great deal of psychiatric treatment is negotiated and much treatment is talking, hardly action at all. Rather perversely, the lack of Responsibility that psychiatrists are held to have for their patients may be confirmed for clinical students by the fact that psychiatric patients are the only ones for whom they themselves can have real and continuing Responsibility, by getting on the supervised scheme to meet a patient once a week for psychotherapy; for consultants to hand over Responsibility in this way to untrained students may further emphasize the lack of the aspects of both ownership and action in Responsibility. To put this another way, no cardiac surgeon would hand over to a student complete Responsibility for treating one of his patients. For all these categorical reasons, then, Psychiatry is the lowest Status specialty in general medical culture; this is confirmed, certainly among clinical students, by a questionnaire study of their attitudes to different specialties (Furnham 1986).

It will be apparent that there are two sorts of hierarchy at work here. Dispositions are themselves ranked in order of importance: Responsibility comes first, Knowledge second, and then Experience, while Economy may be a practical consideration. The resultant combination of the hierarchically ranked dispositional factors found to be practised within any given specialty is given expression in another hierarchy, found in the differential Status accorded to different specialties. But though there is a common value given to specialties in general medical culture, the value that individuals, in their own 'style', give to dispositions (and hence to the Status of specialties) may be very different; indeed it must be so, for otherwise how would any doctor choose to pursue such a low Status specialty as Epidemiology, for example?

That clinical students themselves actually use dispositional categories in this way is quite clear from the example of Abdul's description of Rheumatology as 'the housewife's specialty'; in explanation, he said, 'It's all outpatients, all women and children, all tablets and aches and pains.' In Rheumatology, in other words, not only is the ownership of Responsibility limited to outpatients, and the action of Responsibility to giving tablets, but the patients' problems are seen to be 'aches and pains', not providing any Experience in the form of real pathological findings, and the patients themselves are women and children: this combination makes Rheumatology a low Status specialty, suitable for women doctors, who may well work part-time, so making it 'the housewife's specialty'. The association implied by Abdul between low Status specialties and women doctors, who often work part-time, is in fact quite a strong one.

The demonstration of this involves a different approach from the 'mechanical' structuralist one that I have sketched out above: this different approach to the same phenomena, but at a different level of analysis, is a statistical one (Lévi-Strauss 1977, pp.282–289). In interpreting these figures, it is important to bear in mind both that contingent and personal variables are involved and that, in the gendered institution of medicine, men always feature more largely in the higher ranks of the profession. So, the lowest proportion of women consultants is found in the specialties of Surgery (4.3%) and Medicine (8.6%) – the category of Medicine has been created by lumping the six highest Status subspecialties: General Medicine, Cardiology, Diabetes and Endocrinology, Gastroenterology, Nephrology and Thoracic Medicine. In Rheumatology it is 16.2 per cent, while in Psychiatry it is 29.8 per cent (DOH 1996, Table 7A). In fact, the highest proportion of women consultants is now[3] in Paediatrics (33.6%), which appears to be the subsegment of Medicine thought particularly suitable for women. Abdul's other point about low Status specialties being more open to women because of the ease of working part-time is shown by the proportion of all Senior Registrars (the grade below consultant) who are women working part-time: 0.02 per cent in Surgery, 3.3 per cent in Medicine and 12.7 per cent in Psychiatry (DOH 1996, Table 7D).

It is not my purpose here to discuss cause and effect as regards the interaction of the Status of specialties, gender and part-time training; but these figures lend support to what I have tried to show so far, how students' and doctors' categorization of medical specialties may be understood in terms of the structures of professional thought and practice.

DISCUSSION

In this last section, I shall make some comparisons between my own work and *Boys in White*, a work that must be seriously acknowledged because of the huge amount of time its authors spent with the group of students they studied: four researchers working for two years.

Becker and his colleagues (I shall hereafter refer to these workers by the first named) derived what they called 'perspectives' from what preclinical and clinical students said and did, unprompted, in each other's presence (on the official backstage, in my terms). A perspective is defined as a 'co-ordinated set of ideas and actions a person uses in dealing with some problematic situation, to refer to a person's ordinary way of thinking and feeling about and acting in such a situation'. Perspectives, then, are situationally specific; they have an active or practical as well as a cognitive component; and they are also collective and shared (Becker *et al.* 1961, pp.34–37). But perspectives are limited in several important ways: limited to one or other of the specific levels of training where Becker and his colleagues did fieldwork (preclinical and clinical); limited in their application to the area where Becker studied (the official backstage, in my terms) and sometimes even limited to particular settings found there; and, generally, limited to students and their culture, which Becker considers to be autonomous.

To summarize Becker's findings very briefly, students arrive at medical school with a Long-range perspective (that medicine is hard but worthwhile work); faced with the huge quantity of written work expected of them in the preclinical years, their Initial perspective (of wanting to learn everything) changes, through the Provisional (the recognition that the Initial perspective cannot be practically carried out), to the Final perspective (of working in ways calculated to maximize their chances of passing exams). In the clinical years, when students see patients for the first time, they learn more perspectives: the strangely named Academic one (that their teachers can humiliate them and stop them passing, and so must be accommodated to), and that of Student Cooperation (the need to share out clinical work allocated to them on the services [firms] to which they are attached). All these perspectives (apart from the Long-range one that they arrive with) are said to be the product of the autonomous student culture; clinically, students also learn two perspectives derived from medical culture, that of Clinical Experience (a desirable quality gained from having access to patients) and that of Responsibility (a desirable attribute gained by having patients and doing medical things to them, archetypally found in the surgeon holding the patient's life in his hands).

It is easy to see that the medical dispositions that I have described above have many similarities with Becker's perspectives – my dispositions of Idealism and Status, for example, can be derived from the Long-range perspective and the disposition of Experience differs little from the perspective of Clinical Experience. But it is my proposition that dispositions have advantages over Becker's perspectives in several ways.

The advantages of dispositions over perspectives

When Becker describes the way that clinical students categorize patients (1961, pp.313–340), he finds that this can mostly be associated with the explicit perspectives described above, although some cannot. These he reckons are categorized according to some non-specific perspectives from lay culture and medical culture, as well as to a 'hazy' perspective from student culture. I suggest, on the one hand, that these patients can be more aptly categorized using my dispositions and, on the other, that the non-specific and catch-all perspectives can be done away with, and therefore that dispositions are analytically more powerful than perspectives. So, for example, patients who fit better into dispositional categories are 'difficult' patients, with no respect for doctors' authority and intensely disliked by students (no doubt because of their own ambiguous Status). These are placed by Becker in a category derived from a general and unspecified perspective of medical culture (1961, p.320) but are much better classified under the dispositional categories of denying doctors their medical Status and refusing Cooperation. Conversely, an example of a catch-all category that can be done away with seen in the 'hazier case for the argument that students draw on student culture' when they consider that 'patients should not take up a student's time without giving him something worthwhile in return' (1961, p.335): this hazy category is immediately clarified if the Economic dispositional category is applied.

Again, when Becker describes how students, towards the end of their clinical years, consider which medical specialty they might follow, he is insistent that the 'criteria' students use to do this are speculative and hypothetical (1961, p.368) and are not related to the perspectives they learnt during their training up to this point. This insistence is really rather odd, because students might be expected to use the perspectives that they created together during their preclinical and clinical years to think about their future careers. At any rate, these criteria can be seen very easily in terms of dispositions, again indicating dispositions' greater analytic power. For example, three criteria about specialties (making an adequate amount of money; 'having convenient hours and not being too arduous', and 'requiring a long training') can be collapsed into the Economic disposition, with its emphasis now on the acquisition of money in relation to time. When seen in this way, the rankings of the segments of medicine by Becker's students and students at UCLMS are strikingly similar (see Sinclair 1997, pp.35–37, 242–247).

There are also some real difficulties with Becker's perspectives. Take, for example, the perspective of Student Cooperation: this, in accordance with the definition of perspectives as situationally specific, is located firmly in the clinical years. But, in fact, all his perspectives (except the personal Long-range perspective with which individual freshmen arrive) were collectively worked out by students and Becker found general agreement between students about them. Here then arises a paradox, that students must have somehow cooperated to reach the perspective of Student Cooperation itself; this paradox is resolved by seeing Cooperation as the paramount disposition throughout the years of training and, given that dispositions are found in the profession at large, it is therefore also the paramount general professional disposition. But Cooperation has an inverse, Competition, which is very evident in official frontstage settings of medical schools. Perhaps because his fieldwork took place mostly on the official backstage, Competition appears to have entirely escaped Becker's notice. There is another striking omission in Becker's account: there is no perspective that refers to the 'book-work' which forms such a prominent feature particularly of preclinical students' lives, which Becker describes as the polar opposite to Clinical Experience (1961, p.231), and to which indeed the Initial, Provisional and Final perspectives are all related. This area of 'book-work' I have covered by the disposition of Knowledge.

Probably because of the combination of the situational specificity of perspectives and the location of Becker's fieldwork, conflict between perspectives is not described as occurring. A further reason may be that the one major conflict that Becker does describe – when preclinical students find the Initial perspective cannot be carried out – is itself called a perspective, the Provisional one. This conflict is resolved by the development of the Final perspective, which has many similarities to my Economic disposition. I have derived this disposition, on the other hand, from the explicit conflict between Idealism (the wish to learn everything) and Status (the desire to progress to the next level of training) over the acquisition of Knowledge. But, even in Becker's material, other conflicts can be found (in the Academic perspective, for example) and there are, in fact, others still (that between Cooperation and Competition being an obvious instance). Here then is the last point to make about the advantages of dispositions over perspectives: that medical dispositions, being embodied, are practised by students and doctors at all levels of the medical profession (and not just at the three levels of training, let alone at just the two which Becker studied) and, in one form or other, on most 'stages' too. Being embodied, dispositions may conflict with each other in various ways: these conflicts (such as that between personal Idealism, professional Idealism and Economy for housemen, alluded to briefly above) may in turn allow a greater understanding of some of the problems caused by medical training. Indeed, I have suggested (Sinclair 1997, pp.301–320) that the results of some well-known studies of psychological morbidity in students and junior doctors can be understood simply in terms of conflicts between dispositions.

In summary, I think that, in his great study, Becker seriously underestimated the power of his observations. By limiting the application of his findings to the fieldwork site, he took the view that medical student culture was autonomous. But, in fact, medical training does not lead to an autonomous student culture, and student culture should better be thought of as an integral part of medical culture, crucial to its continued reproduction.

NOTES

1. Here it should be noted that the word 'medicine' is commonly used in two different ways: to denote the medical profession generally and to describe the specialty of General, or Internal, Medicine, practised by physicians. I shall continue to use lower case to indicate the former (so, medicine) and upper case to indicate the latter (so, Medicine) and all such specialties (so, Surgery and Psychiatry).

2. Fieldwork took place in University College London Medical School (UCLMS), to which I am most grateful. My research was conducted for a PhD from the Department of Anthropology at the London School of Economics and was supported by a Postgraduate Student Award from the ESRC.

3. These were the most recent figures available at the time of writing.

REFERENCES

Atkinson, P. (1981) *The Clinical Experience: The Construction and Reconstruction of Medical Reality.* Farnborough: Gower.

Atkinson, P. (1983) 'The reproduction of the professional community.' In R. Dingwall and P. Lewis (eds) *The Sociology of the Professions: Lawyers, Doctors and Others.* London and Basingstoke: Macmillan.

Becker, H.S., Geer, B.S., Hughes, E.C. and Strauss, A.L. (1961) *Boys In White: Student Culture in Medical School.* Chicago: University of Chicago Press.

Bloom, W. (1971) 'The medical school as social system.' *Millbank Memorial Fund Quarterly 49,* 2: Part 2.

Bourdieu, P. (1977) *Outline of a Theory of Practice.* Trans. R. Nice. Cambridge: Cambridge University Press.

Department of Health (DOH) (1996) *Hospital Medical Staff – England and Wales: National Tables.* London: HMSO.

Dingwall, R. (1977) '"Atrocity stories" and professional relationships.' *Sociology of Work and Occupations 4,* 371–396.

Furnham, A.F. (1986) 'Medical students' beliefs about nine different specialties.' *British Medical Journal 293,* 1607–1610.

General Medical Council (Education Committee) (1993) *Tomorrow's Doctors: Recommendations on Undergraduate Medical Education.* London: GMC.

Goffman, E. (1990) *The Presentation of Self in Everyday Life.* Harmondsworth: Penguin.

Goffman, E. (1991) *Asylums: Essays on the Social Situation of Mental Patients and Other Inmates.* Harmondsworth: Penguin.

Lévi-Strauss, C. (1977) 'Social structure.' In C. Lévi-Strauss *Structural Anthropology 1.* Trans. C. Jacobson and B.G. Schoepf. Harmondsworth: Penguin.

Merton, R.K., Reader, G.G. and Kendall, P. (1957) *The Student-Physician: Introductory Studies in the Sociology of Medical Education.* Cambridge, MA: Harvard University Press.

Sinclair, S. (1997) *Making Doctors: An Institutional Apprenticeship.* Oxford and New York: Berg.

12

Lessons From Anthropology

Maurice Lipsedge

INTRODUCTION

Twenty years ago I wrote, together with Roland Littlewood who was then a lecturer in the Department of Psychological Medicine at St Bartholomew's Hospital, a chapter in *Recent Advances in Clinical Psychiatry* (Granville-Grossman 1979) entitled 'Transcultural Psychiatry'. The theme of the chapter was the dictum of Aubrey Lewis, the doyen of British psychiatry, that 'it is by no means easy to decide whether a particular person, living in a culture alien to him or in a culture alien to the examining psychiatrist, is mentally ill or not' (Lewis 1967).

The words 'culture' and 'mentally ill' were taken for granted, as was the diagnostic process itself. In the two decades since that chapter was written, much of the theory and practice of biomedicine in general and psychiatry in particular has been subjected to critical scrutiny by anthropologists, sociologists and some radical psychologists. However, in everyday clinical practice and in the teaching of psychiatry there is little awareness of the self-reflective criticism which anthropology could inject into our professional ideologies and activities. This disappointing impermeability of psychiatry can be demonstrated by a review of the content of the most influential psychiatric textbooks published over the past ten years or so which can be assumed to represent the views of mainstream teachers and practitioners of psychiatry.

TRANSCULTURAL PSYCHIATRY 1979 STYLE

Most of the ethnographic material selected by psychiatrists working with ethnic minority patients in the late 1970s was chosen for its potential relevance to the cross-cultural clinical encounter with its perplexing lack of mutual comprehension encapsulated in Aubrey Lewis's dictum. The psychiatrist was eager to avoid making a false attribution of mental illness, especially psychosis.

I remember combing the classic works of anthropology for ethnographic data which might help a psychiatrist to avoid the cardinal error of misdiagnosis. Devereux's story of the Navajo Indian whose reluctance to communicate was interpreted as catatonic stupor served as a warning (Devereux 1963). The culturally naive psychiatrist was alerted against the error of assuming that when an Azande publicly accepted an unjustified witchcraft attribution, he was not showing that morbid self-accusation which in the West would be pathognomonic of melancholia (Evans- Pritchard 1937). In any case, irrational ideas of guilt and self-recrimination were said to be rarely experienced by Africans, among whom the psychological defence mechanism of projection was assumed to predominate over introjection and self-castigation (Murphy, Wittkower and Chance 1967). While morbid guilt was rare, somatization was allegedly commoner among depressed people in the third world. Wittkower (1969), founder of the *Transcultural Psychiatric Research Review*, attributed this to the incapacity of 'pre-literates' to describe their feelings because there were no words for depression in their languages. Leff (1973) had similarly concluded that depressed people in developing countries lacked the vocabulary to differentiate between unpleasant emotional states. Our own indignant rejoinder cited the subtle differentiation of a wide range of emotional states demonstrated by the lexical categories employed in the Pintupi speech community (Morice 1978).

The reported rarity of guilt-ridden melancholia in Africa and the favourable prognosis for schizophrenia among people such as the aboriginal population of Taiwan (Rin and Lin 1962) now have an idyllic pastoral Noble Savage flavour (but see the paper on the rarity of psychosis in Tonga by Murphy and Taumoepeau 1980).

One explanation for the better prognosis for schizophrenia in the developing world was framed in terms of societal expectation and response (Waxler 1974). Thus, in Mauritius and Sri Lanka mental illness was generally attributed to vindictive and capricious supernatural agents and the patient's 'self' was unchanged. Full recovery from a psychiatric illness was expedited by the rituals of exorcists and the optimistic predictions of astrologers.

The Cornell-Aro project which involved both American and Nigerian psychiatrists and anthropologists attempted to demonstrate sociocultural influences on psychiatric disorder among the Yoruba (Leighton *et al.* 1963). The investigators did not encounter any locally recognized syndromes that were unfamiliar to western clinicians, despite the local attribution of the cause of mental disorder to supernatural agency such as witchcraft, magic, curses, ghosts or breach of taboo. However, there was no Yoruba word for depression and the concept of depression as a syndrome was thought to be unknown (see Kleinman and Good 1985). The psychoanalytically orientated cultural anthropologists' claims that variations in child-rearing practices (such as the use of symbolic sanctions rather than corporal punishment) might account for cross-cultural variations in the occurrence of depression had recently been challenged (Singer 1975).

An oblique influence of anthropology on this 1979 overview of trans-cultural psychiatry was in relation to the culture-bound syndromes whose 'ritualised symptoms convey a message in a socially sanctioned form in response to intolerable pressure or conflict' (Lipsedge and Littlewood 1979, p.106). Well-known examples were *susto*, the response to a situation in which the victim is unable to meet their social obligations (Rubel 1964) and 'Wild Man' in the highlands of Papua New Guinea, which was the culturally standardized expression of otherwise reprehensible emotions (Langness 1965; Newman 1964). Since the brief stylized aggressive outburst of *Negi Negi* is attributed to investment by malign spirits, the 'Wild Man' is absolved of responsibility for his actions and he gains the Parsonian benefits of the sick role. There is an analogy with the possession states described by Ioan Lewis (1966) in Somali nomadic women, whose mysterious complaints have to be treated by bestowing gifts on the spirit's vehicle, i.e. the married woman who feels neglected or rejected by her polygamous husband. The communicative aspects and the secondary gains of at least some of the culture-bound syndromes had led psychiatrists to consign this behaviour to the category of 'hysterical dissociative reactions' (Hollender 1976).

Roland Littlewood and I went on later to describe the instrumental and expressive aspects of some of the exotic culture-bound syndromes and their triphasic structure in the fifth volume of *Recent Advances in Clinical Psychiatry* (1985) and then a similar analysis was applied to the culture-bound syndromes encountered in the West (Littlewood and Lipsedge 1987).

The polarization of views on the influence of culture on the aetiology, symptomatology and incidence of psychiatric disorder was shown by con-trasting a psychiatrist's review of his experience in Ghana (Forster 1962) with an anthropologist's account of conceptions of psychosis in four East African societies (Edgerton 1966). The psychiatric universalist view was represented by the following passage from Forster:

> Psychiatric syndromes or reactions, by and large, are similar in all races throughout the world. The mental reactions seen in our African patients can be diagnosed according to Western textbook standards. The basic illness and reaction types are the same. Environmental, constitutional and tribal cultural background merely modify the symptom constellation. Basically the disorders of thinking, feeling, willing and knowing are the same. (Forster 1962, p.35)

Although there appears to be universal recognition of grossly disturbed behaviour (purposeless self-injury, gross self-neglect, incomprehensible speech and unprovoked violence), Edgerton (1966) found that there were significant differences between the psychotic behaviour of the members of four neighbouring tribes in East Africa and between those individuals and psychotic patients in western Europe and the USA.

In summary, the 1979 chapter dealt with questions of normality and abnormality, mental illnesses specific to a particular culture and problems in the cross-cultural use of standardized diagnostic instruments and issues of epidemiology. The remainder of the chapter considered racism and psychiatry, and migration and psychiatric disorder among immigrants to Britain.

MISDIAGNOSIS

The question of how to avoid misdiagnosis in people from unfamiliar cultures remains a first priority in the teaching of medical students and trainee psychiatrists.

Case history 1

A 40-year-old Nigerian man of Yoruba descent walked into a local district general hospital and asked to be directed towards the hospital chapel. He was carrying his nine-month-old baby. As it was very late in the evening the receptionist asked him why he was visiting the chapel at such a late hour. He replied that on a previous visit to the hospital he had read a notice which invited anybody to drop in at any time if they felt in need of spiritual support. He told the receptionist that he was worried about his baby's health and he felt that she needed a blessing from a priest. The receptionist asked why the sick baby needed a blessing rather than examination by a doctor and the father replied that he believed that the baby's illness was caused by *ju-ju* (black magic). At that point the English receptionist became alarmed and called the duty psychiatrist, who happened to be Scottish. He interviewed the father and examined the baby. The baby was indeed unwell but the doctor concluded that the father's fear of witchcraft was a symptom of a paranoid psychosis.

The psychiatrist called a paediatrician to examine the baby and she decided that she was suffering from a relatively mild respiratory tract infection and did not need admission in her own right. The psychiatrist, however, concluded that the baby might be in danger from her father because of his paranoid illness and called in the duty social worker to arrange for the baby to be taken into the care of the local authority. When the father protested the doctor summoned a team of porters to subdue him and he was given an injection of paraldehyde. He was admitted to the acute ward overnight. Arrangements were being made to have him transferred the following day to the locked ward at the local mental hospital which was situated about twelve miles away. In the event, I received a telephone call about this situation and was able to go to the ward and convince the psychiatrists that the attribution of illness to witchcraft is not necessarily a symptom of mental illness and that seeking a Christian blessing for a sick baby can be routine practice among Christians. Fortunately, the Church Army was able to send a representative who blessed both the baby and his father. The father went home with the baby and has remained perfectly well ever since.

Case history 2

A Yorobo woman from the Nigerian Mid-West was referred by her GP to a south London teaching hospital with a diagnosis of depression. She was assessed by a psychiatrist who elicited the following history: the patient's husband had recently taken a second wife (under the Native Law and Custom). The psychiatrist consulted a Nigerian colleague who told him that it was not uncommon for women to become upset in those circumstances. Accordingly, the psychiatrist sent the patient home and informed the GP that this was 'merely a cultural [sic] reaction'. The Nigerian woman returned to her home and her reactive depression became progressively worse. She found it increasingly difficult to care for herself and her two small children and eventually a social worker became involved because there was concern that the children were being neglected. A case conference was called and on the basis of the psychiatrist's conclusion that the patient was not actually suffering from mental illness, it was decided that the children were the victims of maternal neglect and that they had to be protected by being taken into the care of the local authority. The mother became intensely distressed and eventually set fire to the social worker's office. It was not until she had served six months of a two-year sentence for arson with intent that the prison medical officer identified that she was suffering from a treatable depressive illness.

Case history 3

A 75-year-old English woman from Dorset was interviewed by a psychiatrist from Egypt. When asked about her husband and children she described how she had tried for many years to become pregnant. Eventually she went to Cerne Abbas and sat on the Rude Giant's penis and nine months later she had her first baby. The psychiatrist concluded that she was deluded.

WHAT DOES THE PSYCHIATRIST WANT FROM ANTHROPOLOGY?

Let us look at the document prepared by the Examinations Department of the Royal College of Psychiatrists entitled 'The Basic Sciences and Clinical Curricula for the MRCPsych Examinations'. The section headed 'Social Sciences' has ten subsections (Royal College of Psychiatrists, 25.11.94). These include the social role of doctors, sick role and illness behaviour, family life in relation to major mental illness, social factors and specific mental health issues, life events, stigma and prejudice, and basic principles of criminology and penology.

There are three subsections where one might expect a significant contribution from anthropology:

1.   The sociology of residential institutions.

2.   Ethnic minorities, adaptation and mental health.

3.   'Methodology, particularly surveys, anthropological and ethnological [sic] approaches'. Is this a typographic error for ethology? If not, what is the relevance of ethnology which is defined as, 'the comparative study and classification of peoples, based upon conditions of material culture, language and religious and social institutions and ideas, as distinguished from physical characters. The influence of environment upon culture' (Radcliffe-Brown 1954).

According to Radcliffe-Brown a meeting of teachers from Oxford, Cambridge and London held in 1909 to discuss the terminology of their subject agreed on the word 'ethnography' as the most appropriate term for 'descriptive accounts of non-literate peoples'. In any case, since Radcliffe-Brown the term 'ethnology' appears to have evolved. According to Lucy Mair the main interest of ethnology is in the past history of peoples without written records and is closely allied with archaeology whereas she states that ethnography 'refers to the process of collecting data by direct enquiry and observation, whatever the theoretical purpose of the enquiry' (Mair 1972). It is not clear from this curriculum what the Royal College requires if it is making a distinction between social anthropological and ethnographic approaches. But it is probably fair to assume that the terms are being used interchangeably.

ARE THE COLLEGE EXAMINATION CANDIDATES BEING TESTED ON THEIR KNOWLEDGE OF THESE ASPECTS OF THE SOCIAL SCIENCES?

Analysis of the 30 essay questions set in Part II of the membership examination between spring 1995 and spring 1998 shows that there was not a single essay dealing explicitly with an anthropological topic. The closest one gets to a transcultural theme is in the following essay question: 'There are some countries which do not have an up to date mental health law. Imagine you are asked to draft new mental health legislation for such a country. Give the elements you would like to see incorporated into a new Act with reasons for each point. Give also a list of pitfalls to be avoided, again with argued reasons' (Royal College of Psychiatrists Part II examination essay paper, 23.10.96).

There is an implication that 'some countries' might be 'under-developed' in terms of civil liberties legislation. It is conceivable that the list of pitfalls to be avoided might include some reference to cultural relativism and to whether the legislation developed within the framework of the Anglo-Saxon legal tradition can be appropriately exported lock, stock and barrel. Edward Said quotes the following passage from one of Lord Cromer's collected essays published in 1913: 'Even the Central African savage may eventually learn to chant a hymn in honour of Astraea Redux, as represented by the British official who denies him gin but gives him justice' (Said, 1978).

TO WHAT EXTENT DO THE COLLEGE'S OWN TEXTBOOKS PROVIDE MATERIAL ON ASPECTS OF THE SOCIAL SCIENCES WHICH REFLECT THE WORK OF SOCIAL ANTHROPOLOGISTS?

The textbook entitled *College Seminar in Social Psychology and the Social Sciences* (Tantam and Birchwood 1994) sets out to review 'the current state of the basic sciences, but in topic areas that are likely to be of clinical relevance'. The authors of the social science section are three sociologists, Ellen Annandale, Joan Busfield and Robert Moore, together with M.R.D. Johnson who is a research worker at the Centre for Research in Ethnic Relations, University of Warwick. Moore deals with contemporary ideas on class and includes a critical review of the notion of the underclass and the neo-eugenic arguments of Charles Murray: 'The plight of the most disadvantaged is individualised and pathologised; they become 'cases' needing treatment or punishment' (p.295). In his chapter entitled 'Culture, Race and Discrimination', Johnson defines race, racism and ethnicity. He rejects the term 'culture' in favour of 'ethnicity'. He touches on the issue of somatization and invokes Cecil Hellman (1984) to remind psychiatric trainees that 'the premise for a transcultural approach to medical practice is the recognition that most 'scientific' medicine is based upon the assumptions and codes of expression or behaviour with which its practitioners have been most familiar. Inevitably this has meant that it is geared towards the expectations and experiences of western European society' (p.304). Johnson asserts that anthropology has shown that the ethos of biomedicine is relativistic, transactional and subject to change and he warns that no culture is static and one must avoid relying on stereotypic descriptions of members of ethnic minorities. The remainder of Johnson's chapter deals with the relative rates of psychiatric disorder among ethnic minorities, social factors and the causation of mental illness and migration and mental health.

Of these four social science chapters, the one by Busfield on the social construction of illness and deviance has the greatest relevance for the interface between anthropology and psychiatry. She writes that regardless of their biological or physical basis, both illness and deviance ('wrongdoing') are characterized and given meaning through human thought and action. This is as true of the biological processes we term illnesses as of the behavioural processes we term delinquency (p.316). A corollary of this social construction is that the boundaries and meaning of the concepts of illness and deviance vary both diachronically and across cultures and social groups: 'What is deemed undesirable functioning of body, mind or behaviour at one time, or by one group, will not necessarily be the same as at or by another' (p.317). She tries to reassure the potentially indignant physician that 'the material reality of the biological processes is not called into question by the claim that illnesses are socially constructed' (p.317). Without using the term 'explanatory models' she introduces that notion by reminding the reader that 'lay and scientific understandings compete with one another, often creating problems for effective communication between practitioner and client'. In a useful section on potential conflict between concepts of illness and deviance as held by professionals and by lay people she demonstrates potential boundary disputes between deviance and acceptable behaviour on the one hand and deviance and mental illness on the other. Contested lines of demarcation between deviance and mental illness (badness and madness) involve professional interests which influence the form and content of medical and legal practice (Johnson 1972; Smith 1981).

In her chapter on mental health services and institutions, Annandale summarizes the work of Goffman (1968) and cites the less well-known study by Brown (1987) on psychiatric diagnosis in a walk-in clinic in the USA. Goffman's detailed description of hospital life shows how the patients' previous identities, statuses and social relationships are radically changed by the influence of the structure of the organization, especially the abolition of the normal separation between domestic work and leisure life. But Goffman also shows how patients do not invariably become passive and apathetic and he describes strategies of resistance by which they can influence the formal organization by means of bargaining and negotiation. Goffman's ethnography shows the underlife of the hospital in which the patients work the system within a more or less rigid framework of standard routines.

Annandale refers approvingly to the similarly ethnographic approach of Brown (1987) who showed how the diagnostic process was 'characterised by uncertainty, ambiguity and conflict. Clinicians and supervisors, in the course of routine diagnostic evaluations, engage in many conflicting and ambivalent behaviours. These include humerants and sarcasm about diagnostic categorisation, real or imagined alternatives to the diagnostic schema, evading diagnosis, minimalisation of severity for some patients, and critiques of the various diagnostic models' (Brown 1987, p.37). Annandale summarizes the organizational factors which account for this situation. Within the microcosm of the psychiatric clinic the disparity between the ideal DSM-III diagnostic categories and the actual process of diagnostic work arises from 'conflict between an ascendant biopsychiatric model and the everyday work of a therapeutic service, the tensions involved in providing a service to clients while servicing the needs of public agencies (such as Social Services) and the mixed agendas which surround diagnosis' (Tantam and Birchwood 1994, p.339). This interactionist perspective 'emphasises the fluidity of organisational structure and people's creative roles' (p.339).

One criticism of this interactionist research at the micro-level of institutional life is that it fails to pay attention to how the 'macro' structures of power in the world outside the hospital impinge upon what goes on inside it. Rosaldo makes a similar comment on the suppression of the interplay between power and knowledge in his description of the use and abuse of ethnographic authority. He castigates the historian, Le Roy Ladurie, for following the ethnographer's tactic of minimizing 'discussion of the politics of domination that shaped the investigator's knowledge about the people under study' (1986, p.81).

OTHER RECENT POSTGRADUATE TEXTBOOKS OF PSYCHIATRY

Two psychiatrists, Puri and Tyrer (1992) have written a book which they describe as a basic reference text for psychiatric trainees studying for the membership examination. In their preface the authors write:

> The principles of the basic sciences related to psychiatry are described wherever possible and we hope that this information makes their application more understandable to the reader. This does not mean that factual details are skimped, but understanding their setting helps their retention in memory. (Puri and Tyrer 1992, p.i)

Only three and a half pages of this 334-page book are devoted to what the authors call 'Social Studies'. They recommend five books for further reading: Anthony Clare's *Psychiatry in Dissent* (1980); Goffman's *Asylums* (1961); Hollingshead and Redlich's *Study of Social Class and Mental Illness* (1958); Mechanic's *Medical Sociology* (1978) and Talcott Parsons's classic *The Social System* (1951).

The authors group together social class and social groups and the topics given most emphasis are the total institution and the sick role and illness behaviour. The contribution of medical anthropology occupies a single brief paragraph:

> The sick role and the particular form illness behaviour takes are culturally determined. In some societies it is not a doctor but rather a spirit (sic) healer, witch doctor, or shaman, say, who both defines and legitimises illness. Even in Western societies there exist groups, such as members of certain religious cults, for which a non-medically trained person is the one whose help is asked for by sick individuals. (Puri and Tyrer 1992, p.294)

In contrast to Puri and Tyrer's postage stamp treatment of the social sciences, the fifth edition of Kendell and Zealley's *Companion to Psychiatric Studies* (1993) gives pride of place to Kathleen Jones's chapter entitled 'Social Science in Relation to Psychiatry'. This precedes not only the chapters on psychology in relation to psychiatry and the biological determinants of personality, but also chapters on the basic sciences including functional neuroanatomy and neuropharmacology and neuroendocrinology. In a stimulating overview, Kathleen Jones emphasizes the importance of understanding the social contexts, networks and social relationships which have a critical role in understanding psychiatric illness. She refers approvingly to Caudill's anthropological study of the processes of interaction on a psychiatric ward (1958). While criticizing the anti-psychiatry school because it rejected the physiology and biochemistry of psychiatric disorder, Kathleen Jones also challenges the medical view's five basic tenets:

> Psychiatric disorders are diseases with distinct pathologies, courses and outcomes; psychiatry is a branch of medicine; the aetiology of psychiatric disorder is at present imperfectly understood but the causes are primarily genetic and biochemical; diagnosis and prescription are reasonably exact sciences and will become more so; hospital, clinic and general practitioner services are the appropriate agencies for treatment. (Jones 1993, p.10).

She expresses mild scepticism:

> There is no guarantee that a highly successful medical conquest of the gross plagues will be repeated, or that research in the natural sciences will produce comparable findings…what we know of schizophrenia, which accounts for about two thirds of all severe chronic psychiatric disorder, suggests that the aetiology is complex and probably includes both social and biological factors. (Jones 1993, p.10)

She recommends that both medical and social factors are to be taken into consideration by psychiatrists.

Kathleen Jones's summary of the critique by social scientists of the medical model does little justice to more trenchant criticisms such as those of Zola (1972). She summarizes the social science view as follows:

> 'Mental illness' and 'psychiatric disorder' are medical terms for what are basically problems in human relationships; psychiatry is (or ought to be) one of the helping professions; treatment is an art as well as a science; drugs and electroconvulsive therapy merely suppress distress and may be methods of social control; medical labels are stigmatising; most people diagnosed as psychiatric patients can manage to live in the community if they are accorded some human dignity and reasonable conditions of life. (Zola 1972, pp.10–11)

Kathleen Jones (1993) deplores the inappropriate application of the methodology of clinical drug trials to the study of distressed people. She contrasts the focus of the natural sciences on convergent problems, i.e. those which permit of a 'right answer' with the divergent problems found in the social sciences 'which require the exercise of a high quality of judgement and rarely permit of a clear cut and permanent solution' (p.12). She recommends that 'description and observation must come before the construction of scales and the formulation of hypotheses'.

There is no point in counting heads until the basic situation is sufficiently well understood to make the exercise meaningful. She attacks the absurdity of demanding that all work in the social sciences should be capable of statistical verification. Kathleen Jones writes approvingly of ethno-methodology (which she defines as the examination of the meanings and significance of everyday events without prior mental constructs) and symbolic interactionism which emphasizes the content of interaction rather than the status of the interlocutors. She cites the analysis of the consultation process in general practice (Stimson and Webb 1975) which looks at the interaction between doctor and patient from the patient's perspective.

She then goes on to describe Goffman's *Asylums* (1961). She points out that the empirical base for his study was very limited but she devotes a great deal of space, given the overall length of her chapter, to Goffman's analysis which drew on deviance theory and symbolic interactionism. She explains the encompassing tendencies of the total institution (batch living, binary management, the inmate role and the institutional perspective) and the 'betrayal funnel', and the acquisition of the inmate role through 'mortification' or 'role stripping'. Goffman prefigures Barrett (1996) with this description of the history-taking procedure: 'The events recorded being carefully selected to support the hypotheses that he is the kind of person the institution exists to treat' (Jones 1993, p.16). She describes the four ways in which a patient may react to the 'assault on the self': withdrawal into fantasy life; open rebellion (as in *One Flew Over the Cuckoo's Nest*); 'colonization', i.e. a feigned acceptance of the official view; and 'conversion', i.e. complete acceptance of the official view of the patient's status. She also describes Goffman's attack on the way revelations obtained in group therapy constitute the greatest threat to privacy since they involve 'looping' – the collapse of the patient's defences on himself by using his own evidence against him (p.16).

Finally, she is the only contributor to all these introductions to the relevance of social science to psychiatry to mention Foucault. While critical of Foucault's cavalier attitude to facts (he dismissed them as 'superficial' while he digs for 'underlying unities'), she approves of his demonstration that 'apparent humanitarianism may be a cloak for social control' and that what had previously been regarded as an enlightened reform movement might in fact be an insidious form of repression.

CROSS-CULTURAL PSYCHIATRIC ASSESSMENT

Neither the *Companion to Psychiatric Studies* (Kendell and Zealley 1993) nor the *Oxford Textbook of Psychiatry* (Gelder, Gath, Mayou and Cowen 1996) give any advice to trainee psychiatrists on the issues involved in cross-cultural psychiatric assessment. However, this topic is dealt with in two small handbooks and in two recent papers in the Royal College of Psychiatrists' *Journal of Continuing Professional Development.*

In *Practical Psychiatry* which is one of the Oxford Medical Publications Pocket Medical Reference series, Betts and Kenwood (1992) include a chapter entitled 'Interviewing People Who Speak Another Tongue'. They begin with an admonition to be tolerant:

> You also have to learn to respect (even if you privately disagree with) hallowed cultural and religious beliefs. Although most *clinical* [italics in original] delusions, delusional interpretations, and hallucinatory experiences lie outside culture, not all do. Where does culturally acceptable strong religious belief in practice end and insanity begin? If like us, you have no religious belief you will need to enquire from an adherent of the particular religion in question whether his colleague's beliefs and behaviours are compatible with that religion or whether they are obsessive or have become clinical. The local leaders of most sects (unless they have become politicised) [!] can make this distinction for you and should be consulted. If you do have your own religious belief do not let it blind you to the beliefs of others or compromise your tolerance of different cultural practices. (Betts and Kenwood 1992, pp.23–24)

They warn against the medicalization of the cultural expression of grief and distress and they point out that a 'native healer' is likely to be 'much more effective than you in helping neurotic illness within his community'. The apprentice psychiatrist is warned against trying to rescue:

> the girl [sic] from a strict Muslim or Sikh background who hankers after the apparent liberties and freedom of her English schoolfriends and who finds the differences between her home life and her outside social life impossible to reconcile. You may be tempted to help her escape into a hostel or refuge or other network set up by Social Services for such problems, but if you do this without thinking about it very carefully and consulting with some professional from her original culture first, you may unwittingly make her problems worse. Despite the conflict, she would almost certainly be drawing much strength and support from her home life, which she would lose forever at a time when she would be trying to battle with the problems of her new life. (Betts and Kenwood 1992, pp.27–28)

The three authors of *Pocket Psychiatry* (Bhui, Weich and Lloyd 1997) have studied social anthropology at the postgraduate level. Together with Dinesh Bhugra, Kamaldeep Bhui has written a longer review of the issues involved in cross-cultural psychiatric assessment for the journal *Advances in Psychiatric Treatment* (Bhugra and Bhui 1997, pp.103–110). This paper is important because it appears in the College's 'state-of-the-art' journal alongside reviews entitled 'Practical Pharmacotherapy for Anxiety', 'Interventions for People with Autism: Recent Advances' and 'What a Patient Can Expect from a Consultant Psychiatrist'. Bhugra and Bhui (1997) distinguish 'illness' and 'disease'. They remind the reader that the doctor–patient interaction is affected by the doctor's as well as the patient's past experiences, educational and social background and ethnicity. They warn that 'if cultural variables are over-emphasised the provider is guilty of stereotyping the patient while if racial [presumably the patient's experience of racism] considerations are under-emphasised, the doctor is guilty of insensitivity to influences that may affect the dynamics of the interview' (p.103). They point out that linguistic difficulties, uncertainty about the idioms of distress and the inappropriate application of the biomedical model might lead to diagnostic error, in addition to impeding understanding of the patient's distress and the development of a therapeutic relationship.

The clinician is warned against assuming that life events have the same significance for patients as they do for the clinician. They also remind the psychiatrist that the Anglo-Saxon world view is not universal. Its features include the tendency to divide the world into discrete 'knowable' parts, to keep emotions fairly private, to aspire towards independence and self-actualization rather than collaboration and to subscribe to a linear view of time. They devote some space to aculturation and racism and in the section entitled 'Microskills for the Clinician' remind him/her about eye-contact rituals and cultural variation in patterns of gaze avoidance. The work of anthropologists is quoted most extensively in the relatively brief section entitled 'Psychological/Somatic Mindedness'. Thus, Kleinman (1980) and Shweder (1991) are invoked to support the statement that in Japan, China and India 'internal psychological explanations of suffering are neither sought nor seen as credible'.

Over half the review deals with the limitations of the standard mental state examination. Speaking in tongues, extreme religiosity, trance and possession are adduced as examples of unusual behaviour which is not clearly understandable and which is therefore 'too readily seen as evidence of psychosis without due attention to the adaptive or coping potential of the behaviour' (p.106). Aggression is frequently incorrectly identified as a manifestation of psychosis. The current preoccupation with risk and dangerousness is revealed in the warning: 'do not be prompted to anticipate an aggressive situation through your own fear of assault and uncertainty about a patient with whom you do not share cultural values, norms and mores' (p.107). The clinician is warned not to intervene too early with 'control and restraint', which is the term used to describe a standardized way of physically overpowering a patient.

Bhugra and Bhui (1997) helpfully remind the reader, who might too readily assume that hallucinations are suggestive of a psychotic experience, that nearly half of bereaved individuals experience hallucinations of the dead person for years after the loss. In general 'the experiences of feeling ancestors' presence and hearing their voices or seeing them after their death are related to cultural norms and expectations' (p.107). In order to reduce the risk of diagnostic error 'appreciation of congruence with the patient's own culture is crucial in reaching a diagnosis; it is necessary to understand the culture within which individuals are embedded before deciding whether symptoms or beliefs are pathognomonic of underlying psychiatric disorder' (p.108). The authors recognize that it is unrealistic to expect the psychiatrist to have a detailed knowledge of all the belief systems they are likely to encounter. Information about religious ideas and culturally sanctioned explanations must be obtained from a variety of sources including the patient's family and advocates as well as community or voluntary organizations. The authors conclude that a sign of illness would be a belief that is unfamiliar or inappropriate within the specific cultural framework, coupled with functional impairment. They recommend that the clinician elicits explanatory models (Kleinman 1980) to enhance an understanding of both the patient's and their family's concepts of illness.

RESEARCH METHODOLOGY

The Royal College of Psychiatrists' attitude to ethnographic or indeed any qualitative type of research is revealed by its publication: *Research Methods in Psychiatry: A Beginner's Guide* (Freeman and Tyrer 1992). There are no references whatever to non-quantitative methods and in this respect psychiatric nursing research techniques are far in advance (see, for example, Crawford, Brown and Nolan 1998).

TRANSCULTURAL PSYCHIATRY AND THE LAW

At times cultural issues might be raised in the forensic context. This may not be an effective strategy for mitigation, since the prevailing view is based on 'when in Rome...' Thus, at the Court of Appeal in 1998 psychiatric evidence for the appellant in the case of a Pakistani woman in Bradford who had been convicted of murder relied on Roger Ballard's research (Ballard 1990) in Mirpur and his exposition of honour and shame, the rules of purdah as well as his account of the role of the *Pir*, divine succour, and the *taweez* (*The Times*, 27 October 1998). The three senior judges were not convinced. They concluded that the appellant 'had little of her honour left to salvage...in any case she was certainly capable of striking out on her own'. The court implied that women brought up in this traditional culture are passive, docile and submissive, lacking in financial and entrepreneurial skills. As regards the question of *Izaat*, the court appeared to regard honour as a binary all-or-nothing affair, lacking any subtle gradation of reputation and status.

Paul Bowden, consultant forensic psychiatrist at the Home Office, inserts the culture-bound syndromes into his magisterial *Principles and Practice of Forensic Psychiatry* (Bluglass and Bowden 1990). While it seems fair to give *amok* pride of place in this particular context, it is not easy to imagine the forensic significance of *latah* (echolalia, echopraxia and an enhanced startle response) or even of a morbid preoccupation with penile shrinkage (*koro*). This emphasis on the exotic is, however, counterbalanced by Rosemarie Cope's (1990) impressively thorough and fair review of the literature on forensic psychiatry and ethnicity which appears in the same volume.

Two psychiatrists practising in New Zealand usefully remind their clinical colleagues that the treaty of Waitangi has to be considered in any application of the local Mental Health Act to detain and treat a suicidal patient. They consider the hypothetical example of a 24-year-old Maori woman with a recent history of several acts of deliberate self-harm, who has just taken a large overdose of paracetamol. In the case vignette, she has refused treatment on the grounds that her ancestors have instructed her to die. In this particular case it is recommended that while a psychotic illness has to be excluded, the patient must also be allowed contact with an elder (*kaumatua*) in accordance with Section 5 of the New Zealand Mental Health Act which requires 'proper recognition of the importance and significance to the patient of the patient's ties to his or her family, *whanau, hapu,* or *iwi'* (Hatcher and Samuels 1998).

TERMINOLOGY

Teachers of psychiatry should explain that the notion of 'race' is a social construction. The Royal College of Psychiatrists has issued this statement:

> The College is particularly conscious of the important distinction between 'racial' differences, in terms of appearance and particularly skin colour, and 'cultural' differences in terms of long-established customs, language and social and family structures. For a psychiatrist assessing and treating any individual patient and his/her family, the *cultural* differences are as important as *racial* ones, if not more so. (Council of the Royal College of Psychiatrists 1990)

However, the distinction between 'race' and culture remains blurred. Thus both the first and second editions of an authoritative textbook of psycho-pathology (Sims 1988, 1995) state: 'First rank symptoms [of schizophrenia] cannot be used as a diagnostic check-list…for a psychiatrist to use them clinically, he must first know them. Secondly, he must know how this person from this social and *racial background* [my emphasis] is likely to describe any particular first rank symptom.'

This is not a trivial or pedantic issue. Our own teachers of psychiatry were brought up on the original *Oxford Textbook of Psychiatry*, whose 1956 edition included the following passage:

> It may appear that we are putting a great deal of emphasis on hereditary predisposition and its possible consequences. We make no excuse for doing so. We believe that a healthy diathesis or constitution is of paramount importance for the welfare of the individual and the race; we must take cognisance of all influences that tend, in however remote a degree, to give to the more suitable races, or strains of blood, a better chance of prevailing speedily over the less suitable than otherwise they would have had. The possible application of hereditary principles may make a valuable contribution to the health of the nation, and is a matter for earnest consideration both in the scientific and medical departments of our universities. (Henderson and Gillespie 1956, p.62)

REFERENCES

Ballard, R. (1990)'Migration and kinship.' In C. Clarke, S. Vertovek and C. Peach *South Asians Overseas: Contexts and Communities.* Cambridge: Cambridge University Press, pp.219–249.

Barrett, R.J. (1996) *The Psychiatric Team and the Social Definition of Schizophrenia: An Anthropological Study of Person and Illness.* Cambridge: Cambridge University Press.

Betts, T. and Kenwood, C. (1992) *Practical Psychiatry.* Oxford: Oxford University Press.

Bhugra, D. and Bhui, K. (1997) 'Clinical management of patients across cultures.' *Advances in Psychiatric Treatment 3*, 223–239.

Bhui, K., Weich, S. and Lloyd, K. (1997) *Pocket Psychiatry.* London: W.B. Saunders.

Bluglass, R. and Bowden, P. (eds) (1990) *Principles and Practice of Forensic Psychiatry.* Edinburgh: Churchill Livingstone.

Bowden, P. (1990) 'Amok.' In R. Bluglass and P. Bowden (eds) *Principles and Practice of Forensic Psychiatry.* Edinburgh: Churchill Livingstone.

Brown, P. (1987) 'Diagnostic conflict.' *Journal of Health and Social Behaviour 28*, 37–50.

Caudill, W. (1958) *The Mental Hospitals as a Small Society.* Cambridge MA: Harvard University Press.

Clare, A. (1980) *Psychiatry in Dissent: Controversial Issues in Thought and Practice,* 2nd edn. London: Tavistock.

Cope, R. (1990) 'Psychiatry, ethnicity and crime.' In R. Bluglass and P. Bowden (eds) *Principles and Practice of Forensic Psychiatry.* Edinburgh: Churchill Livingstone.

Council Report 10. 'Psychiatric Practices and Training in British Multi-Ethnic Society.' (1990) London: Royal College of Psychiatrists.

Crawford, P., Brown, B. and Nolan, P. (1998) *Communicating Care: The Language of Nursing.* Cheltenham: Stanley Thornes.

Devereux, G. (1963) 'Primitive psychiatric diagnosis: a general theory of the diagnostic process.' In I. Gladstone (ed) *Man's Image in Medicine and Anthropology.* Independence MO: International Universities Press.

Edgerton, R.B. (1966) 'Conceptions of psychosis in four East African societies.' *American Anthropologist 68*, 408–425.

Evans-Pritchard, E.E. (1937) *Witchcraft, Oracles and Magic among the Azande.* Oxford: Clarendon Press.

Forster, E.B. (1962) 'Theory and practice of psychiatry in Ghana.' *American Journal of Psychotherapy 16*, 7–51.

Freeman, C. and Tyrer, P. (1992) *Research Methods in Psychiatry: A Beginner's Guide,* 2nd edn. London: Royal College of Psychiatrists.

Gelder, M., Gath, D., Mayou, R. and Cowen, P. (1996) *Oxford Textbook of Psychiatry, 3rd edn.* Oxford: University Press.

Goffman, E. (1961) *Asylums: Essays on the Social Situation of Mental Patients and Other Inmates.* New York: Anchor Books, Doubleday.

Granville-Grossman, K. (ed) (1979) *Recent Advances in Clinical Psychiatry.* London: Churchill-Livingstone.

Hatcher, S. and Samuels, A. (1998) 'Medicolegal aspects of managing deliberate self-harm in the emergency department.' *New Zealand Medical Journal 110*, 255–258.

Hellman, C.G. (1994) *Culture, Health and Illness*, 3rd edn. Oxford: Butterworth Heinmann.

Henderson, D. and Gillespie, R.D. (1956) *A Textbook of Psychiatry for Students and Practitioners*, 8th edn. Oxford: Oxford University Press.

Hollender, N.H. (1976) 'Hysteria: the culture-bound syndromes.' *Papua New Guinea Medical Journal 19*, 24–29.

Hollingshead, A.B. and Redlich, F.C. (1958) *Social Class and Mental Illness*. New York: John Wiley and Sons.

Johnson, T.J. (1972) *Professions and Power*. London: Macmillan.

Jones, K. (1993) 'Social science in relation to psychiatry.' In R.E. Kendell and A.K. Zealley (eds) *Companion to Psychiatric Studies*. Edinburgh: Churchill Livingstone.

Kendell, R.E. and Zealley, A.K. (1993) *Companion to Psychiatric Studies*, 5th edn. Edinburgh: Churchill Livingstone.

Kleinman, A. (1980) *Patients and Healers in the Context of Culture*. Berkeley: University of California Press.

Kleinman, A. and Good, B. (eds) (1985) *Culture and Depression*. Berkeley: University of California Press.

Langness, L.L. (1965) 'Hysterical psychosis in the New Guinea Highland: a Bena Bena example.' *Psychiatry 28*, 258–277.

Leff, J.P. (1973) 'Culture and the differentiation of emotional states.' *British Journal of Psychiatry 123*, 299–306.

Leighton, N., Lambo, T.A., Hughes, C.C., Leighton, D.C., Murphy, J.M. and Macklin, D.B. (1963) *Psychiatric Disorders Among the Yoruba*. Ithica: Cornell University Press.

Lewis, A.J. (1967) *Inquiries in Psychiatry*. London: Routledge and Kegan Paul.

Lewis, I.M. (1966) 'Spirit-possession and deprivation cults.' *Man 1*, 307–329.

Lipsedge, M. and Littlewood, R. (1979) 'Transcultural psychiatry.' In K. Granville-Grossman (ed) *Recent Advances in Clinical Psychiatry*, 3rd edn. Edinburgh: Churchill Livingstone.

Littlewood, R. and Lipsedge, M. (1985) 'Culture-bound syndromes.' In K. Granville-Grossman (ed) *Recent Advances in Clinical Psychiatry*, 5th edn. Edinburgh: Churchill Livingstone.

Littlewood, R. and Lipsedge, M. (1987) 'The butterfly and the serpent: culture, psychopathology and biomedicine.' *Culture, Medicine and Psychiatry 11*, 289–335.

Mair, L. (1972) *An Introduction to Social Anthropology*, 2nd edn. Oxford: Oxford University Press.

Mechanic, D. (1978) *Medical Sociology*, 2nd edn. Glencoe: Free Press.

Morice, R. (1978) 'Psychiatric diagnosis in a transcultural setting, the importance of lexical categories.' *British Journal of Psychiatry 132*, 87–95.

Murphy, H.B.M. and Taumoepeau, B.M. (1980) 'Traditionalism and mental health in the South Pacific: a re-examination of an old hypothesis.' *Psychological Medicine 10*, 471–482.

Murphy, H.B.M., Wittkower, E.D. and Chance, N.A. (1967) 'Cross-cultural inquiry into the symptomatology of depression: a preliminary report.' *International Journal of Psychiatry 3*, 6–15.

Newman, P.L. (1964) '"Wild Man" behaviour in a New Guinea Highlands community.' *American Anthropologist 66*, 1–19.

Parsons, T. (1951) *The Social System*. Glencoe: Free Press.

Puri, B.K. and Tyrer, P.J. (1992) *Sciences Basic to Psychiatry*. Edinburgh: Churchill Livingstone.

Radcliffe-Brown, A.R. (1954) 'Historical note on British social anthropology.' *American Anthropology 54*, 276.

Rin, H. and Lin, T.Y. (1962) 'Mental illness among Formosan aborigines as compared with the Chinese in Taiwan.' *Journal of Mental Science 108*, 134–146.

Rosaldo, R. (1986) 'From the door of his tent: the fieldworker and the inquisitor.' In J. Clifford and G.E. Marcus (eds) *Writing Culture: The Poetics and Politics of Ethnography*. Berkeley: University of California Press.

Rubel, A.J. (1964) 'The epidemiology of a folk illness: Susto in Hispanic American.' *Ethnology 3*, 268–283.

Said, E.W. (1978) *Orientalism*. London: Routledge.

Shweder, R. (1991) *Thinking Through Western Cultures*. Cambridge MA: Harvard University Press.

Sims, A. (1988) *Symptoms in the Mind: An Introduction to Descriptive Psychopathology*. London: Bailliere Tindall.

Sims, A. (1995) *Symptoms in the Mind: An Introduction to Descriptive Psychopathology*, 2nd edn. London: Bailliere Tindall.

Singer, K. (1975) 'Depressive disorders from a transcultural perspective.' *Social Science and Medicine 9*, 289–301.

Smith, R. (1981) *Trial by Medicine: Insanity and Responsibility in Victorian Trials*. Edinburgh: Edinburgh University Press.

Stimson, G.V. and Webb, B. (1975) *Going to See the Doctor: The Consultation Process in General Practice*. London: Routledge and Kegan Paul.

Tantam, D. and Birchwood, M. (eds) (1994) *College Seminar in Social Psychology and the Social Sciences*. London: Gaskell.

Waxler, N.E. (1974) 'Culture and mental illness.' *Journal of Nervous and Mental Disease 159*, 379–395.

Wittkower, E.D. (1969) 'Perspectives on transcultural psychiatry.' *International Journal of Psychiatry 8*, 811–824.

Zola, I. (1972) 'Medicine as an institution of social control.' *Sociological Review 20*, 487–504.

The Contributors

Dinesh Bhugra is a senior lecturer at the Institute of Psychiatry, London. He has trained in sociology and social anthropology and heads the section of Cultural Psychiatry.

John Campbell teaches social anthropology in the School for Social Sciences and International Development, University of Wales, Swansea. He has worked as an anthropologist in a number of African countries.

John Cox is President of the Royal College of Psychiatrists and a founding member of the Transcultural Psychiatry Society. He is also Head of the Department of Psychiatry at the University of Keele.

Simon Dein is an honorary consultant psychiatrist at Princess Alexandra Hospital, Harlow and an honorary lecturer in anthropology at University College, London.

Maurice Eisenbruch is a clinical pyschiatrist and medical anthropologist who has worked with Cambodians for twenty years. He teaches international and multicultural health at the Faculty of Medicaine, University of New South Wales, Australia.

Maureen H. Fitzgerald, a medical anthropologist, is a senior lecturer at the School of Occupation and Leisure Sciences, University of Sydney. She maintains a strong association with the Transcultural Mental Health Centre in Sydney.

Gerard Hutchinson is a research psychiatrist and lecturer at the Institute of Psychiatry, London.

Jane Jackson is a physician and worked for ten years as Director of Public Health in Newham, London. Now retired, she plans to conduct health service and anthropological research among young people in East London.

Sushrut Jadhav is a clinical lecturer in psychiatry at University College, London and also works at the Focus Outreach Clinic for the Homeless Mentally Ill, Camden and Islington Community Health Services Trust, Kings Cross, London.

Maurice Lipsedge is a consultant psychiatrist at South London and the Maudsley NHS Trust and honorary senior lecturer in psychiatry and Head of Section of Occupational Psychiatry, Department of Psychiatry and Psychology, Guy's, King's and St Thomas's Hospitals, London.

Roland Littlewood is Professor of Anthropology and Psychiatry at University College, London and co-director of the University College Centre for Medical Anthropology.

Vieda Skultans is an anthropologist working at the Division of Psychiatry, University of Bristol. She has taught Medical Anthropology at undergraduate and postgraduate levels.

Simon Sinclair is a consultant psychiatrist in Co. Durham and an honorary research fellow in the Department of Anthropology, University of Durham.

Els van Dongen is a medical anthropologist with long standing experience of working in the field of psychiatry and medical anthropology. She is a senior staff member of the Medical Anthropology Unit of the University of Amsterdam.

Subject Index

Author Index

Abbott, W. 180
Abu-Lughod, L. 41
Ackernet, E. 80, 81
Addison, J. 51
Adinma, J.I. 204
Adler, L. 236
Affonso, D.D. 203
Ahmed, A. 137
Ahmed, S. 240
Albrecht, G. 236
Alston, R.J. 244
Amariko, A. 19, 28, 29
American Psychiatric
    Association (APA) 43, 45,
    52, 55, 56, 57, 185, 238
Ammann, L. 243
Ang, C. 218, 228, 229
Angermeyer, M.C. 242, 247
Annandale, E. 277, 278, 279
Antonio, R.J. 240
APA Task Force 173
Argyle, M. 179
Aristotle 86
Armstrong, M.J. 186
Asch, A. 246
Atkinson, P. 20, 259, 261
Augustine, St 100
Avruch, K. 186
Ayonrinde, A. 244

Babb, L. 50, 51, 60
Backner, B.L. 240
Baker, F. 239
Baker, R. 61
Bakhtin, M.M. 95, 100
Baldwin, J. 233
Ballard, R. 285
Barley, N. 32
Barnett, B. 202
Barnhouse, R.T. 173
Barrelet, L. 243
Barrett, R. 12, 24, 31, 157,
    281
Barth, F. 95
Bartlett, C.J. 151
Bartlett, F.C. 97
Bataille, G. 123
Bateson, G. 88, 117, 118
Batson, C.D. 173

Bean, G. 241, 243
Beard, G.M. 54, 69
Becker, A.E. 225, 258, 259,
    266–9
Beiser, M 239
Beit-Hallahmi, B. 179
Belenky, M.F. 184, 189
Benedict, R. 23–4, 81
Ben-Noun, L. 236, 245
Bergin, A.E. 173, 174
Berlin, I. 22, 23, 33
Betts, T. 282–3
Bhishagratna, K. 46
Bhugra, D. 28, 233–49, 283,
    284, 290
Bhui, K. 283, 284
Birnbaum, K. 17, 72, 86
Birchwood, M. 277, 279
Black, P.W. 186
Bleuler, E. 71, 72
Bliss, M. 158, 180
Bloch, J. 68
Bloch, M. 68
Bloom, W. 258
Blount, T. 61
Bluglass, R. 285
Boddy, J. 113, 116
Boeles, J.J. 229
Boerhave, H. 60
Bourdieu, P. 66, 111, 259,
    260, 263
Bourne, P. 238
Bowden, P. 285
Bowlin, J. 120
Boyer, P. 88
Boyle, R. 50
Brigham, A. 67, 88
Bright, J.A. 236, 239, 240,
    247
Bright, T. 59
Brill, A. 53
Brislin, R.W. 186, 190, 191
Britten, N. 149
Brockman, J. 237
Brodskey, B. 236
Brody E.B. 173, 190
Bronner, A. 179
Brookfield, S. 188, 191, 192
Brown, B. 285
Brown, G.W. 154
Brown, L.M. 234
Brown, P. 278, 279
Bruning, R.H. 195
Buchanan, A. 238
Burgos-Lingan, M.O. 204
Burke, P. 192

Burti, L. 246
Burton, R. 49, 51
Busfield, J. 277, 278
Byrne, P. 164

Campbell, J. 105–20, 290
Capps, L. 109
Carothers, J.C. 24, 76, 82, 88
Carritt, E. 51
Cassel, J. 163
Cassian, J. 47, 59
Caudill, W. 280
Cazamian, L. 51
Chamberlain, M. 109
Chamberlin, J. 246
Chance, N.A. 272
Chapman, M. 115
Chapman, S. 163, 164
Charcot, J.M. 54
Chaucer, G. 61
Cheetham, R.W. 203
Cheung, F. 235
Cheyne, G. 67
Clare, A. 279
Clarke, B. 45, 46, 47, 48, 51
Clausen, J. 235 237
Clement, D.C. 186
Clemson, L. 197
Clifford, J. 33
Cohen, L. 42, 239
Coles, E.C. 151
Connerton, P. 101, 103
Cooper, J.E. 88, 245
Cope, B. 187
Cope, R. 285
Corrigan, P.W. 242, 244, 246
Cowen, P. 282
Cox, J. 7–33, 139, 201–4,
    228, 290
Cranton, P. 191
Crawford, P. 285
Crick, M. 126
Crocker, J. 239, 246
Crow, T.J. 243
Csordas, T. 126
Cullen, F.T. 241, 243
Cullen, W. 60
Cummings, E. 237
Cummings, J. 237
Currer, C. 155

Daniel, V. 100
Daramola, S.M. 203
D'Arcy, C. 237
Dasberg, H. 236
Dear, M.J. 239